POSTERS

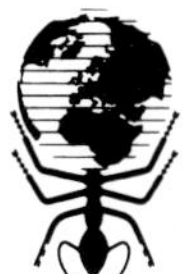

POSTERS
A GLOBAL HISTORY

ELIZABETH E. GUFFEY

REAKTION BOOKS

Published by Reaktion Books Ltd
Unit 32, Waterside
44–48 Wharf Road
London N1 7UX, UK

www.reaktionbooks.co.uk

First published 2015, reprinted 2016

Printed and bound in China

A catalogue record for this book is available from the British Library

ISBN 978 1 78023 371 0

CONTENTS

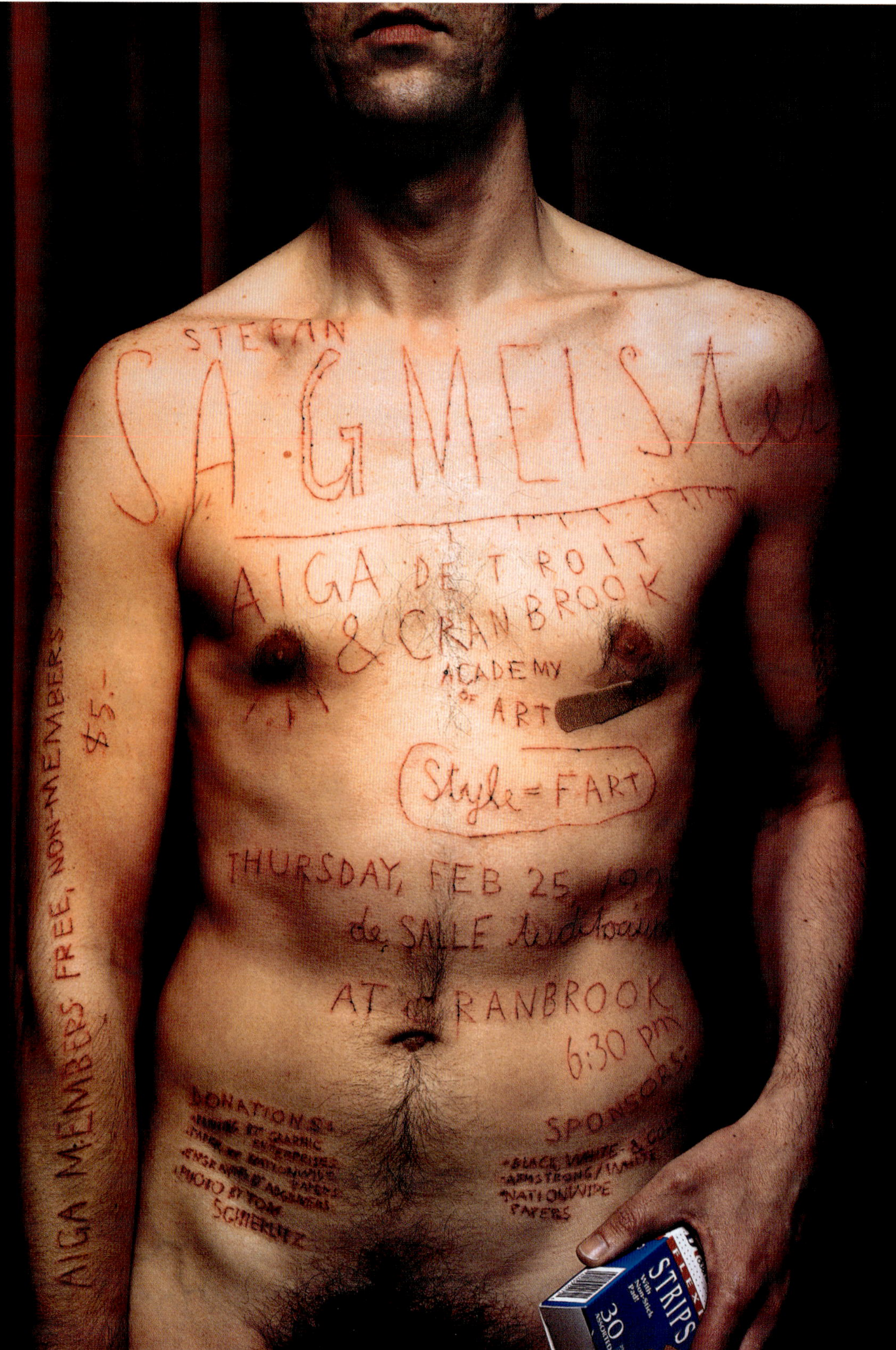

STEFAN
SAGMEISTER
AIGA DETROIT
& CRANBROOK
ACADEMY
of ART
Style = FART
THURSDAY, FEB 25, 1999
de SALLE auditorium
AT CRANBROOK
6:30 pm
$5.-
AIGA MEMBERS FREE, NON-MEMBERS
DONATIONS:
SPONSORS:
PHOTO BY TOM
SCHIERLITZ

INTRODUCTION

In 1999, an intern cut letters into the skin of Stefan Sagmeister's torso and arms for more than eight hours. Then Sagmeister was photographed, and he used the resulting image in a poster announcing his lecture at Cranbrook Academy of Art, near Detroit. Now an icon of contemporary design, the poster opens up multiple discourses about the body in the second millennium, with allusions ranging from exhibitionism and tattooing to sadomasochist subcultures and even the self-injurious practice of cutting. The poster announces the date, time and place clearly enough, but the image of incised flesh and rising welts challenges us to read the information; while functioning as an announcement of a specific event, it serves as well as a desperate cry to draw attention to the poster itself. Sagmeister's plea speaks volumes. But how did we get to the point of Sagmeister's mute blandishment?

Moving from Paris cabaret advertisements to Soviet propaganda to San Francisco psychedelia, the 'history of the poster' is already well ensconced in books, exhibition catalogues and other written records. But this is more than a story of stylistic innovation or a series of topical messages printed on paper: it is also a tale of posters as things, of material forms with which we spend our lives. Posters endure as one of the most permanent and solid forms of visual communication, and they exert a palpable physical presence, shaping spaces while reflecting and altering human behaviour. Posters, for instance, can establish zones of behavioural expectation: 'Work Hard to Increase Fertilizer Production!' They can provide a unified voice to large numbers of people: 'Vote for Green!' They can even assert ownership of space itself: 'Lebanon is Christian.' After a century and a half of innumerable uses by various people, posters remain uniquely positioned to materialize the increasingly immaterial nature of visual communication.

Stefan Sagmeister, poster for AIGA lecture, Cranbrook, Michigan, 1999.

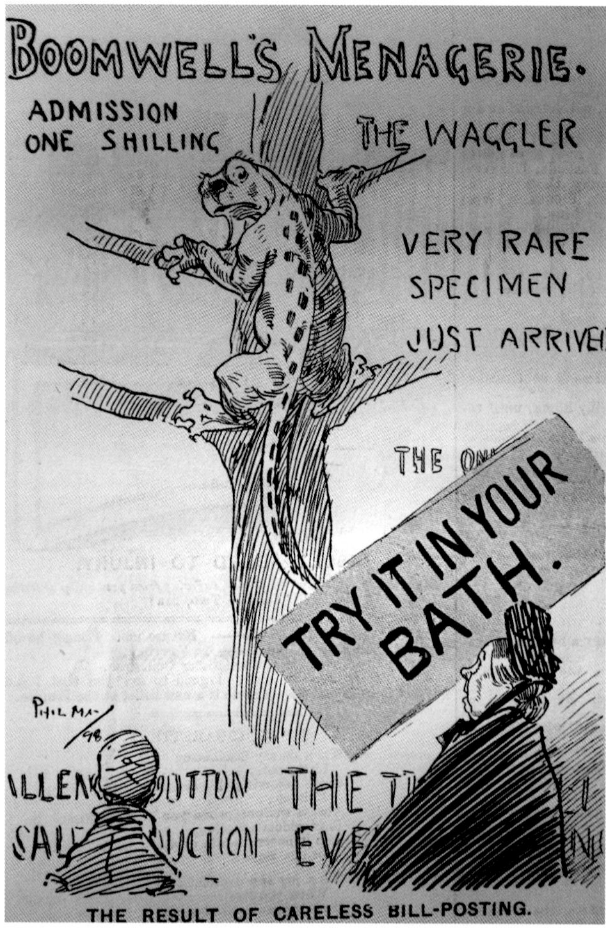

'The result of careless bill-posting': a cartoon from *Punch* (1898).

A history of posters as things may well start similarly to familiar narratives, with posters emerging in the capitals of Europe and North America as an outgrowth of mass production. Indeed, in this early stage of their history, posters were little more than communications of text and/or image, printed as multiples on paper and hung in the public realm. Posters' birth was attended by the Industrial Revolution, in the tight, cluttered walls and side streets of Paris, London and New York. Yet the spaces into which posters were placed were not in any sense a *tabula rasa*: the poster materialized in a culture where printing was already well established and valued, and posters made these spaces over into one of the most visually and verbally saturated environments in human history. The culture of posting only increased throughout the nineteenth century, with nearly any and every available surface of urban space crowded with a dense cacophony of handbills and advertisements. Posters began to reshape this typographic landscape through their sheer size and physical presence. They also transformed the nature of reading and communications: the brash, crass instance of Victorian posters and handbills cut across class lines and bent reading from a leisurely and physically private exercise into a distracted public act.

Traditional histories usually note that posters came into their own with the widespread use of chromolithography in the late nineteenth century, as artists pushed illustrated posters from curious ephemera to become things of beauty. Yet this change also came from significant social shifts and economic upheaval. For instance, the bounding and

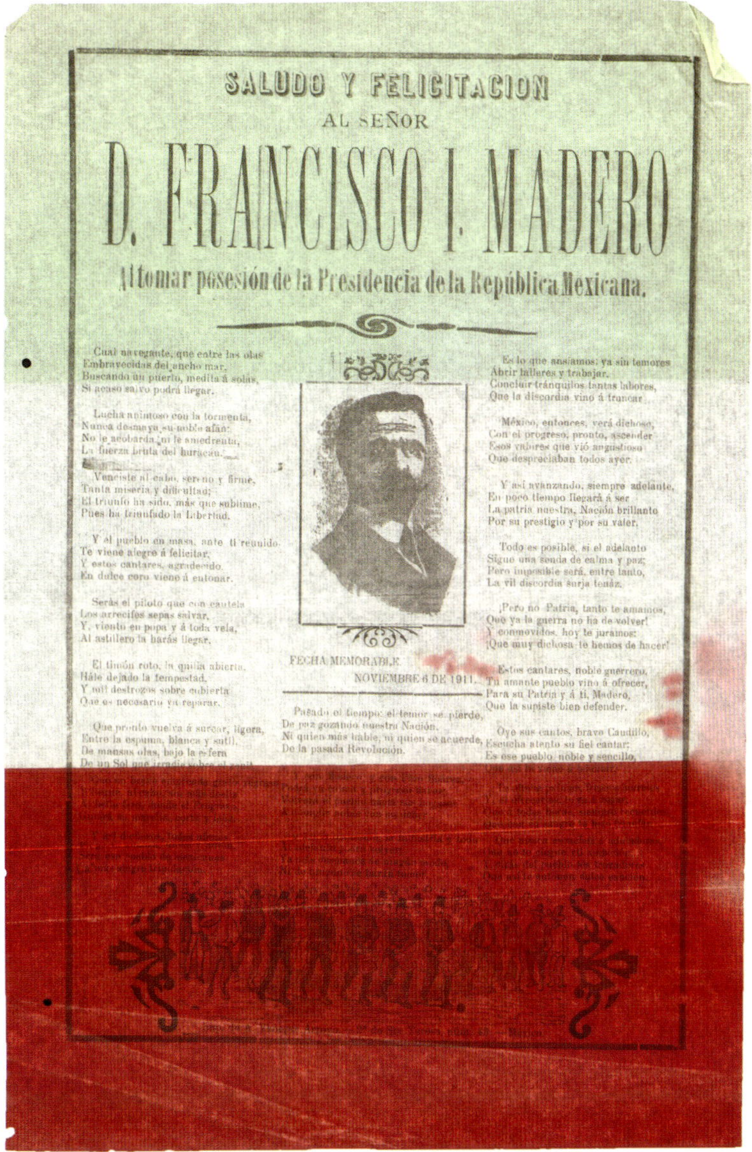

effusive female 'cherettes' that typify Jules Chéret's work were given life
not only through his skilful adoption of lithographic printing techniques
but also by the lifting of France's traditionally strict censorship and
bill-posting laws in 1881. The elegant, daring compositions of Henri
de Toulouse-Lautrec, Théophile Steinlen and Alphonse Mucha echo
the day's artistic avant-garde but also document the near-electric
charge of consumers' new buying power: the rapid profusion of mass-
produced cigarettes, soaps and other consumer goods enabled the
poster to blossom in Paris and spread throughout Europe. For these

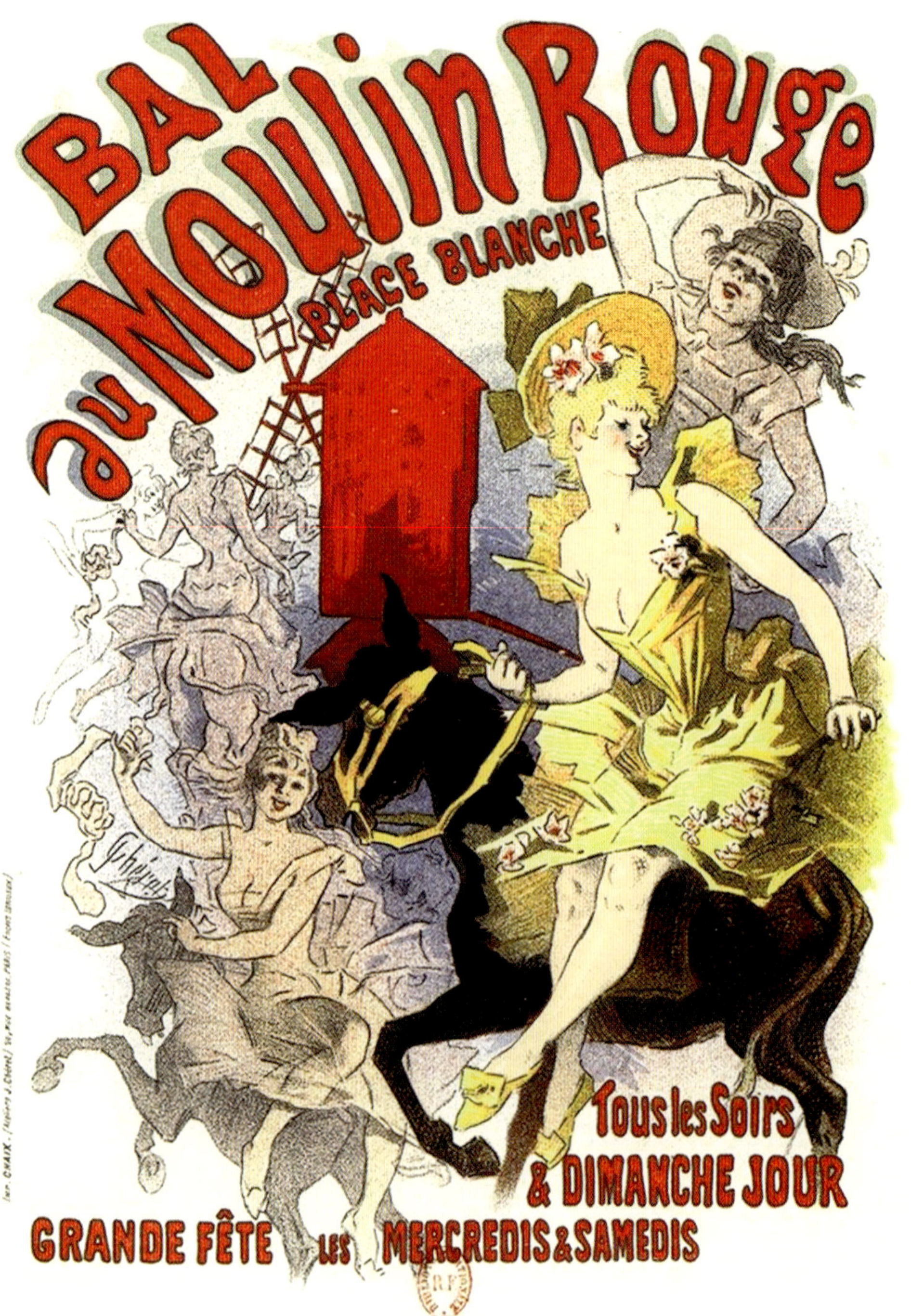

Jules Chéret, 'Bal au Moulin Rouge', 1896.

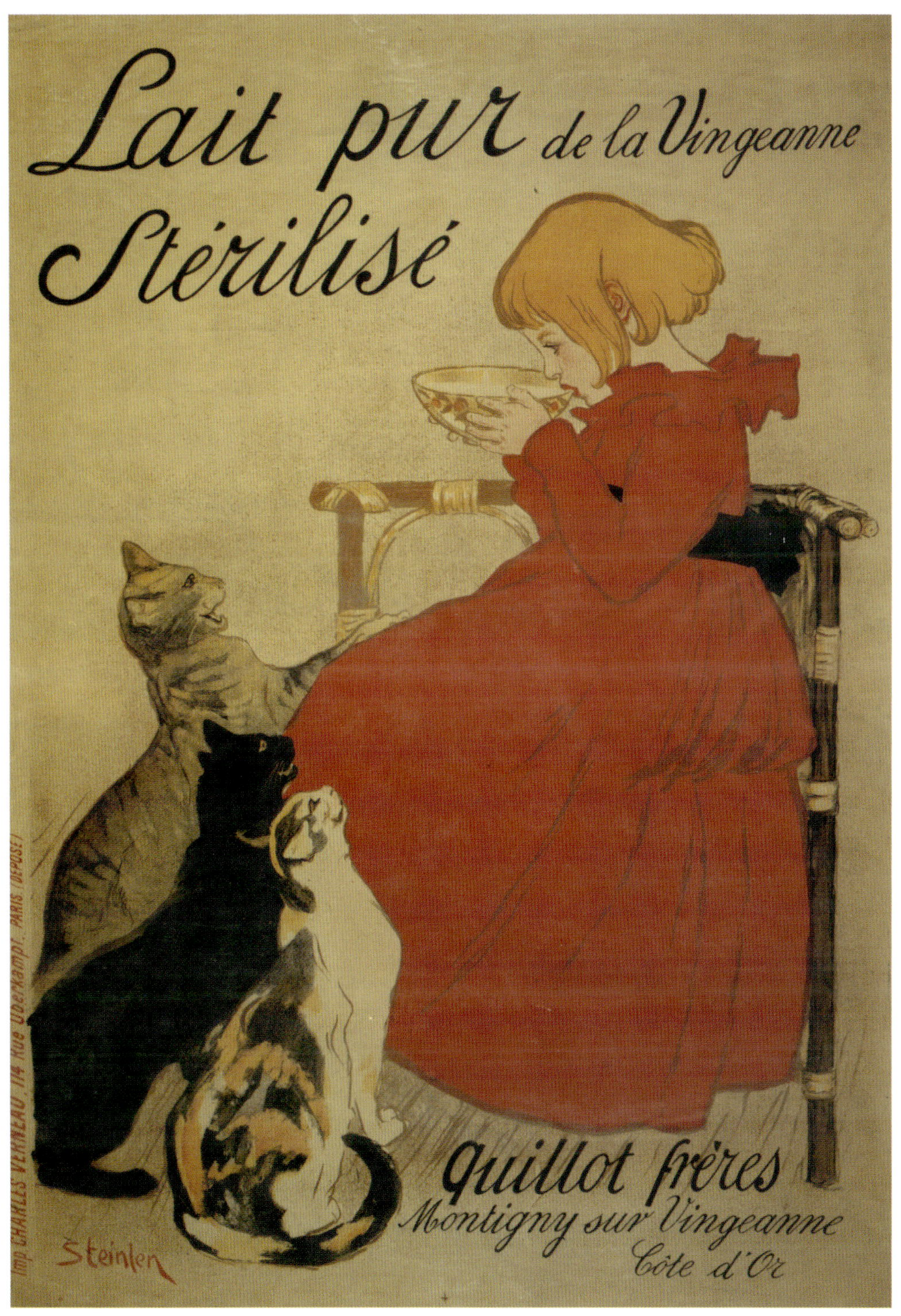

Théophile Steinlen, poster for sterilized milk, 1896.

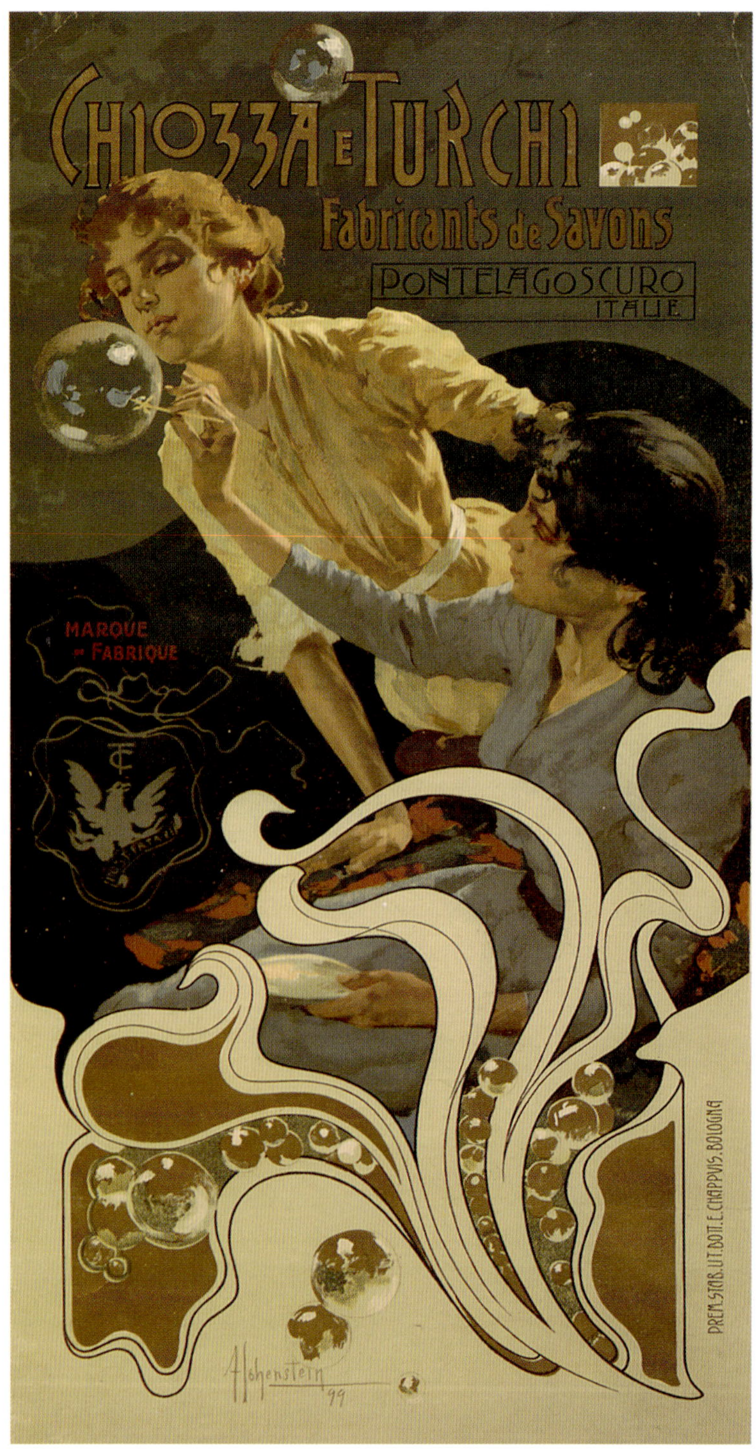

Adolfo Hohenstein, Chiozza e Turchi soap poster, 1899.

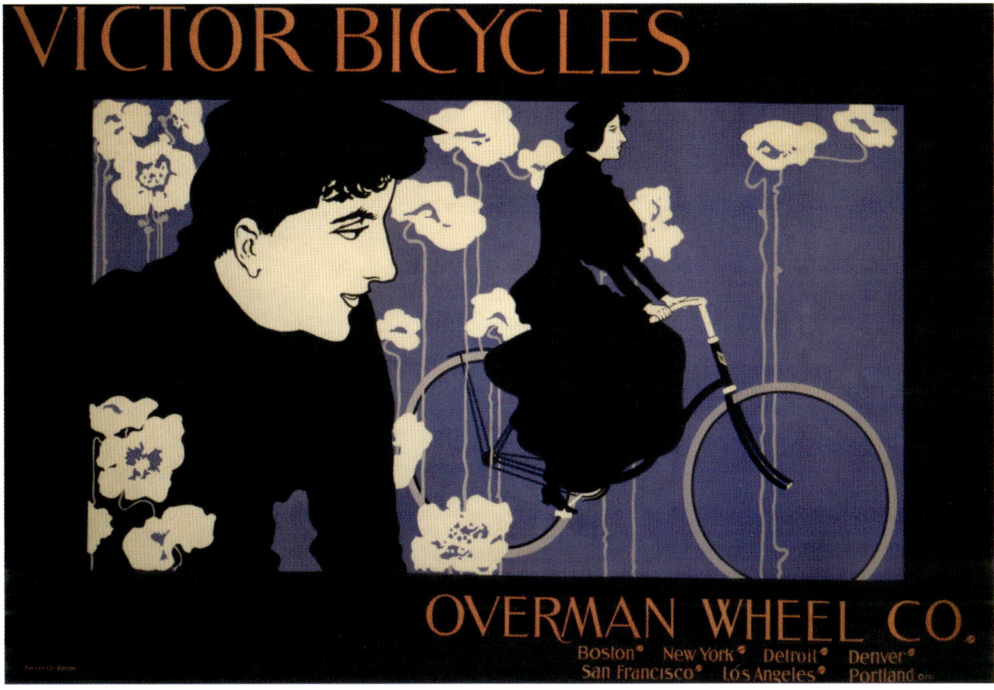

Will Bradley, 'Victor Bicycles', *c.* 1895.

reasons, the late nineteenth century is usually hailed as the 'golden age' of the poster.[1]

Most histories note that the illustrated French poster was quickly rivalled in London and New York. The new presence of illustrated posters throughout the urban spaces of Europe and America changed some public perceptions. As large, colourful posters began to command the spaces of public streets, markets and squares, the format itself took on a civic respectability never afforded to Victorian handbills. The Beggarstaff brothers in Britain, Toulouse-Lautrec and Steinlen in France and Edward Penfield or Will Bradley in North America designed commercial advertising posters that were nonetheless seen as public decorations and even regarded as 'art'; the very streets of Paris, New York and London were lauded as 'the poor man's picture gallery'.[2] While some critics decried the poster as a quick-blooming, big-headed, overbearing upstart, others saw posters as educators; they could make public space into a kind of open classroom, teaching the general public some aesthetic lessons in good taste or even democracy.[3]

Whether perceived as civic art or public nuisance, nineteenth-century illustrated posters were unequivocally capitalist, urging consumption even as they were themselves consumed. As posters

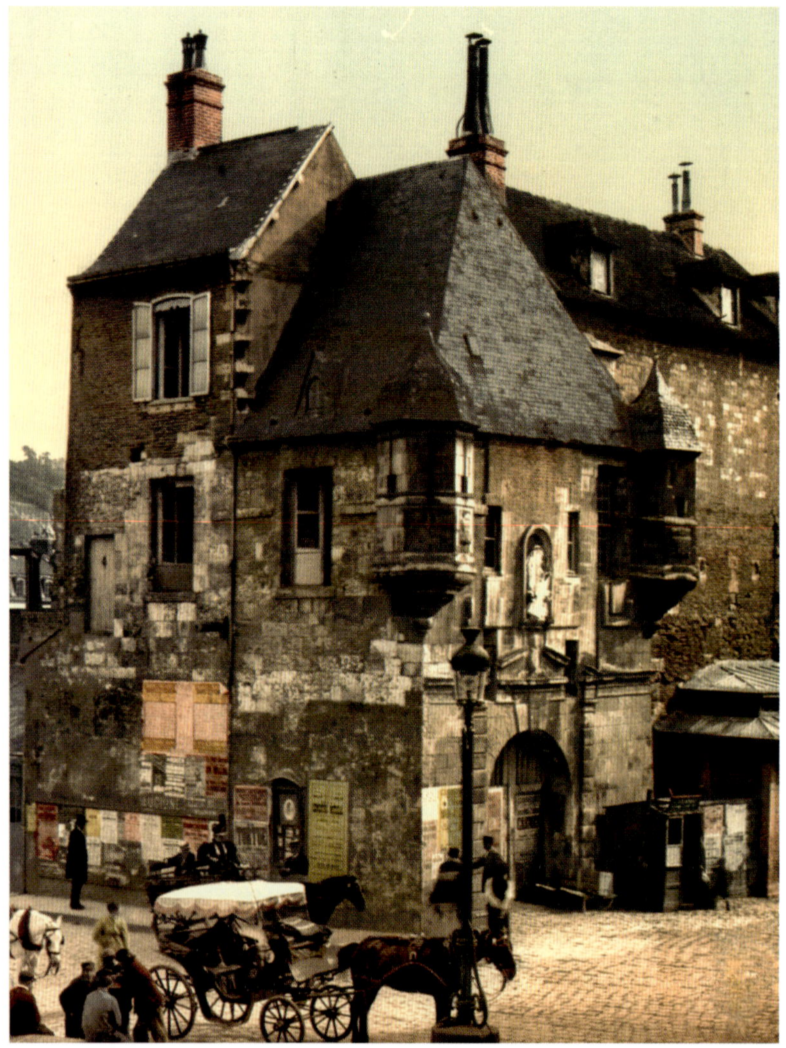

grew in popular appeal, dedicated collectors began saving, trading
and buying them for ever-increasing sums. The poster was perceived
as both public image and physical object: posters still wet with paste
were pulled off the sides of buildings, unpeeled from railway carriages
and even bought directly from printing houses. For the dedicated
devotee, the editor of *The Poster* warned in 1896 that money 'is
mere green paper, [but] posters are worth their weight in gold'.[4] The
popularity of posters also revealed a new geography of consumption:
local governments and property owners began to recognize large, flat
spaces as a potential source of rents, and a large-scale remapping of
cities and towns ensued. Posters not only disrupted the existing visual
order, but they also rendered visible previously disregarded spaces,

including the walls of derelict buildings and berms that ran along
railway tracks; even the sides of goods carts or wagons and boats
were suddenly seen as revenue-generating space ready to be sold.

But the illustrated poster also moved indoors, tracking the
mud and dust of the public sphere inside with it. If posters grew more
domesticated, part of their appeal was their fundamental coarseness.
With their sheer size, sharp colour contrasts, aggressive typography
and insistent messages of mass-market advertising (whether sly or
bombastic), they remained somewhat rude and carried a titillating
whiff of 'the street' into bohemian parlours and mannered drawing
rooms. Collectors could rival orchid enthusiasts as they fussed over
the care of their poster collections, arguing about the merits of
specially built cabinets or flat file storage and parsing the advantages
of portfolio cases or shallow drawers. By 1901, one collector reputedly
owned some 10,000 posters and had constructed a special room for
their storage and display.[5]

While posters helped to reshape the public face of the great
capitals of Europe and America, they also travelled more widely than
is commonly assumed. Commercial enterprises, too, began to distribute commercial and calendar posters: frequently printed in Britain
or Germany, these visually dazzling timekeepers often showcased the
chromolithographic skills of printers as much as advertising particular
products, including dubious patent medicines, borax and baking
powder. Charming, informative and effusive, these posters were
welcomed in homes and businesses from Hamburg to Cheyenne.
But calendars were among the first mass-produced posters that also
had an international presence. The British government used them to
concretize its wide-flung network of political power, providing calendars
to both colonial outposts and local rulers throughout south Asia and
Africa. Commercial firms also distributed showy, colourful posters of
various types as advertising overseas. The British-American Tobacco
Company made significant inroads in East Asia around the turn of the
century, distributing calendar posters as 'gifts' to customers marking
the New Year. In addition, poster design provided an early opportunity for independence groups to flex their muscles. In south Asia, for
instance, the advent of Indian-run presses meant that lithographic
posters were being produced by the late 1870s. Both here and in
China slightly later, posters helped foster independent, nationalist
visual cultures.

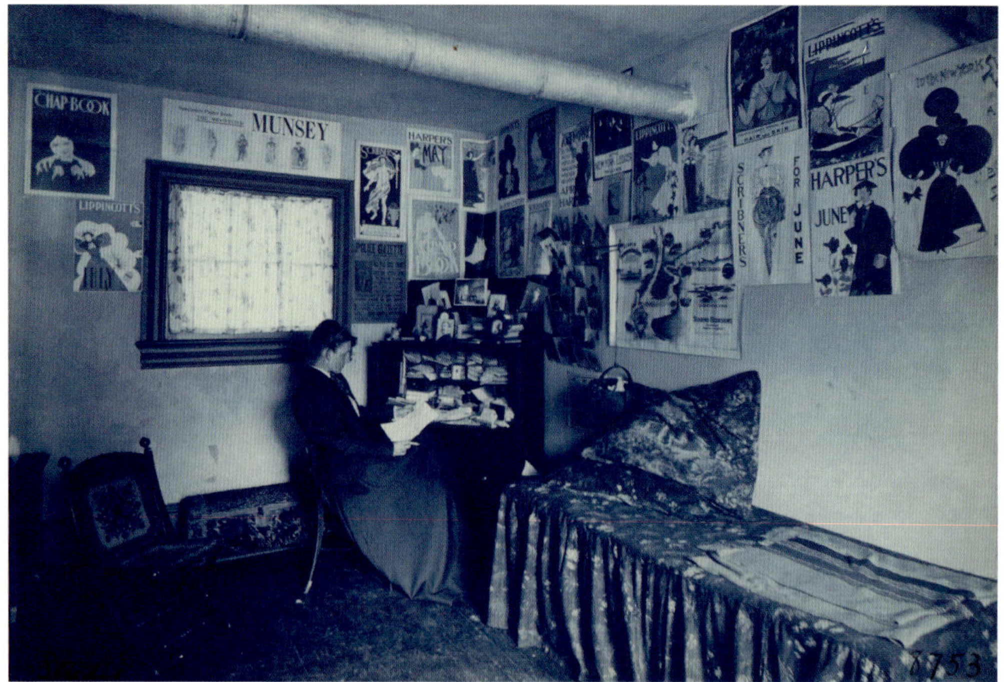

A collection of posters
on the walls of the studio/
office of the photographer
Frances Benjamin Johnston,
c. 1896.

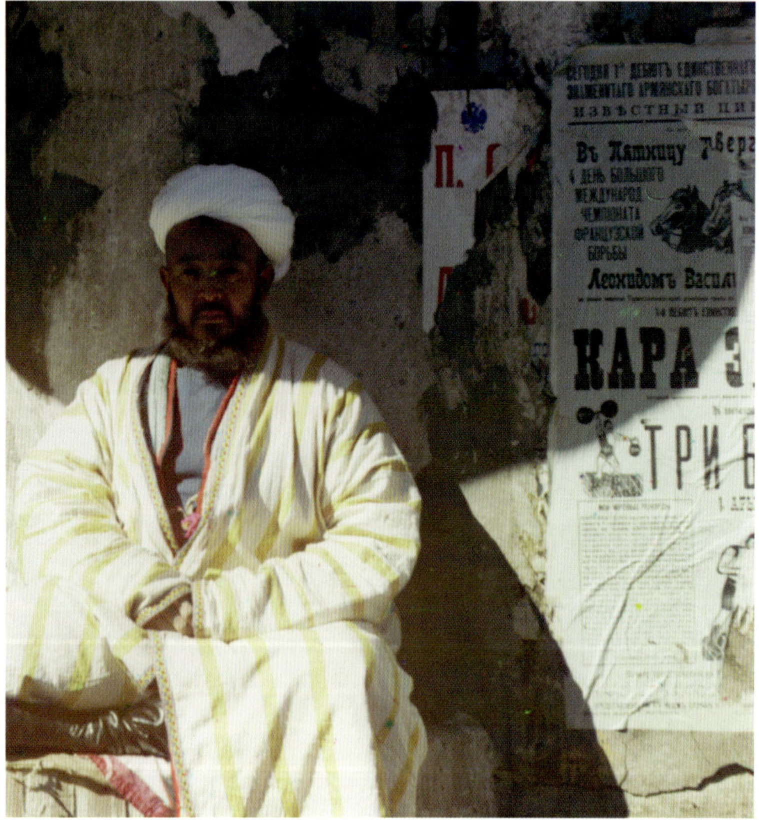

Sergei Mikhailovich
Prokudin-Gorskii,
'Trader in the Registan,
Samarkand', *c.* 1910.

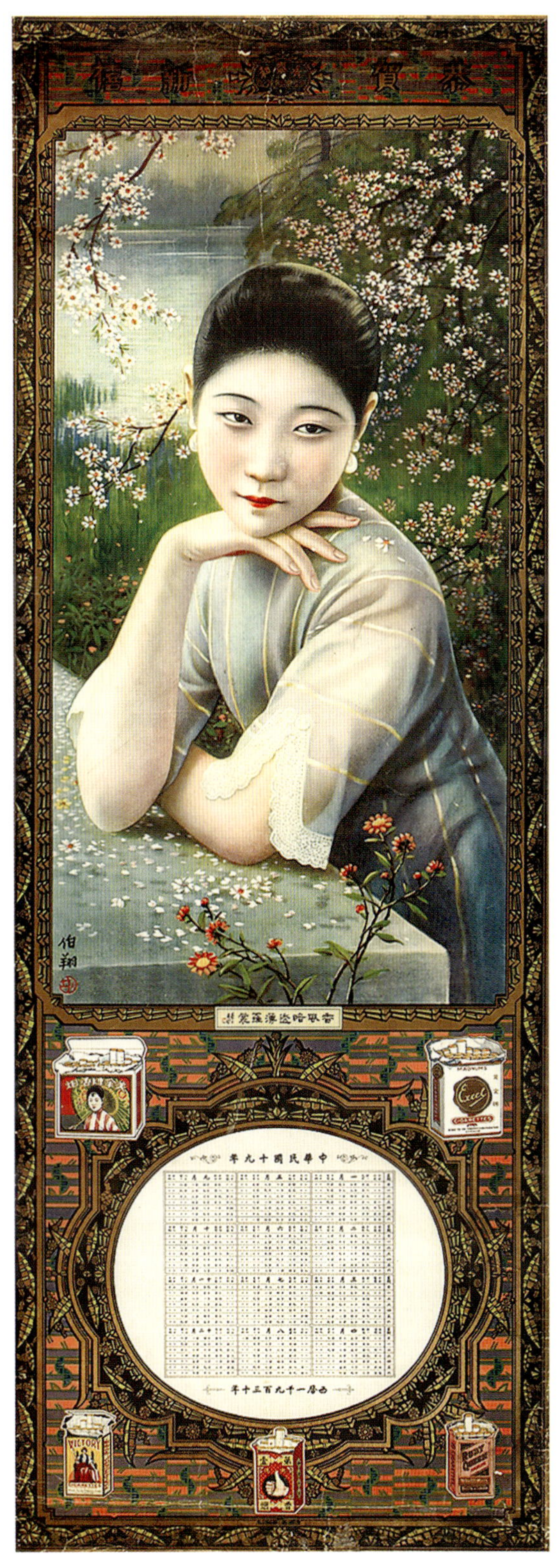

Hu Boxiang, calendar poster, c. 1930.

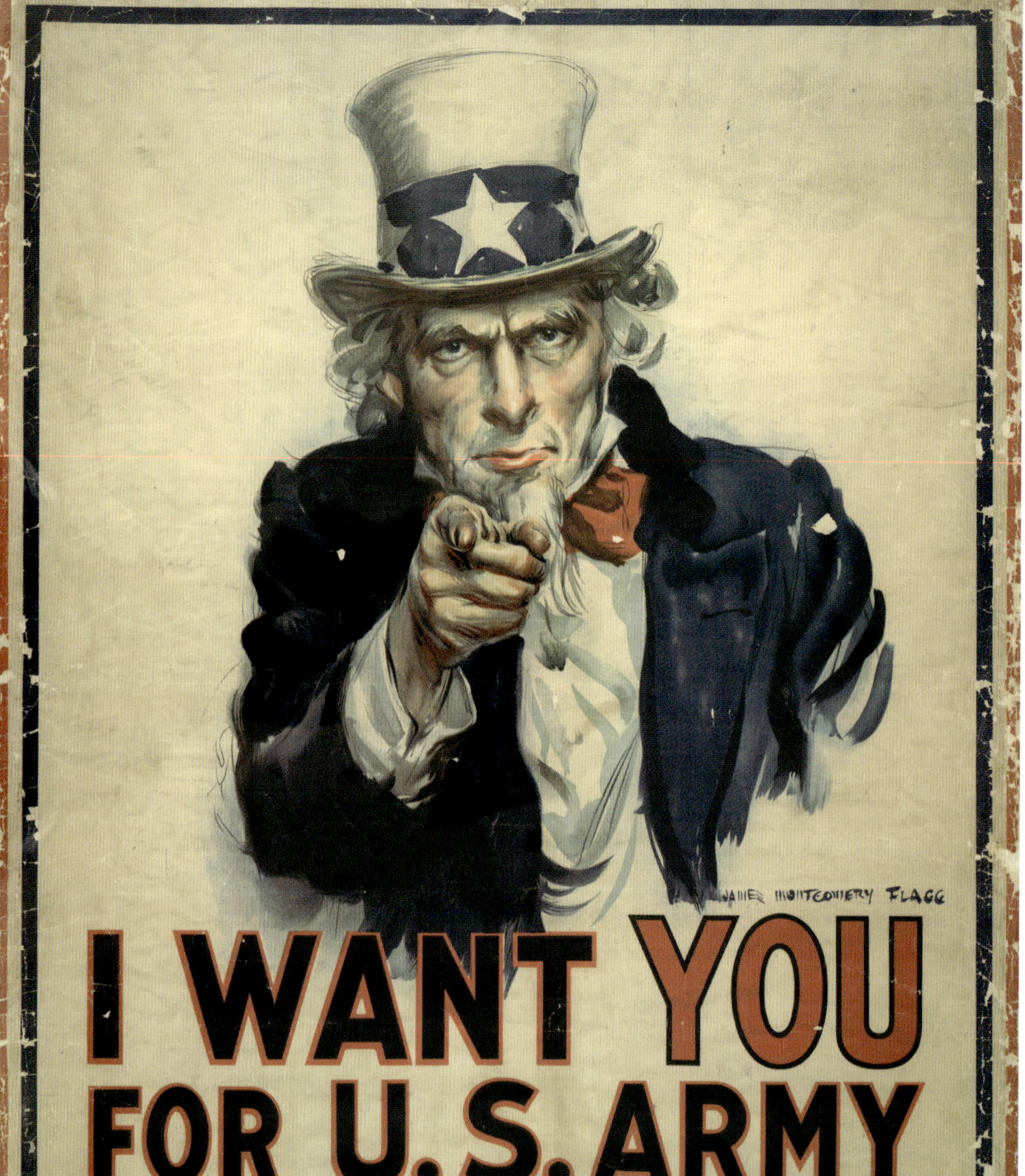

JAMES MONTGOMERY FLAGG
I WANT YOU
FOR U.S. ARMY
NEAREST RECRUITING STATION

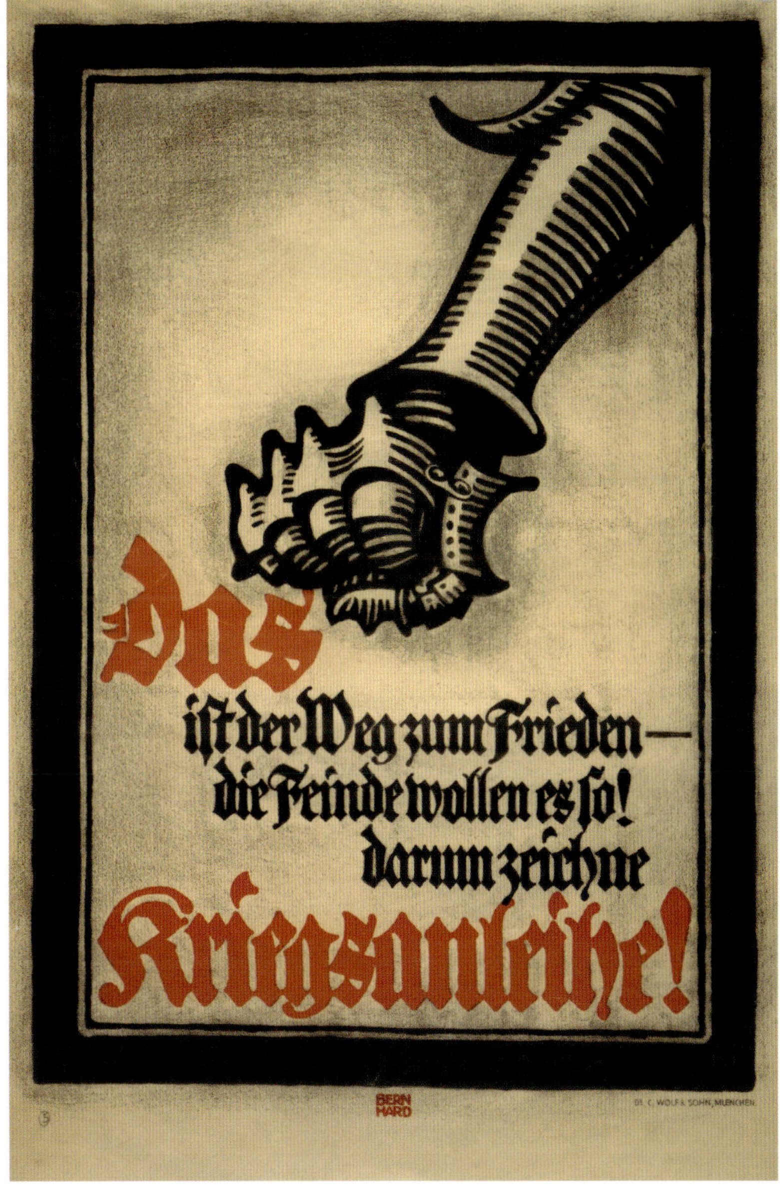

Whether national or international in scope, most histories of the
poster meander slowly through the early twentieth century; justifiably,
most trace a range of visual styles and give considerable space to First
World War posters that alternately pleaded with and admonished
citizens of both sides. While these war posters combined innovative
design and widespread dissemination (in the United States alone,
20 million posters bolstered the nation's relatively short war effort),
they reinvigorated a rapidly ageing form. If the global poster came

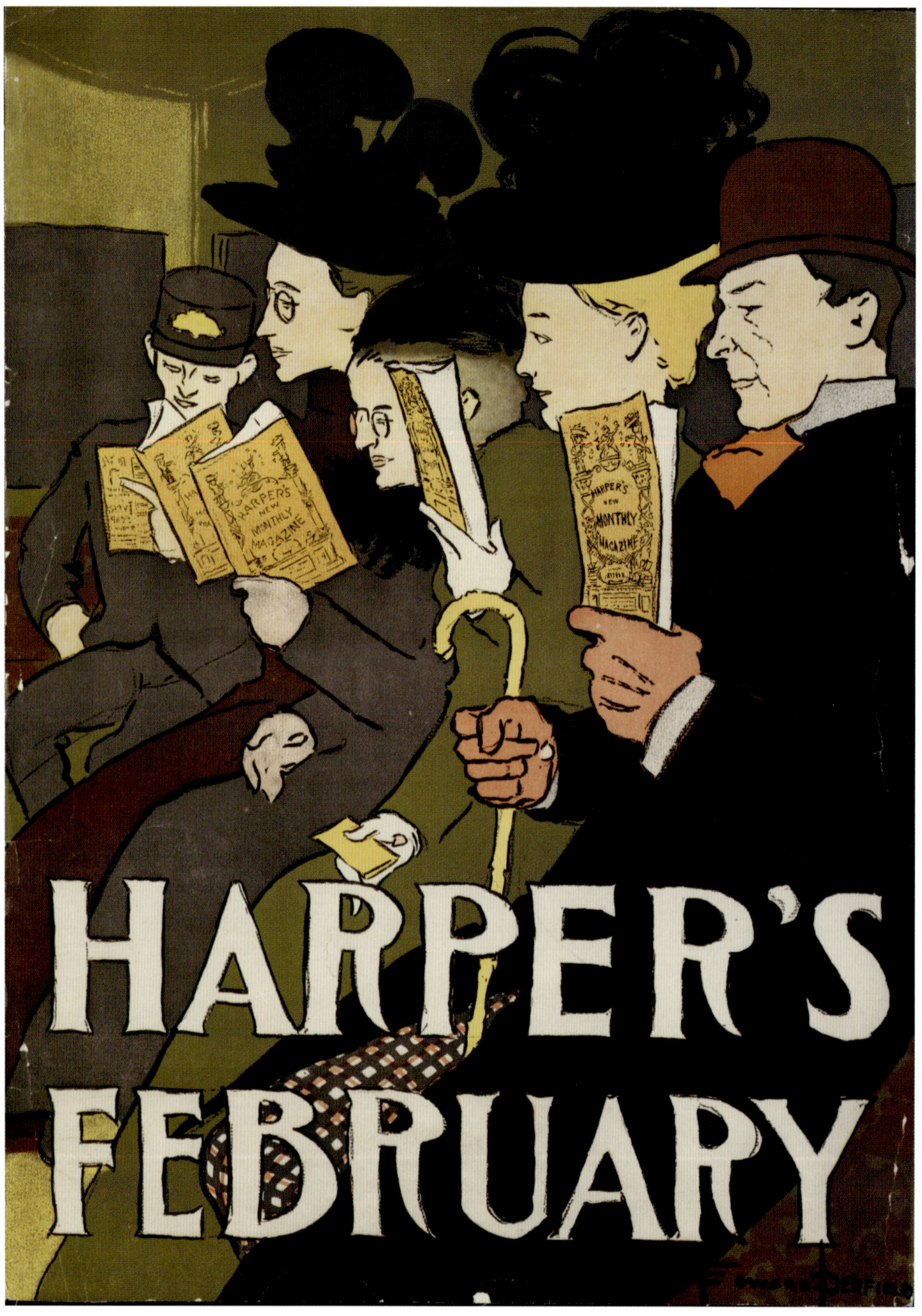

Edward Penfield, *Harper's* magazine promotional poster, 1895.

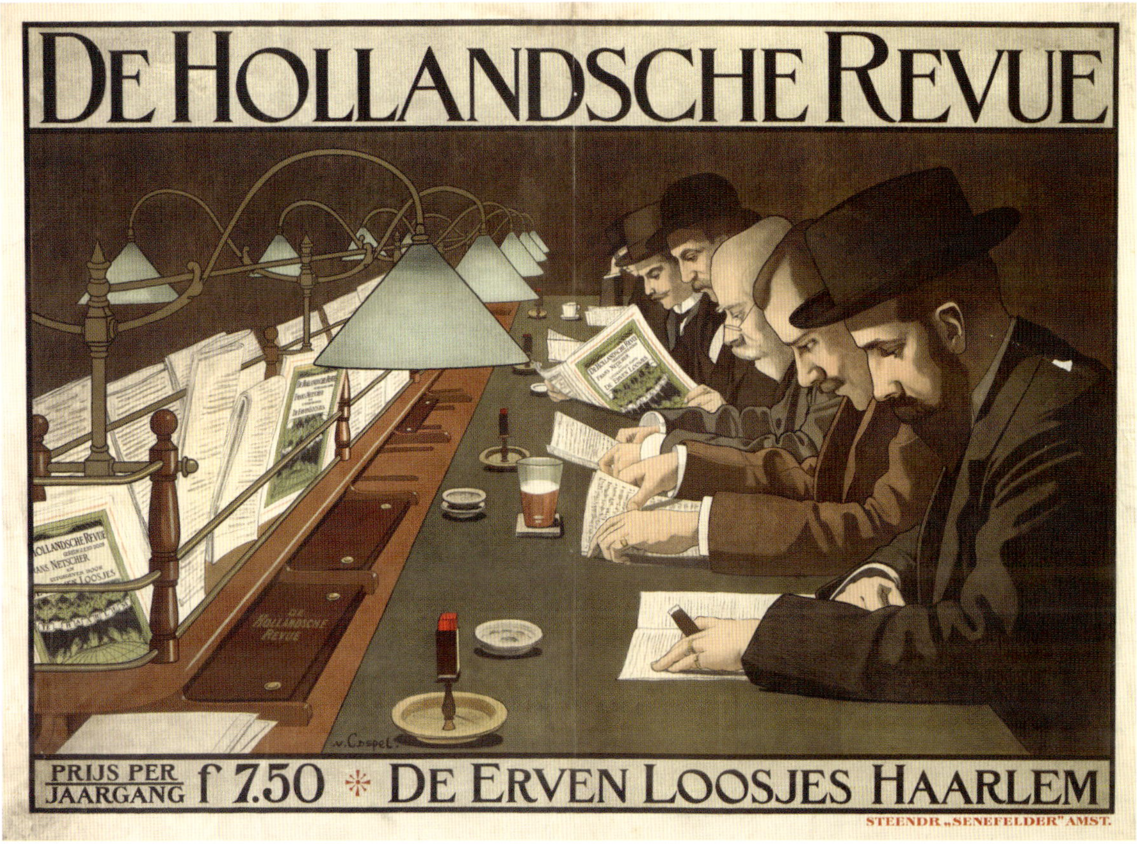

Johann Georg van Caspel,
De Hollandsche Revue
poster, 1910.

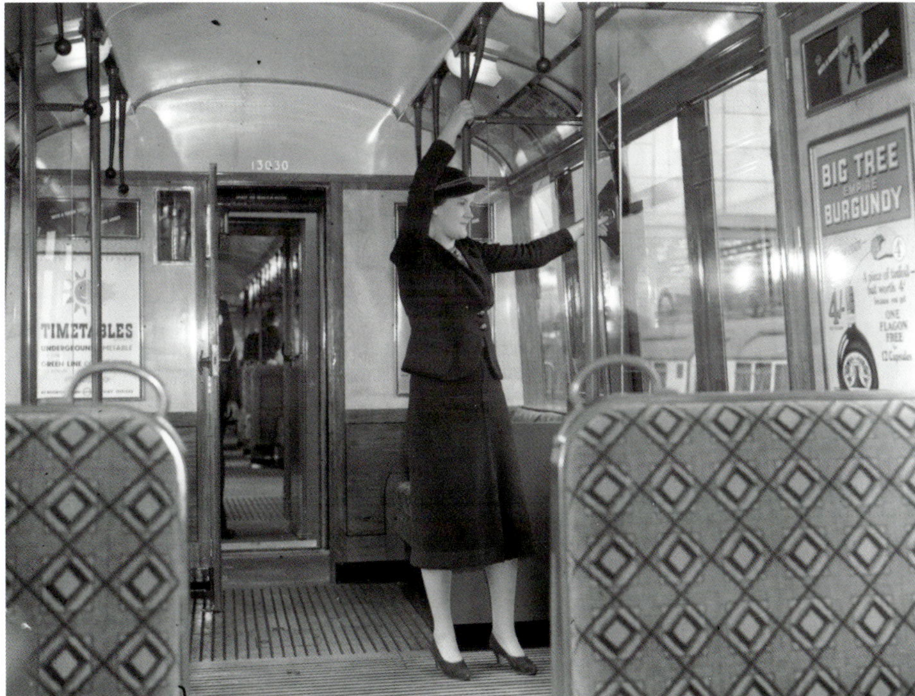

David Saville, a woman
in a 'new design' London
Underground train, 1937.

of age in the noisy excitement of the late nineteenth century, it was never an only child; soon enough it was joined by younger, more clamorous siblings. Mass-market magazines and newspapers arrived first, and radio emerged soon after. Pushy in their boisterous thrall, these new forms of mass communication competed directly with posters for advertising budgets, and they quickly gained precedence. Poets may have lauded the French designer Cassandre (Adolphe Mouron) as the 'stage director of the streets',[6] but the poster itself met with ever-increasing ennui; at best, posters flourished in areas where newer communications technologies were less effective or had not arrived. As today, the terrain of posters began to be constricted. They congregated near the pavements of European cities or dawdled in train carriages and subway stations elsewhere, sticking to zones where consumers were little more than a captive audience.

More traditional narratives often trace the growing ubiquity of the International Style's orderly grids and austere typography throughout the 1940s and '50s, while classifying international poster design into themes like 'activism' or 'travel'. In so doing, they evade a growing problem with posters. Although inventive new designs and production techniques did emerge in the post-war decades, in the eyes of many advertising professionals the poster had entered a dreary middle age. Far from driving budgets and strategies, posters became an afterthought to the large-scale, coordinated corporate advertising campaigns that emphasized consistency and identity in both products and advertising; many advertisers balked at tailoring these campaigns to questions of scale, legibility and other seemingly fussy needs demanded by posters. Posters had done their job during the Second World War, but by the late 1940s

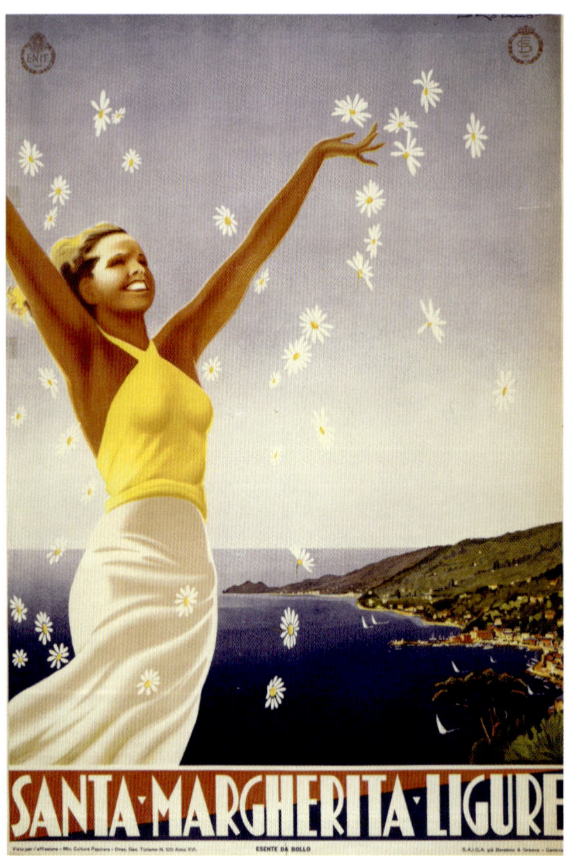

'Santa Margherita Ligure',
Italian travel poster, 1951.

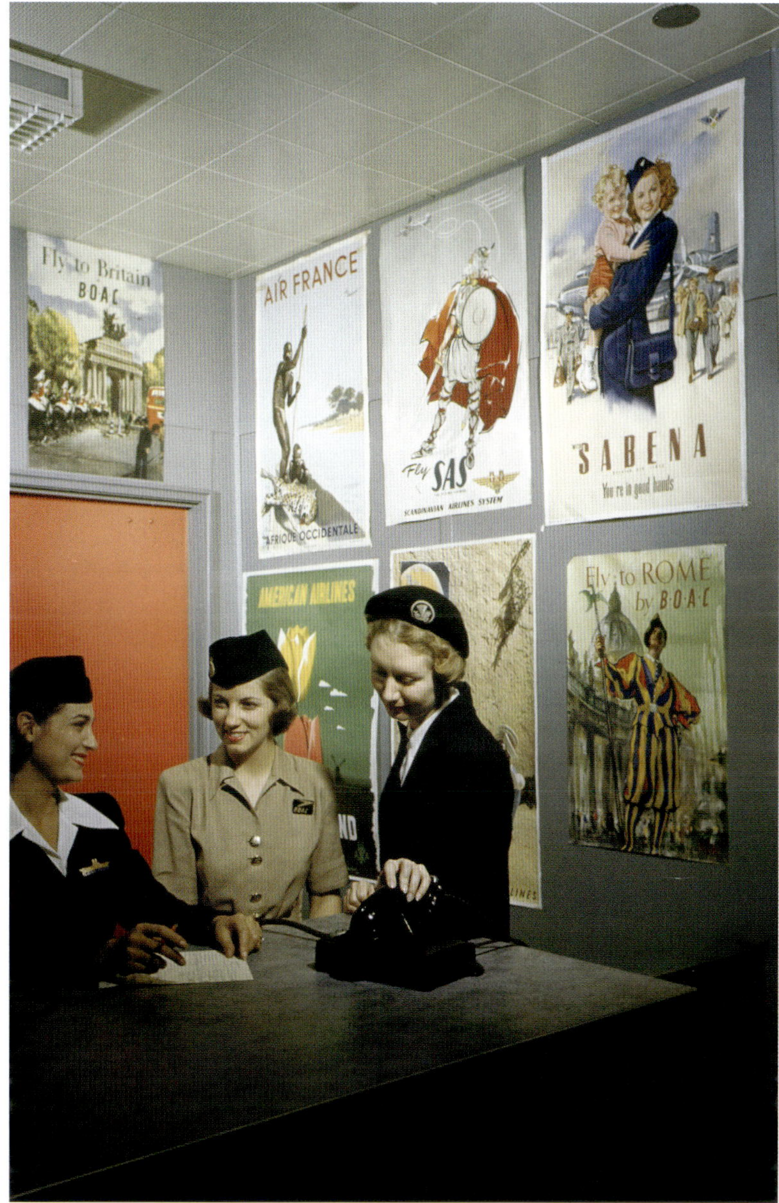

they were back to hawking cheap bus tickets and toothpaste. For
many observers, commercial posters were simply a blight. Perhaps
the nadir occurred when, as part of a broader post-war austerity
regime, the UK Parliament debated taxing posters heavily, with MPs
claiming that posters were a waste of timber, paper and manpower.[7]
Fifty years earlier, posters had been pulled off walls to be coddled
and collected. Here our narrative deepens. At the height of their
commercial eclipse, *Posters: A Global History* argues, they underwent

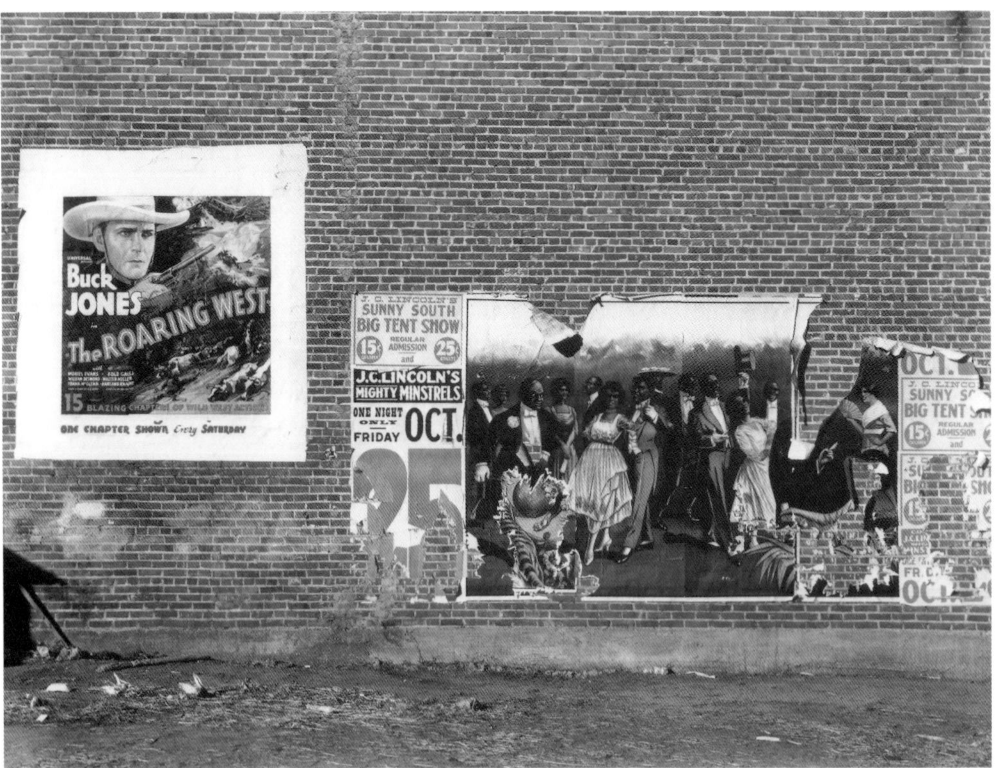

Walker Evans, 'Posters advertising a circus near Lynchburg, South Carolina', 1936.

a remarkable transformation. French Nouveau Réalistes pulled tattered, decaying posters off walls as part of their larger investigation into junk materials and urban decay. They were little more than decomposing rubbish.

Against this picture of decline, *Posters* asserts that the form is reinvented; moreover, posters received an informal reprieve from an unexpected source. As posters lost precedence in Western advertising campaigns, a new type of poster emerged in the Eastern bloc. Behind the Iron Curtain, where consumer economic and technical conditions lagged, posters continued to flourish as a form of state-sponsored propaganda. But in newly communist countries like Czechoslovakia and Poland, posters designed for films and cultural events began to challenge this established pattern with a kind of cultural doublespeak: stylistically diverse, the posters combined idiosyncratic illustrations and hand lettering to create haunting, equivocal statements that performed risky conceptual somersaults around censors and public alike. Not only did these posters deftly sidestep many official ideological prerequisites for printed matter, they also came to inhabit a kind of 'grey zone' between communism and capitalism, serving as official

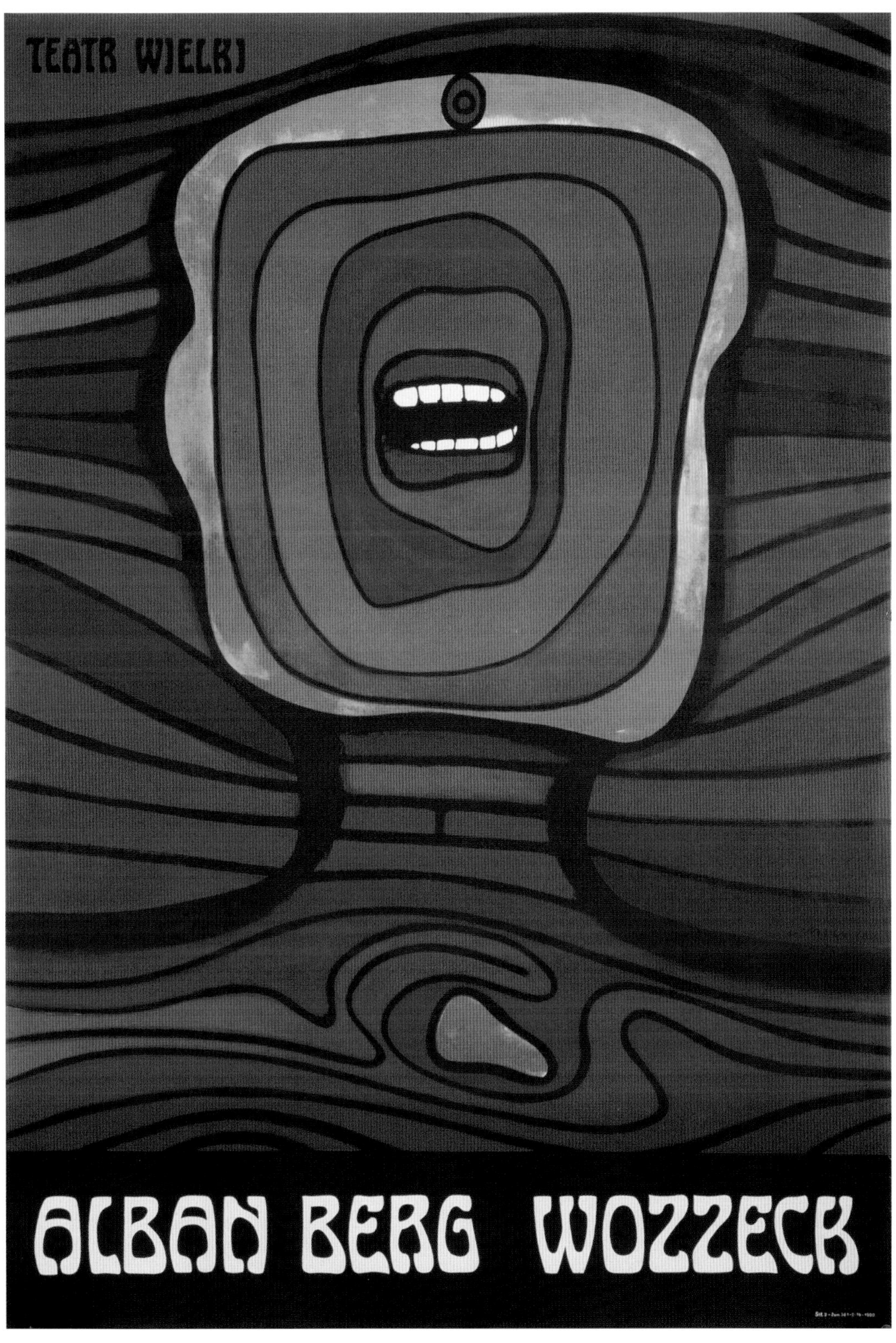

Jan Lenica, poster for Berg's opera *Wozzeck* at the Teatr Wielki in Warsaw, 1964.

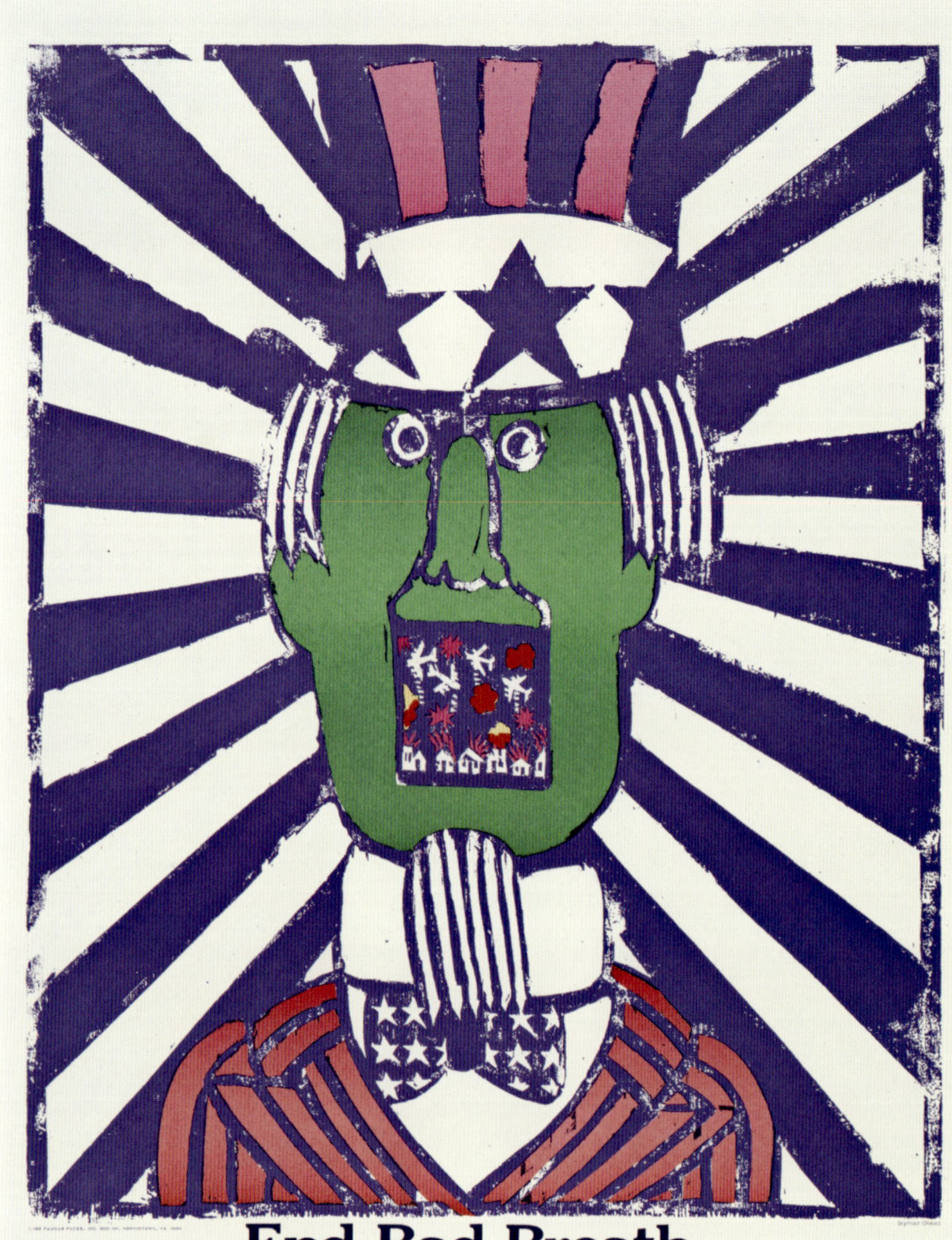

Seymour Chwast, 'End Bad Breath', 1967.

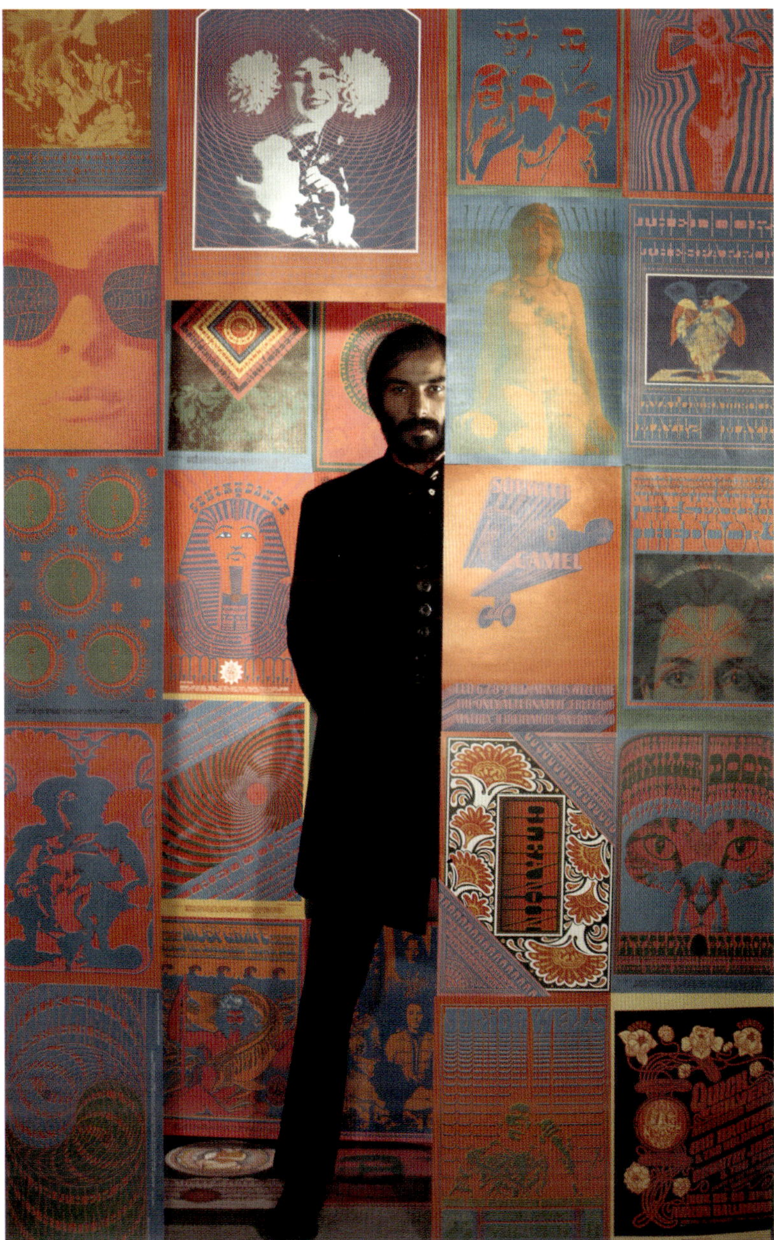

Ted Streshinsky, 'Victor Moscoso surrounded by psychedelic posters', *c.* 1967.

publications while maintaining personal visions; they offered subtle comments on political and cultural power.

Beyond their borders, Polish posters also inspired a new generation of designers in the West, where the political and cultural foment of the 1960s saw the printed poster undergo an identity shift. While losing allure as an overt advertising medium, the poster was newly regarded as a novel means of self-expression, whether of pop

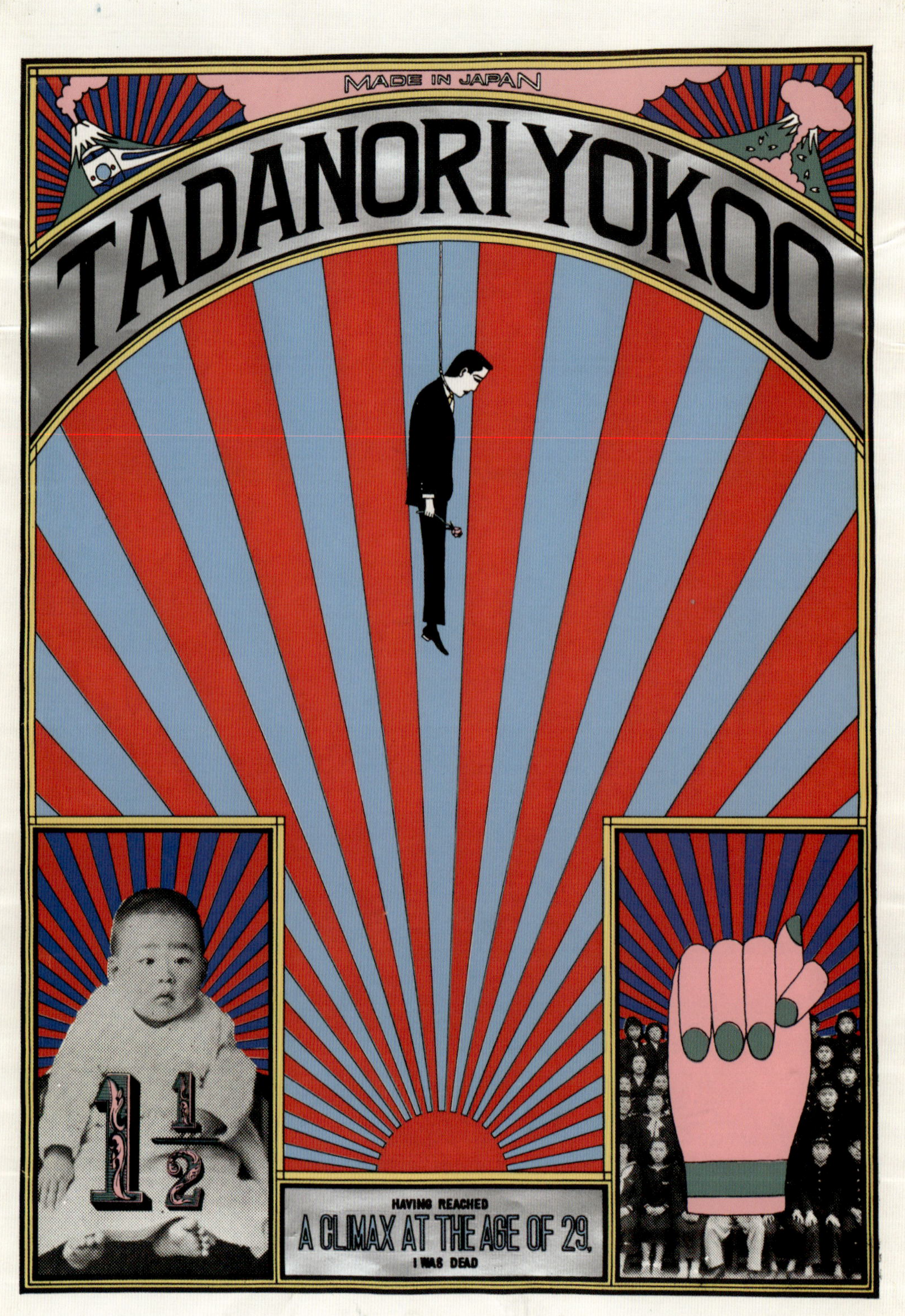

Tadanori Yokoo, 'Having Reached a Climax at the Age of 29, I Was Dead', 1965.

fandom, political rebellion or generational solidarity. The advertising industry itself sought out the informal trappings of a burgeoning 'youth culture' with quirkily allusive posters by independents like New York's Push Pin Studios, which plundered the past for decorative flourishes, wooden type letterforms and antiquated photographs. But by the late 1960s, even these designers were struggling to keep up with posters' new mystique. Indeed, the period experienced a resurgence in poster popularity that rivalled the initial craze some 70 years earlier. Yet the qualities that drove this new 'postermania' were changed: the flashy physicality and trashy disposability, once looked at as detriments, now formed an intrinsic part of their new-found popularity. Some detractors expressed disdain and called them 'pseudo-posters'.[8] Nevertheless, whether psychedelic posters promoting Phil Graham's mid-1960s rock concerts or ones advocating the anti-Vietnam War peace movement, these posters marked out personal spaces and stances while also charting landscapes of the mind.

Beyond a doubt, the poster craze of the 1960s encompassed more than mere fashion; the period also saw posters creep, or rather leap, into view as revolutionary icons. Drawing from the past and anything but subtle, many of these posters emerged as brief, compressed lessons in

Mark Gayn, 'Girls dance in a park before an anti-American propaganda poster in China', *c.* 1965.

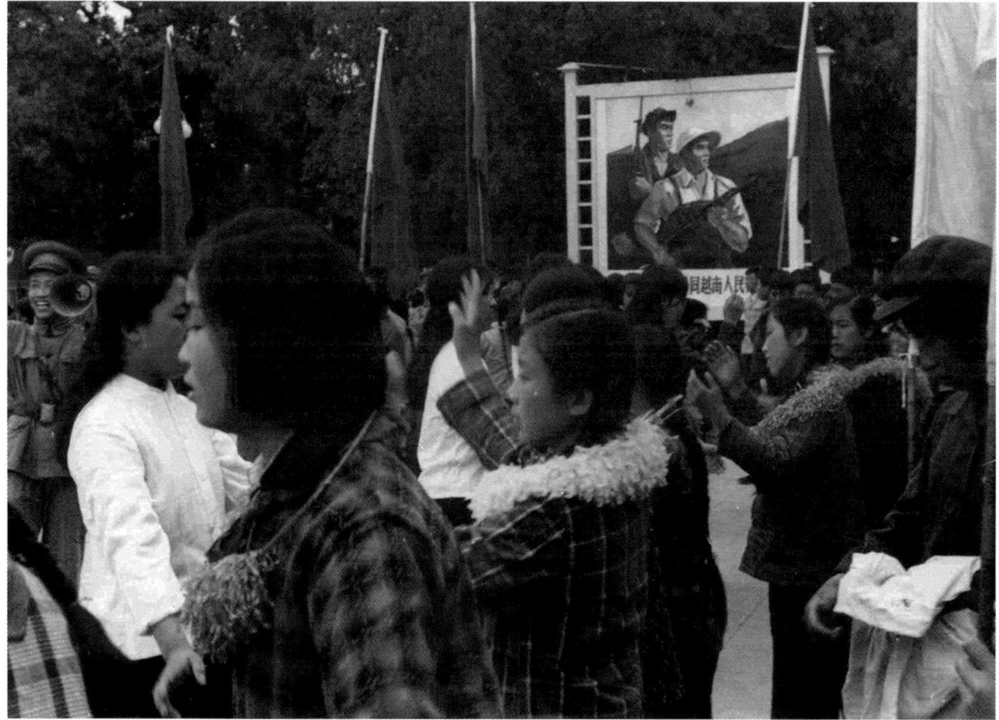

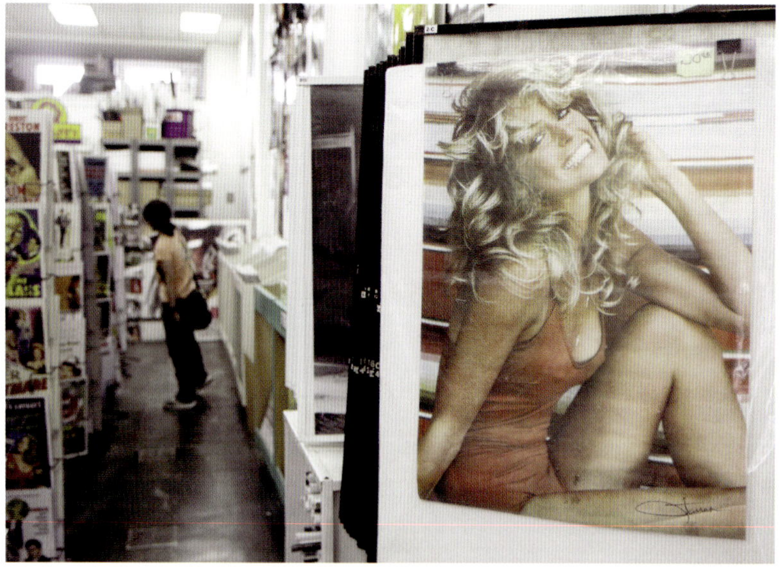

global history and ideology. In China, for instance, posters emerged as an essential element of the Communist Party's public information system. Combining its long history of 'popular folk art'[9] with its more recent adoption of calendar posters and a Stalinist embrace of social realism, Chinese posters echoed their Soviet partners in conflating party goals with larger ethical and moral dimensions. Concurrently, Cuban designers began a vigorous poster effort that courted audiences at home and abroad; in contrast to other communist nations, Cuban designers earned official praise for their assimilation of a wide confluence of visual styles, including Western psychedelia, Pop art and comics. Though largely eclipsed as mainstream media in Europe and America, posters retained a vibrant underground currency, promulgating multiple, alternative ideologies at a time when worldwide revolution seemed a very real possibility.

Since the 1970s, posters have continued to exist as a largely local and relatively low-tech alternative to screen-based media. Useful for constricted urban areas and college campuses, they also remain commonplace as indoor decoration. Both types of posters occasionally hit a popular nerve, whether the million-selling Farah Fawcett poster of 1977 or any number of dour typographic variations of 'Keep Calm and Carry On'. Creative, timely posters could harness the public imagination about specific causes, such as the Guerrilla Girls' use of insistently acerbic humour to quantify sexism within the art world or the spiky and driven posters created by ACT UP and Gran Fury. Occasionally, this

Guerrilla Girls, *The Advantages of Being a Woman Artist*, 1989.

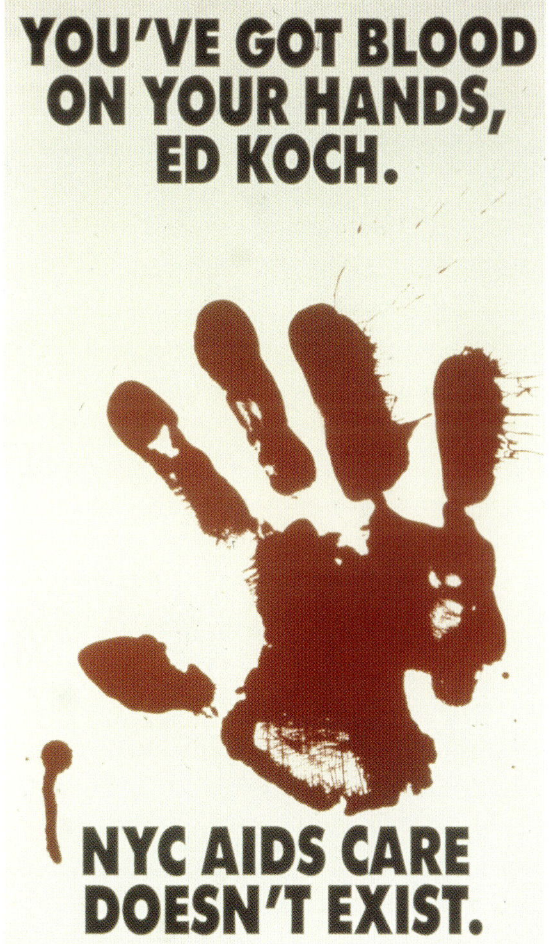

Gran Fury Collective, 'You've Got Blood on Your Hands, Ed Koch', campaign poster for ACT UP, 1986–7.

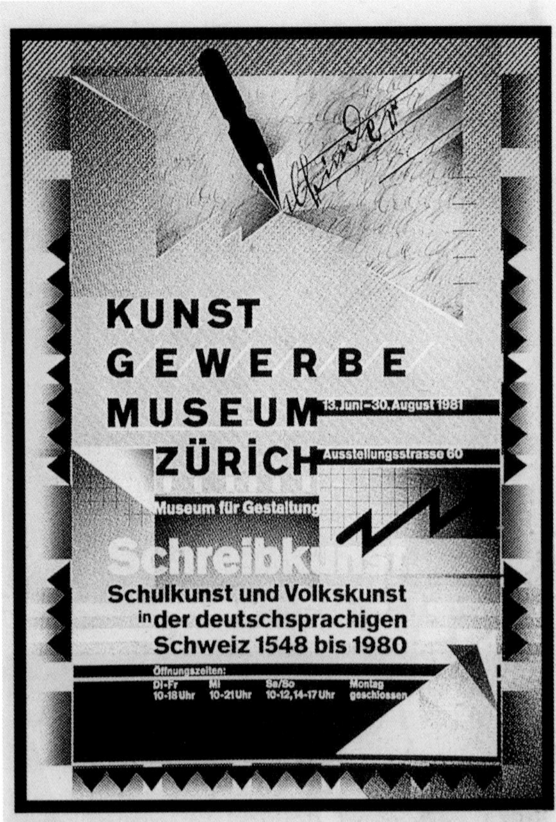

Wolfgang Weingart, poster for a calligraphy exhibition at the Kunstgewerbemuseum, Zurich.

vein of issue-driven poster design influenced commercial campaigns: the Body Shop's 'education and agitation' shop window campaigns, for example, fused commerce with activism. Borrowing from the 'issue-driven' poster, these crafted a sly twist on Madison Avenue's typical advertising campaigns.

Even as designers themselves have increasingly questioned the form's relevance, posters have grown in importance within the design profession. Often described as over-large and under-used, the poster is, as another design professional put it, a 'dead' medium.[10] Still, from the 1970s on, designers have consistently sought to define themselves as a profession, and the poster reflects this effort, forming a common visual currency. With few commercial opportunities, designers have focused on posters for cultural, political or charitable organizations, or even simply make and publish designs for themselves. At first, a small cadre of inventive designers used posters to question the tenets of mainstream society and the principles of modernist design: France's Grapus studio; Switzerland's Wolfgang Weingart; the partners Gunter Rambow, Gerhard Lienemeyer and Michael van de Sand in Germany; and Tadanori Yokoo in Japan. In the mid-1980s, April Greiman and Katherine McCoy designed posters to make complex statements about the nature of technology and communication itself. Such posters were feted in museum exhibitions and reproduced in trade journals as well as textbooks of design history; like paintings and sculpture, posters were more widely seen as small reproductions in books and magazines, even as they began to form the basis of many 'standard histories' of twentieth-century design.

But, if we turn our gaze outside this tightly cropped narrative, posters have begun not only to look but also to do inventive things.

The Palestinian martyr poster, often the product of digital assembly and printing, functions in ways unthinkable in nineteenth-century Paris. Here and elsewhere, artisanal and craft traditions are rapidly being replaced by digitally designed posters that can be output at business communications shops – now as ubiquitous in urban areas of south Asia or sub-Saharan Africa as they are in Europe and North America. The new global poster is changing, in part through new materials, and today can be laminated or printed on vinyl almost as easily as paper. But it also taps into emerging transcultural networks, where the prime mover is the Internet. A poster designer in Nigeria can download images, be they of popular hairstyles or war in the Ivory Coast, from a website, paste them into a layout program, add captions and colours, print on demand and distribute a new poster through urban and rural networks of pedlars and small shop owners over the entire region. At a barber shop in Burundi, a poster is purchased by the store's owner, who hopes to titillate customers with news and hair-styling fashions. Unlike the painted posters found in earlier barber shops, these are digitally made and form a crucial, often overlooked, element of the global information network. Rather than waiting for a shabby funeral and unremarked death, the poster has moved on. Though often discounted and so changed as to be unrecognizable, the unremarked poster is indeed enjoying yet another golden age.

The Social Life of Posters

Elias Khoury's detective story *White Masks* (1981) details the brutal murder of Khalil Ahmad Jabir in Beirut during the early years of the Lebanese Civil War. He was killed, the book suggests, by posters. The story begins with Jabir's funeral, but it pivots on his son, a local militia member who died in the war's opening days, being declared a martyr. Posters announcing his and other martyrs' deaths begin appearing around the city; some are given to the family by the militia. As the impact of his loss deepens, the sorrow-crazed Jabir tries to pretend that the child never existed; he then begins to obliterate all traces of his son. Starting with family photos, then newspaper clippings, he methodically scratches or tears any image of the young man. Later he turns his attention to the posters, tearing them down or whitewashing them. Jabir is arrested for this latter act, the local militia leader sanctimoniously asking:

How could we let the posters of our martyrs, our war heroes,
be torn down? You know how precious such pictures are to
the relatives and friends of the dead, don't you?[11]

Jabir's body later turns up in a rubbish dump. The murdered father is
then himself declared a martyr, and posters bearing his likeness appear
on the walls of Beirut.

The idea that a poster, or any thing, can be anthropomorphized
and said to have a 'life' of its own is not new. Human history is full of
'angry skies' and clouds 'crying rain'; Juliet is Romeo's 'sun' and a car 'hums'
along. Anthropomorphism has made the inanimate simpler and more
comprehensible for millennia, or so the Greek philosopher Xenophanes
suggested when he coined the term. Beginning in the late nineteenth
century, many observers began to assign human qualities to posters,
claiming that they helped mute walls speak. One of these was Jean
Cocteau, whose poster 'Homage to Fernand Mourlot', for an exhibition in
1955 at Mourlot Studio, one of the best printers in Paris, imagines posters
and walls passing through our consciousness like living beings:

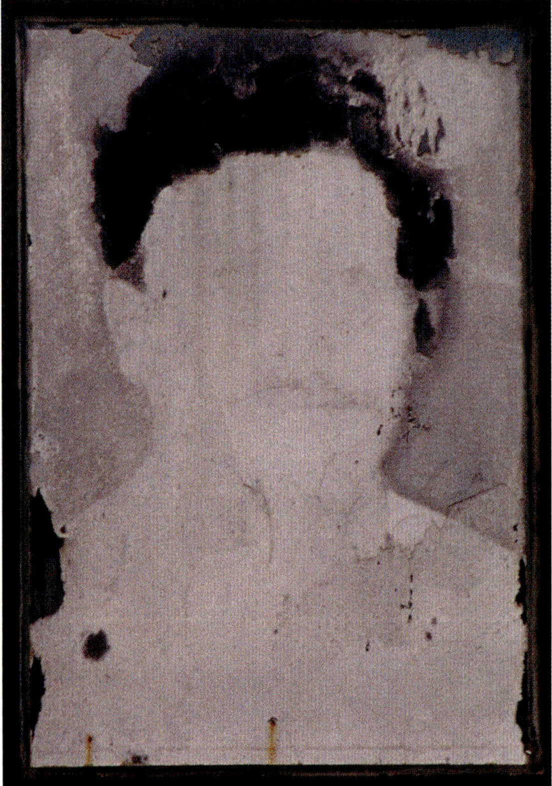

Joana Hadjithomas and Khalil
Joreige, 'Faces-B', from the
series *Faces*, 2006–9.

Walls have ears
They even have mouths
Mourlot Posters
Present some
Of their songs,
Some of their screams.

Cocteau's metaphor, however, is rarely extended to a larger aware-
ness of a poster's 'life'; too often we focus only on posters as if they
exist just off the presses – seldom do we delve into the materiality
of their youthful pasts or worn and faded futures. It is this lingering
material presence that Joana Hadjithomas and Khalil Joreige's project
Faces tries to encompass. Based on the lingering presence of martyr
posters, and tracing their slow disintegration as a muted but omnipresent facet of city life, the pair argues, the project 'reflects a Beirut
in which people are constantly observed by images of the dead'.[12]

When we look at a 'social life' of things,[13] we can take a broader
view of their conception, birth, career, where they lived, retirement

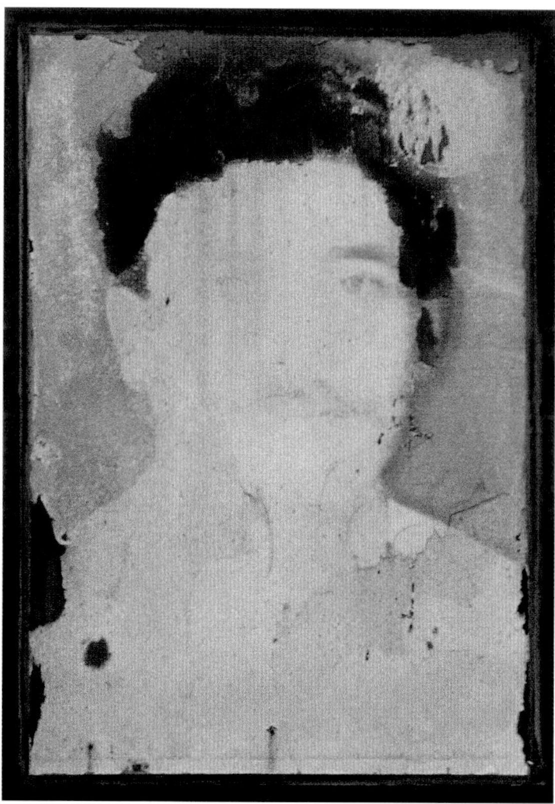
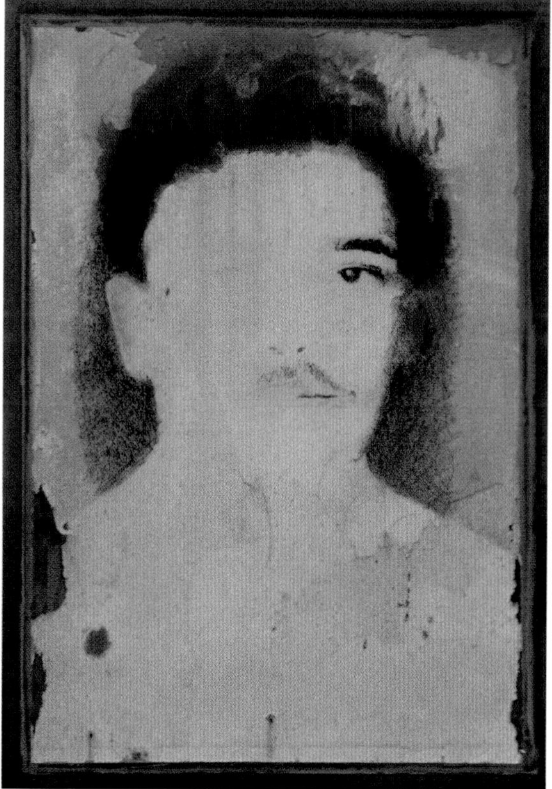

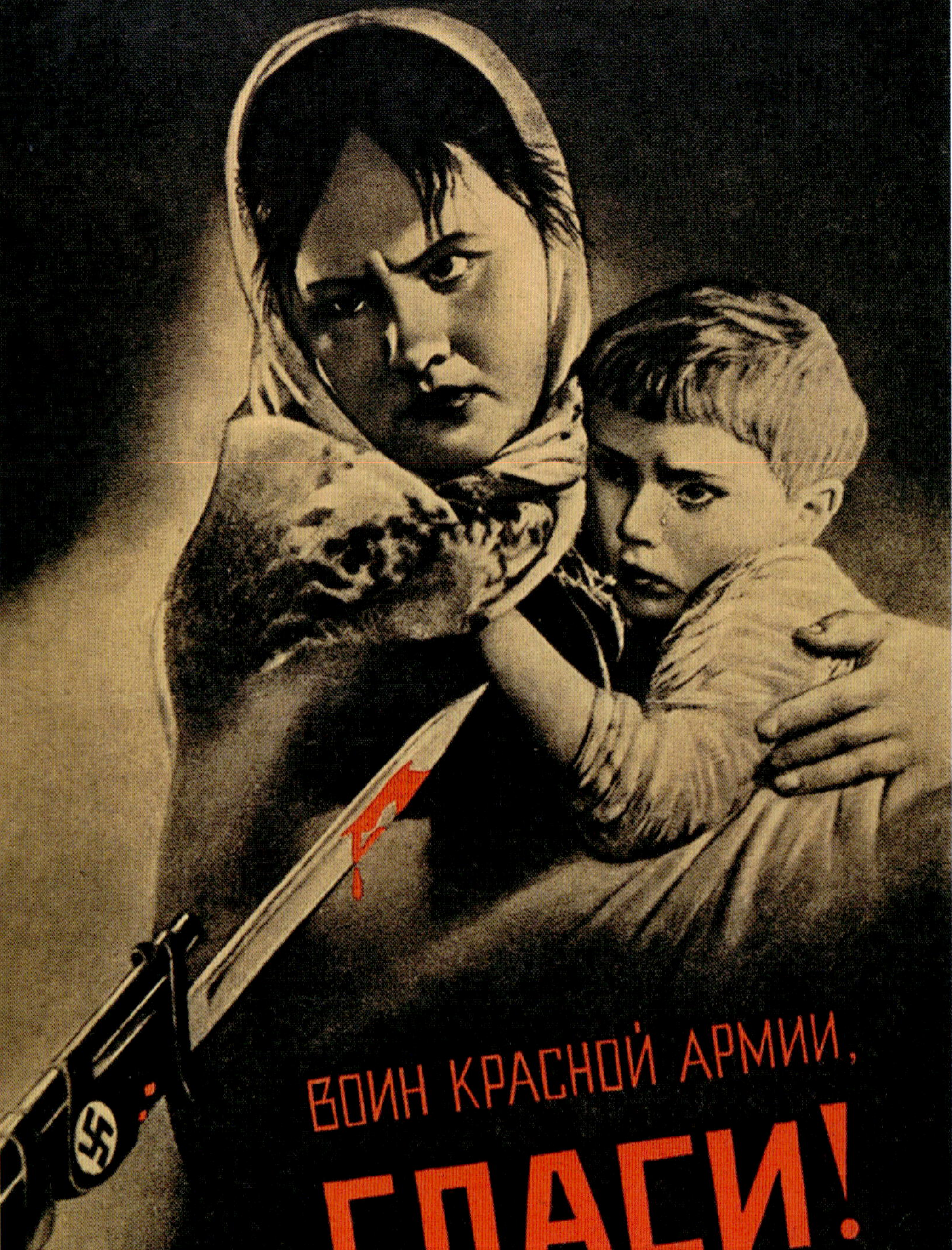
ВОИН КРАСНОЙ АРМИИ,
СПАСИ!

and death. Why, when and how were they made? What would be the 'ideal career' for a particular poster? And where did the poster actually end up? Do posters ever actually die or can they experience a second or multiple lives when repurposed or recycled? Whether conceived in a simple drag-and-drop software template or laboriously drawn on a lithographic stone, posters are born into a world that offers multiple careers. Some are vagabonds and take up rough – and often short – lives on construction fences or the sides of abandoned buildings. Others pass their lives quietly, perhaps seen but ignored on the walls of offices or waiting rooms. Indeed, few of the iconic posters associated with the Depression-era Works Progress Administration actually made it to America's streets; a great many simply ended up on the walls of WPA offices. Posters have marched into war: on the Eastern Front, Soviet soldiers carried posters into battle in a manner much like the religious icons taken into battle by their grandfathers. German commanders quickly noted this semblance and told their men to take aim at the posters, as if bullets could kill these paper icons.[14] A lucky few, like Sagmeister's Cranbrook lecture poster, may make it into museum frames or flat files. These continue to live in a kind of suspended animation. They may see the light of day on rare occasions, but generally live lives outside the public eye. Often seen only by curators and art handlers, they can pass months and even years alone, perhaps envying the posters that have passed a rough but livelier life.

A Harbinger of Change

In this age of immateriality, as mobile phone apps and e-mail blasts add new marketing potentials undreamed of in the age of Chéret and Mucha, it may seem curious to look at posters as a distinct form. But posters' format provides a snapshot of broader epochal transition. To be sure, posters are no longer the darlings of most advertisers, but they have hardly died away. Indeed, how and when they are deployed becomes all the more interesting. When the Apple iPod was launched, the company chose a poster campaign, presenting silhouettes of listeners dancing against backgrounds of screaming, saturated colour, to convey the physicality and sensory depth of the iPod experience. Even – perhaps especially – in a digital age, the materiality and life of a poster can maintain a powerful hold on us.

Victor Koretsky, 'Red Army Soldier, Save Us!', 1943.

This book examines posters not only as designs that reflect avant-garde aesthetics or novel marketing strategies or emphatic political beliefs, but also as material things that live among us. In exploring how the poster creates, shapes and reflects the material world, it examines the spaces where posters live and the functions that they have served. The resounding visual rhetoric of the Russian Revolution, for instance, or the familiar favourites of the Art Nouveau movement, are discussed along with West African street posters and advertising for Bollywood films. Many, for example, posters of Chairman Mao or Che Guevara, are already familiar, only to be contextualized slightly differently here. This approach aims to look beyond the aesthetic regimes of art and design history and begin to see posters as part of everyday life. Seen from a slightly different angle, we discover that posters in the digital age continue to live, and even thrive, in surprising places and with unexpected roles, or even lives. Observed in terms of their social lives, we find a veritable constellation of posters living not in textbooks or museums but in the alleys of Ramallah, the barber shops of Lagos and the market stalls of Chennai. From the nineteenth century onwards, posters have been born with commitments, responsibilities,

Uri Baruchin, iPod poster display, New York, 2005.

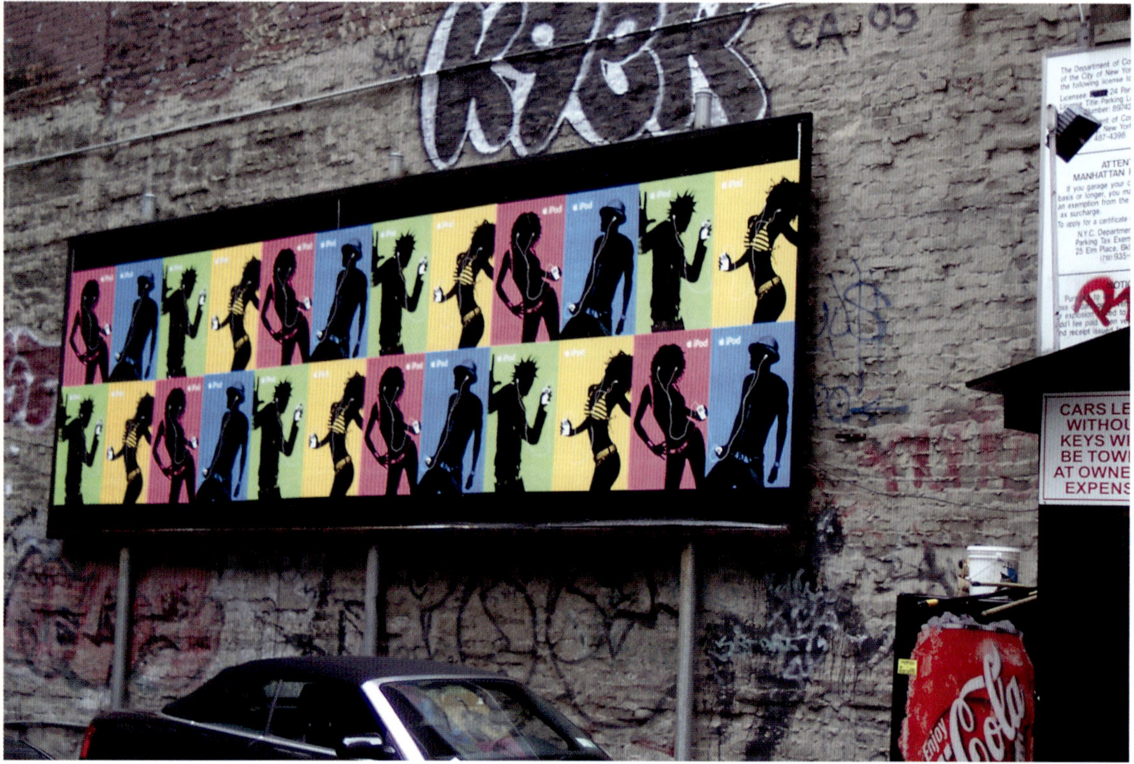

38

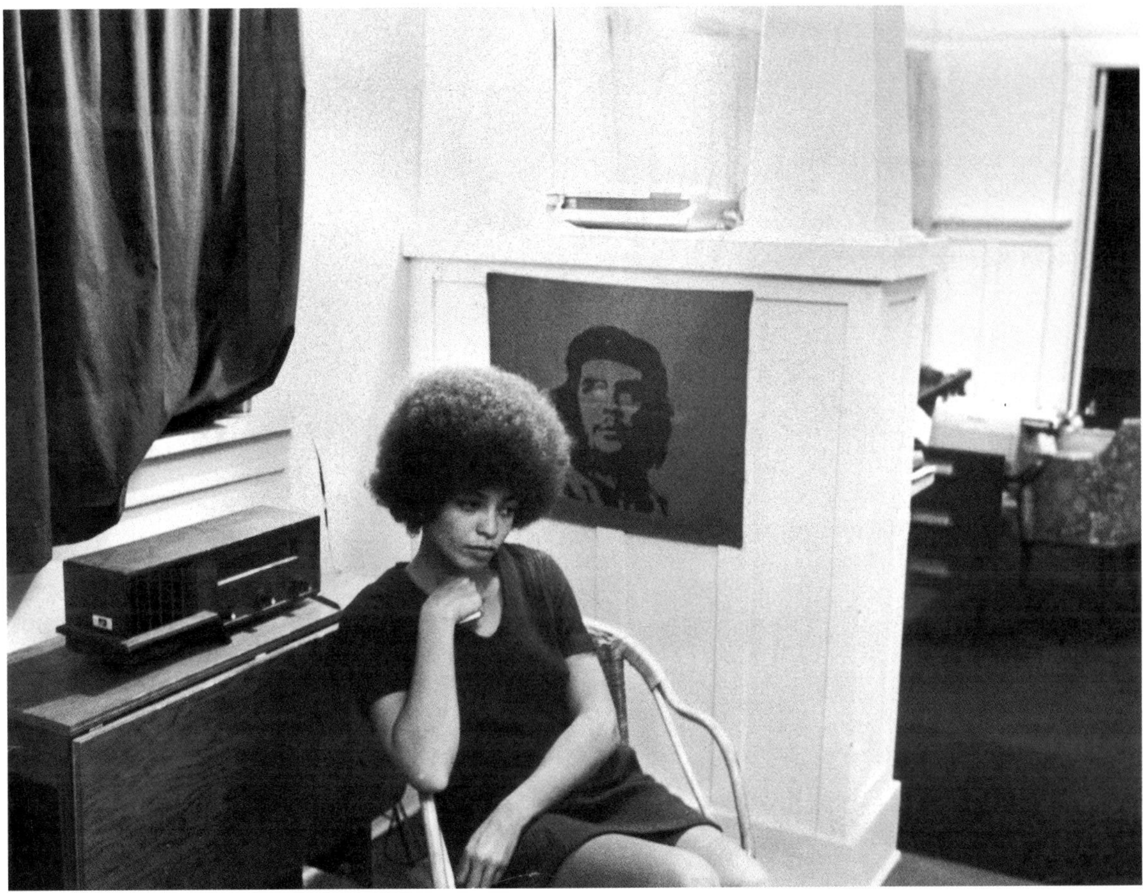

Lucas Mendes, 'Angela Davis', 1969.

dependents and emotional ties; they leave marks on history. Taken singly, posters are essentially short-lived. Their principal talent lies in exposing and expressing their conditions of time, but they are easily dated. Studied more broadly, however, groups of posters can seep into our consciousness, describing not only artistic but also technical, social and political revolutions alongside modes and rhythms of everyday life. Few forms provide a better example of evanescent notions of modernity and globalization long before these became buzzwords. Chapter by chapter, this book aims to build a composite picture of the lives of posters over time. As Khoury's desperate old man discovers, in their very materiality, posters carry a significance that can mean the difference between life and death.

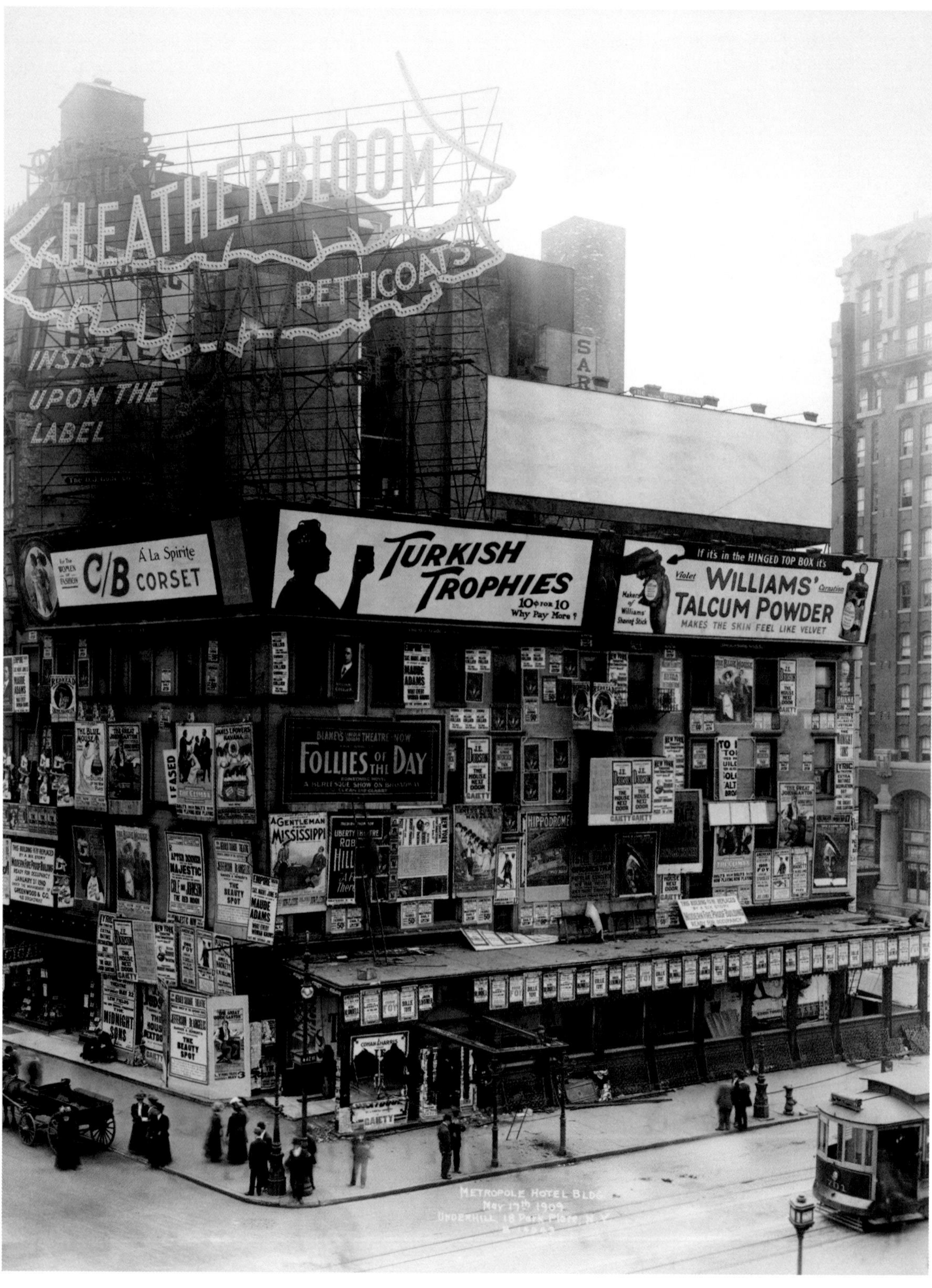

HEATHERBLOOM
PETTICOATS
INSIST UPON THE LABEL
C/B CORSET
À La Spirite
FOR THE WOMEN OF FASHION
Turkish Trophies
10¢ FOR 10
Why Pay More?
If it's in the HINGED TOP BOX it's
Violet WILLIAMS' TALCUM POWDER
MAKES THE SKIN FEEL LIKE VELVET
Makers of Williams' Shaving Stick
BLANEY'S THEATRE NOW
FOLLIES OF THE DAY
A BURLESQUE SHOW ON BROADWAY
A GENTLEMAN FROM MISSISSIPPI
MAUDE ADAMS
MAJESTIC
THE BEAUTY SPOT
MIDNIGHT SONS
HIPPODROME
METROPOLE HOTEL BLDG
May 17th 1909
UNDERHILL 18 Park Place N.Y.

1 CONSUMING WORDS ON THE STREET: 1840–1950

In an article of March 1851 in the periodical *Household Words*, Charles Dickens described the perfect way to kill a man in Victorian London. He would uncover a secret about his victim and print it on a poster, and would then place a large impression in the hands of an active billsticker. 'I can scarcely imagine a more terrible revenge. I should haunt him, by this means, night and day.' In this way, provocative posters would be

> glaring down on him from the parapets, and peeping up at him from the cellars. If he took a dead wall in his walk, it would be alive with reproaches. If he sought refuge in an omnibus, the panels thereof would become Belshazzar's palace to him. If he took [a] boat, in a wild endeavour to escape, he would see the fatal words lurking under the arches of the bridges over the Thames. If he walked the streets with downcast eyes, he would recoil from the very stones of the pavement, made eloquent by lamp-black . . . If he drove or rode, his way would be blocked up by enormous vans, each proclaiming the same words over and over again from its whole extent of surface.

Dickens concluded that his rival would naturally grow thin and pale, reject food and die, his revenge complete.[1] He may have exaggerated the pull of the man's conscience, but his understanding of words in the cityscape was only a slightly inflated one. By the middle of the nineteenth century rapid developments in printing technology dwarfed the gradual transformations that had occurred in the 300 years following Gutenberg's 42-line Bible. Based on a fortuitous alignment of emerging lithographic print technology, steam-driven presses and a ready availability of cheap ink and paper, the modern

The Metropole Hotel covered in advertising, New York, 1909.

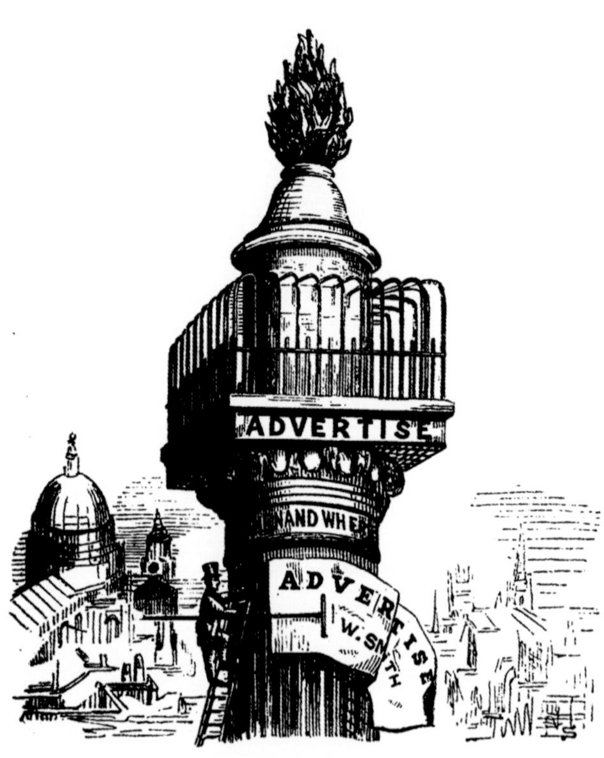

William McConnell,
'Advertise', 1863.

poster is a product of the Industrial Revolution. While Plato imagined Athens as a logopolis, a 'city of words', he would probably have been astounded at Victorian London. If buildings were not enough, printed advertisements were placed on pavement flagstones, covered commercial carriages and vans that slowly trundled through city streets and even appeared on the sides of boats on the River Thames. At one time, many busy London thoroughfares featured poster-covered cabinets that supported large clock faces. The poster may have made London into a new kind of city of words, but the words were predominantly urging sales. Dickens's posters announced a world of mass consumption.

The world described by Dickens has disappeared, and another has appeared in its place. And yet we still sense the urgency behind Victorian posters and handbills. Cutting across class lines, these typeset town criers hawked 'genteel comedies' and railway timetables; they drummed for local and national politics, lost children or goods, trade-union strikes and rewards for escaped felons. But their primary purpose was to sell. Posters served as classified advertisements, announcing sales of houses, household items and other objects frequently sold in an urban marketplace upon a move, bankruptcy or death. The poster was not just a communicator but also a seller; it was so well established that it was hard to imagine selling goods any other way. 'How, our commercial forefathers contrived to announce what commodities they had on sale,' one observer remarked, 'in this our long famed commercial country, is difficult to discover.' [2] Posters opened our horizons, allowed us to look far afield, see new lands and bury ourselves waist deep in the products that they hawked.

Walter Benjamin would later decry how 'script is pitilessly dragged out into the street by advertisements'.[3] Certainly, the brash, bold visual styles representative of the dynamic cities that came of age in nineteenth-century Europe and North America were hard to ignore. Using bombastic, fat faces and other decorative and display type, Victorian handbills carved a new terrain of readership, a space dominated by the strategic use of short declarations, exhortations and aggressive questions intended to catch the eyes of consumers on the move. When Susan Sontag claimed the poster as a capitalist invention, she was not far off;[4] with wildly daring abandon, posters materialized an emerging culture of consumption.

The Gallery of the Streets

But this consumer landscape was still quite beyond advertising as we understand it today; only when illustrations arrived did posters truly begin to animate streets, alleyways and boulevards while also leaping off fences and into collectors' portfolios. In 1869 Jules Chéret introduced to France a system of three-colour lithographic printing that assured accurate colour registration, transmuting the poster into artistic gold; a happy confluence of technology, talent and legitimacy made posters into 'frescos, if not of the poor man, at least of the crowd'.[5] Printed in what the poet Camille Lemonnier called 'electric ink',[6] common street posters were rapidly reconceived as art. Watching with a kind of passive wonder, residents of Paris saw boulevards and alleyways transformed into a 'gallery of the streets'.

Of course, posted images were not new. Hand-painted signs sometimes included pictures, and from time to time woodcut posters might contain limited illustrations. For many years, Barnum & Bailey, for instance, covered barns and fences alike with crudely worked but bright and vividly illustrated advertising, all carefully timed to precede the circus's arrival in town. The bootblacks on a stereoscopic card from about 1866 stand before a hoarding in New York's City Hall Park; they are overwhelmed by P. T. Barnum's huge advertisements touting Tom Thumb's wedding, among other posters. But these relatively crude woodcuts were gradually swept aside by the chromolithograph. In France, Chéret's innovation received a huge boost with the advent of the democratic Third Republic and the passage of the *Loi sur la liberté de la presse du 29*

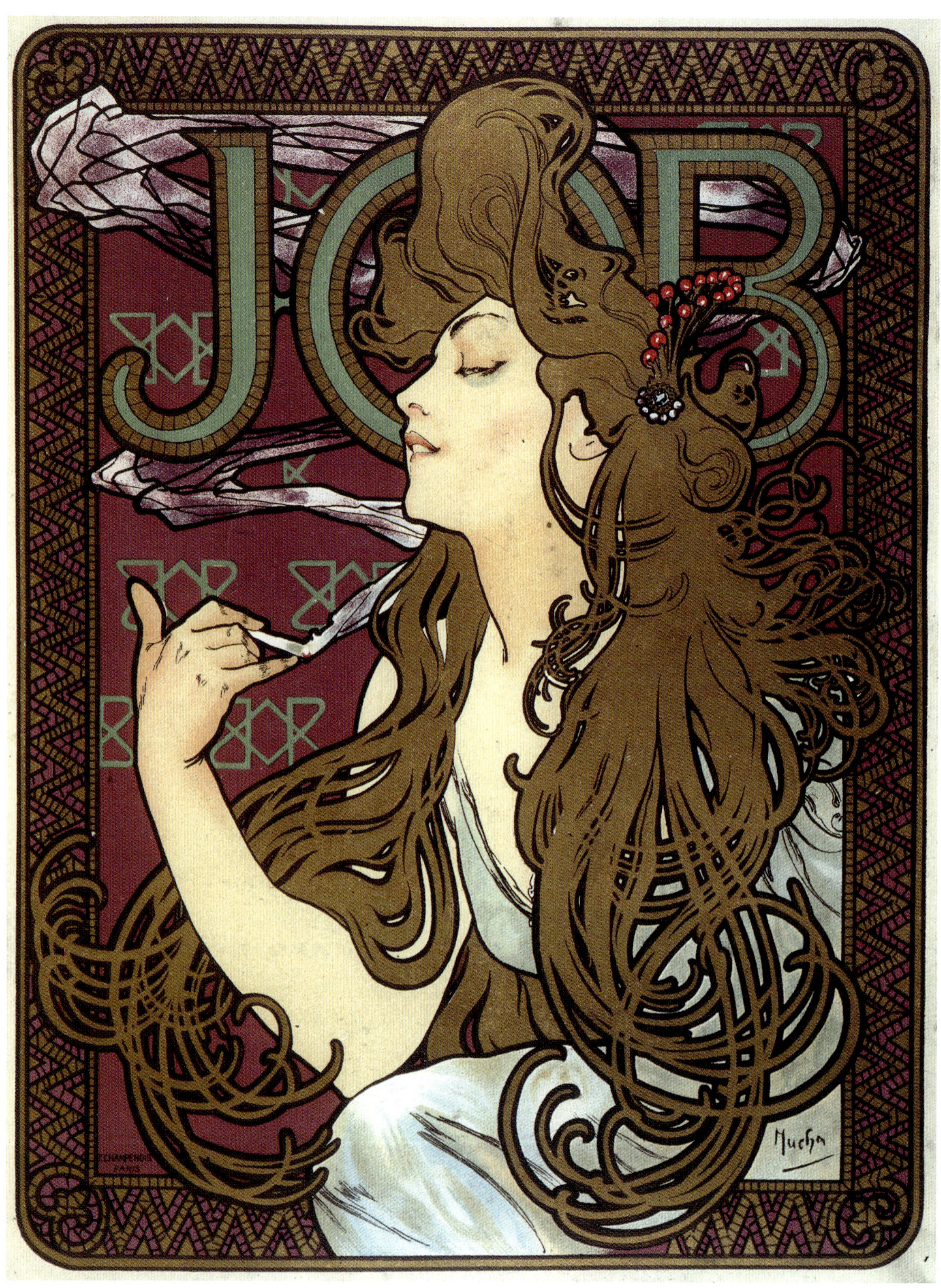

Alphonse Mucha, poster for Job cigarette papers, 1898.

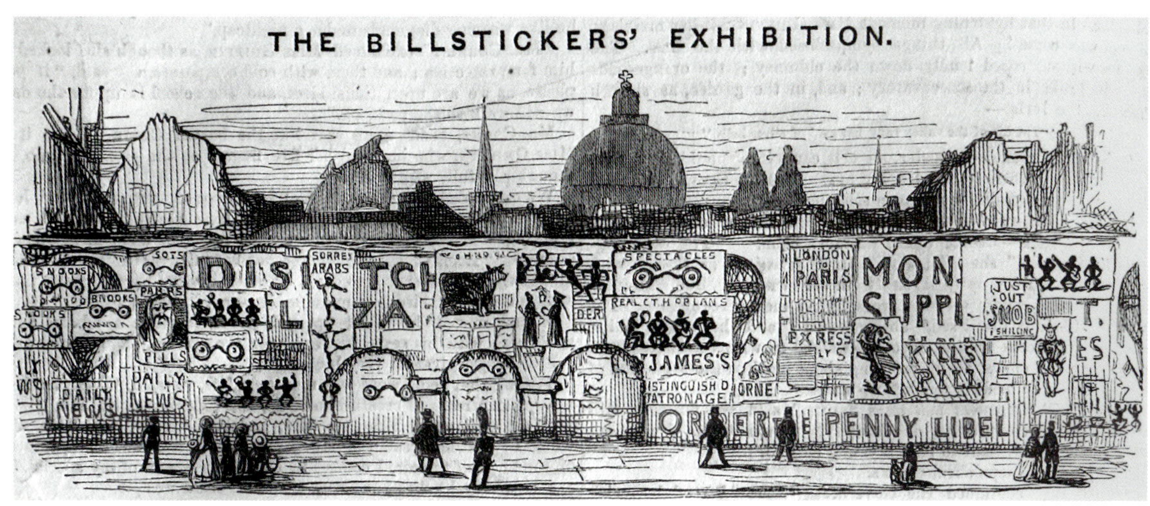

'The Billstickers' Exhibition', cartoon from *Punch* (1847).

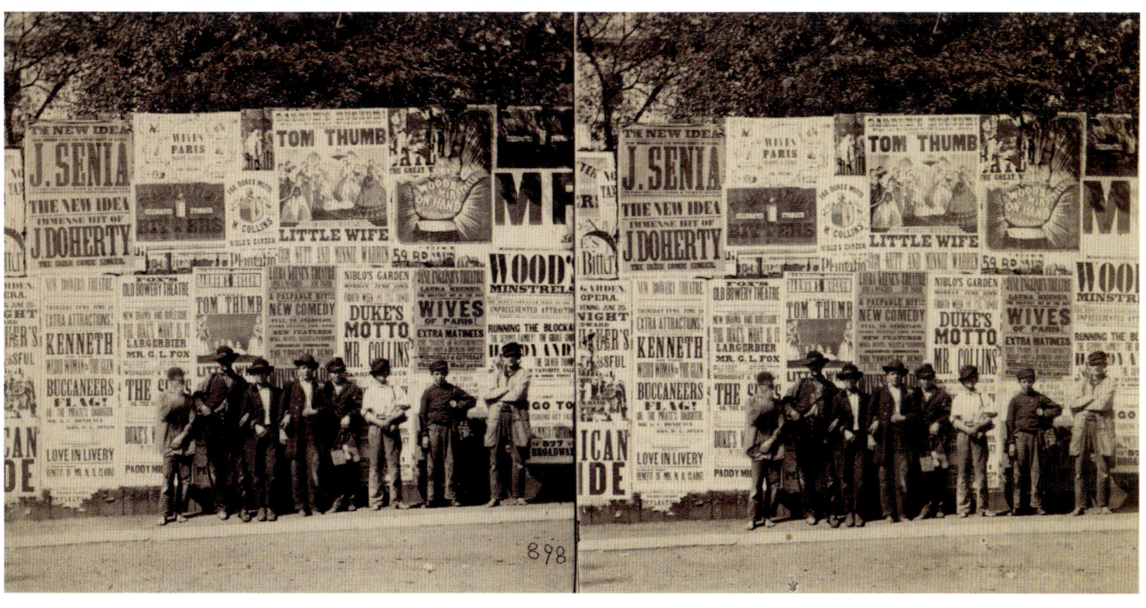

'The Brigade of Shoe Blacks, City Hall Park', *c.* 1866.

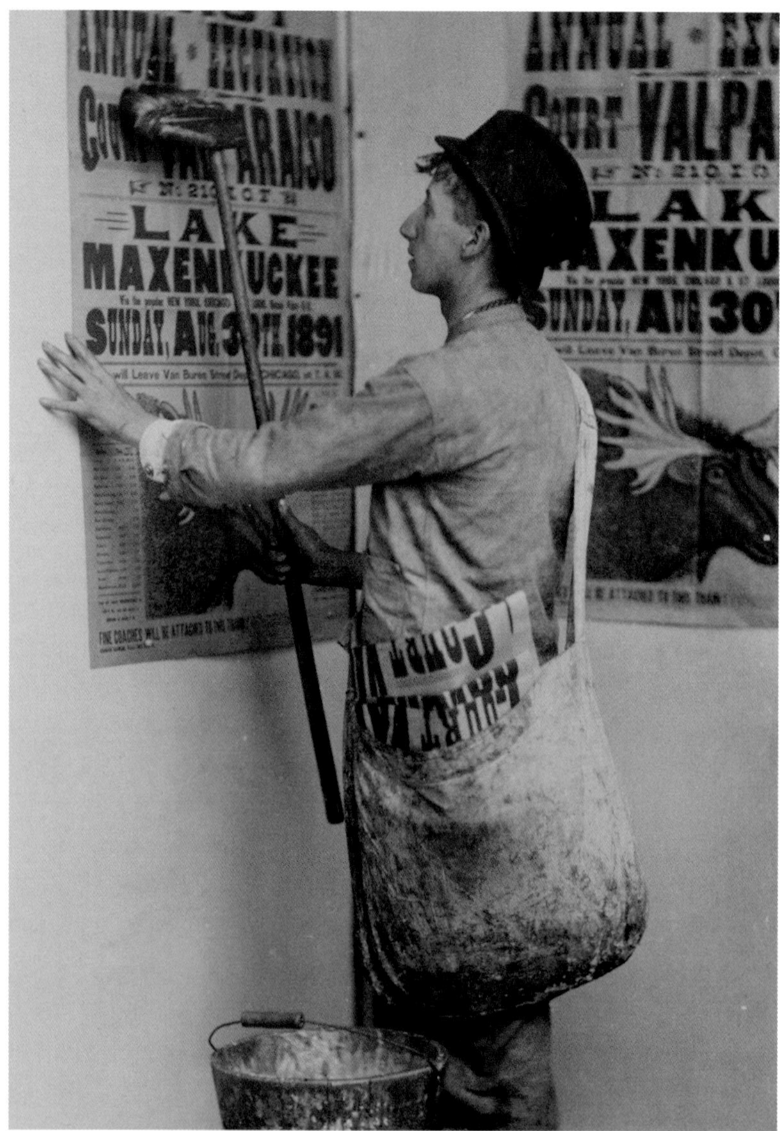

juillet 1881, or Press Law of 1881. Posters rapidly came of age. This
new legislation not only granted posters protection from censorship,
but also from vandalism; furthermore, it inadvertently opened up
physical spaces where posters could hang freely and ply their trade.
In a sweeping shift, bridges, moving carts and major monuments
were all fair game to the city's legions of billstickers. At first working
as freelancers, these unrefined men, often ex-cons or otherwise
unemployable, took up the task of papering nineteenth-century
cities. Female billstickers were rare, but men quickly took advantage
of a new freedom tolerated everywhere except on churches, voting

46

halls and areas designated by local mayors. All else became a backdrop for selling.

Illustrated posters advertised soap and patent medicine, tickets for travel on steamers and to plays, but they could also hawk new ideas and behaviours. Posters marketing bicycles for women also bespoke freedom to go around the city unencumbered; advertisements for cafés and bars shook off associations of dingy slothfulness and instead suggested an easing of social class lines while cultivating a veneer of cheerful depravity. Alphonse Mucha, for example, began his career promoting theatre productions, but quickly branched out, hawking gas lamps and tyres, chocolate and beer. Advertising was a kind of ether, translating things into products. Mucha's posters for 'Job' cigarette papers promoted paper that could wrap tobacco into cigarettes. Other designers' work announced dairy milk transmuted by Nestlé into 'Swiss milk, richest in cream'. Pears Soap was touted as easing ' the White Man's Burden [by] teaching the virtues of cleanliness'. Nevertheless, before the late 1890s most political posters developed haltingly and often exhibited an almost literary sense of decorum; striking workers, for example, exhorted their fellows in posters covered in huge blocks of texts, their complex arguments meant to be read and digested.[7] Occasionally, some posters using wooden type included crudely cut or garishly printed images. But it was only at the very end of the century that politically active artists like Théophile Steinlen and Jules Grandjouan germinated forceful images. Even these, however, were most often used to sell special issues of left-leaning periodicals and books.

In effect, the first picture posters were linked more with capitalism and less frequently with politics; chromolithographs captured buyers' imagination in ways that were impossible for text-only posters. They tried to foist on the consumer a series of obligations, first insisting that their images be viewed, then pushing the reader to read their text and finally expecting them to buy what was being recommended. They required readers to give themselves up to a fantasia of shaving creams and soaps, theatre productions and circuses. They animated streetscapes, allowing the passer-by to travel into unreality, driven by the imaginary breezes of Turkish cigarettes, cheap chocolate and 'dirt-killing' chlorine bleach. Throughout the period, commentators feared that posters appealed to the basest instincts. Many, one British commentator feared, were 'deplorably bad, from a moral standpoint'.[8]

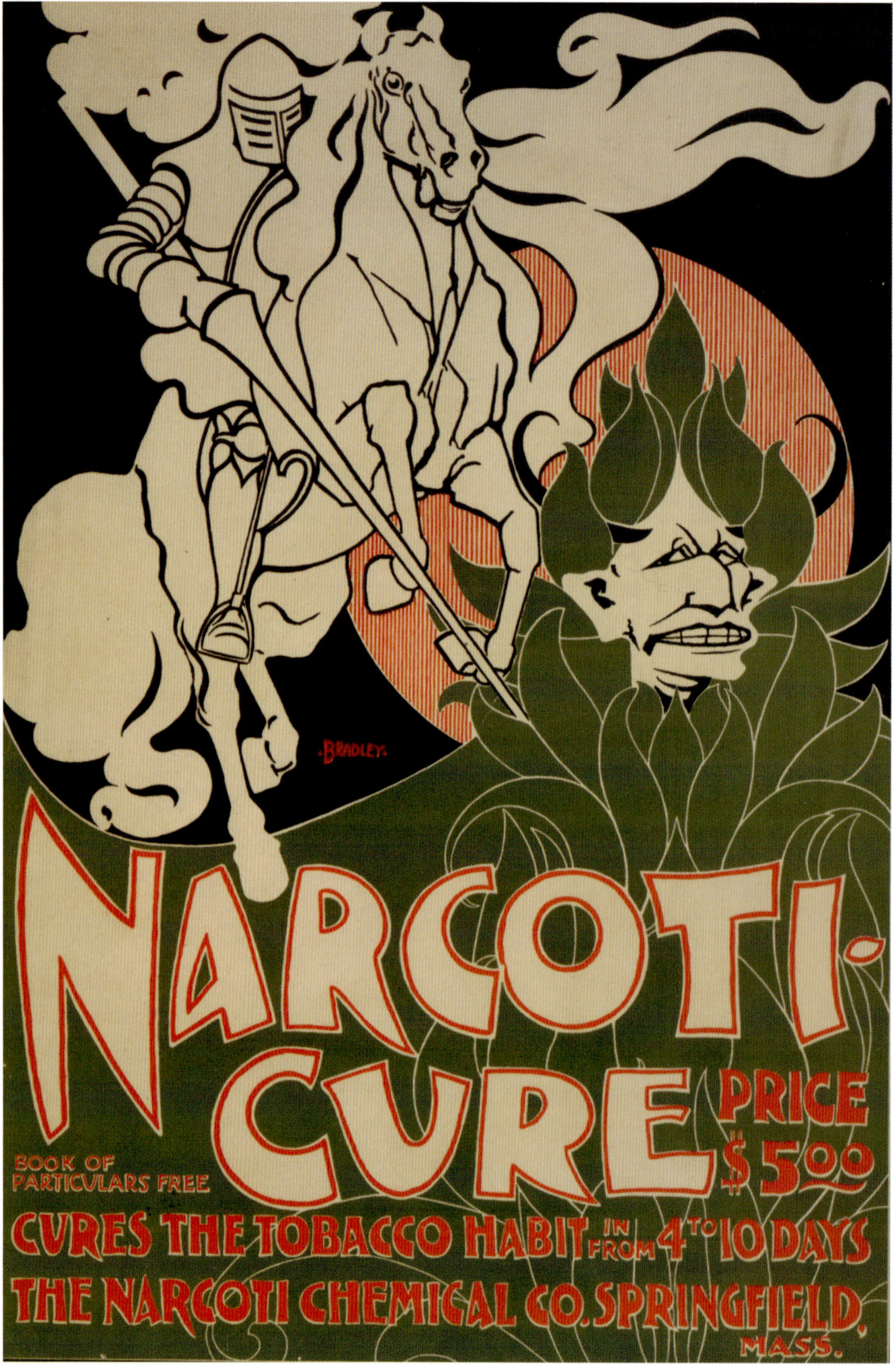

William H. Bradley, 'Narcoti-Cure', 1895.

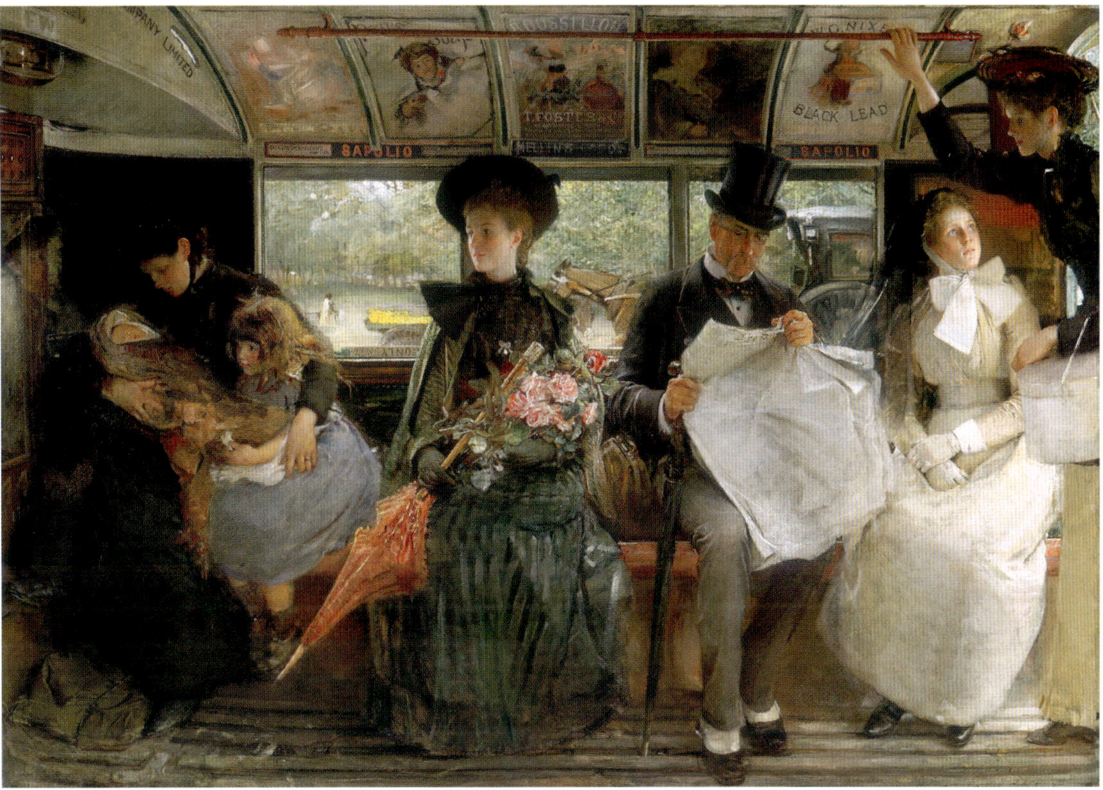

George William Joy,
The Bayswater Omnibus,
1895, oil on canvas.

Another decried the 'pandemonium of posters', while also fretting that 'much ill' could 'be wrought through the eyes'.[9] As one worried French politician nervously reflected in 1880, an illustrated poster

> Startles not only the mind but the eyes . . . stirring up passions, without reasoning, without discourse . . . [addressing] all ages and both sexes . . . speaking even to the illiterate.[10]

For good or bad, the French were usually blamed as the first to treat public imagery as potent tools of communication. The illustrated poster came of age in Paris, the art capital of the nineteenth century.[11] On the one hand, cheap penny prints had circulated in France for many years; on the other, the elite French Ecole des Beaux-Arts and annual Salon were widely known and imitated across Europe. Unsurprisingly, once censorship laws were lifted, large-scale, easily legible posters with dazzling colours quickly burst on the scene, filling alleyways and omnibus interiors alike. Art, the English aesthete Vyvyan James explained, 'is laying violent hands on the bill-postering stations'.

49

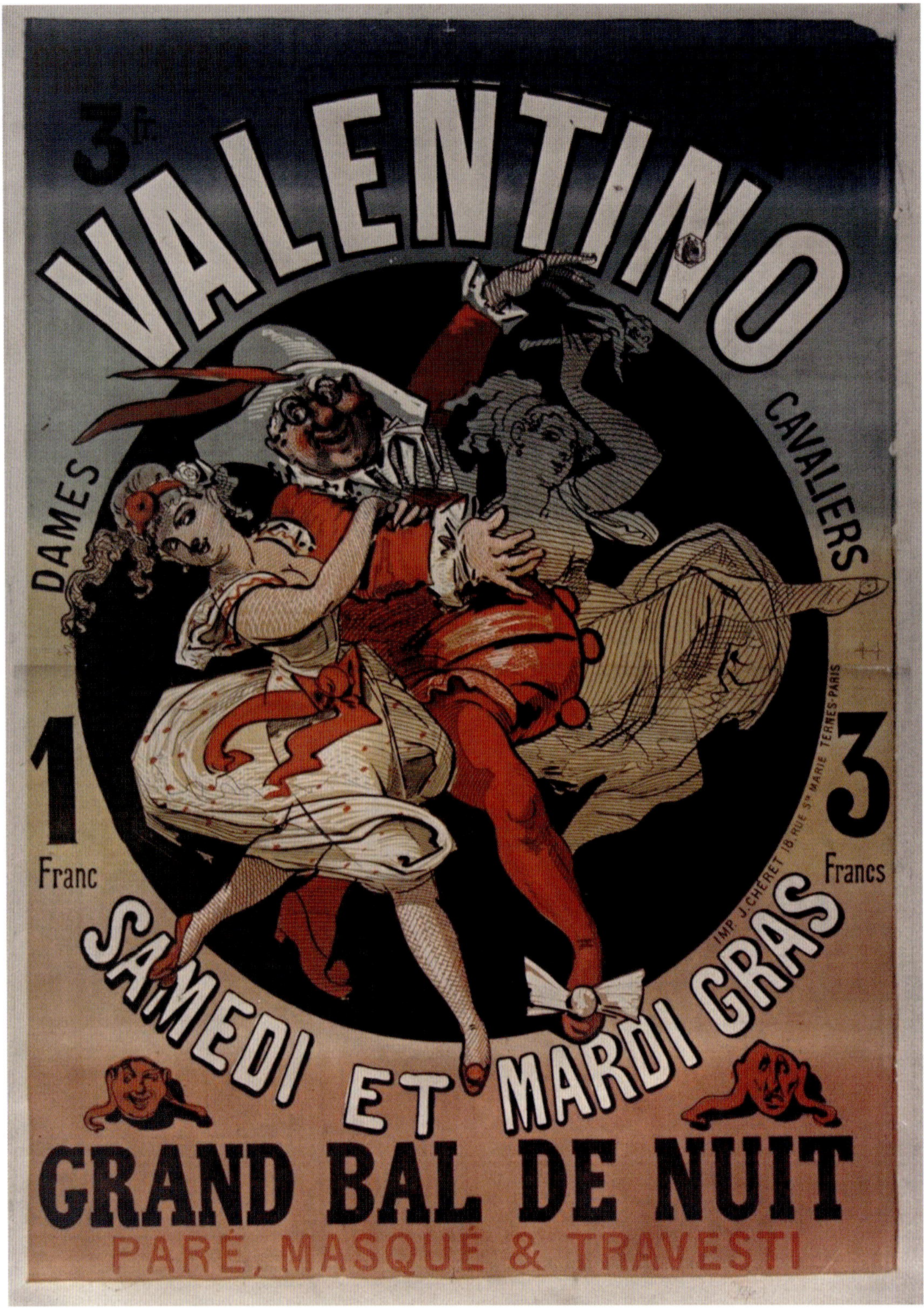

Jules Chéret, poster for the Valentino ball, 1869.

But, he argued, this transformation of poster hoardings was good, 'transforming their hideousness into galleries of pictorial beauty'.[12]

As the lowly handbill was transformed, some commentators argued that the poster pushed to one side more traditional forms of art. The writer Joris-Karl Huysmans, for instance, finished his review of the Salon of 1879 by concluding that most of 'the 3,040 catalogued paintings . . . certainly do not measure up to the commercial posters on view on street walls and boulevard kiosks'.[13] Art historian and critic Roger Marx went further, insisting that Chéret's poster art 'has no less significance . . . than the art of fresco'.[14] The rise of the 'art poster' highlights how quickly the pictorial poster was adopted. But it also signals how, no matter how gluttonously, urban spaces would gradually be turned into 'the poor man's picture gallery'.[15]

At a time when theorists like William Morris believed that 'Art will make our streets as beautiful as the woods', this was a welcome change.[16] By the late nineteenth century, both critics and urban planners hoped the poster could soften harsh public spaces. Comparing Paris to Florence, a city filled with dignified town squares and elegant building facades, writer Jules Claretie believed that though 'Florence, in its streets and plazas, [is] a museum of marble and bronze . . . [the] poster gives Paris its image museum, its exhibition of master water-colour artists in the open wind'.[17] Posters not only decorated streets but also, proponents claimed, could help wrest the public sphere out of the hands of profligate industrialists and the lazy government bureaucracy that dominated French politics in the Third Republic.[18] Political reformers embraced the attitude of the nineteenth-century collector, writer and publisher Ernest Maindron, that 'It was a great joy . . . to note that the factory walls and the cold and naked palisades of buildings under construction had become veritable museums where the masses, reflective and attracted to art, now found some of their aspirations satisfied'.[19] But underneath the fine words, posters in fact had a love–hate relationship with fine art.

The Seller is Sold

Deep one night, in December 1891, billstickers plastered Paris with some 3,000 copies of a poster for the Moulin Rouge nightclub. Soon after, most of the posters had disappeared – torn down, not because they were unpopular, but because they were being collected. The poster's jagged silhouettes, variegated lettering, flat colours and unusual perspectives gave a tantalizing impression of the licentious cancan then sweeping Montmartre, but its overnight popularity also exemplified the 'postermania' of the 1890s; placards from the street figuratively jumped from fences and exterior walls and landed indoors, only to be hung in gilt frames. Indeed, Toulouse-Lautrec's iconic poster of La Goulue was placed on placards outside the Moulin Rouge and mounted on donkeys that walked around Montmartre. 'I still remember the shock I had when I first saw the Moulin Rouge poster . . . carried along the avenue de l'Opéra on a kind of small cart,' one Paris observer recalled years later, 'and I was so enchanted that I walked alongside it on the pavement.'[20] Years later, the increasingly dour and taciturn Cubist Georges Braque could still remember the thrill when, as a boy, he trailed a billsticker in the provincial town of Le Havre, carefully pulling down freshly glued posters by Lautrec.[21]

In some ways these posters compressed modern life into easily understood snatches, their magic comprehensible to millions of passers-by. Fine artists like Mucha, Steinlen and Toulouse-Lautrec created startling and original combinations of word and image, and, like pouring nectar into a brimming cup, collectors began paying substantial sums to own them. Edmond Sagot, a bookseller by trade, founded the Librairie des Nouveautés et Librairie Artistique in 1881; one of the first dealers to sell posters from his tiny Right Bank shop in 1886, Sagot was quickly joined by others. These vendors treated the new illustrated posters as a type of modern print that simply updated the lithographic tradition. When Galerie Rapp celebrated the one-hundredth birthday of the lithographic print with an exhibition, it drew attention to the lithograph's development in an advertising poster showing an elegant lady holding up an early black-and-white lithograph of a Napoleonic

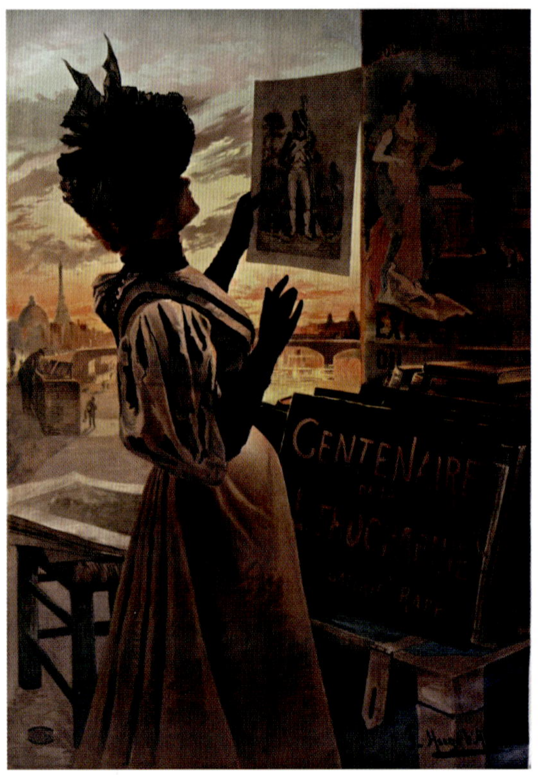

Frédéric Hugo d'Alési, poster for the Centennial Exhibition of Lithography at Galerie Rapp, 1895.

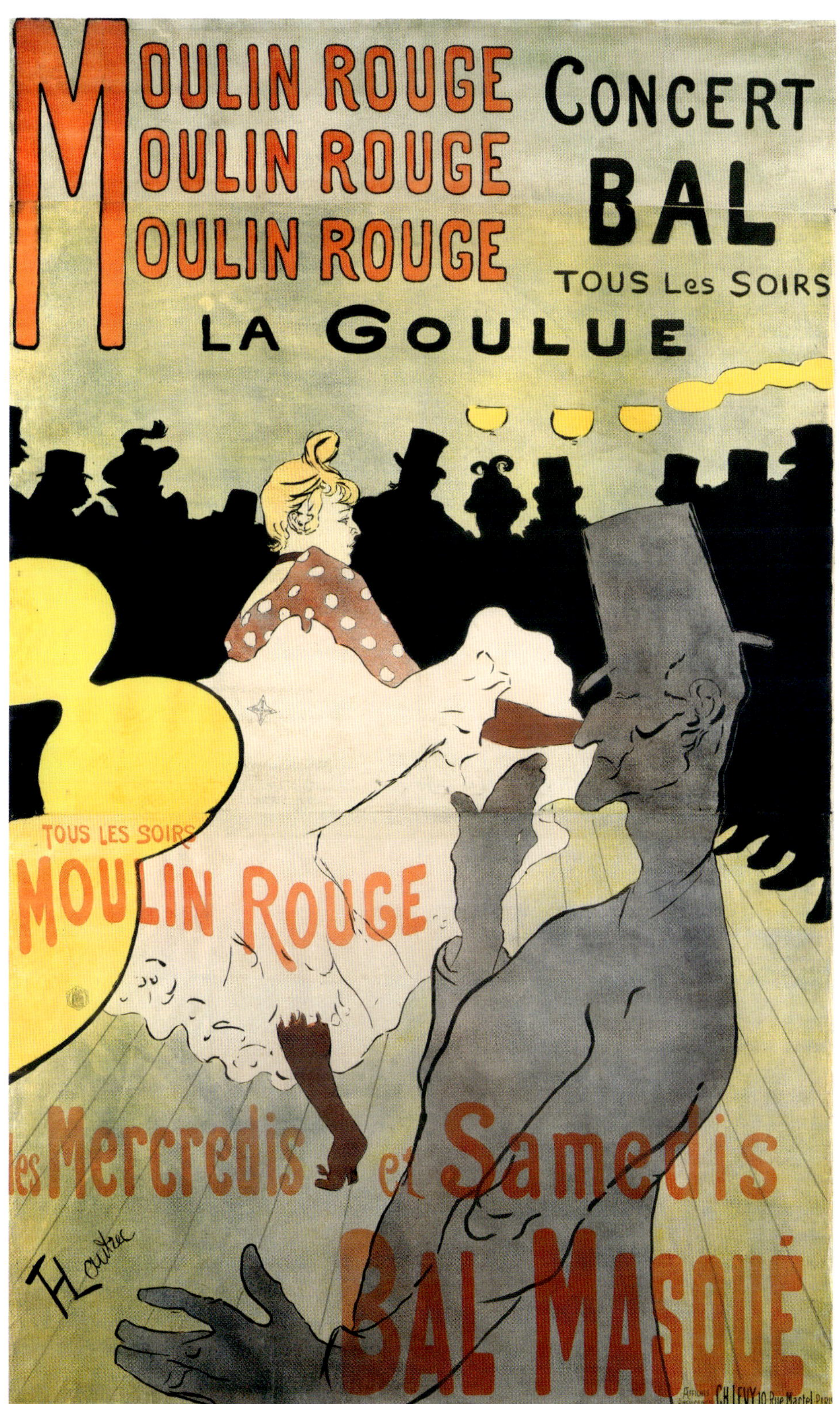

Henri de Toulouse-Lautrec, 'Moulin Rouge, La Goulue', 1891.

soldier. The simple image is juxtaposed against a colourful contemporary poster stuck on a wall. Galerie Rapp's poster mutely describes the poster's evolution. Some dealers, including Sagot, even began publishing collectable posters using good-quality ink and paper, as opposed to the newsprint and cheap dyes found in street posters. Yet, like Braque, any person who desired such strange prizes could simply follow a poster hanger; both serious collectors and art students alike stalked city streets, following in the billsticker's wake and tearing down fresh treasure; like big-game hunters on safari, they were ever-ready to grab and rip down dubious trophies at every turn. The illustrated poster was becoming a consumable product.

As the poster was itself sold, it invaded middle-class homes in unpredictable ways. Daring young couples issued wedding invitations using pictorial poster forms; charades were built around posters and their messages; party guests were invited to come dressed as poster characters and dinner party hostesses used small poster reproductions as name cards at formal meals. Some aficionados even staged *tableaux vivants*, interpreting posters.[22] Collectors could subscribe to series like *Maîtres de l'affiche*, a collaborative effort coordinated by Roger Marx and Chéret that issued slightly smaller versions of popular posters by well-known artists such as Lautrec and Mucha. For a time, such journals thrived, while books described how to classify and collect posters. Critics and poster artists founded poster salons and even discussed opening poster museums. Yet few commentators meditated deeply on the implications of these developments. Collector Charles Hiatt, for instance, was one of the few to notice the 'contrast' between 'how posters look on hoardings vs. what ones will appeal to collectors'.[23] As a consumable art form accessible to the middle classes, its utilitarian function was ignored.

Making Emptiness Profitable

When William Henry Fox Talbot photographed Trafalgar Square in April 1844, the imposing edifice of St Martin-in-the-Fields lay in the background, but Nelson's Column was still under construction and the scaffolding surrounding it was covered with posters advertising anything from an evening of 'Polkamania!' to railway timetables. Loosely hung on a caretaker's shed, a hapless sign reading 'Bill Posters Will Be Prosecuted' was ignored. In Talbot's photograph, these sly posters

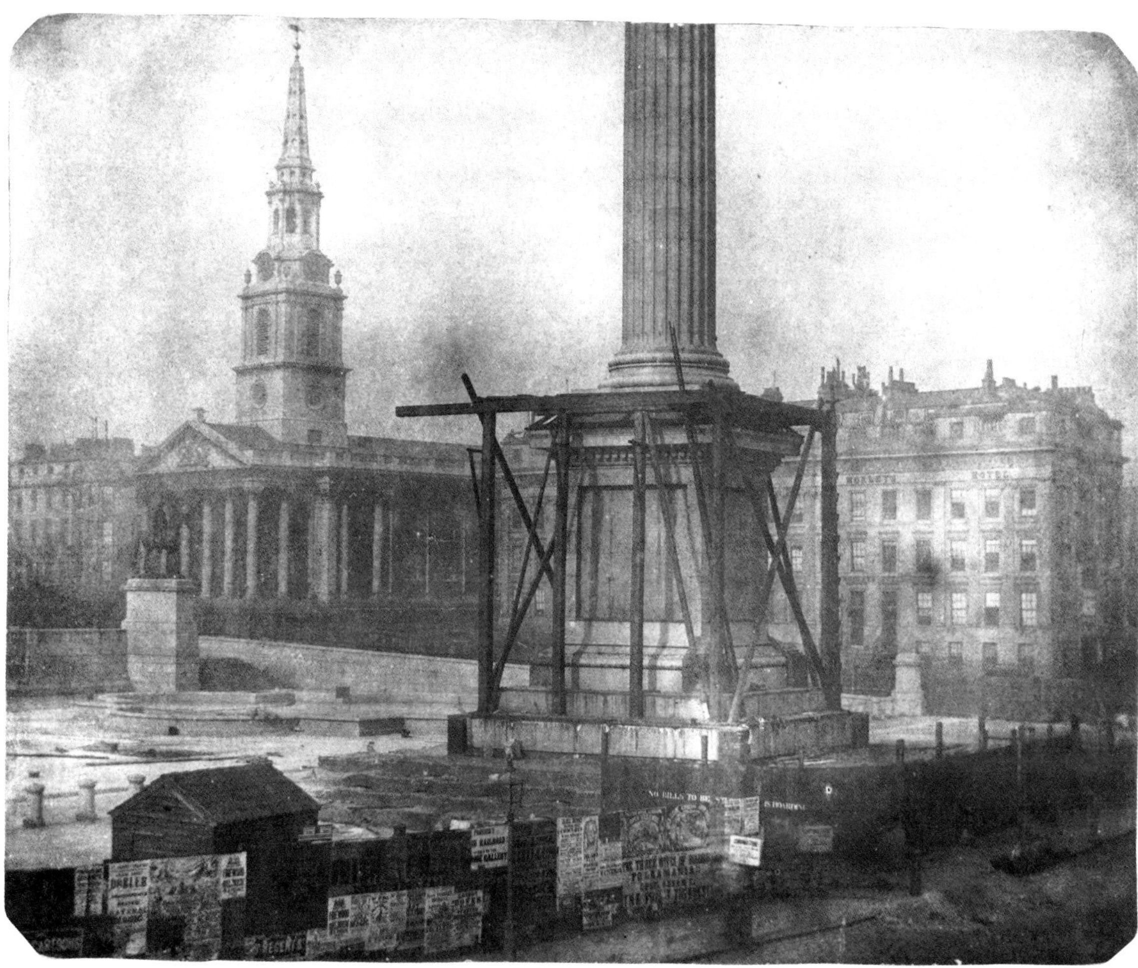

William Henry Fox Talbot, 'Nelson's Column under Construction, Trafalgar Square, London, April 1844'.

insinuate themselves onto London's temporary fences. They register a casual disregard for the law, but also hint at something broader: a vast urban terrain of urban space newly discovered and profitably ripe for the picking. Fifty years earlier, empty walls and casual work sites were of little worth. Ramparts around cities and the doors of official buildings might occasionally sprout authorized announcements. Graffiti was common enough on walls. But advertisers did not pay to put things on walls. With a surprising intensity, posters changed all that, and altered the complexion of urban spaces at the same time. Once considered little more than 'empty' space, windows and walls facing bustling streets, like the sides of wagons, carts and carriages that moved around the city, were suddenly reconceived as valuable space.

By Talbot's day, it was only beginning to become clear that the gold fields in California were not the only places to find easy money.

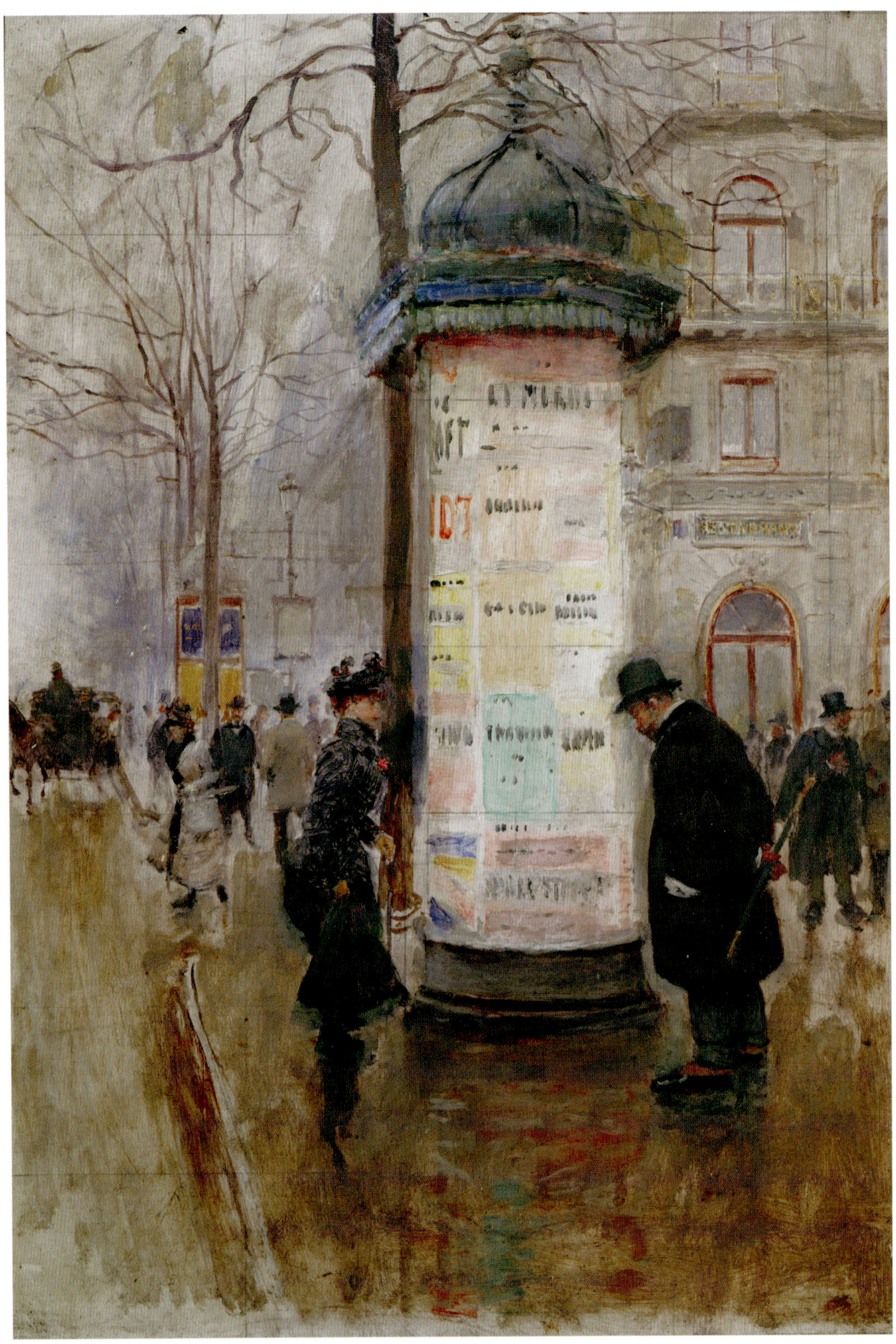

Jean Béraud, *The Morris Column*, c. 1885.

Legal niceties made France a little slower. In 1884, scarcely three years after vast changes to the government's censorship laws, the city of Paris began charging an annual rent of 15,000 francs for advertising on the exposed sides of buildings.[24] Railway companies discovered that station platforms presented sellable space. In bustling New York, advertisers soon discovered that the prices charged could be staggering; during the erection of a new building on Broadway in Manhattan, the owner charged an unheard-of sum of $3,000 a year for access to the temporary boards surrounding his building site.[25] Kiosks with poster space, along with poster-bearing urinals and other 'street furniture', became standard equipment in the broad boulevards of Paris and Berlin. Constructed by the city or private firms, they too were rented out for advertising. Rather than being considered awkward or even embarrassing, these amenities were provided in prosperous districts, where they dotted wide streets and were placed in front of grand hotels, theatres, restaurants and department stores. These hubs of upper-middle-class life were, as one contemporary commentator suggested, 'all the places where the interesting clientele is found'.[26]

With the loosening of advertising strictures in places like France, a plain fact emerged: posters could be very profitable. For several generations, bill posters led hard lives and often competed with one another, fighting their way through the terrible odds to find posting space in overcrowded cities. Energetic poster hangers competed for space and passers-by often witnessed the alarming spectacle of ongoing rivalries, fights and outright wars between different factions. It was not unusual for rivalries to end up in court and in New York several billstickers were sent to the state penitentiary for fighting. Others proudly accepted the challenge of posting in the congested cities of the late nineteenth century. As one observer put it, this kind of billsticker

> will cover the ash-can that a forgetful servant girl has left in the areaway . . . It's all fish that comes to the billposter's net. He will decorate a broken-down moving van or an automobile that is half way up a tree.[27]

The publisher of a contemporary advertising journal went further, praising the 'wide-awake' billsticker who might specifically seek 'a destructive fire in a business house. Before the ruins cease smoking

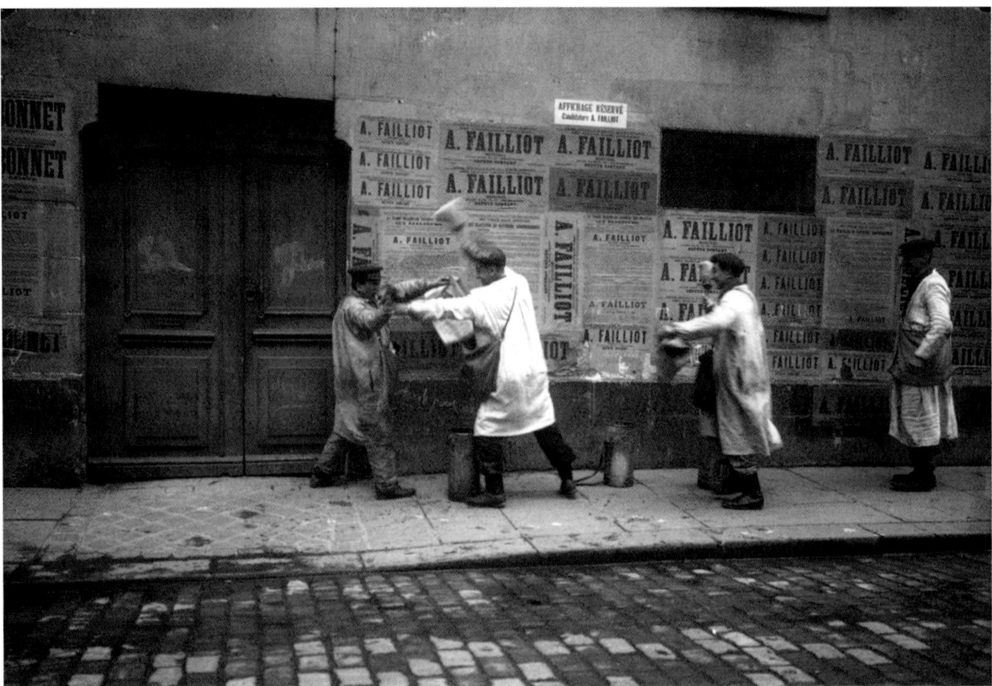

Battling bill posters: poster hangers in Paris fight over profitable street territory, 1910.

the windows are smoothly boarded over' and ready for posting.[28] Space was in such demand that one enterprising billsticker in Pittsburgh purportedly posted on 'the carcass of a horse while the body was still warm'.[29]

At the time, few people realized it, but these cadres of men were also charged with the task of poking and prodding the invisible lines of custom and habit that knitted city neighbourhoods together. In Britain, billstickers were allowed to post on the fences of buildings, but not on private residences. Across the United States, it was common to put large posters on the sides of barns. Advertisers pushed poster hangers to take risks. Urging billstickers to post anywhere, even on private property, Artemus Ward told them to let a property owner

> indulge in profanity of the bluest and most odorous variety, but ten chances to one they read the posters, and, if they happen to need what is advertised, they remember where the goods are to be found.[30]

Needless to say, the phrase 'post no bills', as well as its multiple variants, '*Défense d'afficher*', 'Billstickers beware' and 'Stick no bills', was often ignored. On occasion, poster hangers were involved in violent turf wars, but only rarely were professional billstickers arrested for illegal posting.[31]

But, as the century progressed, advertisers learned that bill-stickers could accomplish something previously ascribed only to alchemists: they turned emptiness into gold. City lots with no buildings on them could hold wooden fences ripe for the posting. 'Gable walls' – that is, the blank, windowless ends of rows of houses – were claimed by cash-strapped cities like Paris, and were soon 'reserved' for paying customers. Government buildings were soon festooned with empty frames, presenting new spaces that could be rented out to advertisers. Even the greasy strip that ran along the sides of railway tracks became, quite suddenly, profit-making space. Areas racked with tidal restless-ness, where waves of cash-flush pedestrians passed every day, were of premium value, and were in special demand. Low-rent districts, the waste places of the town, were also papered over, but more messily and in a haphazard manner. These zones were less well regulated. Cities were cut in pieces, riddled with invisible lines. The first advertising agencies were rudimentary. In the United States, they blossomed in the years following the Civil War; in France, they began to take shape after the fall of the Second Empire in 1870. Agencies like Renier in Paris established domains or 'concessions', for instance, buying monopolies

Walker Evans, 'Posters covering a building near Lynchburg to advertise a Downie Brothers Circus', 1936.

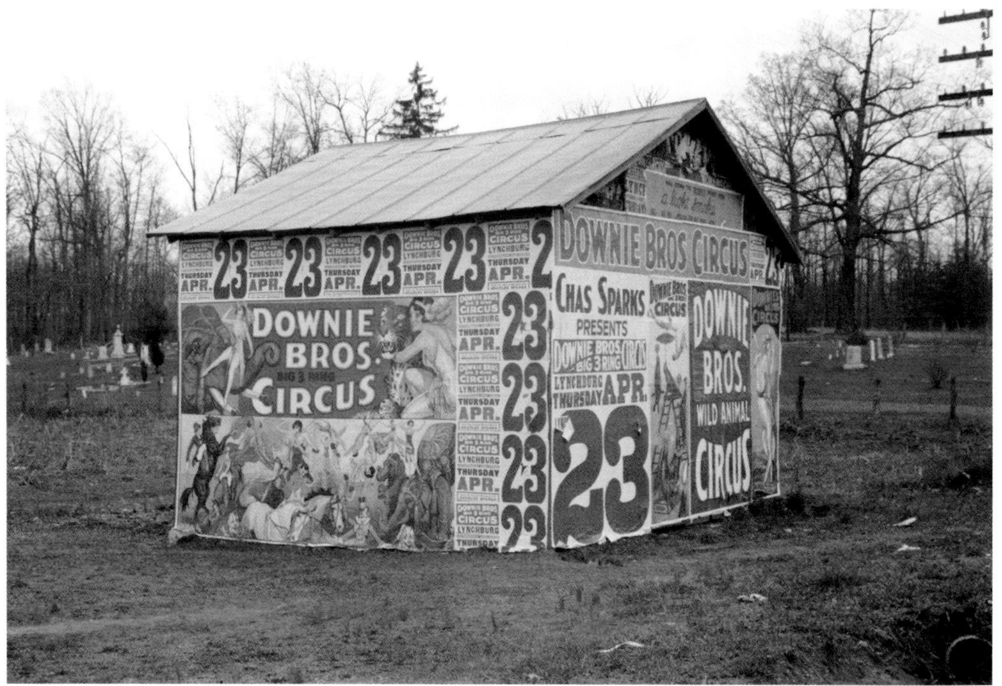

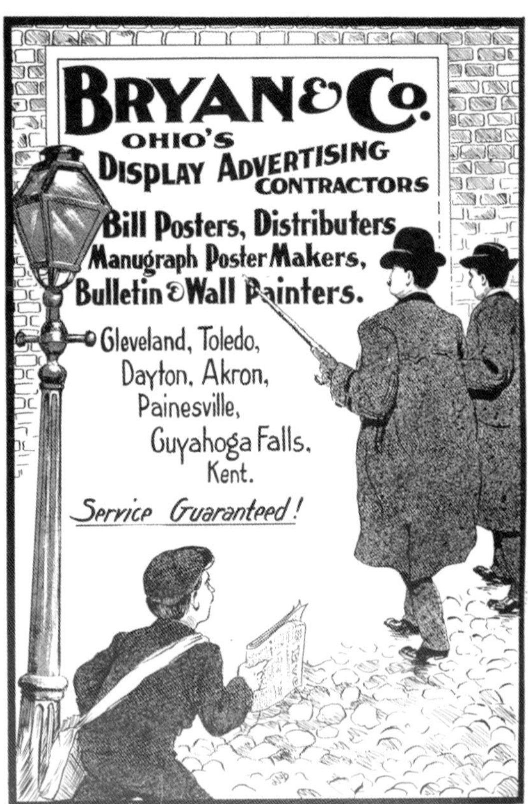

'Bryan & Co. Ohio's Display Advertising Contractors', from *Current Advertising* (1902).

for advertising on Paris Métro stations or trams and omnibuses.[32] Invisible to the general public but drawn up and well understood by billstickers, city advertising was held together by a myriad of undrawn, unwritten borders. These might periodically be re-juggled as one group might sublet parts of their monopoly to other agencies. But they were carefully respected.

By century's end a second transformation had progressed more quietly, in the form of a virtually invisible invasion. As advertising became more established, poster hangers professionalized. Groups like the International Billposters' Association of North America, which was formalized in 1872, were formed. Members were sworn to adhere to a code, in which they avoided 'the malicious covering of bills to gratify private animosity of opposing billposters' and swore that 'we will endorse no bill poster guilty of this offense'.[33] Purified after years of practice, enforcement could be strict; most poster hangers saw 'violators' – in other words, anyone who overstepped this invisible map and independently hung their own posters in prime spots – as threats to their livelihood. That said, many of these changes were invisible to the general public, who might not notice any change. But the old free-for-all was gone and most paid space was extremely orderly. Some billstickers began 'blocking' their posters to hang in large, choreographed series, both horizontally and vertically. Other stickers preferred lining up groups of the same poster. Having purchased the right to hang bills in a spot, poster stickers took pride in their work. Eventually, out of wild disorder came order. But technological change, including film and radio, would soon push the poster in other directions.

Old New Media

The career of screen actress Mary Pickford was on a stormy if meteoric rise when the United States entered the First World War; with her tousled blond curls and endearing manner, fans knew that the Canadian-born heroine was adept at the art of silent acting. But, as Hollywood geared up for war, its favourite actress not only hawked war bonds, but also unveiled the emotional richness behind the American war effort, which ran as much on patterns of belief as steel and cotton. In the one-reel short *One Hundred Percent American* (1918), a film made in collaboration with the Liberty Loan Committee, Pickford plays the perky if flighty Mayme. Our heroine flits perilously close to the chasm of selfish comfort, but is called back from a moral error through the power of the poster. As Mayme and a friend go out for a stroll, the pair casually pass a firebrand 'four-minute man', a specially trained barker who, fuming with energetic excitement, delivers an on-point speech promoting war bonds. Mayme steps up her pace, but is haunted. When the girls enter the Oasis, an ice-cream shop, the friend orders a sundae with shameful carelessness. But Mayme pulls herself back and indulges in a silent, if guilt-ridden, reverie. Remembering the moving Liberty Loan poster 'Hun or Home?', itself a follow-up to the popular 'Halt the Hun' issued earlier in the year, Pickford ponders war at its most beastly. Part of the Fourth Liberty Loan drive in 1918, artist Henry Raleigh's latest poster played on war's unarticulated fears, identifying a small girl, a babe in arms, fleeing from an approaching

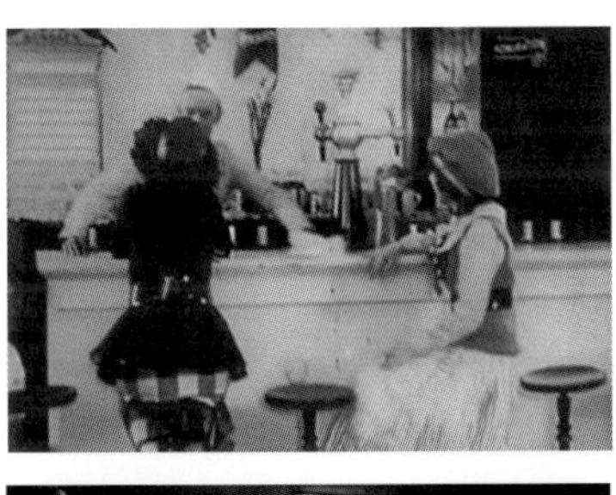
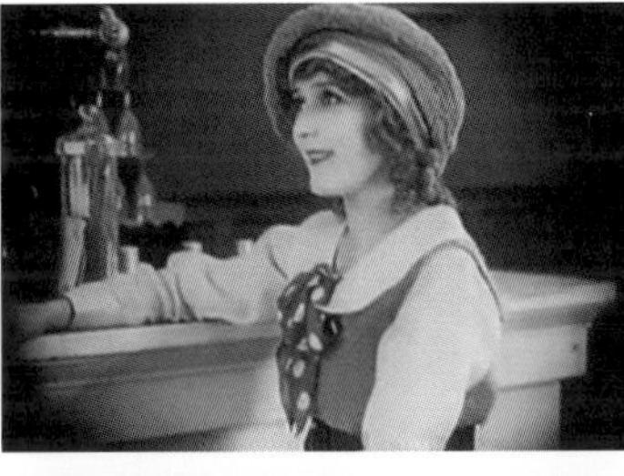
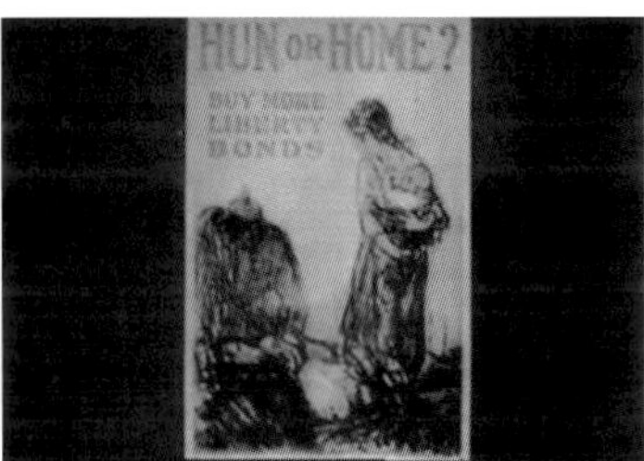

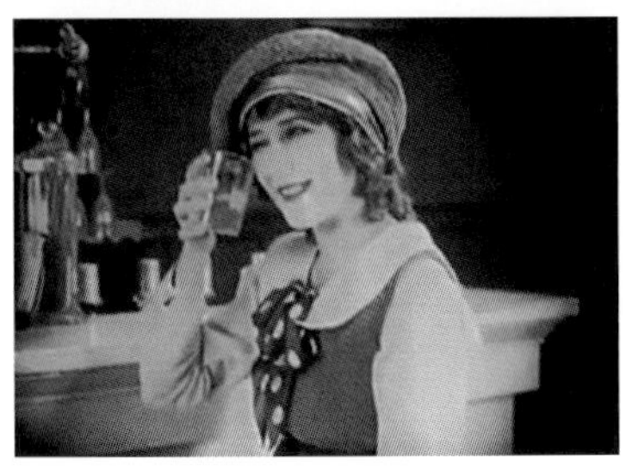
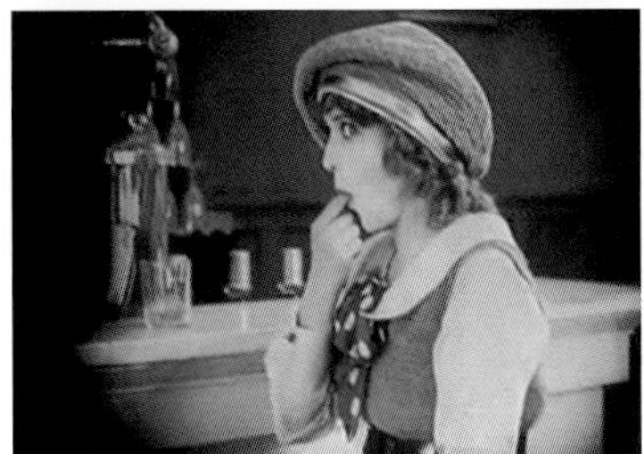
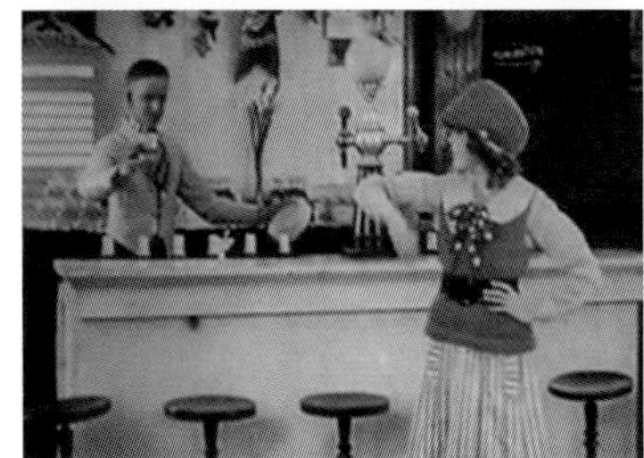

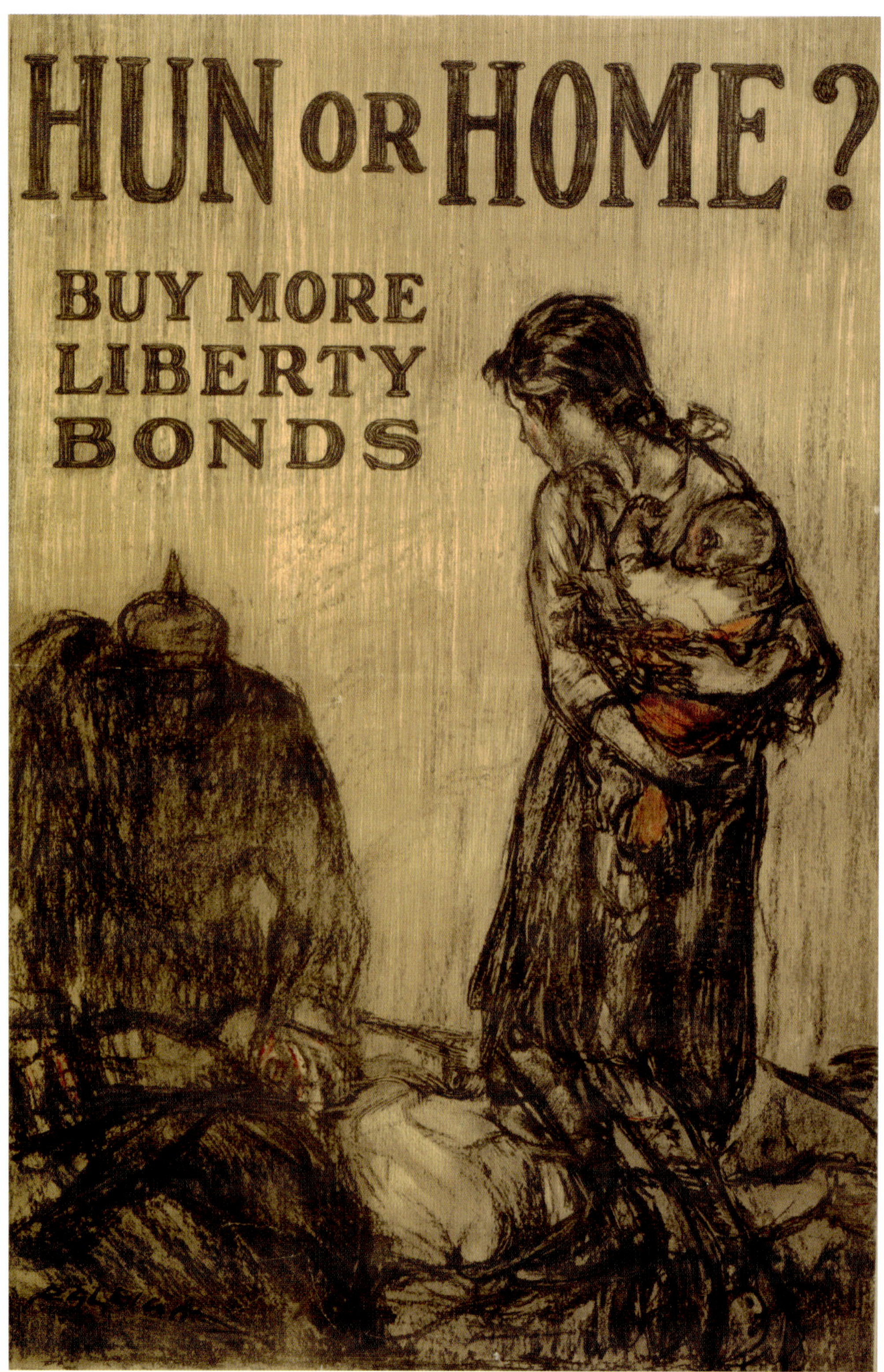

Henry Raleigh, American First World War propaganda poster, *c.* 1917.

German soldier. Depicting a scene of dreadful peril, Raleigh's scratchy lines gave his poster a crude immediacy, but its threat also strikes a note of obligation. With all the grace she can muster, Pickford is reminded of the home-front war effort. She decides to forego the sundae and turns to simpler satisfactions. Mayme changes her order to a glass of water. And yet, everything in her movements, her expression, her balance as a performer, tells her audience that she craves the delicious satisfaction of the ice cream; with studied nonchalance, Pickford dips her finger into her friend's sundae for a small taste. Of course, the film and poster do more than remind viewers to exert culinary caution; while acknowledging her human desires, Pickford saves her money to buy a Liberty Loan bond, but also conserves milk and sugar – precious resources at home. From promoting rapid-fire speeches before keyed-up crowds to issuing threatening posters, the US Treasury Department's Division of Pictorial Publicity engaged stomachs, as well as hearts and minds, to promote the war effort. Across Europe and America, posters gained renewed vigour; they were one of the few reliable forms of communication that governments could use to speak to their citizens. But, in a curious turn, the poster was also participating in its own eclipse. Utterly unacknowledged by Raleigh and other wartime designers, however, these wartime messages subverted the interests that had brought posters to attention some 50 years earlier.

While the furious effort to raise funds promoted arousing pleas like 'Hun or Home?' in both American and British poster-making at this time, German propaganda tended towards more emotional sobriety. In the years leading up to the war, avant-garde German graphic design favoured the Sachplakat, a simple style featuring flat backgrounds and presenting an unmoored object, seemingly floating in space. Some German designers hewed to this style during the war, while others aspired more to its emotional simplicity. Fritz Erler, a scenic designer and painter, produced war-loan posters. Although not a member of the Sachplakat school, his solemn exhortation of 'Help us win! Buy war bonds' echoes the generally subdued approach of the Central Powers towards fundraising. Erler's young, preternaturally calm soldier is the antithesis of the bloodied Hun who approaches Raleigh's girl like a wolf homing in on his prey. Erler's soldier maintains a dreamy idealism, even as he gazes through barbed wire and carries a gas mask. For Germans, trench combat was one of war's many grim surprises; troops and civilians alike expected war to be a purifying or even

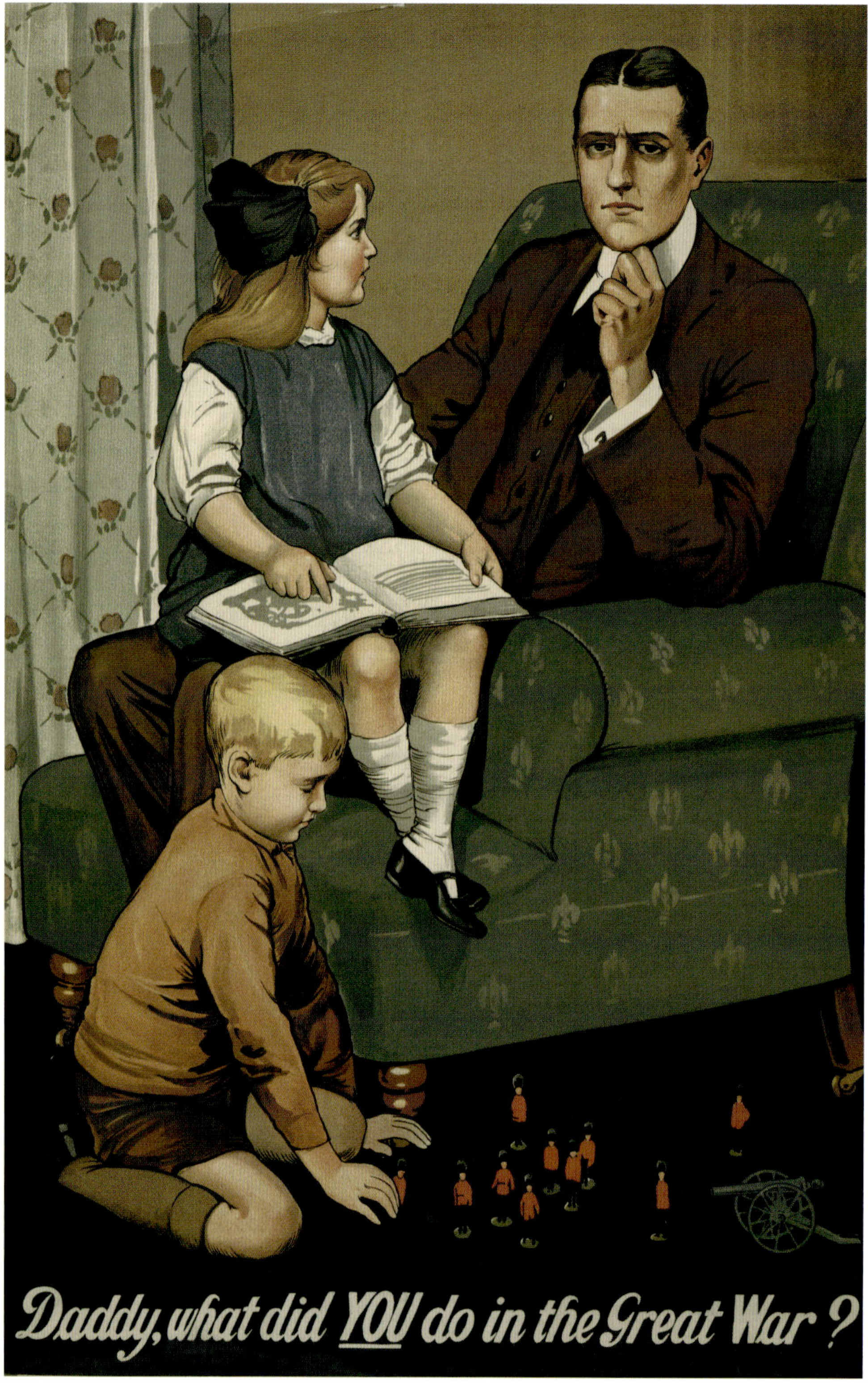

Savile Lumley, 'Daddy, what did YOU do in the Great War?', 1914–15.

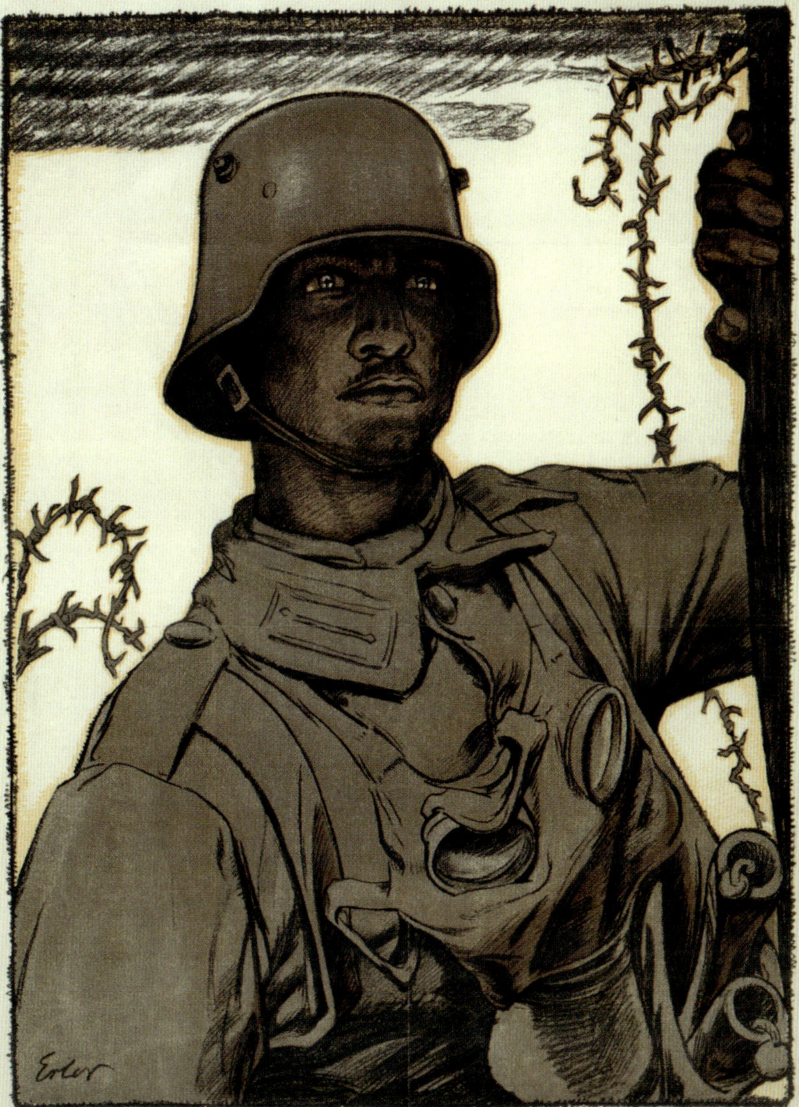

Fritz Erler, 'Help us win! Buy war bonds', 1917.

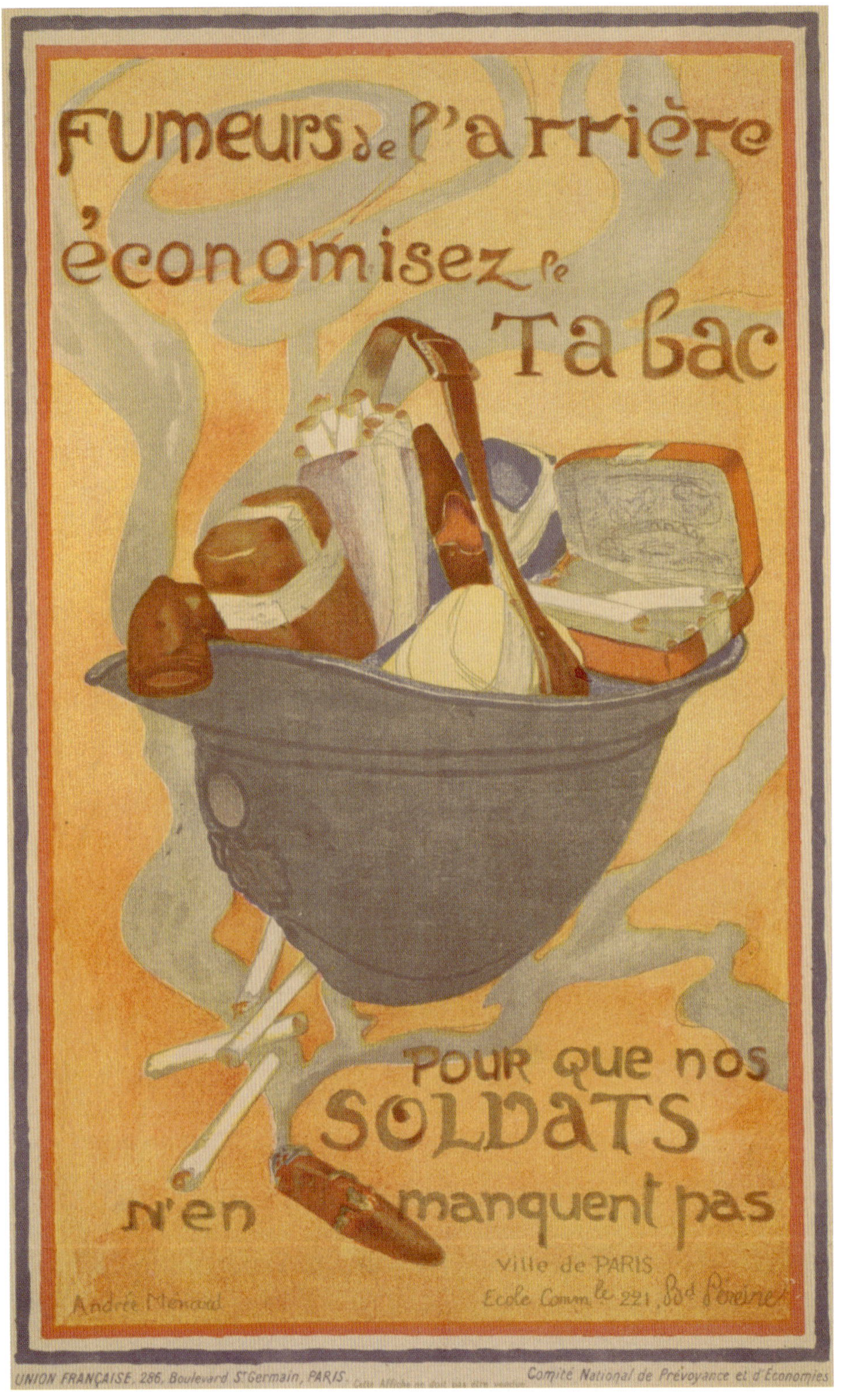

Andrée Ménard, 'Smokers, conserve your tobacco so that our soldiers won't go wanting', 1916.

cathartic experience, and Erler's poster of 1917 did little to correct this impression.

At a time when steak was hard to come by and fresh bread meant long lines, posters begged consumers to transfer their buying power to the government. Good sense implies that the dictates of war could not stall hunger entirely. But posters could shame dutiful citizens into working against their own wills and wishes. Andrée Ménard's 'Fumeurs de l'arrière' poster, for example, depicts a French army helmet turned upside-down and overflowing with a smoker's wartime bounty – cigarettes, cigars, tobacco and a pipe – while urging the public to curtail their consumption so that men at the Front would not want. In the First World War, citizens were asked to give everything – their loyalty, their faith and their money. But these messages were, in some ways, short-sighted. In a curious turnabout, the thriving poster culture of the First World War cut into the texture of a consumer society and turned its back on bicycles, beer and soap. These are all fine things in moments of non-hysteria. But war prompts austerity, not consumption.

In the years immediately after war's end, the poster attempted a near-impossible comeback. Before the war, London Underground pioneered a form of 'soft sell' publicity, clearing its walls of distractions and providing orderly frames and mounts for poster advertisers. When London Transport asked artist Frederick Charles Herrick to design a poster that would encourage visitors to the 1920 International Advertising Exhibition in London to take the Tube to the show, his poster celebrated the Underground's debt to pre-war branding. The Exhibition sponsored a 'Pageant of Publicity' through the London streets, featuring humorous embodiments of well-known brands, such as the Kodak Girl, the Michelin Man and Rowntree's Cocoa-Nibs children. Many of these figures filled pre-war publicity on the Tube; with great eagerness, the Underground's promoters were determined to continue this successful relationship, packing poster spaces on stations, buses and trains. Herrick's poster image depicts a brief, if magical, moment when these famous figures climb down from their perches on the walls of the Underground. True to each brand's nature, some gather to chat, some revel in their new-found freedom and then, of course, the Kodak girl urges them to stop so she can snap a picture of the scene. Like it or not, Herrick's figures come to life, crowding the platform like actual passengers; the artist implies that they are all on their way to the advertising exhibition. But where to from there? The sad truth is that

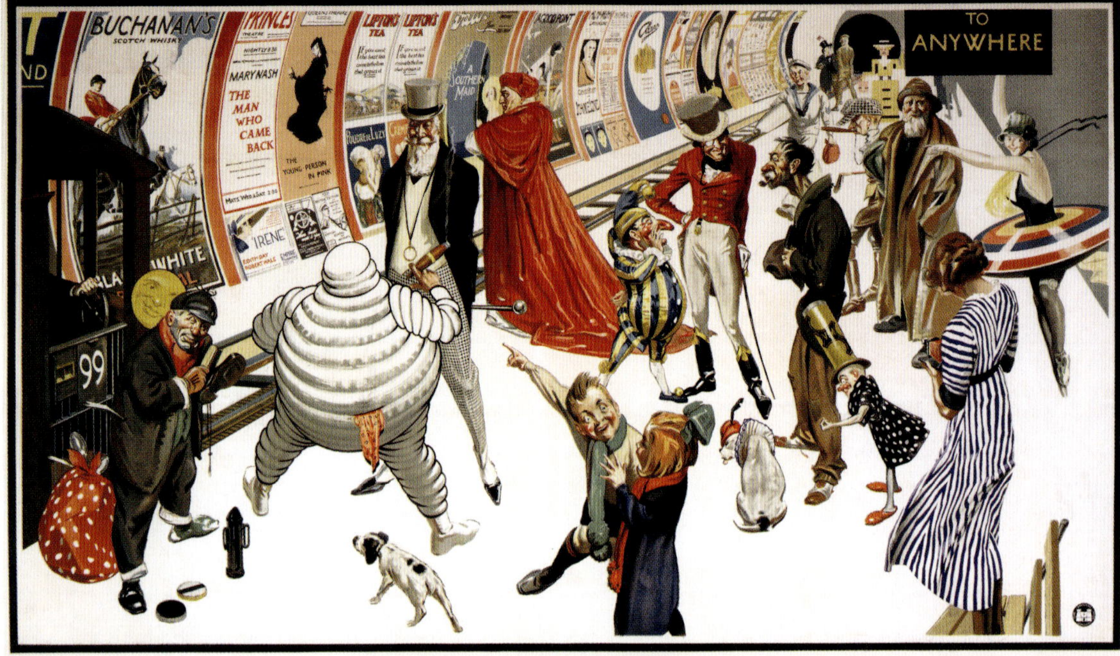

Frederick Charles Herrick, London Underground poster, 1920.

some migrated to newspapers and others to magazines. A decade later, more would make their way to radio. Once unleashed, few wanted to get bogged down and stuck within the sharply confined borders of the poster.

That said, London's transport system provided a bright, shimmering spot of poster activity during these years. Writing in an Arts League of Service bulletin in 1923, Herrick's colleague and contemporary Edward McKnight Kauffer despaired that 'few people realize the importance of the hoardings.' And yet, he insisted:

now that England, after a pause of a dozen years, is again interested in the poster, let this feeling be so genuine and broadcast as to make the hoardings amusingly interesting and vitally important.

Designers like Herrick and Kauffer argued that billsticking should not be taken lightly. Some of the best poster work between the wars decorated London Transport's bus decks, Underground tunnels and passages. Moreover, railway companies and shipping lines in France and Britain, as well as subway and bus lines there and in the United States, still gave extensive work to these and other poster artists. But Kauffer's optimism was ill-founded. Things would not be the same; writing just after war's end, the publisher of the German journal *Das Plakat*, Hans Sachs, announced the *Gotterdammerung* – or twilight – of the German poster, but he might as well have been describing its condition elsewhere, too.[34]

Although a sturdy stalwart, the poster lost some fickle advertisers at war's end and a few wearied of its ardent appeals for all-too-real austerity measures; but war or no war, the problem with posters began earlier, and was fierce and longstanding. At least since the 1880s, critics had discounted posters on aesthetic and moral grounds, accusing them of pressing a kind of dubious, almost extra-sensory, pull. Émile Zola's 'A Victim of Advertising' (1866), for instance, tells the tale of a country naïf who arrives in Paris eager not to 'buy anything, do anything that wasn't recommended by the voice of publicity'; sadly, the story concludes with his death (from a surfeit of drugs and chocolate).[35] While some naysayers worried about the posters' content, others decried the posters as an ugly means to a brutal end. Some critics may have believed that the 'gallery of the street' countered industrial blight, but others argued that posters 'tyrannise over harmless citizens by sheer force of capital'.[36] It was not lost on observers, too, that women seductively touting chocolate and bicycles most often sold products. At least one moralist decried 'The Moral Aspect of the Artistic Poster', not only

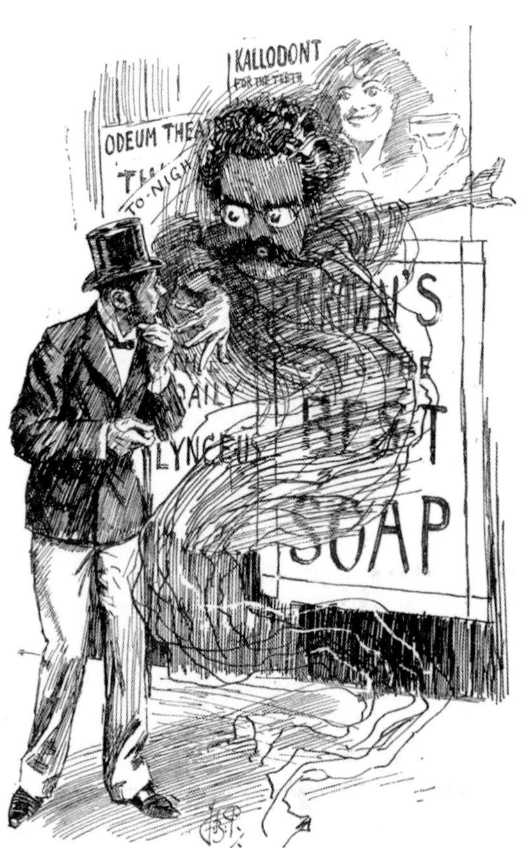

In the 1893 cartoon 'A Pathetic Lament', *Punch* satirized aesthetes' complaints about the lurid and overly tantalizing effects of advertising appearing on posters in London.

cultivating 'vulgar taste' but also leading to depravity.[37] Posters' voluptuous imagery might, some feared, sway men's minds. Other critics believed posters to be like some kind of dirty starched lace that besmirches an otherwise-regal gown. In 1870 the architect Charles Garnier blasted posters as a blight on the city of Paris. Some urban observers, Garnier conceded, may not care about the proliferation of 'monstrous' printed postings, but

> How can I travel through certain districts of Paris, admiring at my ease the buildings which are built there, without being blocked in my admiration by enormous advertisements which attract and wound my sight![38]

A British critic believed that posters heralded a new 'age of disfigure-ment'.[39] Detractors debated the efficacy of boycotts organized against advertisers.[40] Not only did they exert an ugly, or even shameful presence, but they were also accused of being unsanitary. Posters were prey, some city physicians argued, to drifting clouds of disease, since they were 'always decaying, thus providing a prolific forcing bed for all sorts of disease-producing germs'.[41]

Gisèle Freund, 'Cleaning of a house facade, Paris', 1935.

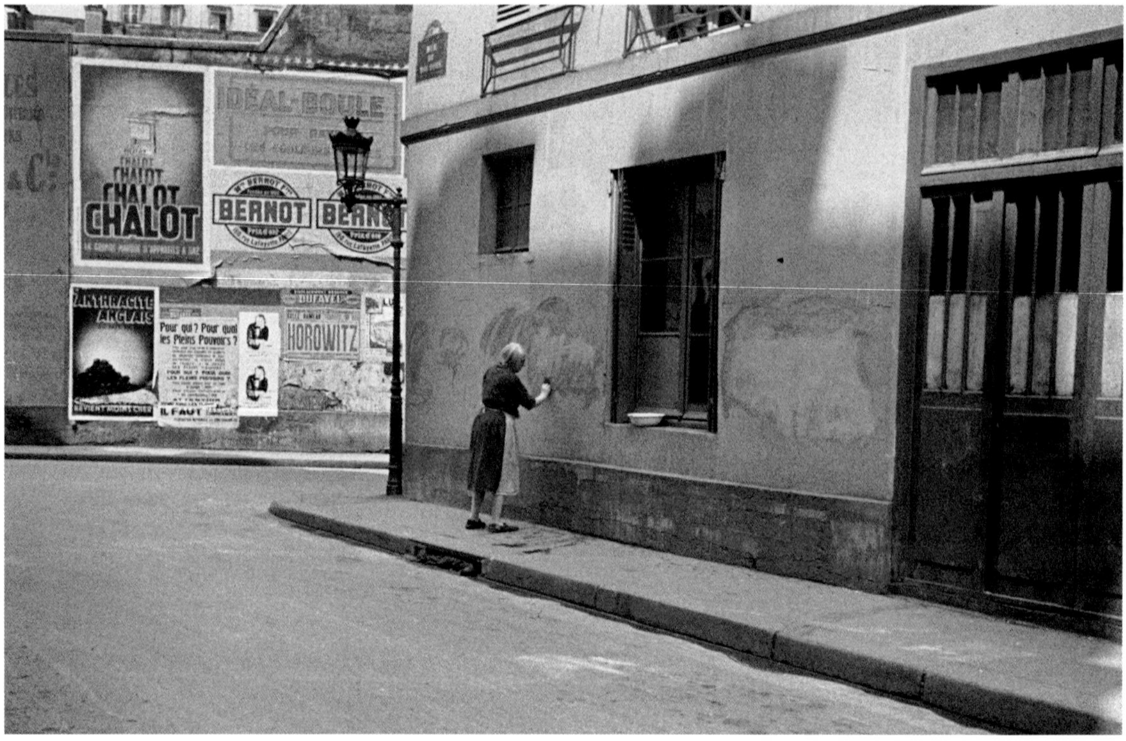

While such rhetoric was often cranky and humourless, posters' real problems came not from critics but from rival forms of media. Already skilled in announcing the latest events, mass-market newspapers drew away advertisers in steadily increasing numbers. By the end of the century, papers began to offer eye-catching, full-page advertisements, and then double-page spreads, too. As early as 1897, American magazine *Fame* struggled to push aside industry gossip that the poster had 'outlived' its usefulness. The journal's editor urged billposters not to fear, because audiences

> are bound to grow in popularity as population increases . . . the poster can not do the work of the newspaper. The newspaper can not do the work of the poster.[42]

But *Fame* was published for billstickers and printers. Rather like parents who over-praise a much-loved child, blind to its faults, *Fame*'s readers were biased towards their own product. Some newspaper publishers argued that the two media were 'complementary', because the poster was still efficient 'out-of-doors', especially in small business districts in which consumers walked to shops.[43] Nevertheless, lured by the easy promise of huge national audiences, advertisers gradually turned not simply to newspapers, but also towards mass-market magazines; hard-to-reach consumers living on isolated farms subscribed the same as purchasers living in big cities. But advertisers themselves changed. Where theatres made up some 80 per cent of poster advertising in 1880s New York, the advent of films cut box-office receipts. By 1905, theatre posters accounted for only 20 per cent of posters' business.[44] Rather, posters still received admiration in urban centres or on public transport; ideally observed at eye level, in a limited fashion, readers walking or sitting could best absorb their message. Buses, trams and trains, however, were themselves soon faced with newer competition.

A breathless sense of discovery swept along proponents of outdoor advertising in the 1920s, but their enthusiasm centred on the car – the poster lost further ground to its car-friendly cousin, the billboard. All manner of roads became 'buyways', ready to be plastered.[45] As cars sped down roads, billboards went higher and bigger, clinging to dizzying heights while badgering and dominating the spaces that they conquered. There may have been a lesson in all of this. A new generation of poster designers had to try harder. In France, Cassandre

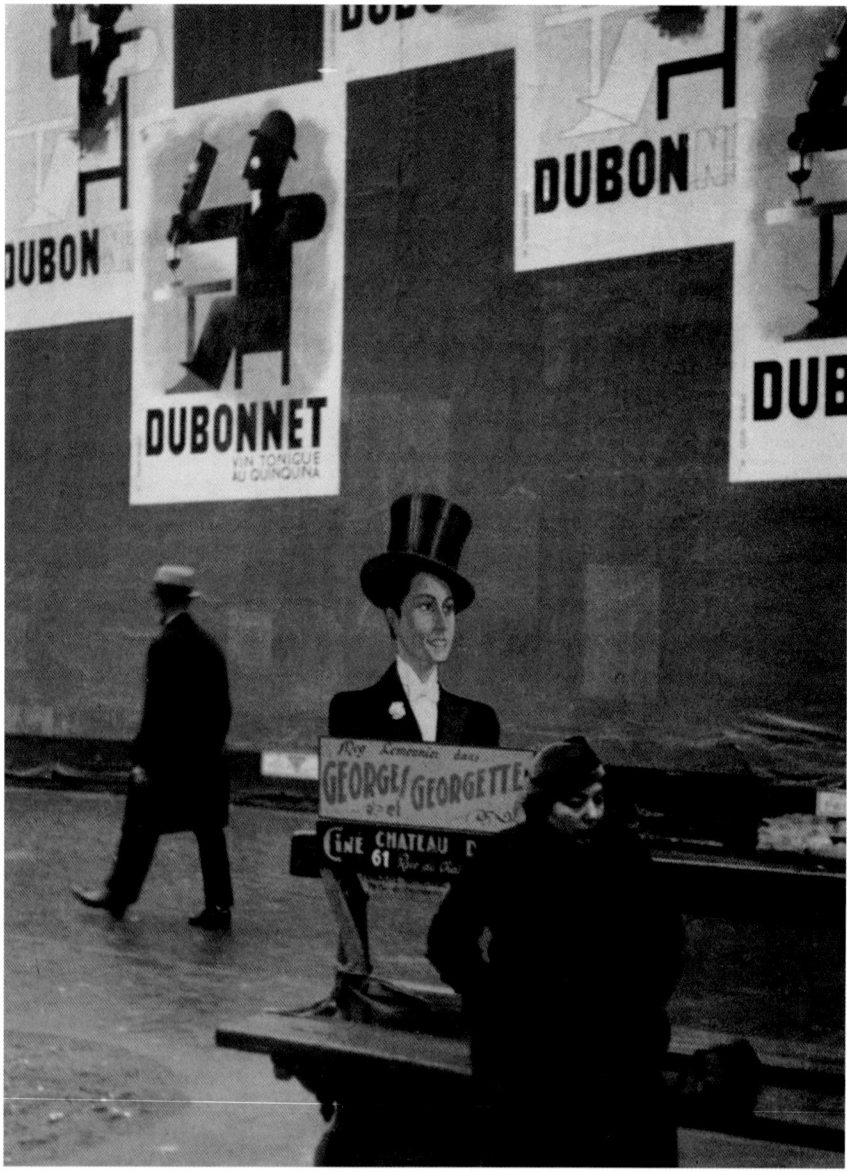

André Kertész, *On the Boulevards, Paris*, 1934.

(Adolphe Mouron) introduced sequential posters for Dubonnet, managing to convey a sense of motion in his advertisements and also allowing them to be grouped together so that they covered large spaces (such as billboards). With the changing climate of bill posting, it comes as no surprise to find that Cassandre's great obsession was placement, or what has been called 'scene design'.[46] As posters got bigger, it became hard to distinguish them from billboards. Posters began to be measured in square metres, a size that gave even Cassandre pause. American advertising was most often associated with this explosion of scale, but Europe was hardly immune. In 1919 Cadum soap was introduced by the American businessman Michael Winburn, who energetically proceeded to paper Paris with the face of a baby just emerging from a bath. Nicknamed Bébé Cadum, a gigantically enlarged image of the baby colonized the city, spreading across several key Paris traffic hubs, including the Place de Clichy and Place de la Bastille. Although beloved of millions, Bébé Cadum's domineering face seemed to fill public spaces with a kind of mass hallucination, or so the painter Fernand Léger insisted. Writing in 1926 in an issue of *L'Art Vivant*, Léger compared Cassandre's work with the Cadum poster. It seemed to Léger that

> we are confronted with two levels of poster: Cadum, or the bare object without any value, and the works of Cassandre who is unquestionably an innovator in the 'art' of the mural poster.

Itching for a fight, Léger asked: 'which are the more tranquillizing: the multiple, hallucinatory images of the Cadum baby or the images created by Cassandre? The latter, of course.'[47] For Léger and a new generation of avant-garde artists, it mattered little if posters were

Miguel Medina, Bébé Cadum advertisement celebrating the brand's 100th anniversary, 2011.

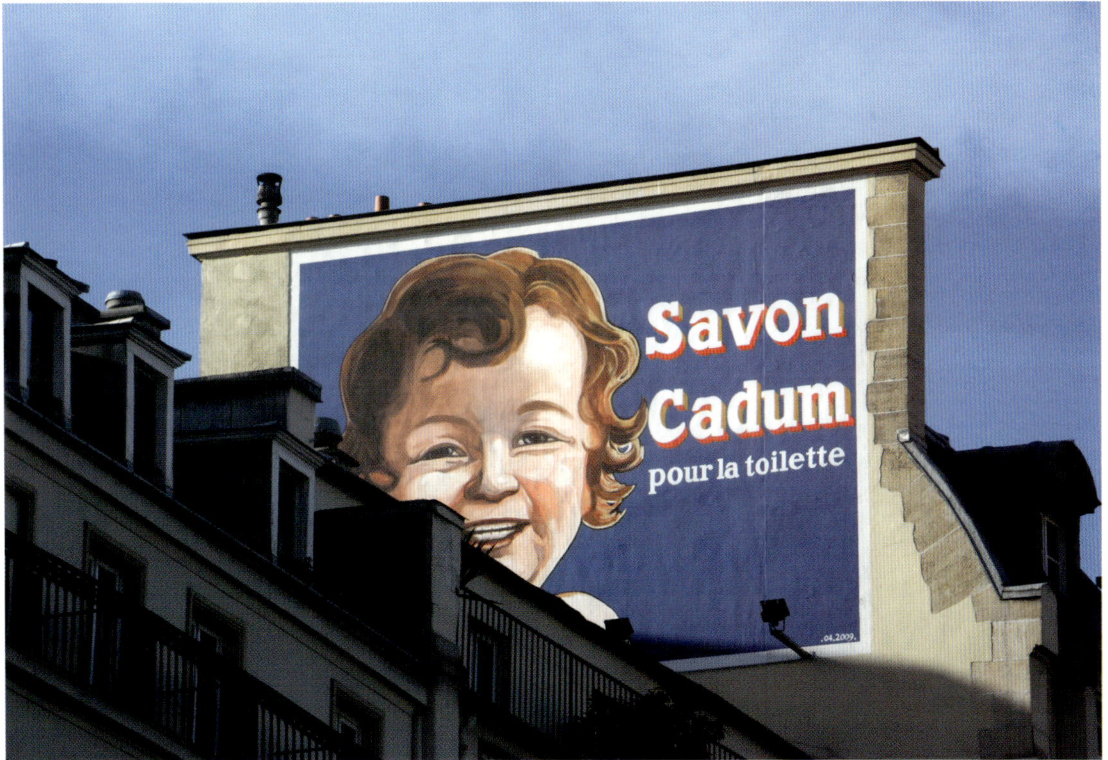

engaged in battles for advertising budgets; instead, posters were a byword for modernity. Léger gave ample space to their disembodied forms in paintings like *The City* (1919). As one part of a dense textile of urban life, for Léger posters were a key element of the modern city.

Of course, as everywhere, posters still existed, but the hurly burly populism of the modernist movement brought posters into the view of avant-garde artists in the early years of the twentieth century. Léger's allusions to the near-mystical Bébé Cadum and all posters of the period found new life in the curious imaginations of both Dada and Surrealist artists. At the 1920 Dada art fair in Berlin, poster-like placards were mounted on the exhibition walls; Dada artists like John Heartfeld put collages into the poster format with cunning impertinence. As one scholar notes, these were 'hung, in other words, not to facilitate individual contemplation and spiritual immersion, like a conventional exhibition, but to arrest, buttonhole, shock and amuse the public'.[48]

The legacy of such hangings resonated in literature for decades. Alternatively, some Surrealist artists pushed still further, casting posters as interpreters of our most elemental dreams. Bébé Cadum has a telling cameo in *Entr'acte*, an experimental film made by Francis Picabia and René Clair in 1924. Here a funeral cortège chases an out-of-control coffin as it careers through city streets and roads plastered with posters for the flaky soap. With ambivalence, Surrealists like the Italian artist Giorgio de Chirico took note of the 'gigantesque' baby, too. De Chirico ignores the content of the poster and its call for better infant hygiene, describing the giggling child as an 'antique god'.[49] In Robert Desnos' novel *La Liberté ou l'amour!* (1924), the poet goes still further, imagining a monstrous fight between Michelin's friendly but bumptious icon, M. Bibendum, and Bébé Cadum. He later revisited the Cadum baby brand, investing it with more dignity; in the essay 'Pygmalion and the Sphinx' (1930), Desnos asks:

> Why must it be that advertising, which furnishes the modern world with so many strange creatures, has not yet entered the domain of statuary? . . . I would love a porphyry Cadum baby getting out of a marble bath . . .[50]

These references gave poster icons a strange kind of durability, fixing them in both vanguard literature and art. And yet, although the Dada and Surrealist artists usually referred to Cadum's advertising as 'posters', in scale and function they quickly approach the poster's cousin, the billboard. After all, *Entr'acte* depicts the advertisement as seen from the road. The thin line between smaller posters and larger billboards is porous, but the difference between both is a question of scale, placement and intended viewing. The billboard is meant to be seen from a speeding car. And so, after the First World War, posters occupy a peculiar position. They continued to grace city kiosks, walls and omnibuses, all meant for pedestrian viewing. But they were no longer the darlings of top advertisers. Apart from a few bright stars like Cassandre, avant-garde artists expended their energy and imagination on an eclipsing tradition.

Nowhere was the poster more prominent in this post-war period than Lenin's Russia. The Bolsheviks gave space and a new rationale to artists like El Lissitzky and Alexander Rodchenko, encouraging them to use the poster to remake the Russian landscape and society. A perplexing group of tardy pioneers, the Russians sifted through the well-worn poster form, utterly remaking it. Some scholars suggest that the Soviet political poster essentially fulfilled the functions of advertising in the West; rather than selling products, though, they promoted ideology.[51] But their imagery was alien to the branded corridors of the London Tube and Paris streets. Of course, these fine artists turned to poster-making in an attempt to rebuild Russian society; in so doing, they aimed to transfer political teachings to a sizable, if largely illiterate, population. New techniques like photo-montage were used and plans drawn for game-changing kiosks that would highlight poster displays for the masses. But their makers were also busy laying the groundwork for a new world order divested of consumption. Lenin in particular supported 'live propaganda' and agitprop actions in which workers and students might carry avant-garde images into the streets; in one 1920 photograph, for instance, students carry posters whose stylized imagery of oil wells and bolts of fabric urge production goals in the realm of metal, oil, coal and textile manufacture.

Later, leaders such as Hitler and Stalin could also deploy posters in complex roles, using their belligerent ubiquity to make over the poster like a quick-change artist. Used in large spaces, and often depicting fascist leaders, posters could dominate Germany's densely populated old towns and Italy's wide piazzas; poster portraits of Hitler and Mussolini were omnipresent and functioned as free-floating

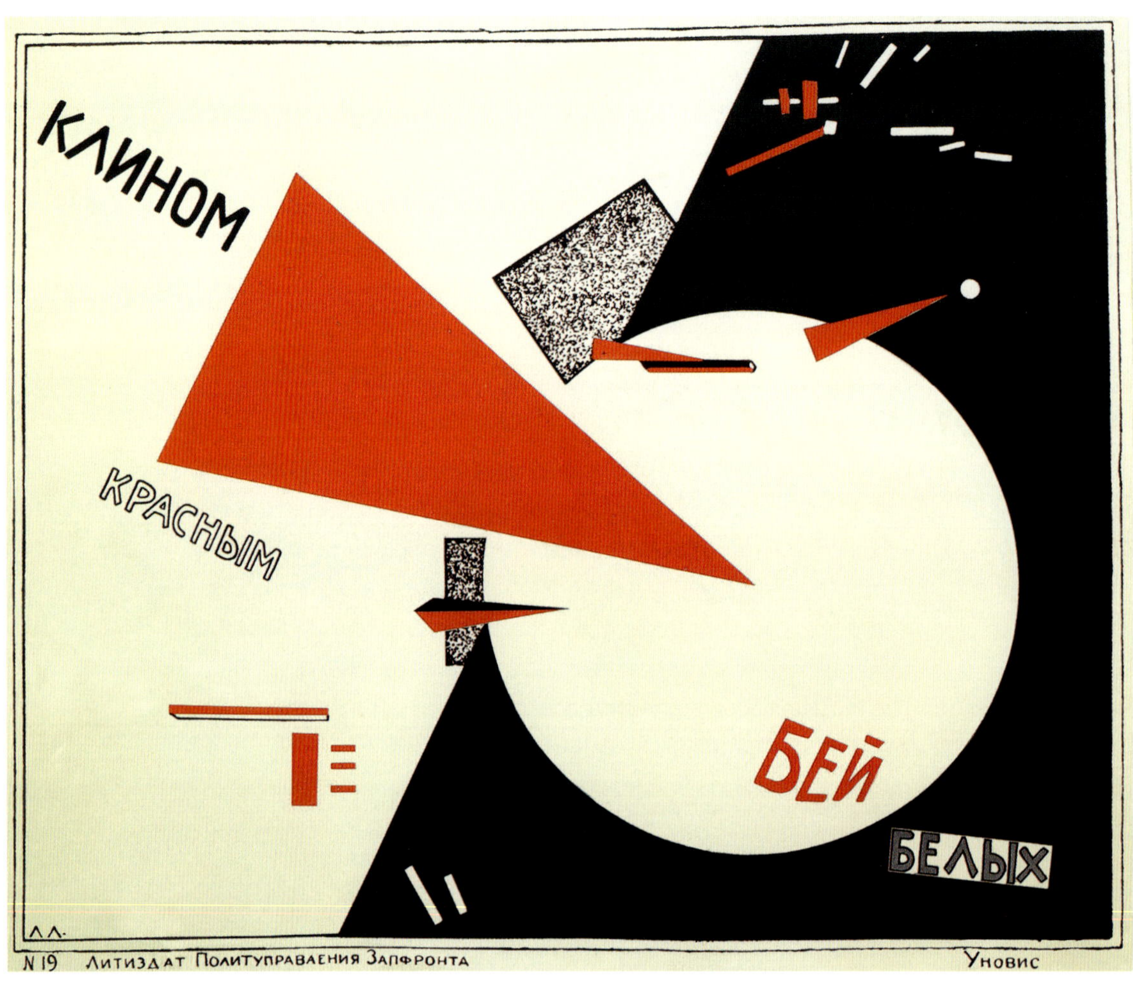

El Lissitzky, 'Beat the Whites with the Red Wedge', 1919.

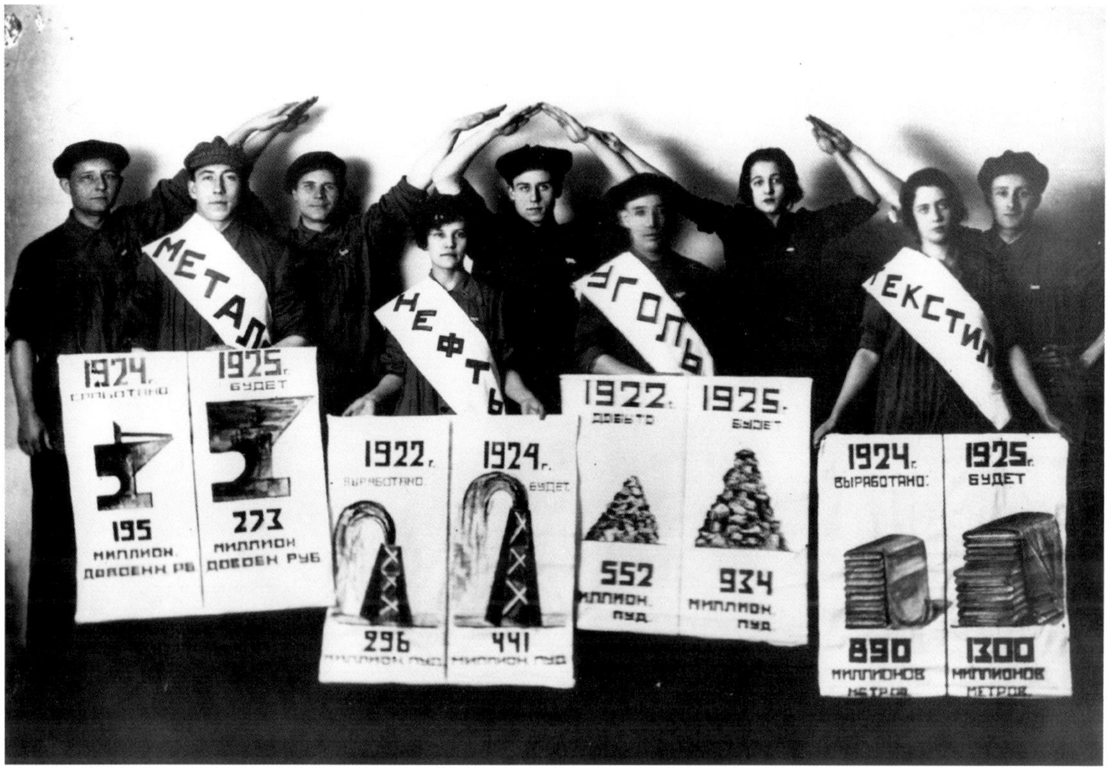

Russian students carrying posters depicting Soviet achievements in industry; the posters advertise metal, oil, coal and textiles, 1920.

signifiers, embellishing government offices and schools or carried in rallies and parades. Speaking a language of mass persuasion, posters like those installed at the entrance to the Apollo Theatre in Nuremberg followed larger rules and rituals. Prominent buildings were often mounted with the swastika or depictions of Hitler. Other important Nazi leaders were positioned slightly lower down and smaller, in this case Nuremberg's mayor Willy Liebel and Julius Streicher, editor of the Nazi tabloid *Der Stürmer* (see p. 78). By the beginning of the Second World War, posters increasingly depicted hard-eyed politicos who urged the public to consume ideas.

Both fascist propagandists and Madison Avenue advertisers knew how best to deploy posters. In densely populated parts of Europe and the United States, where they could bully and cajole in crowded, confined settings, posters still carried relevance and even power. In the United States, much attention has been centred on the dazzle of magazine design in the 1930s, and in the 1940s and '50s on the glamorous work of art directors like Cipe Pineles and Alexey Brodovitch still dominate. But when the Depression prompted the government to form the Work Projects Administration (WPA), the

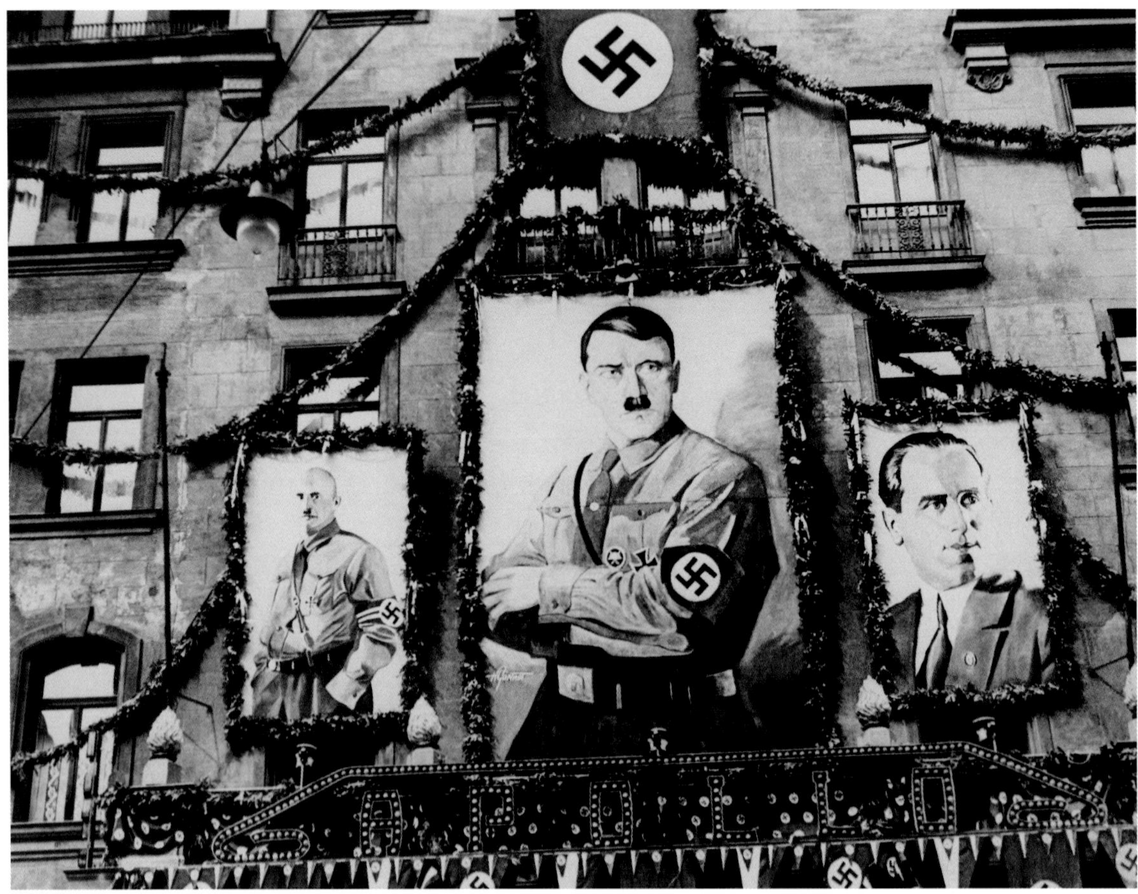

Posters of Hitler, Liebel and Streicher at the entrance of the Apollo Theatre in Nuremberg, Germany, *c.* 1930.

poster saw another lift. Hiring artists like Lester Beall, the Federal Art Project (FAP), an extension of the WPA, produced almost a thousand posters to encourage federal work projects. Although these posters promoted great public works like the rural electrification programme, as well as arts, literacy and health programmes, not everything celebrated in these posters was commercial, or even purely practical. From a soapbox derby in Du Page County, Illinois, to a father–son banquet sponsored by the Chicago Urban League, all fell under the FAP's purview. Nevertheless, many of these posters made it no further than the WPA's offices, where they hung neglected on walls and doors. Indeed, during the First World War, many government-issued posters were hung inside – usually in government or aid offices – and were intended to motivate workers as much as the larger public. Many WPA posters continued this tradition. Several private American firms also adapted the form and began publishing motivational or work-incentive posters. Deploying simple graphics and sturdy slogans like 'I Am Responsible' and 'Drifters

Lester Beall, 'Radio', US government poster, 1937.

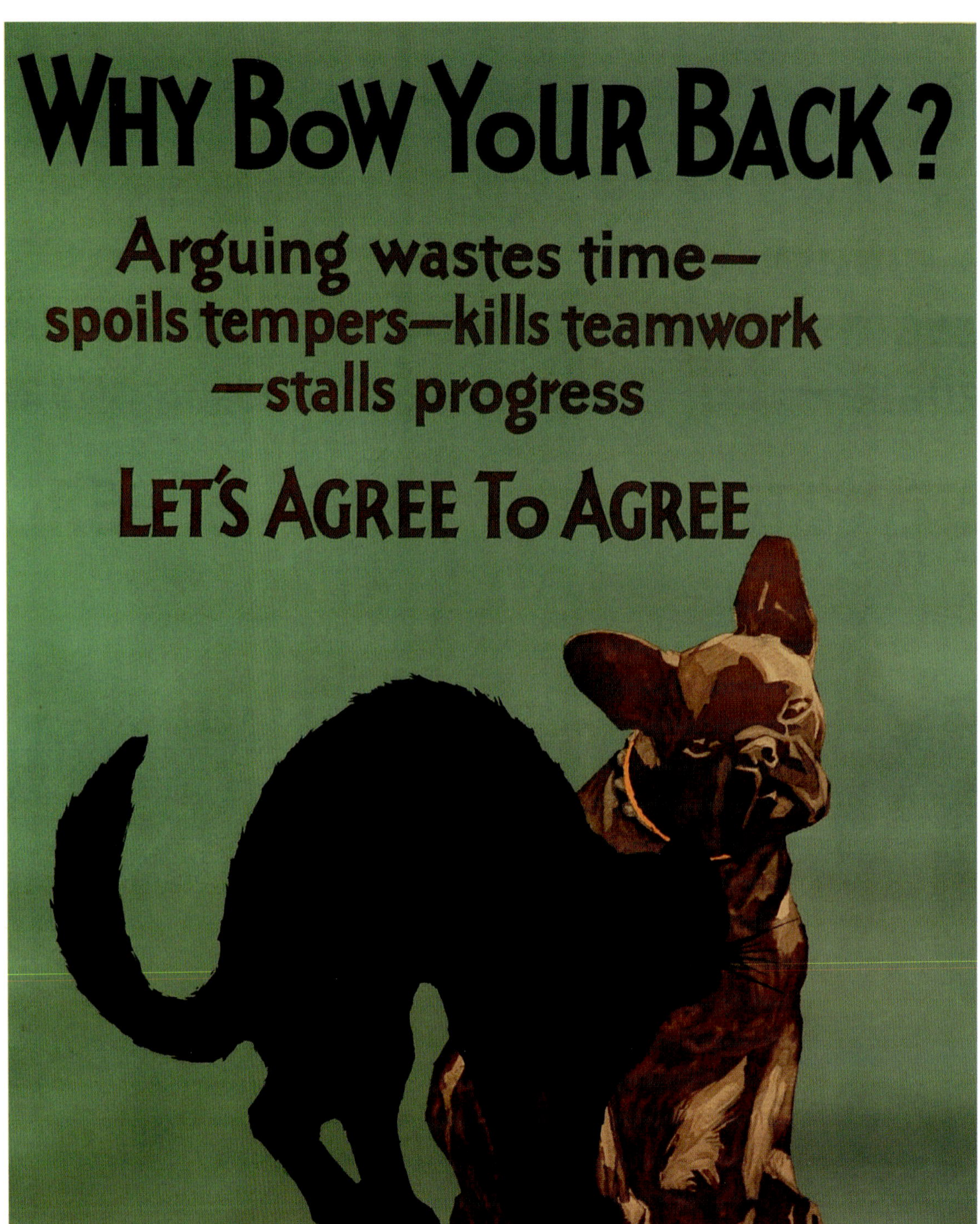

Willard Frederic Elmes for Mather & Company, 'Why Bow Your Back?', 1929.

Never Harvest!', these were intended to improve morals and manners in the workplace.[52]

Posters' most significant impact was beginning to shift. Like a great cresting wave, posters had shaped urban spaces in Europe and America for nearly half a century. But, almost as an afterthought, their presence was only just beginning to be felt on further shores. From Cape Town to Shanghai, and especially in regions where the impact of newer communications technologies were less immediate, posters could still be counted on to engage the public.

Emerging Mediascapes

Lost somewhere in the buzz that still surrounds WPA, Russian and avant-garde posters of the 1920s and '30s, posters outside North America and Europe are still easy to overlook. But gradually, as happened in London, Paris and New York half a century earlier, cities and towns across the globe began to sprout posters on walls and in alleys. There are, of course, places such as India and South Africa, once integrated into the British Empire, where posters arrived in the late nineteenth century; but in regions like West Africa, posters were less common before the mid-twentieth century. In such cases, the poster format seemed a safe, reliable form of advertising for newer markets that lacked dependable radio and print media. And still, such posters followed Western forms closely. Advertising sugar as 'fine food' might set an epicure on edge, but Tate sugar's happy baby proves that the art of eating is not wholly a matter of the stomach. When this sugar-loving infant appeared above the well of a small village in Ghana in 1956, he exerted a familiar appeal, having clearly graduated from the same charm school as France's soapy Bébé Cadum. Few observers pondered Tate's curious legacy of geopolitics; 200 years earlier, the rich Caribbean sugar industry was built on the backs of slaves taken from this very region of Africa. Instead, it was assumed that the format that worked for Paris housewives could work for colonized peoples as well. With a quick change of complexion and the addition of an advertising slogan in the local pidgin patois, the formula was little changed. And yet, posters could also work double time in places like rural Ghana or Nigeria, where they helped barbers' clients choose the latest hairstyles. Waves of paper posters began to sweep over colonies and independent nations alike, buoying new classes of consumers

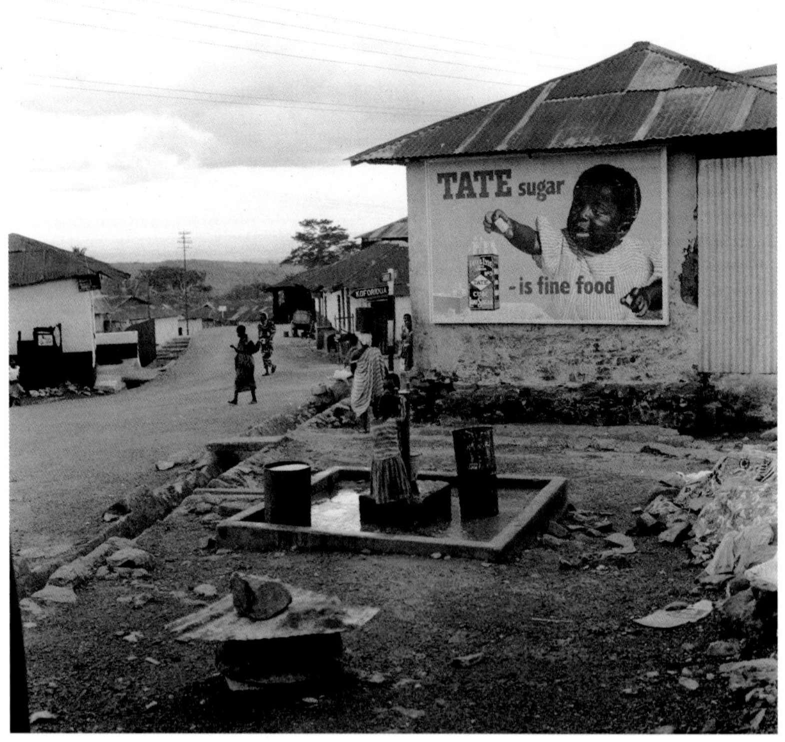

even in societies where forthright barter and other trading systems
were still current.

Small and lightweight, any kind of poster travels well, but, in
the global spread of posters outside Europe, some formats were more
easily assimilated than others. The large commercial posters favoured
by Tate and countless other European manufacturers circulated widely.
Especially in Asia, posters spread quickly – Japanese companies like
Shiseido, for instance, used posters to pitch purchases across Japan
(see p. 84).[53] But the curious standout across Africa and Asia was the
emergence of the advertising poster's more humble stepson, the
calendar poster. Combining a cheerful chromolithograph image
with tiny annual calendars, these small posters differ as much as
the countries in which they circulated. But they also diverge from
the avant-garde posters usually included in design histories of this
period. Most point to modest origins; whether advertising flour, like
the calendar poster published by Lang & Robinson in New York, or
batteries or absinthe, the original placards were, of course, made to
promote purchases. Nevertheless, finely calibrated calendars were
either attached to – or printed directly on – a sheet of advertising.

Some were grand in their aspiration and purpose. Intended for indoor use, calendar posters were favoured by merchants and officials. Advertising small local shops or large companies with widespread business interests, calendar posters began to spread, usually aiming to establish a brand with as much aplomb as they could muster. On the one hand, these often did double duty: introducing a form of timekeeping that followed the tides and rhythms of European life, they reflected the kind of confidence that helped establish the Gregorian calendar globally. On the other hand, many posters were strangers in a strange land. Born in the first burst of the Industrial Revolution, these illustrated posters were soon doing gymnastics by trying to straddle cultures.

If calendar posters had to meet Western and non-Western expectations, they were also rapidly adapted. In some countries, the European-style calendars met with little resistance. In others like China, which had its own long-standing print culture, the Gregorian calendar flew in the face of older timekeeping traditions. By the turn of the twentieth century, cheap woodblock prints were commonly used to celebrate holidays – especially the lunar New Year – and decorate interiors. Equally notable, the Chinese had a long-established

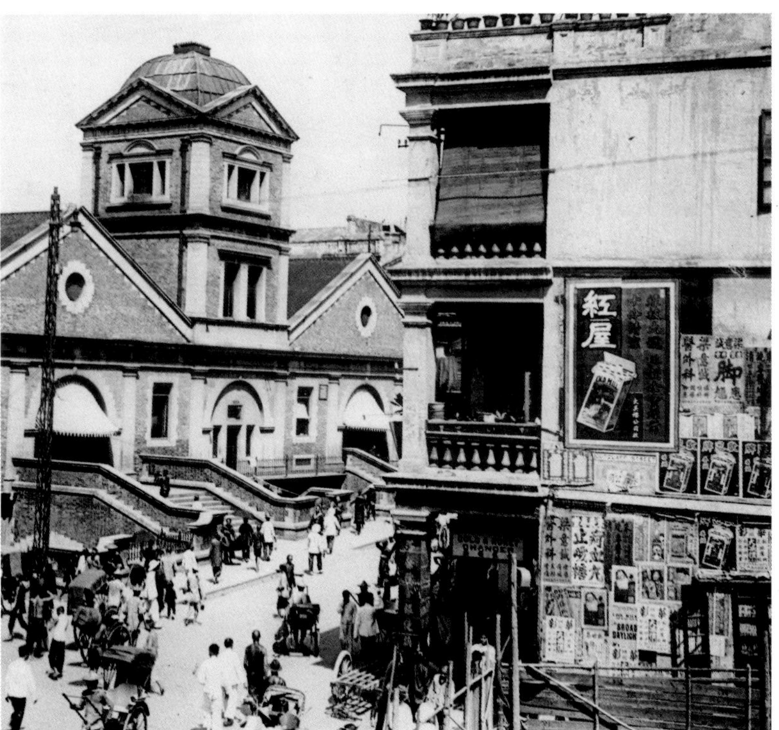

Mee Fong Studio, 'Central Market, Hong Kong', *c.* 1900.

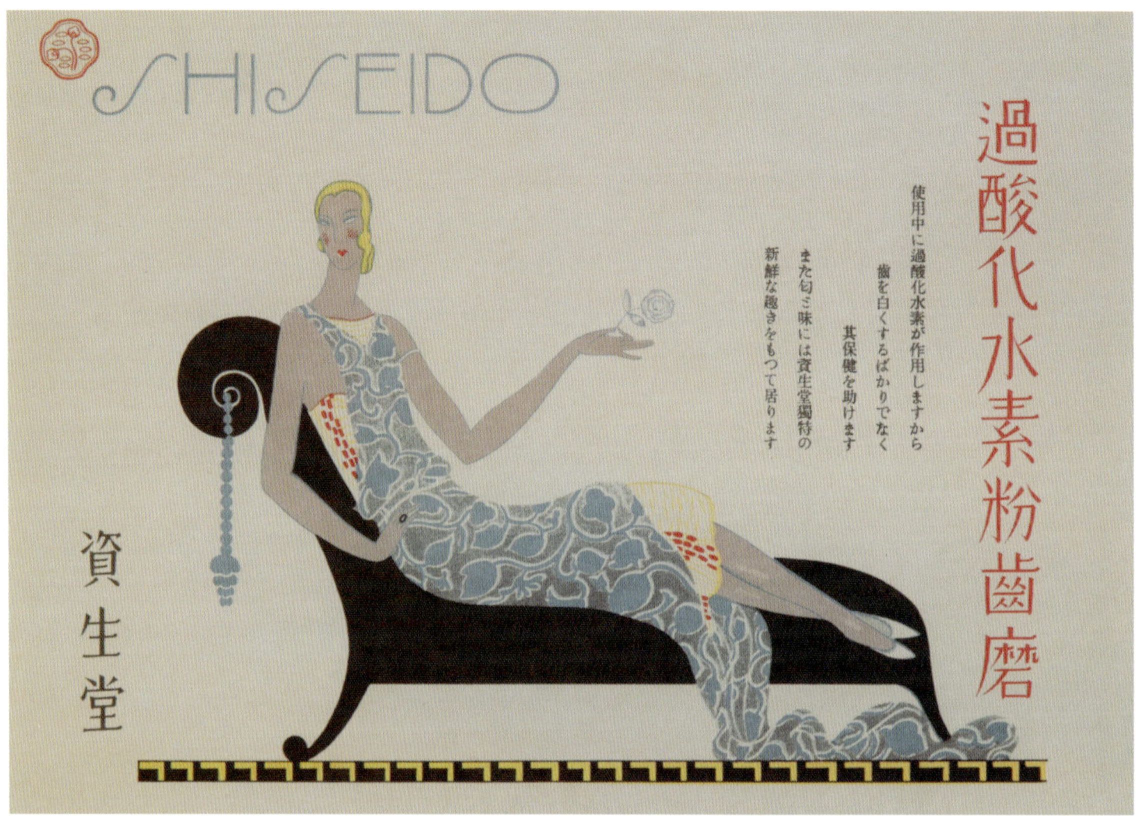

Reika Sawa, poster for Shiseido hydrogen peroxide tooth powder, 1927.

system for measuring time, tracking the progress of the lunar year and ordering a series of long-standing rites and festivals.

Whichever calendar was in use, after losing the First Sino-Japanese War, China saw its borders open and almost inevitably Western merchants began touting their wares. They hawked consumer-friendly products like tobacco, cosmetics and batteries; in so doing, these capitalists often packed with their product the same calendar wall posters that proved popular in Europe and America. Grimms' fairy tales, portraits of the presidents Washington and Lincoln and other strikingly anomalous imagery appeared on these early calendars. And, even when given away free, these wall hangings had limited success; at best, Chinese consumers admired the brilliant precision of their chromolithographed images. Only when the imagery began to be recalibrated, and local artists were hired in the 1910s, did the calendar poster really begin to prosper. Commonly given away for free around New Year, these were pitched to the Chinese market and circulated in consumer hubs like Shanghai with a ferocity that scarcely dimmed over the next 30 years. By the 1920s and '30s, well-known Chinese artists

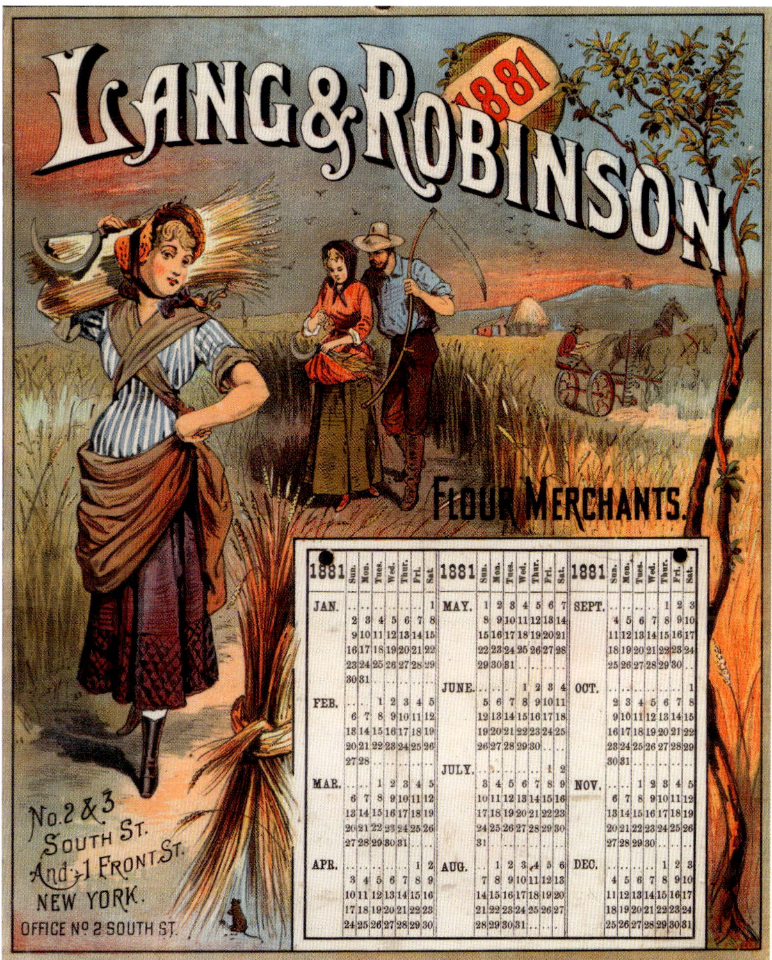

designed hybrid posters that included Chinese imagery but advertised cigarettes sold by British American Tobacco and Eveready batteries. Most favoured were images of women, some beguiling with gentle allure, impassively smelling flowers or sitting on park benches, while others pulse with seductive energy, elegant in their tight-clinging cheongsams and smiling cheerily while drinking cola or smoking cigarettes. The plumage and make-up of these women changed year after year, but behind their well-groomed preciosity they consistently traded on their sexuality while hawking products. Some of these calendars used the Gregorian calendar, aligning with broader ideas of modernization, but others kept to the Chinese lunar year.

This forthright salesmanship was widespread and global. Even earlier, in colonial India, technology contributed to a fast-growing local print culture. Mass-produced, hand-painted images, usually depicting

Hindu deities and Muslim saints, had long circulated in the subcontinent. The introduction of chromolithography, however, burst like a bomb. As in China later, many early posters hawked consumer products like colour dyes from Britain and safety matches from Sweden. With proud independence, however, by the 1870s commercial chromolithographic presses in Calcutta and Poona, near Bombay, began printing posters on the subcontinent itself. Many printers also fixed their imagery to older Hindu and Muslim religious traditions. Their artists, though, were trained in the Western visual arts, and many of these early posters mix, mingle and entwine various cultural influences. A depiction of the goddess Lakshmi from the 1890s, for example, was printed as part of a portfolio and follows a format used in earlier hand-painted icons. She is heavy and voluptuous, and her gown, veil and pose recall the maidens depicted in Hindu woodblock prints, but her attire also bears more than a passing resemblance to the red and blue garments of the Virgin Mary. Published by groups such as the Calcutta Art Studio, there is nothing humble, timid or placatory about these prints, and many were displayed on walls. Indian print shops began producing swathes of individual prints as well as poster advertisements and calendar posters whose imagery teemed and roistered with Hindu gods and goddesses. Some were designed in India and printed in Europe, then shipped back to the subcontinent. But many were designed and made locally. These passed under a variety of names, including 'market art', 'calendar art' or even 'god posters'.[54] Not only did god posters adorn shrines in homes and offices, but, over time, their content became increasingly Indianized as part of a larger 'religious nationalism'.[55] Forms of 'magical realism' were well established in the Hindu canon. Deities sprouted multiple heads and arms, while gods, freed of gravity, could career through the skies or hover in the air over lakes and forests. But they also diverge from traditional European depictions of the divine, shaking off Western ideas of the deity's separateness. Where the Christian tradition taught artists to retain a sense of the sacred, Indians expected their gods to engage directly with worshippers. As Indianized imagery developed, and the pictorial dominance of Western art receded, god posters began to stare searchingly at onlookers. These posters sometimes still advertised products – Indian and European – but they also brought the divine further into the ordinary world.

In India, these moves led to an increasingly complex visual culture. But this process of reimagining what the poster is, and what it could be,

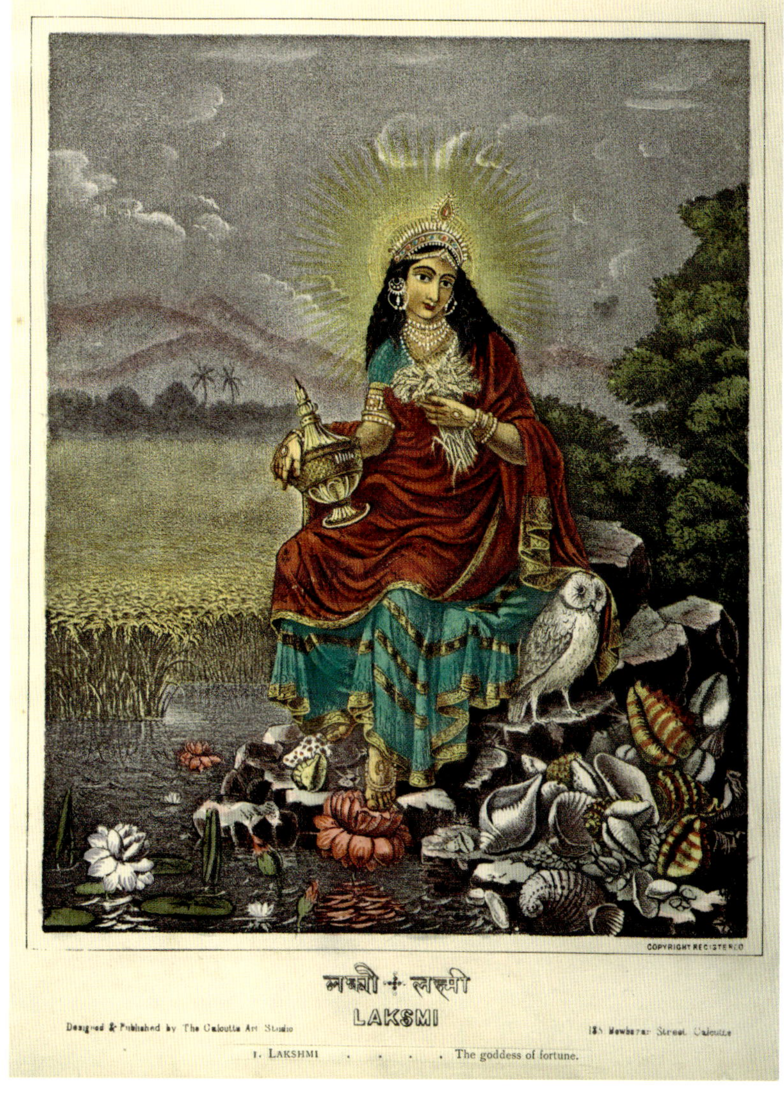

would also substantially change the poster. Historian Dawn Ades has suggested that the poster had 'a spectacular energy' when it bounded onto the nineteenth-century scene; nevertheless, 'this energy has never really been recovered since WWII'.[56] The truth here lies in how we consider the poster and where we look for its development. In many ways, the nineteenth-century poster was but a prelude for the form as we know it today.

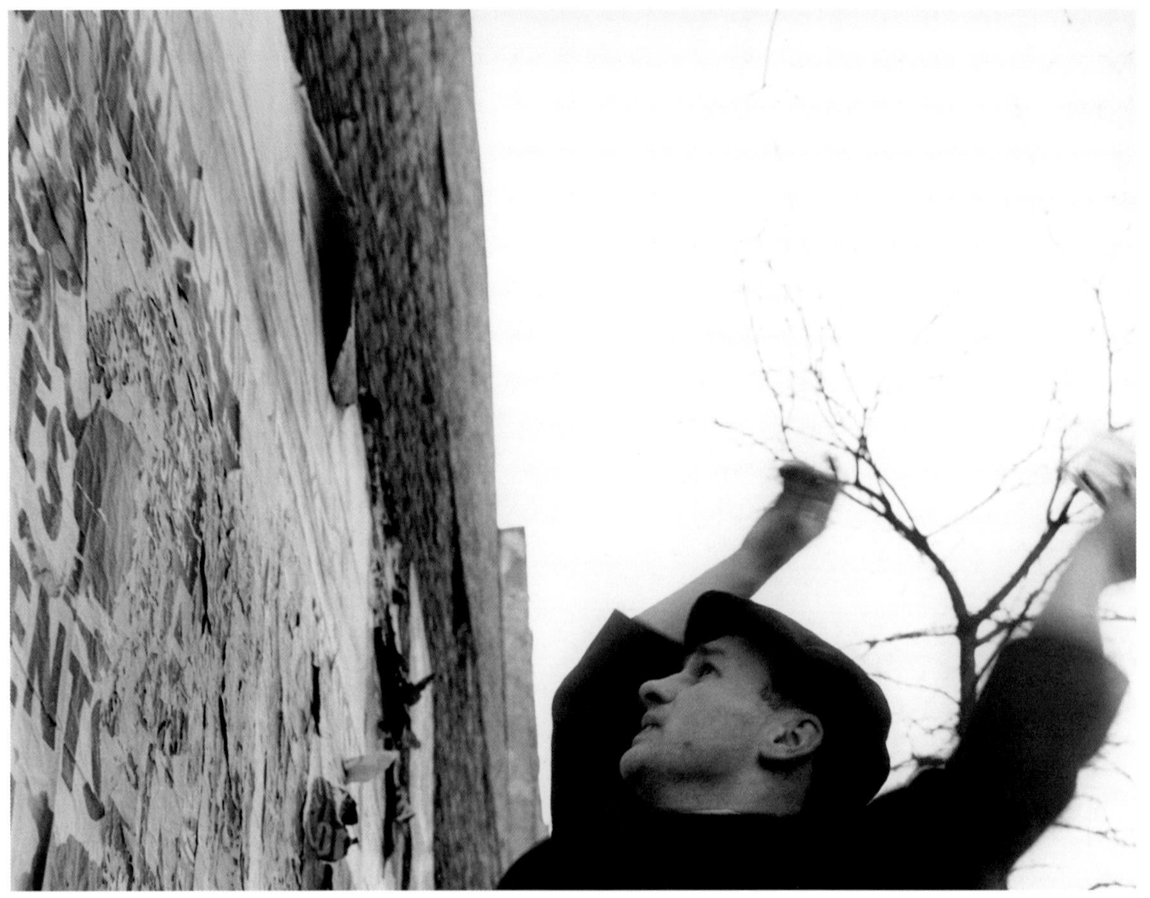

Harry Shunk and János Kender, 'Jacques Villeglé in Paris, 14 February 1961'.

2 TRASHING TRADITION: 1945–1965

In August 1962 a short Pathé newsreel followed a short, furtive man scampering over a poster-encrusted wall, slipping out a knife and then gouging into the wall itself. The man deftly runs the knife along the surface of the wall; with a few precise jabs, slashes and tugs, he pulls a large chunk of posters off the wall, hoists the fragments over his shoulder and briskly walks away. By his clandestine actions and quick pace, we sense that we have just witnessed a crime. Instead, the newsreel announcer suggests that this man 'may be the up and coming Rembrandt of the 1960s'.[1]

Jacques Villeglé, the artist highlighted in the newsreel, could easily be termed the 'Jack the Ripper' of post-war Paris walls. Beginning in the late 1940s, he cut, ripped and tore posters, then remounted them onto canvas in his studio. Some of his contemporaries called Villeglé's work *l'art vol*, or petty theft, a term that he embraced.[2] Still others called it a masterpiece.[3] Yet the work of Jacques Villeglé also represents an utter rethinking of what the poster was, is and could be. In those brief, deft slashes, Villeglé honed an unusual art practice; where artists to date had been engaged with *making* posters, here the poster is being *unmade*. It is being 'trashed'.

During hostilities, the wartime poster was a gift to imaginative Allied and Axis propagandists alike. Using terse messages or inspiring slogans, posters followed armies on the move, motivating soldiers and factory workers and speaking both to troops and subject peoples. When the photojournalist Weegee captured a sombre rally in New York's Lower East Side in 1942, he ushered us into an urban immigrant neighbourhood where shopfronts for 'Shoe Repairing', a 'Meat Market' and a 'Cutlery Grinding Shop' were overwhelmed by wartime flags and bunting; while war banners reading TIME IS SHORT and EVERY MINUTE COUNTS drape from crowded fire escapes, and posters decorate walls

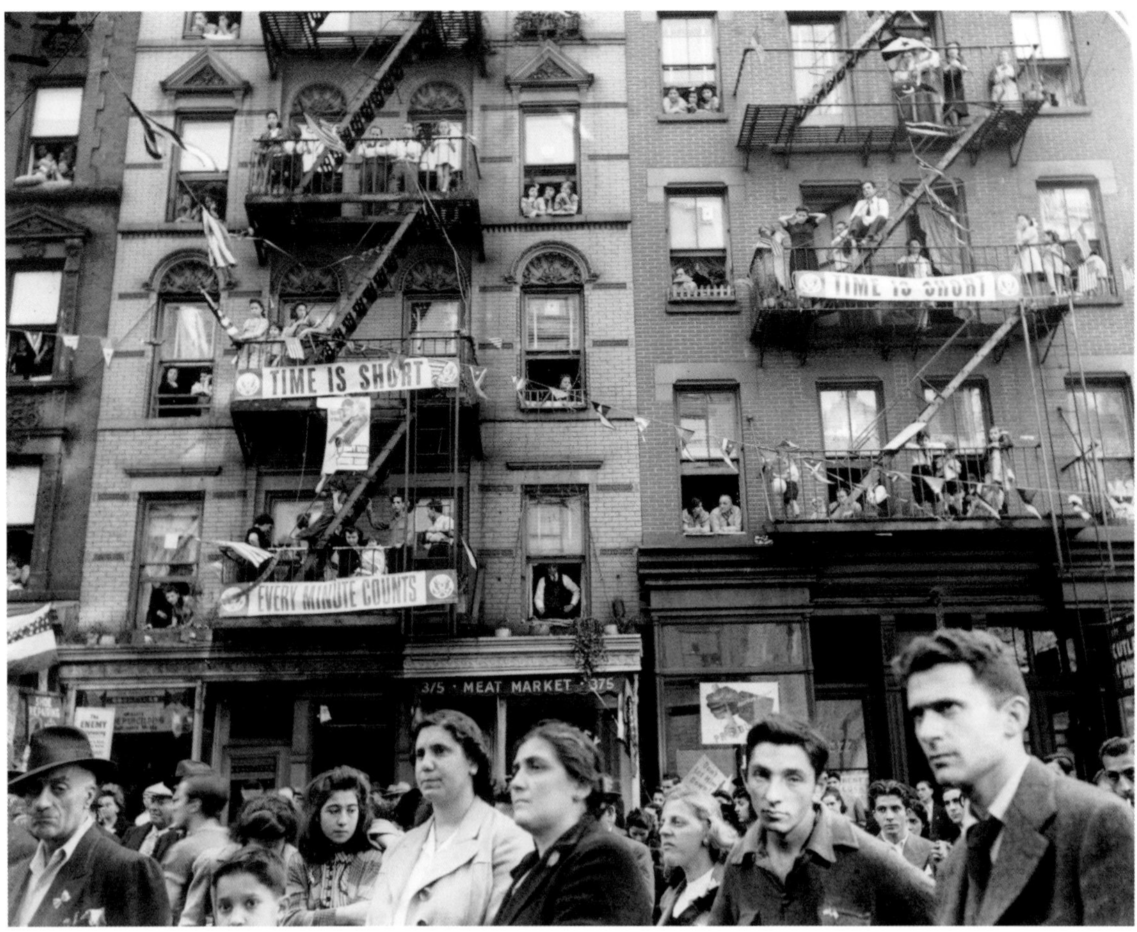

Weegee, 'Time is Short', 1942.

and shop windows. In Weegee's photograph, practically everyone stares, as if hypnotized, their attention focused on something just outside the picture. A tall, relatively young man is one of the few to see us. Behind his head, barely glimpsed in an empty shopfront for rent, hangs Jean Carlu's iconic poster of 1942: 'America's Answer! Production'. Carlu had already made a name for himself in France, where he vied with Cassandre for prominence. Having come to New York for the World's Fair in 1939, he stayed on after the Nazis had invaded France. His poster's aggressive confidence contrasts with the mordant mood of the crowd. A magnet for Italian immigrants, the Lower East Side and its inhabitants must have entered the war with mixed emotions (feelings that Weegee, himself Hungarian-born, understood all too well). The casual swagger of Carlu's poster would seem more at home on the floor of a Midwestern or Californian factory than the overcrowded streets of New York. The wartime banners

90

announcing that TIME IS SHORT were prescient. A year hence, most of this youthful crowd would be working in factories or serving in the Armed Forces; the man who stares out at us would just as easily be in the Pacific theatre or southern Italy than the streets of Manhattan. But time was ticking away for the poster, too.

The insistent presence of posters in Weegee's world did not continue into the post-war years; between 1945 and 1965 this powerful messaging device became unmoored. The decline was not in quality, since inspired designers continued to consolidate years of experimentation. Posters continued to be produced by well-trained and imaginative designers like Saul Bass and Josef Müller-Brockmann. But, in the commercial bonanza of the post-war years, advertisers shifted their priorities. This change did not pass unremarked. Using fewer words and grander gestures, this period of flux was noted by vanguard artists. Channelling a generation's worth of cynicism and provocation, they alluded to the problem with posters more meta-phorically. In the hands of artists like Jacques Villeglé and Marcel

Jean Carlu, 'America's Answer! Production', 1942.

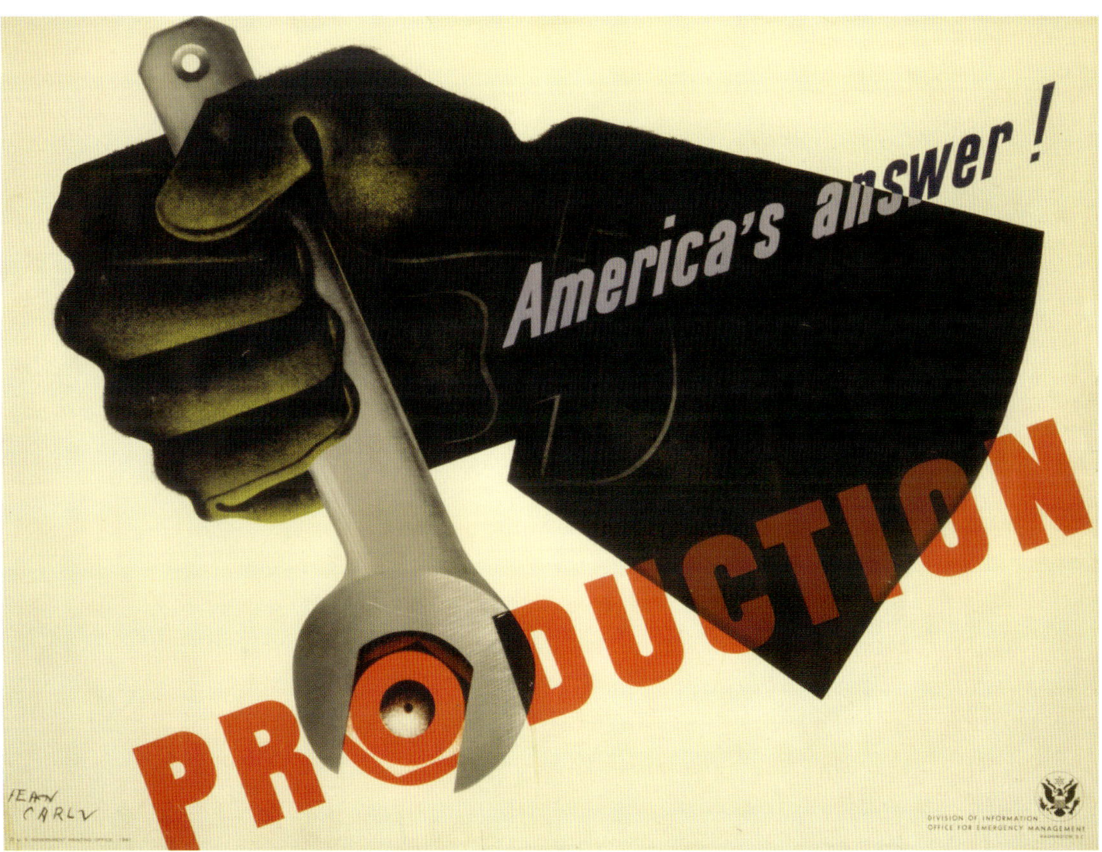

Duchamp, the familiar poster seems suddenly strange. Their use of posters in art was often inchoate and largely symbolic. But they also expressed just how, in the post-war period, the street poster had fundamentally changed.

'When a poster fails,' critic and publisher Charles Matlack Price observed as early as 1922, 'its failure is utter and irretrievable, and its inevitable destiny is its consignment to the limbo of waste paper.'[4] But most paper posters slowly make their way to the rubbish bin, whether they are successful or not. This is the fundamental condition of the poster itself. Nevertheless, as the traditional poster was coming undone, the recognition of this reality laid the groundwork for posters' different, altered existence.

A Paper Resistance

During the Second World War, posters experienced an undeniable, if brief, resurgence in importance. Consumer and travel posters were replaced by instructional placards that urged the public to conserve energy, grow more food, obey orders and protect the secrets of respective combatants. As if to make up for the cool and abstract posters issued by Germany and other Central powers during the First World War, the Axis powers circulated emotionally gripping posters to subjugate, inform and recruit. In France, posters urged collaboration, sometimes calling for 'guest workers' with slogans showing German soldiers and phrases in French, such as: 'They give their blood . . . you give your work.' Other themes were less explicit; public-service posters, for example, enjoined 'abandoned populations' to 'trust the German soldier'. As the war endured, newer posters reminded people of food shortages by announcing grim realities; posters, for example, warned citizens by pointing out the dangers of eating rats. Posters were a conduit of occupiers' edicts, including ordinances against private possession of firearms or radio transmitters. But, in the end, they were only paper, formed a captive, mute embodiment of Occupation and were a focus of long-simmering rage and passive-aggressive resistance.

In 1942, the same year that Weegee documented his sombre war rally, the photojournalist André Zucca photographed a busy pavement in occupied Paris. The two photographers could not have been more different. Zucca published his colour photographs in slick magazines; from 1940 to 1944 he joined the staff of *Signal*, a glossy Nazi propaganda journal published in Paris. Specializing in crime scenes, Weegee documented murder scenes and tenement fires, selling his images to tabloids. Like the posters that he documented, Zucca was part of the Nazi war machine. But these German wartime posters often bore messages that were more significant than their design; as such, they left little room for rejoinders. The stylized simplicity of one particular poster destined to hang on the walls of Paris in 1942, for instance, advertised the Legion of French Volunteers (LVF). Conceived as a French military unit under Nazi command, the LVF fought with Norwegians, Poles and other subject peoples on the perilous Eastern Front. Here an over-life-sized soldier wears the characteristic white uniform of German-backed troops fighting in the winter. The general colour scheme of blue, red and white echoes the small tricolour *écusson* on his sleeve; the yellow-orange fire in the background, across a seeming desert of war, is the only break in this colour scheme. The message – of French solidarity with the Germans – overwhelms the simple image. When the Nazis invaded the capital of their French neighbour, their posters proselytized for collaboration.

As elsewhere in Europe, the Nazis then began their protracted retreat; their soldiers left or were rounded up, but their posters were fair game for reprisal. After Allied troops marched up the Italian peninsula, posters also became a marker of opposition and defiance. One form of resistance took place when fascist postings were torn down and anti-fascist ones mounted in their place. In Italy, where Mussolini's fascist regime crumpled and was replaced by Nazi hardliners, the age-old slogan '*Fuori i tedeschi!*', or 'Out with the Germans!', was resurrected. Centuries of animosity between Italy and its northern neighbours palpitate perceptively in a poster showing a schematically drawn fist, backed with Italy's national red and green colours; it delivers a sucker punch to Hitler's disembodied, but bawling, head. Twenty years earlier, this casual mix of stylized lines, sans serif type and photo collage would have been considered avant-garde. But the poster carried a very different message by the war years. Throughout Nazi-occupied Europe, the very hanging of this or similar posters was illegal; descriptions of poster opposition, and its attempted suppression, are depressingly similar across the continent. In Rome, seven boys, the oldest thirteen, were arrested for hanging anti-fascist posters and executed by the Fascist Republican police.[5] In Genoa, local socialists papered the

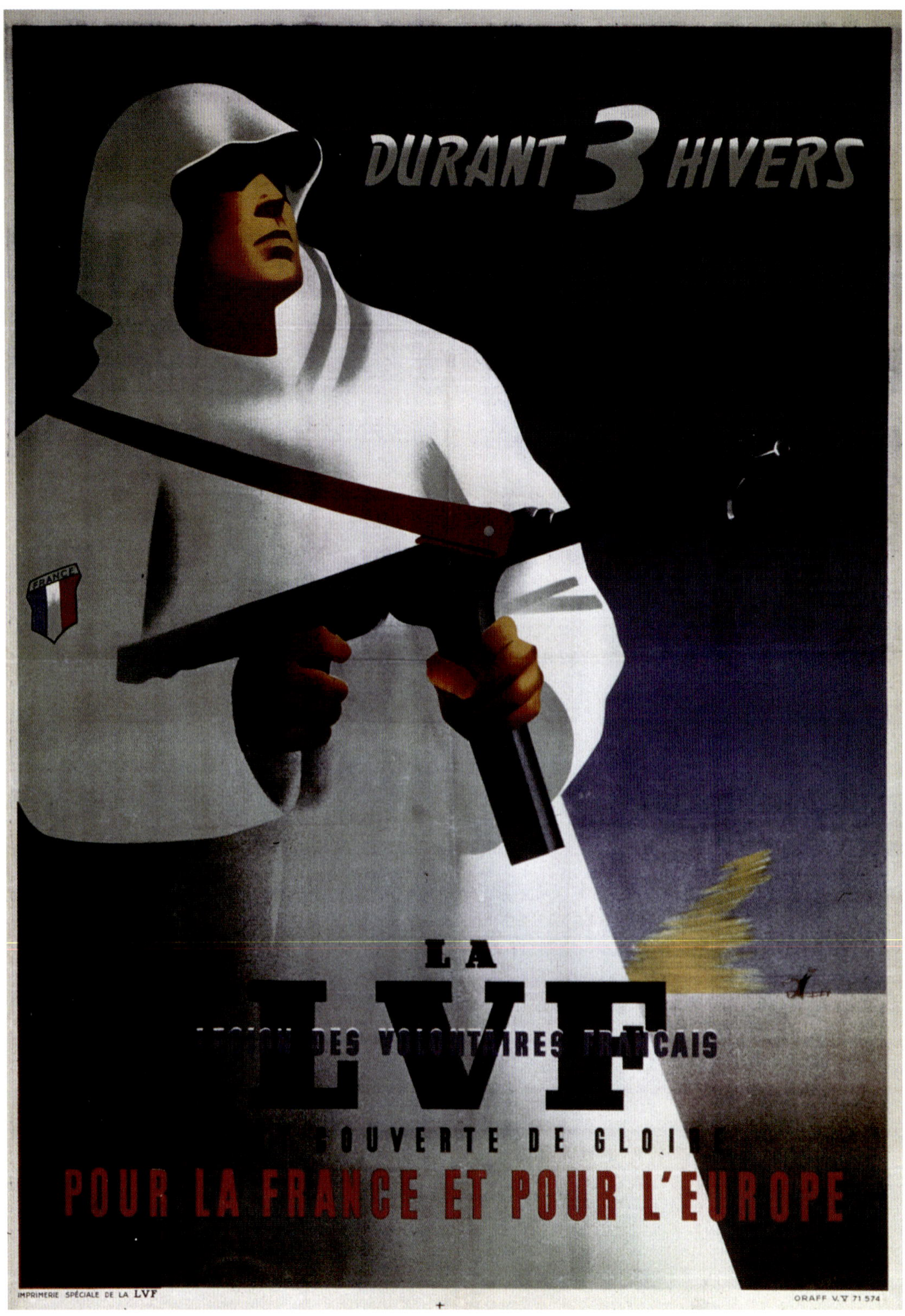

'For 3 winters, the LVF has covered itself in glory, for France and for Europe', Legion of French Volunteers poster, 1942.

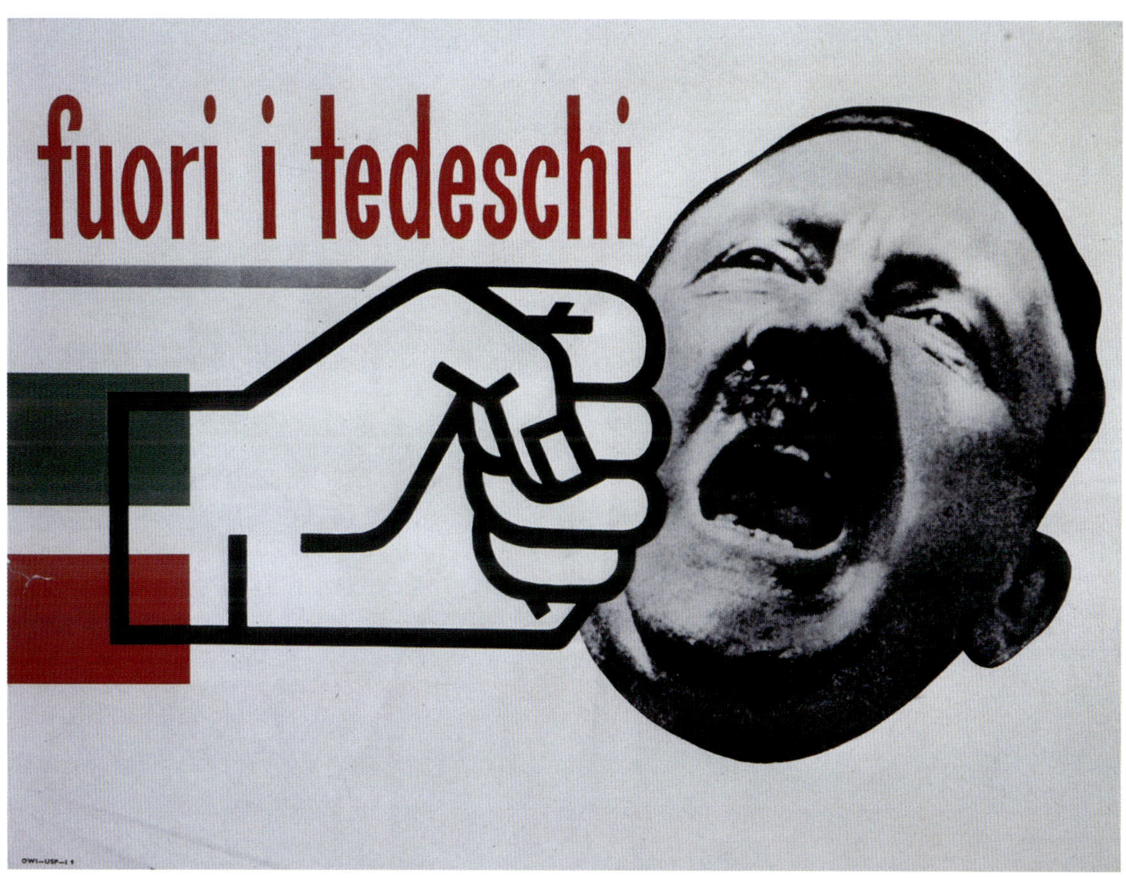

'Out with the Germans!', 1943.

Allied propaganda
in Italy, 1944.

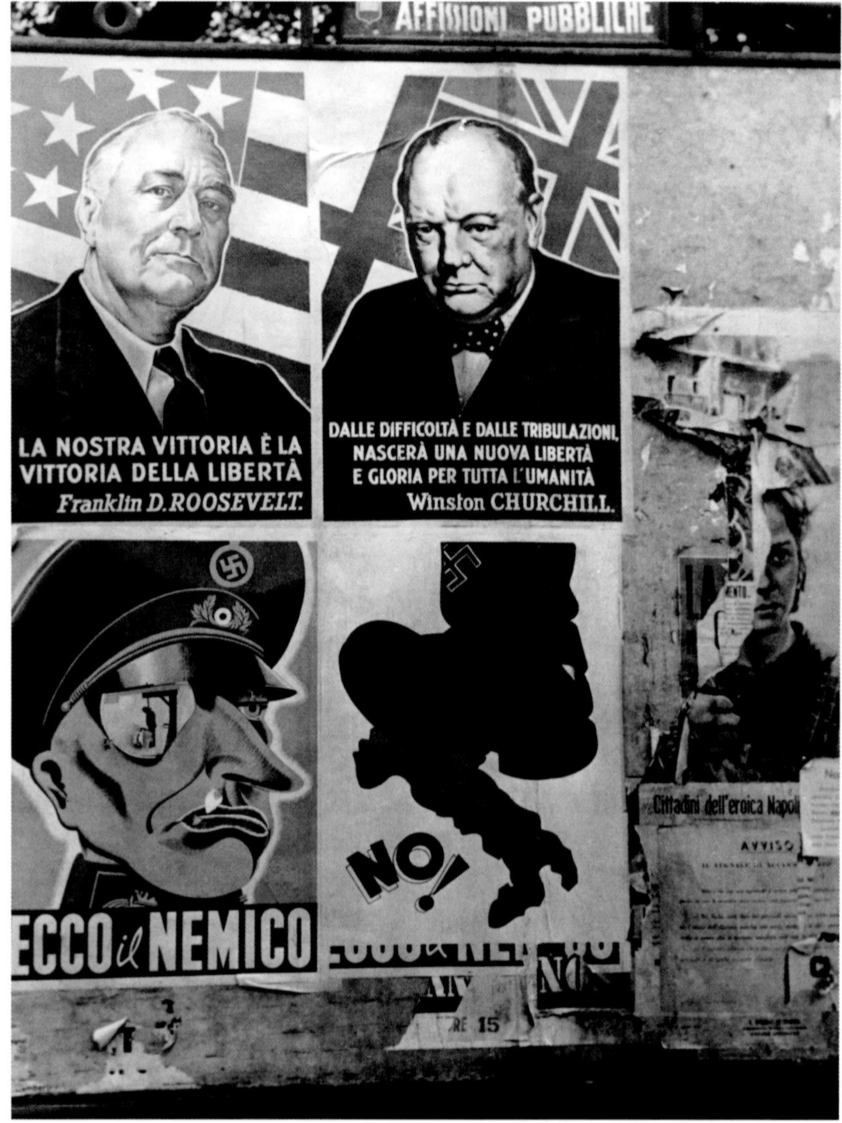

streets with anti-fascist posters and then saw crowds – at the urging of
their posters – gather in these streets to rally together, only to be shot
indiscriminately by soldiers.

In Italy, Allied forces quickly slapped poster propaganda over
fascist posters as they slowly inched their way up the peninsula. During
the war years in France, Allied propaganda made much of Resistance
efforts to subvert Nazi posters. But it was only after the Allied invasion
that the French did violence to these posters with liberating fury. In
closely packed urban areas, where skirmishes were still being waged
between German troops and the French Resistance, Occupation posters

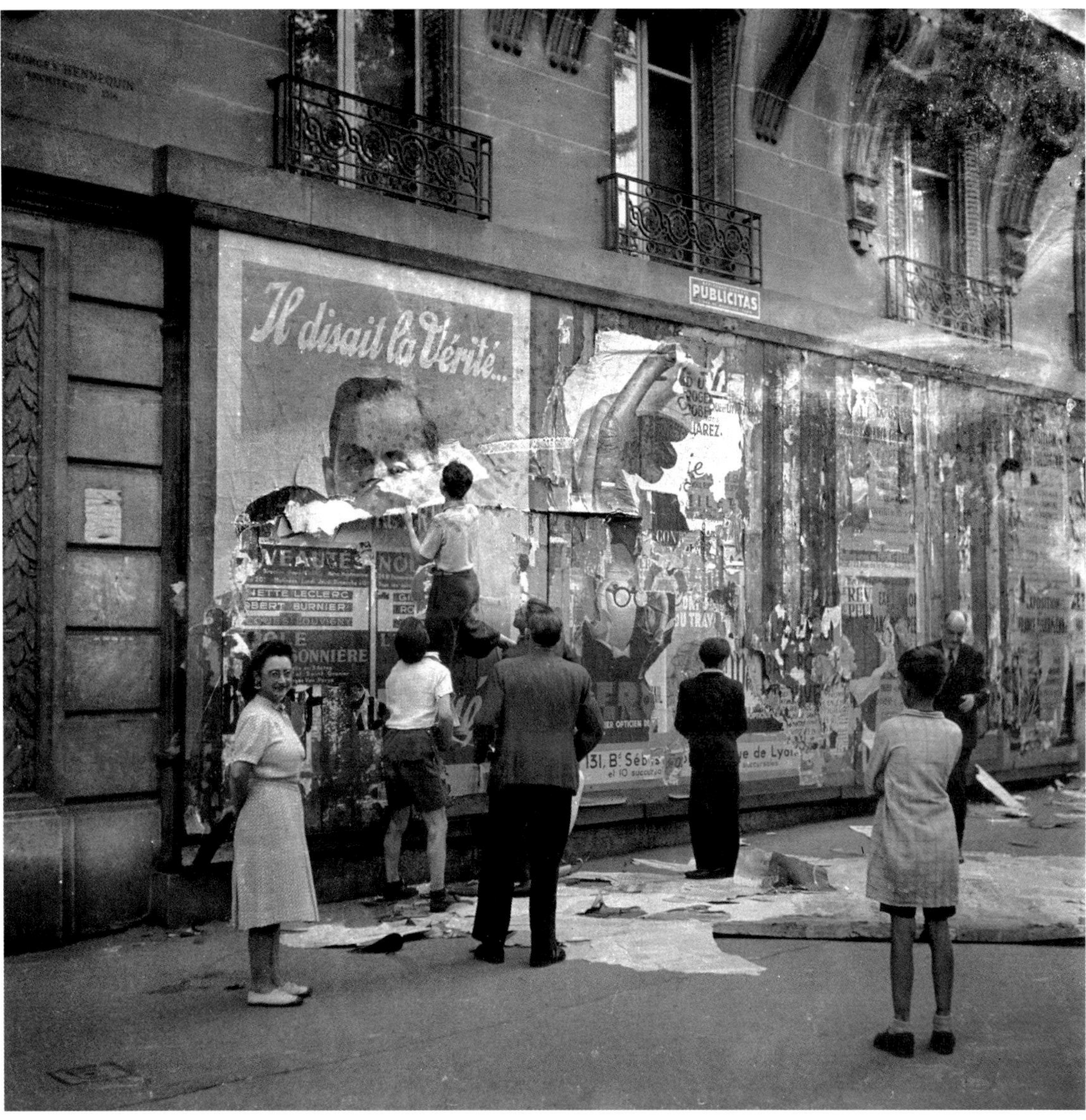

Paris residents destroying
Occupation posters, 1944.

were spontaneously torn down and burned. In April 1944, British Pathé news crews moved in advance of the official front lines, recording the crumpling of German forces in Paris; they featured scenes of the 'Maquis', Resistance / French Forces of the Interior, roaming Paris streets. Along with building barricades, occupying buildings and evading Nazi snipers, citizens began tearing down Nazi posters in large chunks; as if to free themselves of every last vestige of Nazi rule, they lit bonfires that marked the spots where the poster shreds were destroyed. Sometimes there is a very fine line between use and abuse. At few times in the poster's short history was this clearer than after the initial cessation of hostilities and upheavals of the early post-war years; these seemingly simple gestures grew into a curious, but also common, preoccupation in the years following the war.

A Poster about Posting

The Italian Realist film-maker Vittorio De Sica released *Bicycle Thieves* in 1948, and his tale of Italy's painful post-war period focuses on the plight of a poster hanger. He made a curious choice of protagonist. A shambling everyman, Enzo Staiola plays De Sica's flawed hero Antonio. He is so eager for work that he takes the job eagerly enough, but soon learns that it hinges on his owning a bicycle; only with a bike can he move around Rome, plastering walls with movie posters. Early in the film, the bicycle is stolen; as Antonio and his young son search for it, De Sica takes us on an informal tour of a country reeling from years of conflict, its populace living in soulless modern building blocks, pockmarked and peeling, on the outskirts of the city. Haggard women line up for buckets of water, to be carried to their apartments, and laundry hangs out of windows; overgrown plants cover houses while empty lots scar the landscape. When the billsticker leaves the sad suburbs for the centre of Rome, the medieval streets and twisting alleys of the old city change the locale but continue to add force to De Sica's portrait of a society unhinged. Hired to hang publicity posters for a Rita Hayworth movie, Antonio introduces an element of effervescent Hollywood glamour to the bedraggled city walls; the pin-up girl may have destroyed men's lives in Hollywood films such as *Blood and Sand* and *Gilda*, but her 'keg of gunpowder' persona and 'bombshell' looks are utterly out of place in the war-weary, bomb-torn country. De Sica lingers on these scenes. Mutely grinning from overcrowded walls, the Hayworth poster is culpable, an interloper from a new and different world. After war's end, the street poster silently stood accused of great sins.

When the first signs of economic resurgence began to exit Italian factories in the form of Vespas and typewriters, a shift to peacetime production was clear. The very epitome of the capitalist economy, De Sica used the poster of pin-up Rita Hayworth to signal Hollywood's crass commercialism. But, in hindsight, the infiltration of American popular culture also signalled the beginning of sustained industrial growth and the shift from an agricultural to a consumer economy. For at least the next decade, as the country industrialized, rural Italians

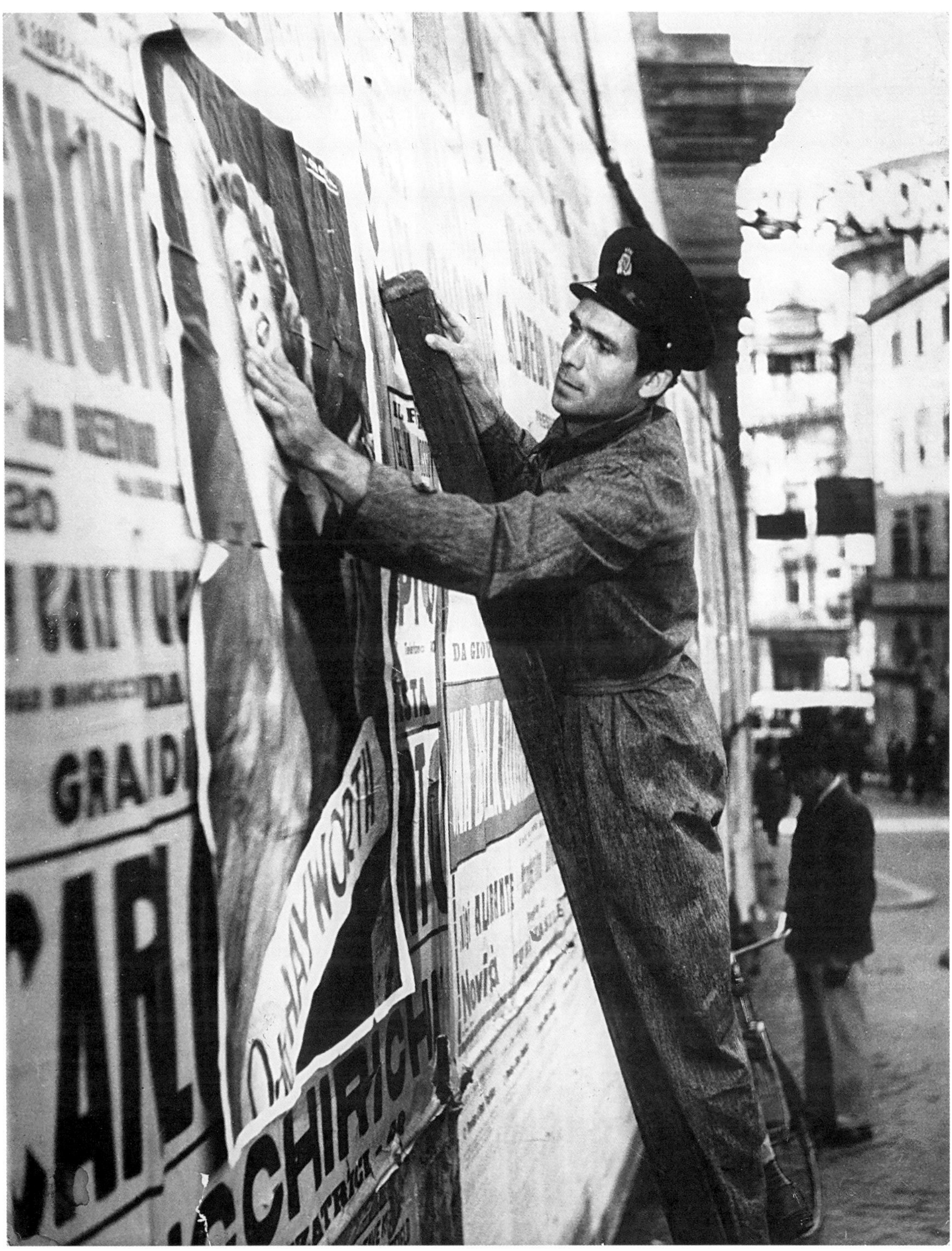

Still from *Bicycle Thieves* (dir. Vittorio De Sica, 1948).

were driven northwards to the churning factories of Milan and Turin;
in the glory years of Olivetti and Fiat, the country's GNP doubled.
Il miracolo economico marked an even larger transformation hinted
at bluntly in De Sica's film.

Bicycle Thieves hinges on one key moment – the instant in which
Antonio's only form of transport is stolen; in this scenario, the poster is
deeply culpable, bringing on a series of woes. As he hangs the publicity
image, his bicycle is stolen. De Sica's film quietly castigates Hollywood's
vision of cinema and the advertising that ensured its success in Italy.

While less dramatic than Italy's post-war transformation, France
was undergoing what one scholar calls 'a moment of spectacular,
unprecedented modernization' that amounted to a 'reordering' of
post-war French culture.[6] While few in France cared to delve into the
country's recent travails, the poster format itself was under scrutiny,
eliciting both fascination and contempt.

Unmaking a Tradition

But, even more than cinema posters, a genuine critique of bills and
poster hanging began to emerge in post-war France. When he first
met the artist Jacques Villeglé in 1947, Raymond Hains's own artwork
consisted of 'deformed' photographs that employed fluted, distorting
lenses. He applied this technique to film-making, and it was during a
film shoot in 1949 that, Villeglé recalled, he and Hains 'took our first
torn poster' near the brasserie La Coupole in Paris.[7] The two not only
tore down the dense, overlapping accumulation of red and black
letterforms, but then mounted it on a canvas and titled the work
Ach Alma Manetro. The title is taken from the few words still legible

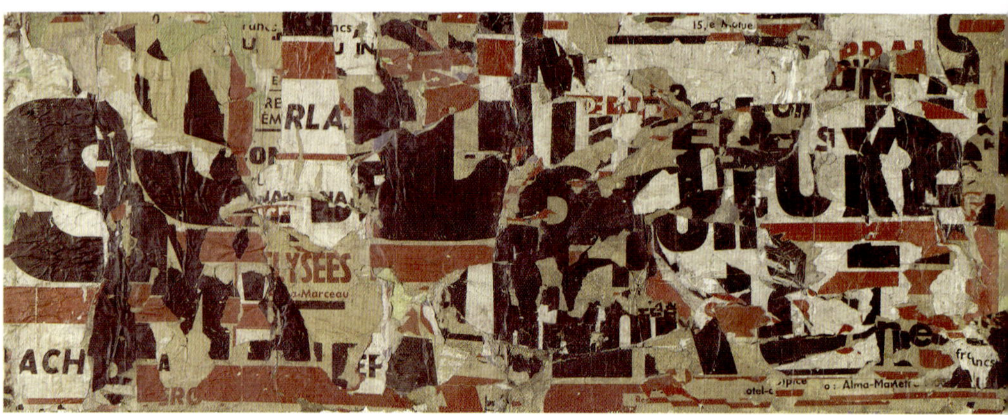

Jacques Villeglé and
Raymond Hains, *Ach Alma
Manetro*, 1949.

after this process was completed. Their use of poster art was, at first, inconsistent since they also dabbled in photography, film and painting. But they kept coming back to the poster format, working at ever-more-striking ways of unmaking the form.

Villeglé, along with Raymond Hains and a small circle of others, began using poster material found in urban streets to create large-scale collages. Their work was termed *affiches lacérées*, or 'torn posters'. Often grouped with post-war French artists working in a variety of media, they pioneered an art movement that would be named Nouveau Réalisme by the French critic and curator Pierre Restany. Sometimes called *décollage*, Villeglé's slashing technique was a nod to the strange alchemy of scribbling, rubbing and other autonomic methods propagated by the Surrealists. In their selecting and claiming of sections of posters, Villeglé and other *affichistes*, or poster artists, drew from Surrealist automatism but, as critics at the time asserted, so mixed high and low art that we cannot straightly think of one without the other. Theirs was an interesting but odd art, alternately plain and ugly or exultant and ennobling. And it was quite unlike the Abstract Expressionism then in ascendance in the United States. Whether pulling down sheets of posters or splattering their detritus over canvases, Villeglé and his peers claimed a sort of detachment or cynicism. Indeed, this aligns best with European developments after the war, like Arte Povera and the Fluxus movement. But Villeglé also paved the way for an entirely new art technique, upsetting the staid rhythm of the post-war art world and lending a kind of rich excitement to a moribund tradition. Or was he simply creating poster rubbish?

Décollage – that is, the process of taking apart or unravelling – is often used to describe the working method of Villeglé and his

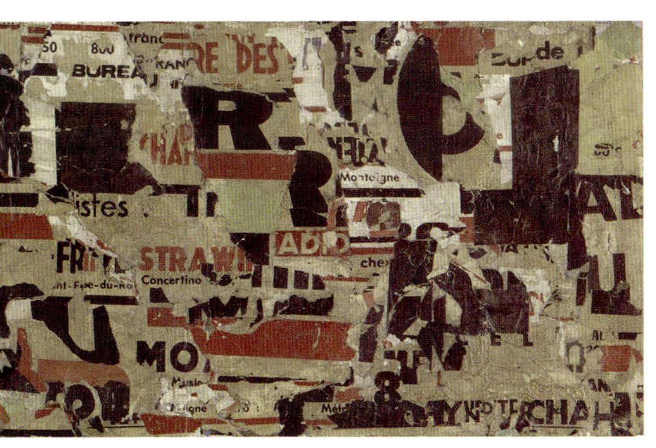

peers; the opposite of collage, that is, the bringing together of various parts, to many observers *décollage* could also seem a mirror of the decline of French elite culture in the late 1940s and 1950s.[8] The British newsreels from 1962 show Villeglé practising an art that appears utterly spontaneous, but his practice more often looked like out-takes from a silent film comedy, revealing less of a Chaplinesque pathos

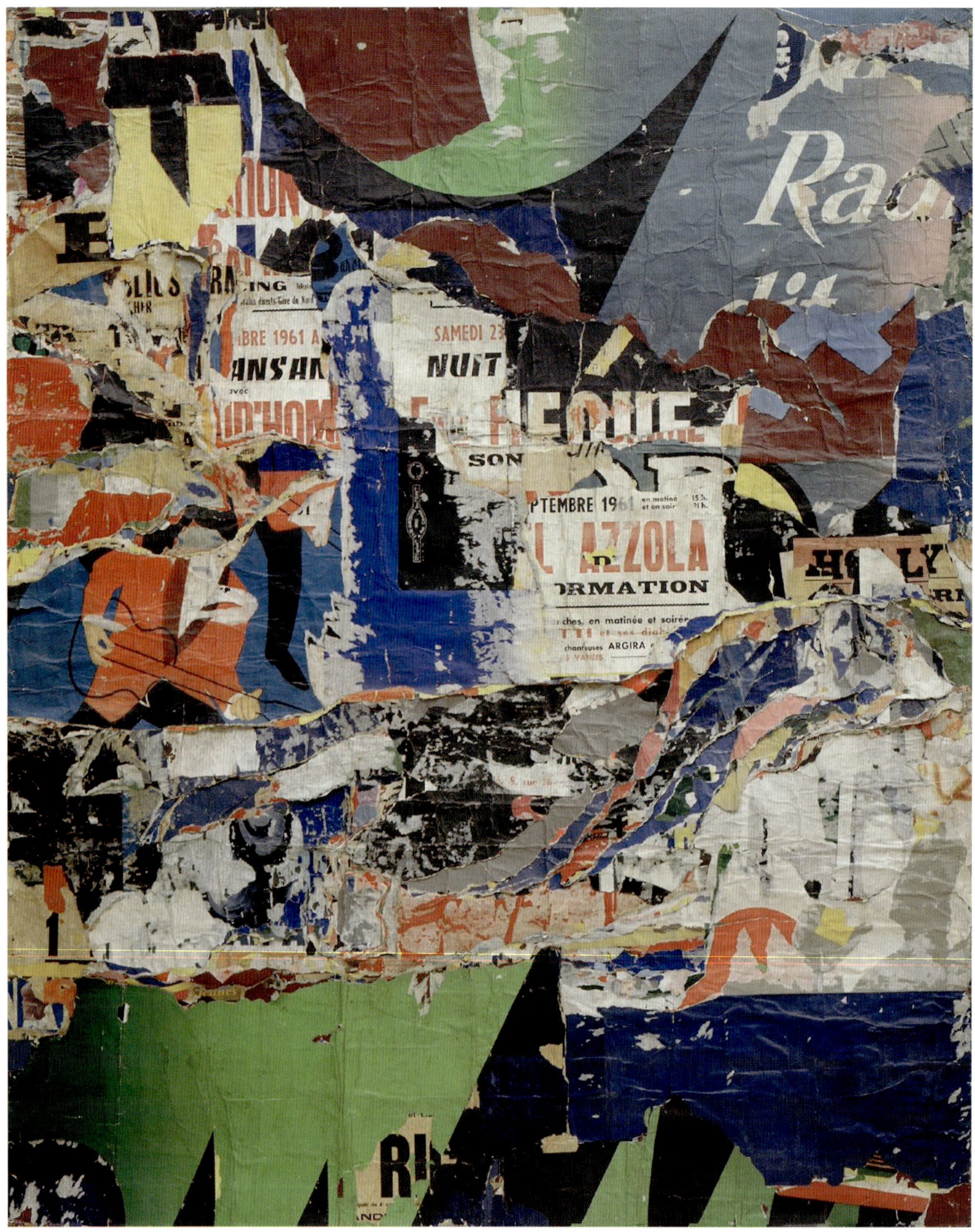

Jacques Villeglé, *The Jazzmen*, 1961, printed papers on canvas.

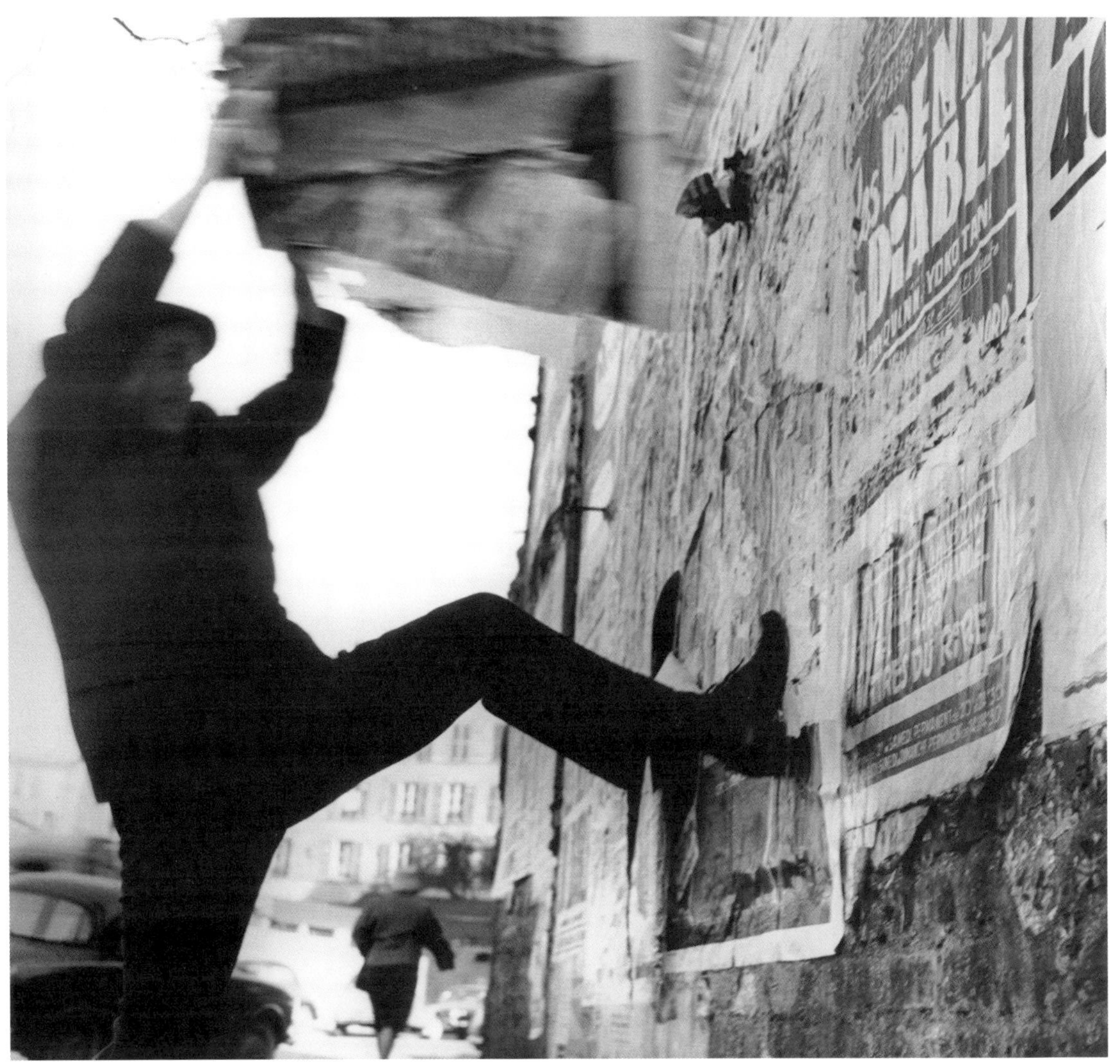

Harry Shunk and János Kender, *Jacques Villeglé*, 1961.

and more slapstick guffaws. To cut and cleave single pieces of a poster off a wall requires considerable technique as well as brute force. Because paper is a relatively elastic material, one must break the adhesive energy adhering it to the wall surface.[9] Harry Shunk and János Kender's photographs of 1961, documenting Villeglé's working process, depict a much more laborious method than is shown in the newsreel footage. The pair were no strangers to contemporary art practice; collaborating with Yves Klein, Shunk and Kender staged a series of photographs that they and the artist then knitted together into the iconic photomontage *Leap into the Void*, depicting Klein gracefully leaping off a building and seemingly hanging in space. The Pathé newsreel shows Villeglé quickly slicing a section, hoisting his cut poster onto his back and briskly walking away in the shadow of Notre-Dame. Shunk and Kender's photos of Villeglé are less rapturous than the film footage and grittier than the carefully doctored Yves Klein image. Here, Villeglé grapples awkwardly with the pasted posters, grabbing and yanking at them. The posters resist, and Shunk and Kender capture yet another artist, in this case Villeglé, in mid-fall.

While a number of different artists claim to have 'invented' the *affiche lacérée*, it is Villeglé and Raymond Hains, two former art students from Brittany, who showed the steadiest and most consistent interest in the poster as a medium. They met in the late 1940s, when Hains had already mounted a solo exhibit at the Galerie Colette Allendy in Paris. Studying art in his native Brittany, Villeglé came of age just as the war ended; but the German withdrawal left a sprawl of waste that haunted the post-Nazi landscape. Shortly after D-Day, Villeglé began to collect German debris and waste, especially the remnants of the Atlantic Wall, an extensive German defence system that, like a barbed wire necklace, laced beaches from Norway to France's border with Spain.[10] Years after the wall, once propagandized by the Germans as 'impregnable', was torn apart during the Allies' landing, these motley cast-offs of steel cable and rope, broken bricks and other detritus were only slowly picked up and cleared off French beaches. Pain, guilt and other memories caused most French people simply to ignore these ruins as they slipped quietly into disrepair. Villeglé was probably right to turn his attention in a different direction; slowly he realized that posters could convey a series of associations even more complex than the remnants of Hitler's 'Fortress Europe'.

Confronted with the role and nature of French collaboration with the Germans during the war, the nation was also deeply enmeshed in a

Posters for the 'No' vote
on the referendum on the
Constitution of the French
Fifth Republic, 1958.

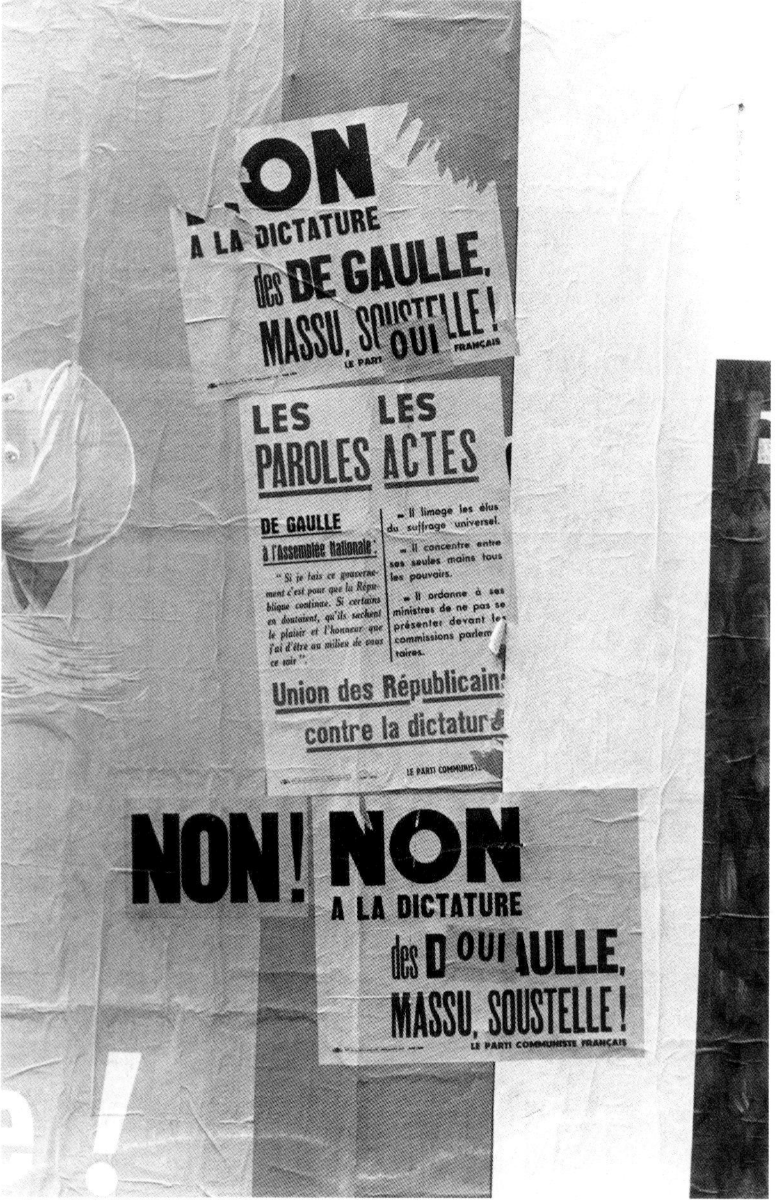

painful decolonization process in the Suez, Algeria and Indochina;
Villeglé's 'lacerated' poster proved an ideal vehicle for commenting on
post-war French politics and art. By the time that Villeglé started his
poster-hunting expeditions in earnest, the French street poster was
alive, but not well. The eventual outcome, a practice that eerily recalls
the poster-tearing by residents of Paris at the end of the Second World
War, found more resonance in printed paper than torn barbed wire.
The turbulent post-war years saw France renegotiating its identity.

Many of these posters were paralysingly ideological; often the poster was subsidiary to carefully written pamphlets and other political tracts filled with propaganda and tailored to specific voting blocks, including young people, miners and North Africans on the Left, Gaullist conservatives on the Right. As late as 1958, observers noted of de Gaulle's presidential campaign that its 'most extraordinary spectacle . . . was the sea of posters'.[11] France's dense urban spaces were a natural home for posters and pedestrians, but these quickly designed and hastily produced posters were unlike the striking visual statements of Lautrec and Steinlen. The form was still alive, but was a shadow of its former self, reduced more and more to fly bills announcing cheap concerts, Hollywood film releases and ephemeral political bills, designed rapidly and shoddily printed on thin paper. The posters used by the *affichistes* were urban detritus that they 'unmade', literally unsticking and ripping through successive layers of glued paper. For Villeglé, this process changed the nature of the poster itself.

Whether or not Villeglé's methods were rooted in rage and were more arduous than he liked to admit, they were also technically illegal. While France's seminal statute of 1881 on Freedom of the Press was part of sweeping reforms, it is best remembered today for the ubiquitous phrase '*Défense d'afficher*', which appeared nationwide on public buildings and historical monuments. Although now often interpreted as an injunction not to post bills, it was originally intended to make clear where posters might be hung. After centuries of censorship, the 1881 law indicated that they may appear almost anywhere, except on public buildings – usually government offices and schools – where local authorities have posted the '*Défense d'afficher*' warning.

The poster craze of the 1890s may have showcased Lautrec and Mucha, but it was fuelled by this legal injunction. More than half a century later, Villeglé and his circle flagrantly disobeyed this law; carefully posed, Villeglé even stood before one of the prohibitive signs for a publicity photo. Moreover, an early group show of *affichiste* work at Colette Allendy's gallery in 1957 was titled 'Le Loi du 29 juillet 1881' (The Law of 29 July 1881). But, as Villeglé seems to intuit, the stealthy, even illegal, actions speak less to the law than to the odd obsessiveness that drove his art. While some malicious critics suspected, not too silently, that Villeglé's technique was more vandalism than art, we must not overlook its subtle distinctiveness; like a cross between

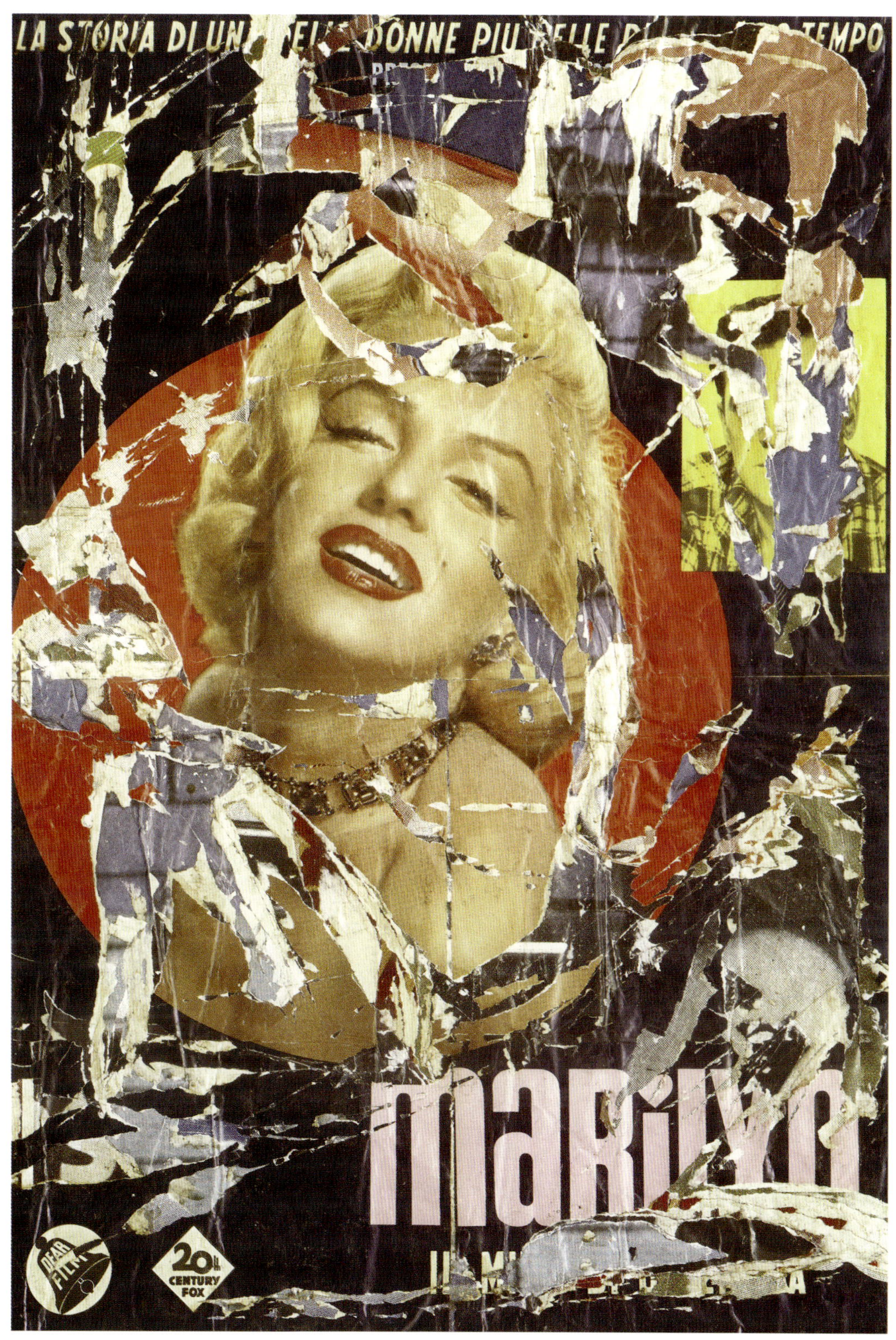

Mimmo Rotella, *Marilyn Monroe*, 1963, décollage.

Shakespeare's impish Puck and a modern-day Shiva, the Hindu god
of destruction, Villeglé might be read as a transformer or harbinger
of things to come.

If Villeglé's practice resembled a form of theft, his utter unmaking
of the poster was not shared by all his Nouveau Réaliste colleagues.
Artist Mimmo Rotella was brought into the fold by Restany, but the
Italian used shredded posters to a different end. A poet as well as
visual artist, and originally affiliated with the Lettrist movement,
Rotella had turned to torn advertising by the mid-1950s. In many
ways, Rotella's practice recalls that of Villeglé. Both artists use peeled
and torn fragments of street posters; both redeploy them on canvas
and each introduces them as fine art. But there is one key difference:
where Villeglé claimed to simply pull these ads from walls, then glue
them directly to the canvas, Rotella always edited his finds. Unlike
Villeglé, Rotella 'improved' the finds by tearing and gluing bits and
pieces together.

Some of Rotella's most memorable décollage work is his cinema
series, a set of works that pays homage to the fabled Italian movie
studios founded by Mussolini just outside Rome. Along with stars
such as Marilyn Monroe and Marlene Dietrich, Rotella even devoted
one work to Rita Hayworth. Recalling the Hollywood glamour shot
featured in *Bicycle Thieves*, Rotella celebrates his seductive star by
reusing a pin-up photo and surrounding it with torn shards of poster.
The piece uses the trashy shreds and clips of advertising in contrast
to Hayworth's irrepressible sensuality. Rotella's unabashed admiration
for the star enhances her mystique in an entirely predictable manner.
Villeglé's slashing act was inchoate and largely symbolic, but it also
marks a turning point, making room for something new, experimental
and rather more original than the dogged posters that advertised Vichy
water and train schedules spotted around Paris at that time.

A Dying Form?

Want to design a poster? It's easy. Here's the community formula
guaranteed to be acceptable in any part of the country. Select
a slogan, pun, rhyme, jingle, or any inane play on words. Get a
realistic illustration to match . . . Finish off this composition with
the client's favorite logotype placed conspicuously on the poster.
There you have it. Send the artwork to the lithographer and get it

plastered all over town . . . The new poster replaces the old, but it makes hardly any difference.[12]

Books and journals including *Printer's Ink* and *Advertising and Public Relations at Work* were filled with advice on how to update the poster and tried hard to sell its advantages. Writing in 1946, J. I. Biegeleisen (quoted above) began publishing 'Poster Gallery', an annual compendium of the 'best' posters to appear each year. Biegeleisen saw himself as fighting a one-man crusade against the corrosive influences of television and lazy poster designers alike. His was a voice in the wilderness. Television made inroads with the 30-second commercial. Magazines offered cheap, full-colour printing for advertisements. Agencies offered poster design as but one – often subsidiary – service within a package that included direct marketing, market research, package design and product-sample distribution. Most damning of all, as the media executive Roger Parry writes, 'creative people in advertising agencies started to look on posters as a poor cousin to other commercial media'.[13] While the Nouveau Réalistes literally tore the poster to shreds, advertising gurus lashed out against the form verbally. David Ogilvy, head of one of the chief New York advertising agencies in the period, expressed a singular dislike for the poster.[14] The 1940s and 1950s were a 'slack' season for it. By 1955, just before commercial television was introduced in Britain, desperate poster advertisers introduced the 'teleposter'. The London-based company behind this venture offered to place posters around built-in televisions 'in bars, lounges, canteens, [and] clubs'. The promotion never advanced beyond promotional ads.[15] Posters fared somewhat better elsewhere; just as the poster form was being trashed in avant-garde art, for a while it seemed as if it might be rescued by post-war designers.

As the climate for post-war advertising shifted, poster advocates in Madison Avenue ad offices were few and far between. For a vertiginous moment after the Second World War, as modernist design tumbled out of its wartime home in neutral Switzerland, there was fresh hope. Sweeping through professional design circles in the former Axis and Allied powers, proponents advocated a rational design vocabulary of simple abstract forms, reduced ornament and the politically neutral presentation of clear messages. Brash and energetic, this broadly apolitical 'International Style' cleaved to an aesthetic shaped by pre-war Suprematist, Cubist and Bauhaus ideas that quickly dominated

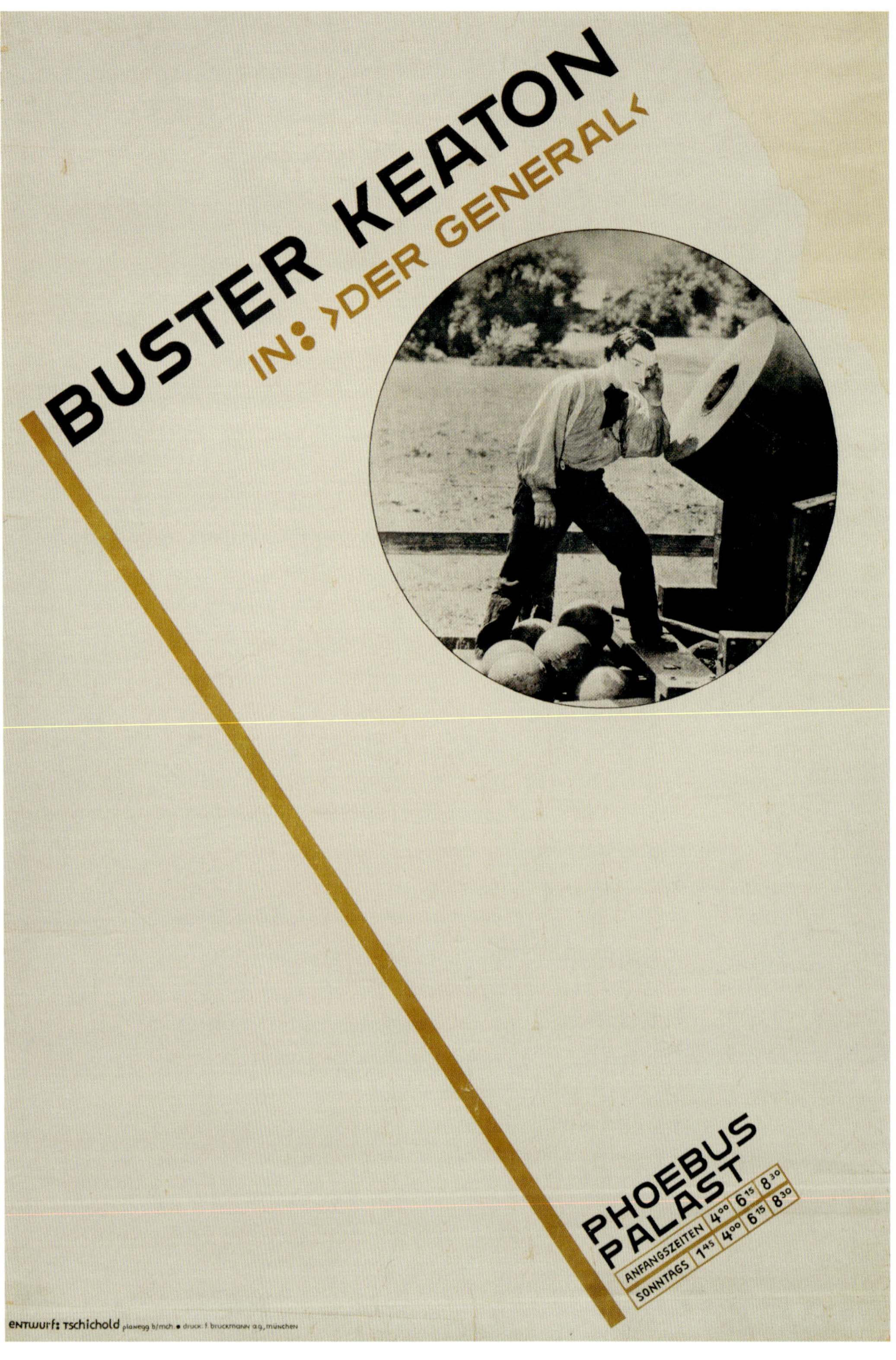

Jan Tschichold, 'Buster Keaton in *Der General*', 1927.

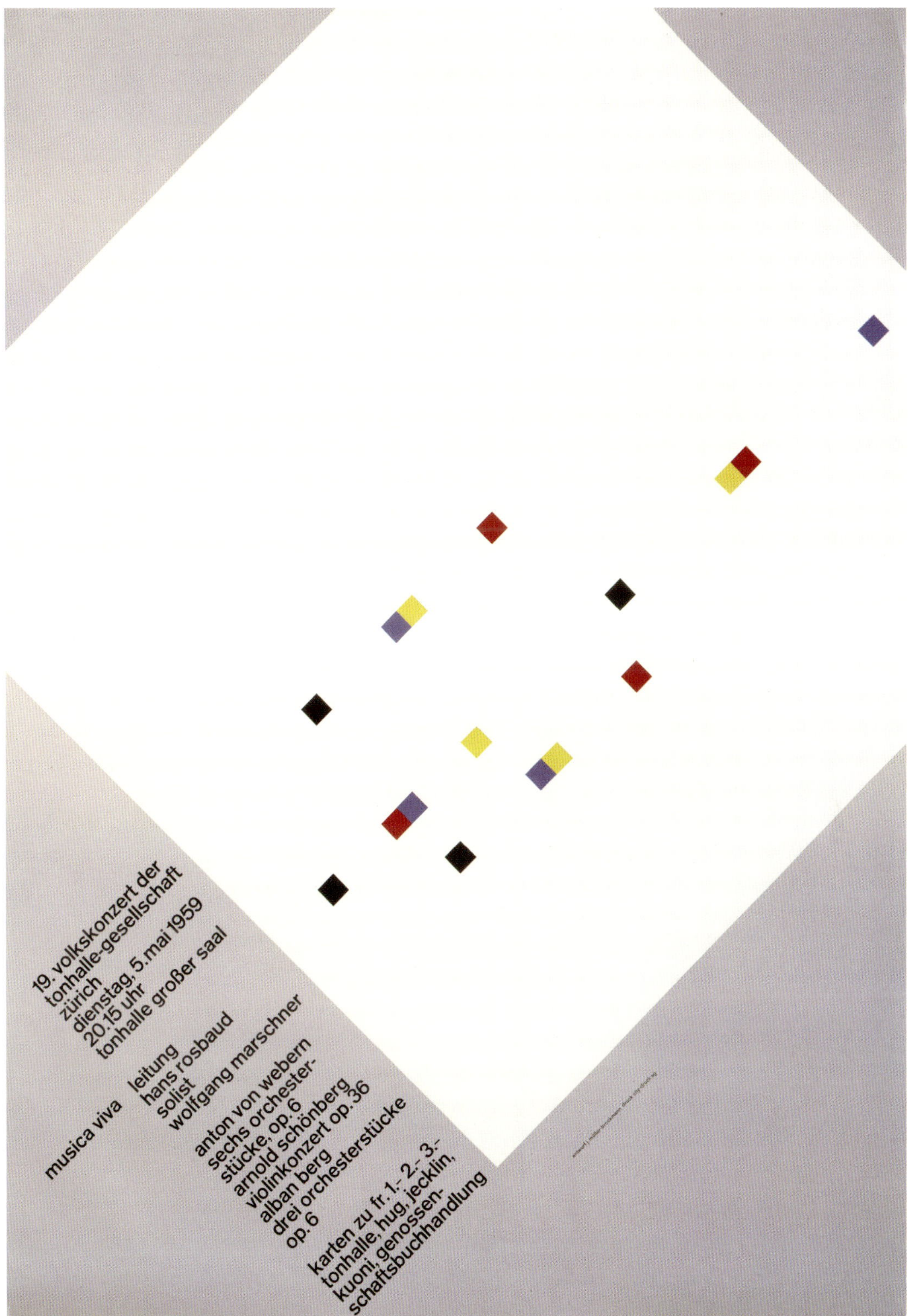

Josef Müller-Brockmann, 'Musica Viva', 1958.

architecture, as figures like Le Corbusier and Ludwig Mies van der Rohe rose higher and higher in public esteem. Bathed in late modernist asceticism, they propounded simple and austere building forms. These architects were joined by a generation of designers who advocated that posters follow a similar format, avoiding foolish nonsense or idle chit-chat; instead, these designers opted to limit themselves to the most essential fundamentals of their messages. Not only did Switzerland shelter famous modernist designers like Jan Tschichold during the war, but also native designers like Max Bill and Josef Müller-Brockmann advocated these clean-lined posters in the years following the Second World War. Brockmann, founder of the magazine *Neue Graphik* in Zurich in 1954, fought a rear-guard battle, arguing that these simple but carefully calculated posters should aggressively 'penetrate' the consciousness of passers-by. For him, a well-made poster is 'not like a gentleman going through the door with a painting easel, but like a burglar through the window with a crowbar in his hand'.[16] To achieve this impact, Brockmann advocated a series of 'laws' for poster design, including the careful and strategic use of colour, form and composition. For example, his poster of 1958 advertising a performance of 'Musica Viva' at Zurich's Tonhalle Gesellschaft not only announces the concert but also lays out a startlingly distinctive structure: super sleek, maximally minimal and rigorously rectangular. Balancing asymmetry with clarity, Brockmann deployed texts and shapes on paper as if they were unstable, dynamic and mutable. His composition looks as though it is hovering weightlessly, but about to be pulled in different directions – an effect that was only magnified when the poster was placed on stone walls, probably in spaces set aside for official concert advertisements. It brought remarkable vitality in contrast to the more conventional designs surrounding it.

To this day, there is a sense of urgency to the designs of Brockmann and his colleagues. Their mission stretched deeper than promoting commerce or Madison Avenue-style advertising; they opted to remake the world itself through clear, rational design. Nevertheless, in spite of Brockmann's efforts, he and other designers ultimately did little to help the predicament of the poster. In New York, it may be a short walk from Madison Avenue to MoMA, but the clear, emphatic modernist aesthetic embraced by Brockmann and other International Style designers was of little use to leading advertising agencies like Ogilvy & Mather, where marketing budgets were heavily weighted towards mass-market magazines as well as radio and television spots. Indeed, by the late 1950s, trendy American advertising agencies such as Doyle Dane Bernbach (DBB) and Papert Koenig Lois (PKL) took the short, punchy messages and clipped visual clarity of Brockmann and other European poster designers and applied their lessons to magazine ads.[17] When the post-war technology giant Olivetti, for example, hired top designers to integrate its showrooms, products and advertising alike, the results were widely publicized in design journals. International competitors – often companies with a global reach – took note. But one point must be stressed here: while corporations like IBM and Columbia Broadcasting System (CBS) were converted to the gospel of International Style design, even they had little use for posters. Instead, as priority was given to 'corporate identity', they aimed to shape the public's general impression of their own sprawling enterprises and activities. These corporations asked designers like Paul Rand and William Golden to bring a simple, rational vision to products, logos, brochures, packaging, print ads and instruction manuals alike. Working for corporate clients, these designers eagerly plundered modernism's stylistic larder, taking almost everything but the free-standing poster.

This is not to suggest that posters simply disappeared. Like distant cousins who over-extend their stay, posters continued to haunt subways, linger in government offices and loiter in school hallways and classrooms. But the form was increasingly relegated to second-class status; few leading advertisers or designers focused on them. Instead, most marketers consigned posters to design limbo, at best approaching them as an afterthought. Professionals barely disguised their disdain for a form that simply reproduced images and messages from print campaigns published in newspapers and magazines. The poster had all but 'lost its creative edge'.[18]

Posters' few corporate advocates stand out. Walter Paepcke, founder and director of the Container Corporation of America (CCA), made a conscious point of commissioning posters as part of the cultural campaign 'Great Ideas of Western Man'. Under the guidance of Charles Coiner, an art director at CCA's advertising agency, 'Great Ideas' began commissioning vanguard artists and designers in 1936. Printed on glossy paper and issued as 'portfolios', however, these were no ordinary street posters. Instead, they were issued in series, with their own case, and were meant to be contemplated or framed.

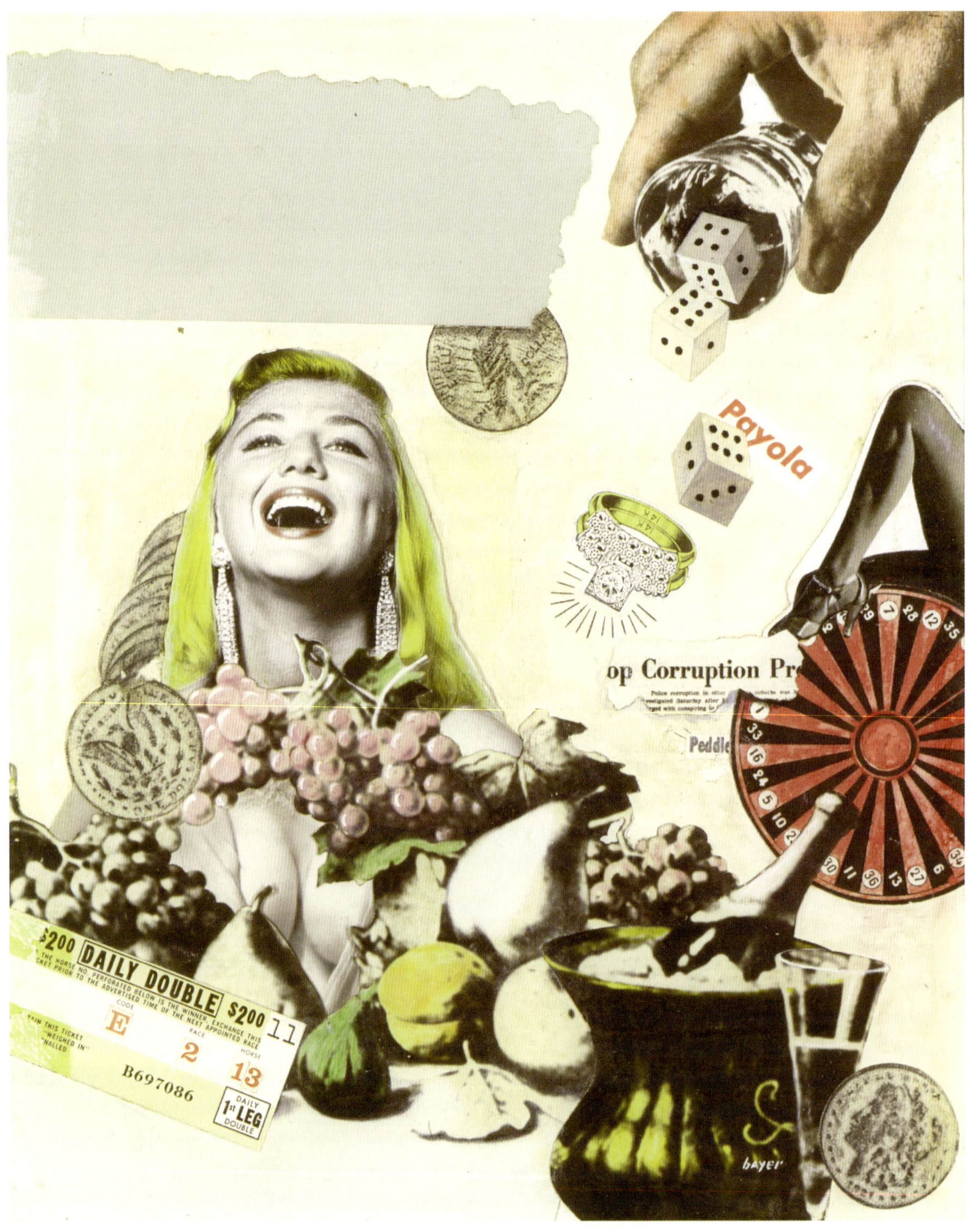

Herbert Bayer, from the series 'Great Ideas of Western Man' by Container Corporation of America (1950–75), 1959.

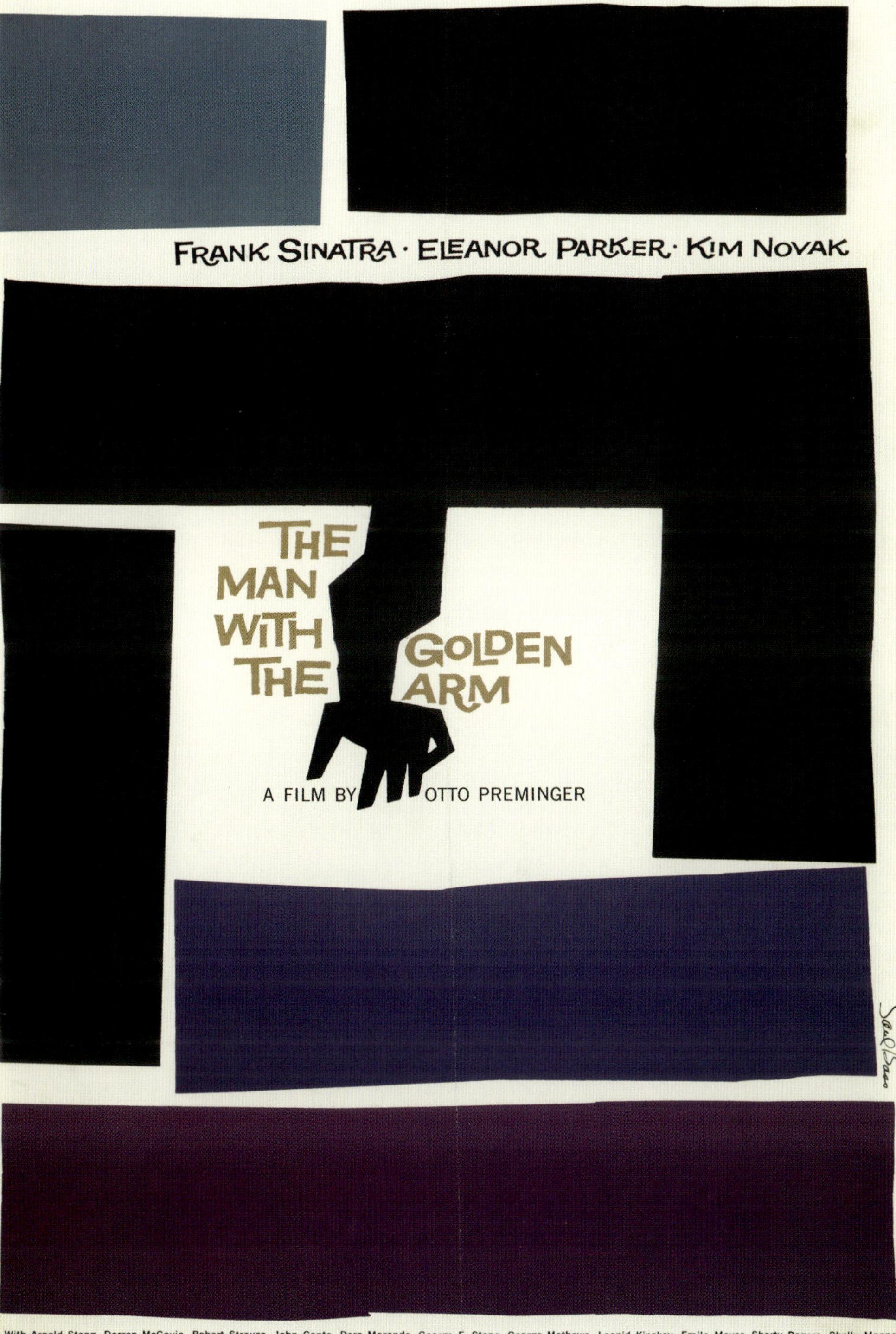

Saul Bass, poster for *The Man with the Golden Arm*, 1955.

If the furniture company Knoll used posters to bring attention to products, but issued brochures to make the final sale, this does not mean that posters were suddenly removed from everyday experience. Public-service posters continued to fill schools and government offices. Moreover, working in the entertainment industry, designers like Saul Bass and Alvin Lustig did use their respective practices to eke out a productive space between explicitly commercial advertising and artful design. Walking a tightrope between the cerebral, highly rational design of the International Style and the no-nonsense approach of Madison Avenue marketers, the Los Angeles-based designer Bass designed a series of brilliantly creative posters for films and music. Bass's poster design from 1955 for the release of Otto Preminger's *The Man with the Golden Arm* effectively announced a series of motifs and used a jagged arm as its logo, echoing the system design for corporations. It employs a rough grid, but oddities like the irregularity of the flat rectangles of colour and the strangely serrated and bent hand and arm, as well as the crude lettering that looks hand-drawn, introduce an element of movement. The motifs are carried through the credits and recall director Preminger's purposefully claustrophobic views of drug-addled addicts in tight, quivering shots. Bass's poster is skittery, looking something like a school art project executed by an excitable group of eight-year-olds. Therein lies its subtlety. The large blocks of coloured rectangles recall Matisse's late-career cut-outs. But the provocative use of empty space and silhouetted figures, and its reliance on a grid (however rough), gives a significant nod to the Swiss School; Bass's quirky typography and wobbly composition almost make paranoia, psychosis and drug addiction charming.

Reviled by post-war advertising gurus, even International Style pioneers like Jan Tschichold began to question the fundamentals of modern poster design. The godfather of rational design in the years that followed, Tschichold knew almost too much about rules. Attacked and even arrested by the Nazis in 1933, when he was living in Munich (he was indicted for owning Soviet posters), the designer was held under charges of 'Cultural Bolshevism'. In the short term, he fled to Switzerland, where he helped shape the post-war International Style. But he also developed a hostility to rigid policy and regulation; his anger was so molten that he spoke out against the ideas that shaped his earlier practice. Broad-based precepts seemed to him to be constructed from the same fascist equipment as Huxley's soma or Orwell's thought crime. Strict rules about design can evoke a frightening vision of state control, the designer insisted, and evinces a 'mania' for order.[19] But, while Tschichold's post-war double-take may have furrowed the brows of fellow designers, artist Marcel Duchamp tried to bring the poster back into the realm of the capricious, improvisational and intensely imaginative.

Trashing the International Style

Not pure art, but not fully commercial either, the poster occupied a position in post-war culture that was hard to articulate. Villeglé and other Nouveau Réalistes assaulted the venerable advertising poster head on, but the best summarizing statement in this period was formed by the artist Marcel Duchamp. Asked to curate the exhibition 'Dada, 1916–1923' (1953) at the Sidney Janis Gallery in New York, Duchamp also created the show's poster. At this point in his life, Duchamp's ideas and art were beginning to be better known and the artist was capable of attracting midge-like clouds of followers. There is an element of bravura in this poster, which was designed and printed on large, thin sheets that resembled tissue paper. It included a list of all 212 works in the exhibit and also featured short texts by key Dada artists Tristan Tzara, Jean Arp, Richard Huelsenbeck and Jacques Lévesque. Beyond the vivid orange title overprinting and irregular blocks of text, however, the poster was a piece of Dada art. On receiving the printed posters at the gallery, Duchamp selected one and crumpled it into a ball; he then directed that each poster be similarly crumpled and thrown into a rubbish bin for visitors to retrieve. As Richard Hamilton rather drily noted, if few copies of the poster exist today, this treatment may 'account for its comparative rarity'.[20]

In this startlingly cold-blooded gesture, Duchamp channelled a generation's worth of cynicism and provocation. 'Dada, 1916–1923' relentlessly probes the dynamic tension between 'art' and 'trash/rubbish', and it is no accident that Duchamp used the poster as both medium and message. While the notion that posters could hold any value beyond their transient messaging function was still relatively new, the exhibition also acknowledges posters' long history of being perceived and described as 'rubbish'. Indeed, where do most posters end their lives, but as rubbish?

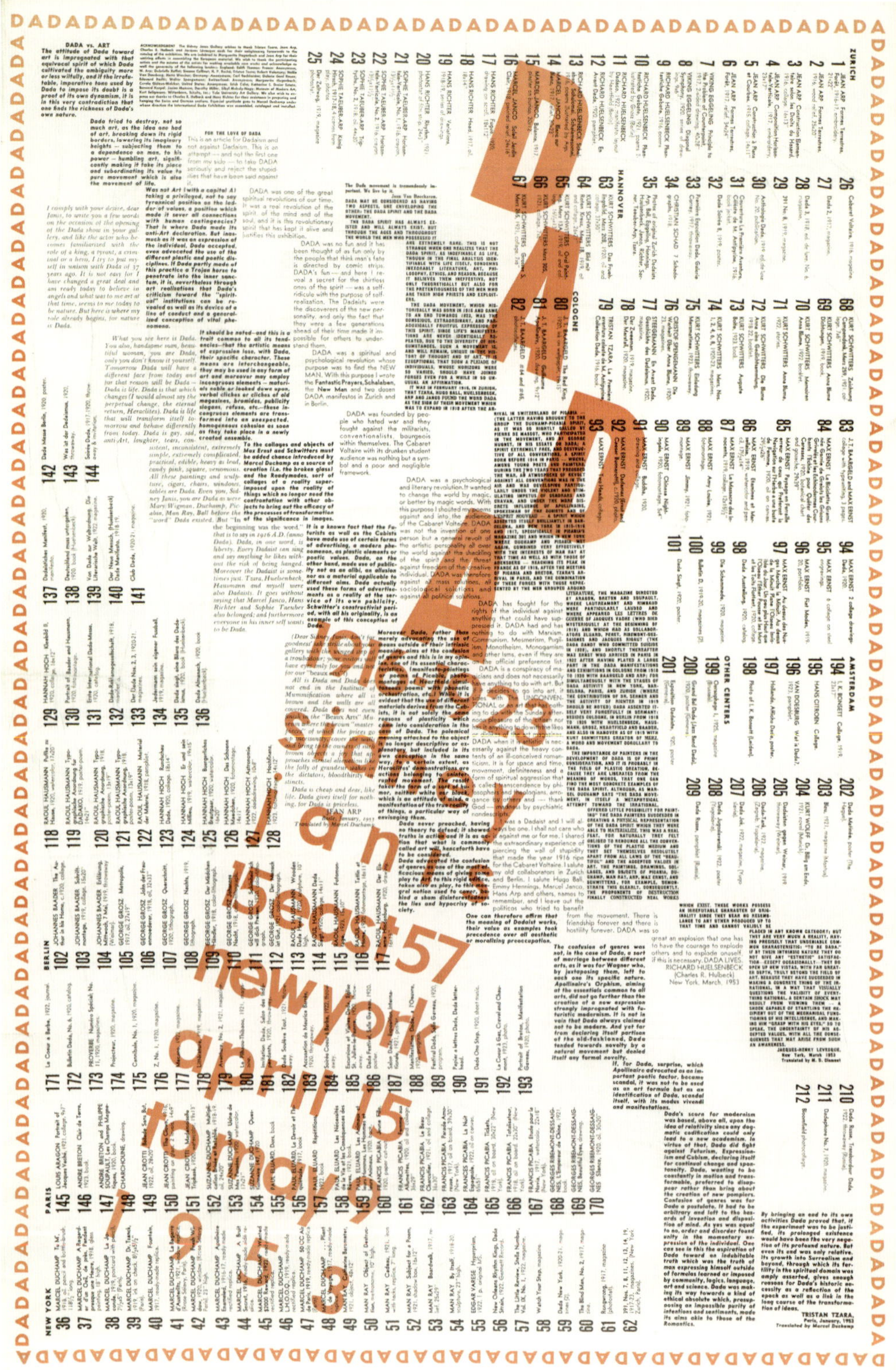

Marcel Duchamp, *'Dada, 1916–1923,' Sidney Janis Gallery, New York, April 15 to May 9, 1953*, 1953, photolithograph.

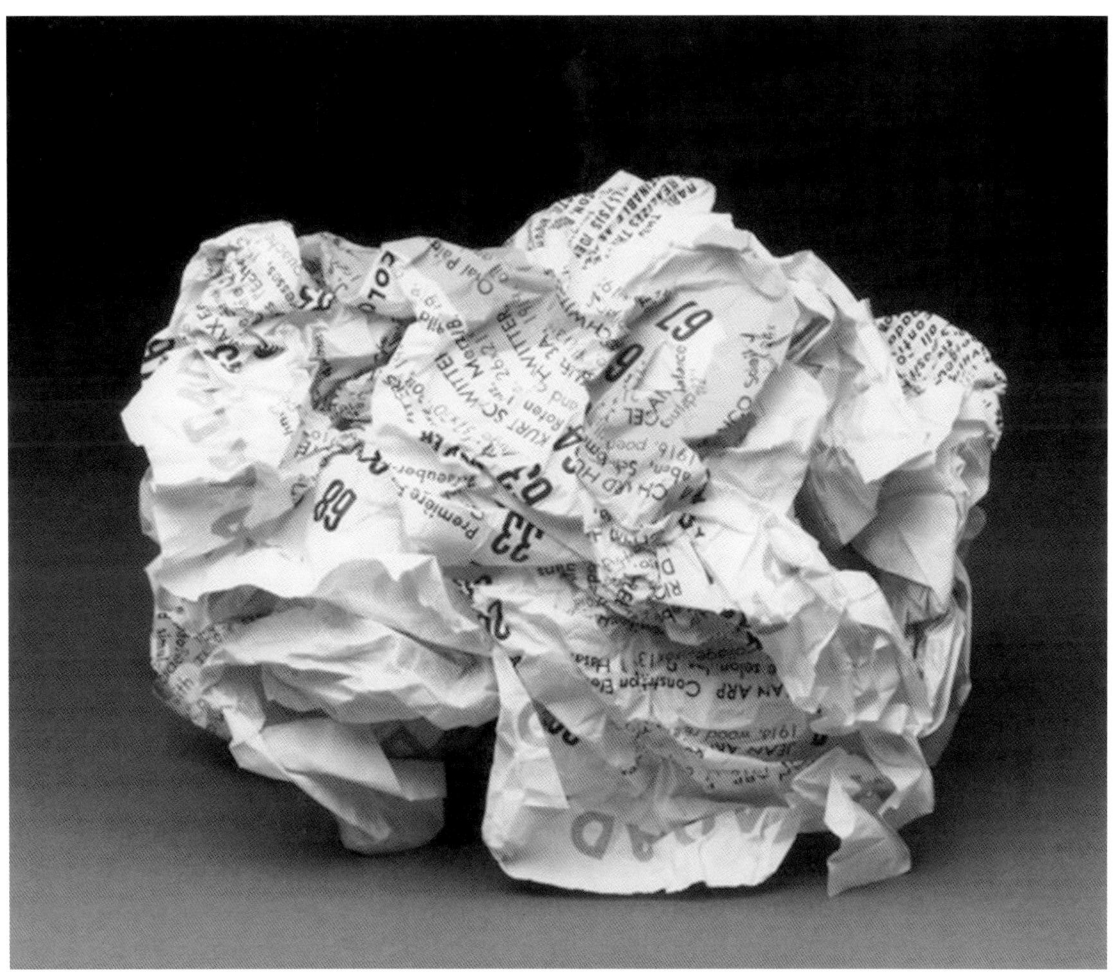

Marcel Duchamp, *'Dada,1916–1923,' Sidney Janis Gallery, New York, April 15 to May 9, 1953*, 1953, crumpled version.

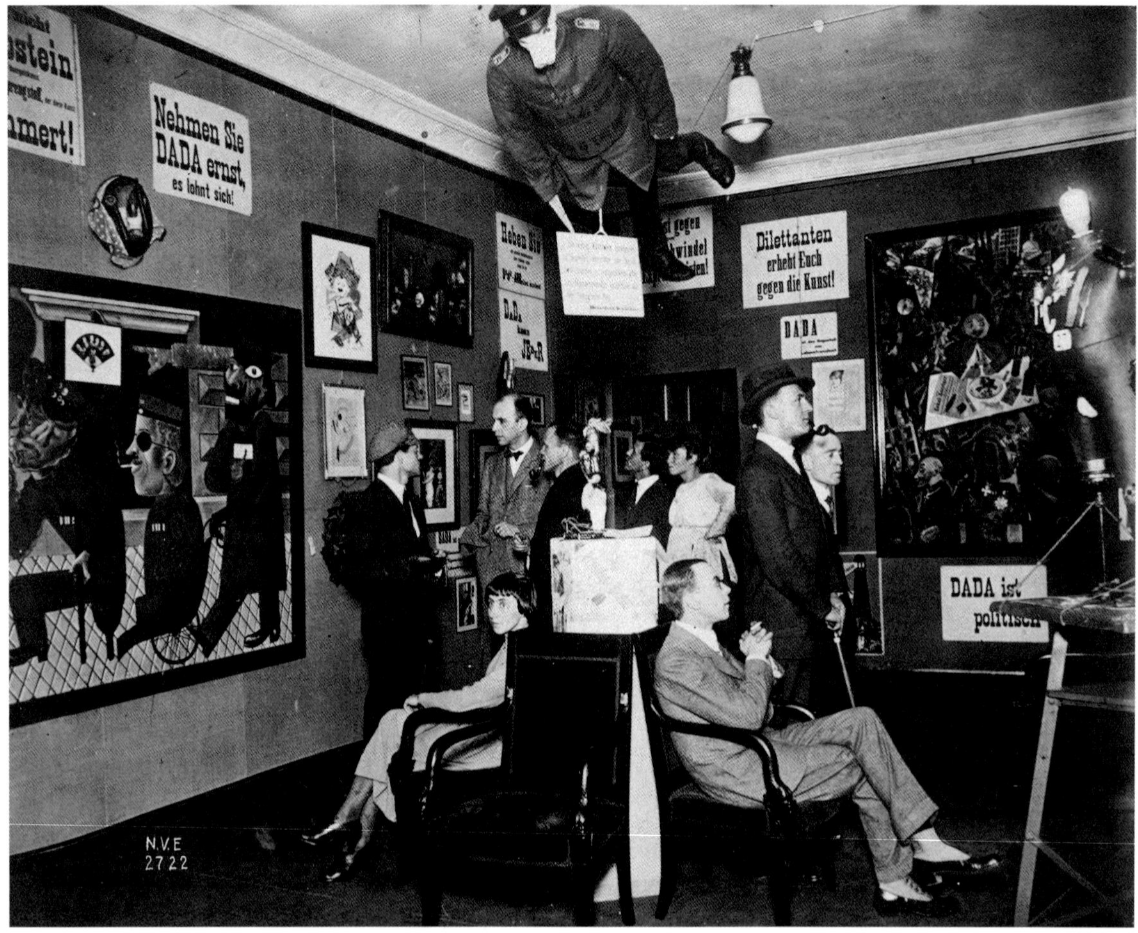

As Duchamp's use of the Janis gallery wastebasket reminds us, rubbish brings with it a startling moment of clarity. Scholars argue that the very act of casting a used thing aside or throwing it away is a form of critique; if something is valued, it is saved. If they stay outdoors, most posters, however, are subjected to what can be called an 'allegory of contemporary capital',[21] discarded or simply left to hang on walls until they slowly disintegrate or are covered up by newer posters. In economies based on scarcity, cast-offs will have other utilities; only wealthy societies create waste. Duchamp's deliberately wasteful gesture signalled a culture of ephemerality and excess.

For all its impermanence, this poster hungrily, even greedily, courts attention. Like a thunderbolt from Zeus, Duchamp's zigzagging orange overprinting looks like a parody of the International Style poster. Beating down the careful, systematic order of Brockmann's grids, the show's title runs in one direction while its text scampers off in the other. Any reader seeking solace in a clear and rational reading experience will be sorely disappointed.

The ambitious scope of 'Dada, 1916–1923' represented Dada as an international art movement dominated by an enduring, provocative and sometimes exuberant strain of irrationality; it also signalled the re-emergence of Dada strategies in contemporary work by artists like Robert Rauschenberg and John Cage. Yet photographs of Duchamp's installation depict a somewhat haphazard affair, perhaps magnified by its curator's droll sense of humour. Instead of the spare aesthetic considered standard for a gallery exhibit, various paintings, prints, collages and posters were splayed across the walls and are even affixed to the ceiling. With pieces stacked one above the next, and sometimes overlapping each other, the main gallery resembled nothing so much as that great rubbish heap of the nineteenth century, the poster hoarding. In its earlier incarnation, the hoarding's free-for-all played with posters' fundamental meaning, garbling messages and providing a kind of metaphor for the 'confusions and collisions' of urban life.[22] Duchamp's gallery installation capitalized on a long-standing Dada fascination with the poster hoarding as a point of flux and chaos. The First International Dada Fair held in 1920 in Berlin featured a similarly haphazard installation. Then, and later, many Dadaist works imitated traditional publicity methods, using leaflets and newspaper articles as well as posters to imitate modern messaging techniques but also to imbue them with contradictory or nonsensical messages.[23]

Duchamp's treatment of posters at the Janis exhibition was highly subversive. In it, he engaged printmaking's puny half-sister, the exhibition or gallery poster. In both Europe and America, the post-war gallery poster carried considerable prestige, functioning as more than an advertisement aimed at a narrow cultural elite. Exclusive American galleries like Leo Castelli, André Emmerich and Pace Gallery as well as museums used the poster format to announce shows, but also sold these posters at more moderate prices. Presented as limited-edition prints, the posters could be signed and numbered by the artist. Many cash-strapped collectors sought these half-breeds out, seeing in them an inexpensive opportunity to buy an 'original' work of art. Duchamp 's unconventional act – crumpling his own show's poster and throwing it into a waste bin – uses a simple gesture to send up the entire genre. Taken at face value, he was engaging with this emerging practice subversively.

At the height of his career, while on his urban rambles, Jacques Villeglé sometimes came across committed Marxists who objected to his practices. Years later, he recalled:

> I had many discussions with militant communists who reproached me for having torn apart their posters. I replied to them that the posters would go into museums, and that thereby their story would be told.[24]

Such discussions were in some ways pointless; Villeglé and his Marxist contemporaries were talking at each other, but speaking different languages. The French communists were still putting their faith in posters as an egalitarian mode of communication; Villeglé saw them as something else. He may have been unmaking the traditional poster, literally tearing them apart while stripping them off walls. But the poster was also rapidly changing. If Villeglé was tearing them down, he might be construed as making space for a very new kind of poster.

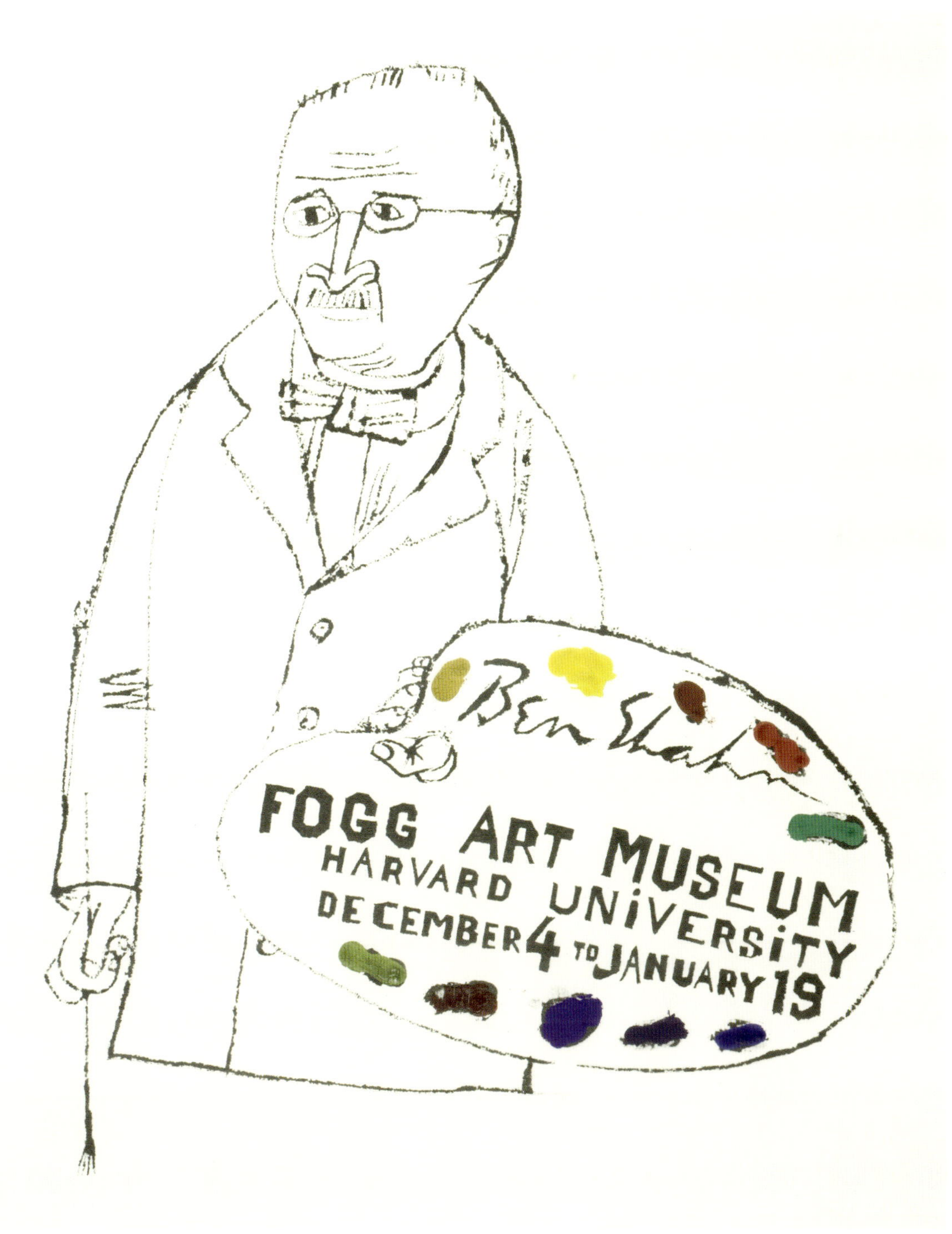

Ben Shahn, Fogg Art Museum exhibition poster, 1956.

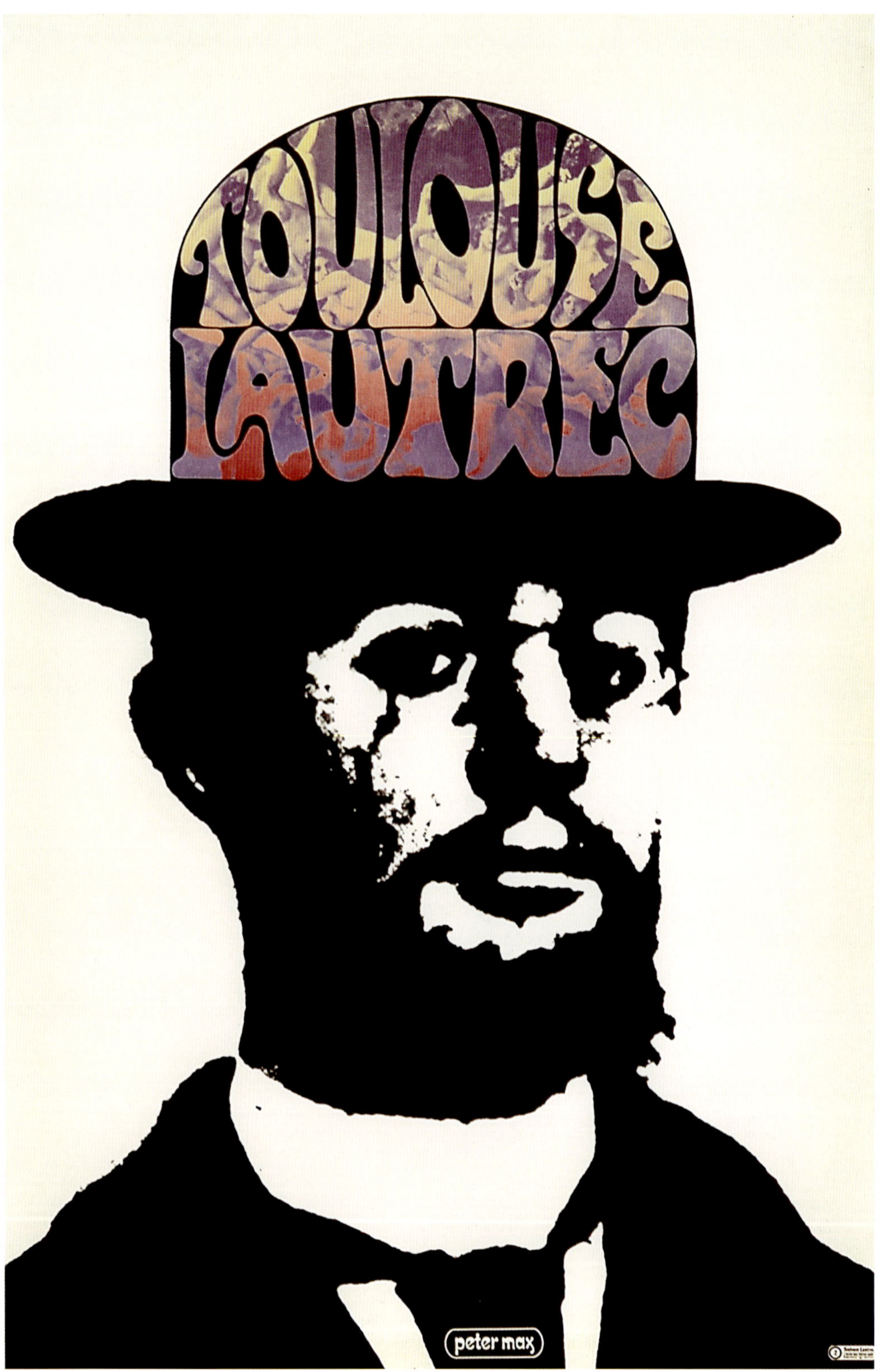

Peter Max's poster 'Toulouse Lautrec', 1966, updated the older poster artist's work by altering a contemporary portrait of him.

3 NEW ART, NEW SPACE: 1960–1980

Beginning in the early 1960s, America and Europe erupted in what one commentator called 'a benign rash of posters'.[1] Remarking on the following decade, one American historian declared that the 'decade of the 1960s was the most innovative and diverse in the history of the poster in this country'.[2] A vast market for new designs, including life-size photos of the supermodel Twiggy, psychedelic announcements of rock concerts and reproductions of famous works by nineteenth-century artists like Mucha and Toulouse-Lautrec, proved that posters were popular once more. Although some commentators called it a 'second flowering', the poster's popular resurgence in the 1960s also marked a turning point. Proclaiming allegiance to bands, the counter-culture and values outside the mainstream, the new art poster became a bellwether, not just of the counter-culture, but of seismic cultural shifts. More than a cheap form of wall decoration, posters of protest or popular entertainment literally brought public spectacle into new spaces; in an era of paradoxes, where 'individualism' was more than rhetorical, many believed that posters could reveal the inner self. By 1968 the poster craze was described as 'half way between a passing fashion and a form of mass hysteria'.[3]

Labels like 'renaissance' are misleading; they imply that the old familiar ground is simply being crossed and re-crossed. While posters continued to hang crookedly and all but forgotten above bus seats and on Underground station walls, by the middle of the 1960s they began to creep, wheedle and charm their way into the homes and offices of a new generation of aesthetes. In some cases, these posters mimicked the modes of fine art, though often with fantastic exaggeration. They were shown in museums and lauded in prestigious biennials. At first it seemed that this poster extravaganza was a simple shadow of the bubble that had boomed, and then burst, some 80 years earlier.

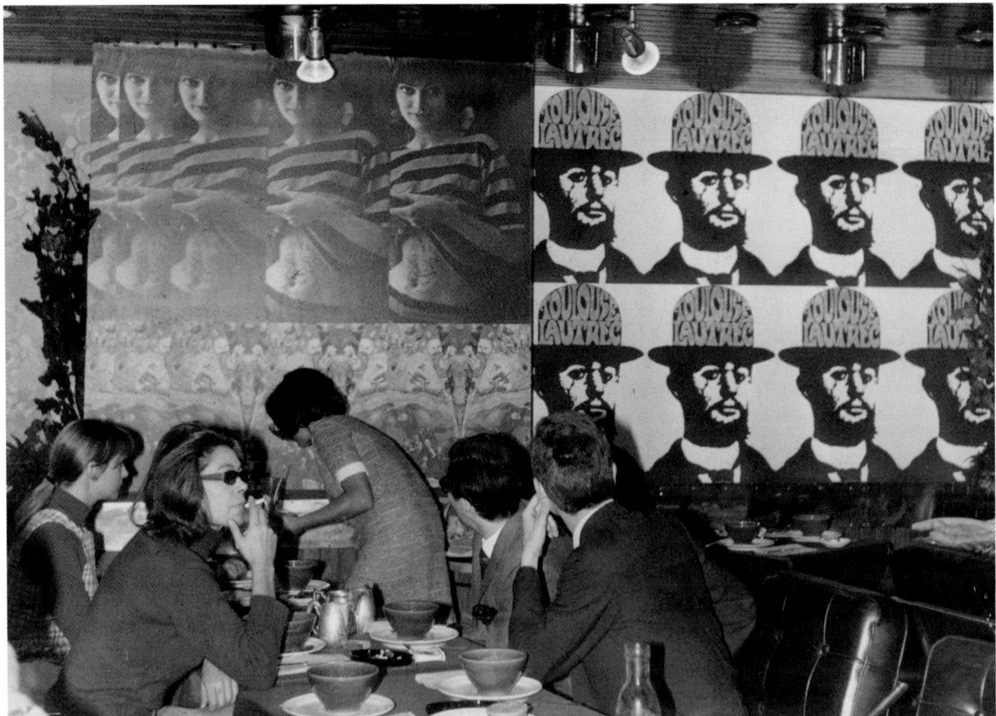

Café displaying the first
'Op', 'Pop' and 'noodle'
posters to reach Paris,
1967.

George Maciunas,
'Fluxorchestra at Carnegie
Hall, New York, September
25, 1965', 1965.

But, as shadow gradually out-leapt original, the post-war explosion took on new contours. Poster fans covered entire walls of student rooms, unheated flats and hip workplaces with them. Hanging in free health clinics and shops that sold drug paraphernalia alike, they signalled not just hipness, but a form of knowing. The medium that had advertised liver pills and bicycles 80 years previously suddenly shone with a new, youthful glow.

Duchamp and Villeglé literally crumpled and tore the poster apart less than a decade earlier. But they were also in the process of making something new. Never a particularly discreet medium, posters became flamboyant, making powerful statements of personal identity for designers and public alike. The French geographer Henri Lefebvre argues that space can be social as well as geographical; our reading of it can reveal cultural and sociological realms indiscernible in ordinary maps. Construed in this way, as markers of social, cultural and psychological spaces, posters in the 1960s become revelatory. Assuredly, posters have little or no connection to the walls they cover. Transient and potentially disorderly, when pinned to a fence, taped above a bed or slipped into a window, they create landscapes that are emotional as well as physical. Posters continued to be used outdoors and were

GREENFIBER - TRUMPET, JOE JONES - VIOLIN, H. KAPPLOW - VIOLIN, SHIGEKO KUBOTA - VIOLIN, DAN LAUFFER - VIOLIN, JOAN MATHEWS - HORN, JONAS MEKAS - ACCORDION, YOKO ONO - VIOLIN, JAMES RIDDLE - TRUMPET, LINDA SAMPSON - VIOLIN, STAN VANDERBEEK - VIOLIN, HELEN VASEY - MELODICA, STEVEN VASEY - HORN, CHRISTOPHER WILMARTH - RECORDER, JOHN WORDEN - TRUMPET, ROBERT WATTS - TUBA, SPECIAL GUEST - SAMURAI SWORD, ORCHESTRA MEMBERS: LA MONTE YOUNG - CONDUCTOR, AYO - TRUMPET, STEPHEN BARRY - MELODICA, LYNN BUNN - FRENCH HORN, JOHN CAVANAUGH - GUITAR, ANTHONY COX - VIOLIN, HENRY

fluxorchestra at carnegie recital hall sept. 25 8 pm.

conductor: la monte young

orchestra costume: by robert watts

ben vautier: audience piece no.4

chieko shiomi: falling event

george brecht: symphony no.3 "on the floor" from "cloud scissors"

yoko ono: 4 pieces for orchestra to la monte young

chieko shiomi: disappearing music for face

anthony cox: tactical pieces for orchestra

olivetti adding machine: in memoriam to adriano olivetti

robert watts: trace for orchestra

yoko ono: sky piece to Jesus Christ

george brecht: octet for winds "in the water" from "cloud scissors"

shigeko kubota: piece

la monte young: 1965 $50

tomas schmit: piano piece number 1

anthony cox: sword piece together with

chieko shiomi: music for late afternoon together with

robert watts: 2"

robert watts: c/t trace

willem de ridder: intermission event

stan vanderbeek: moviee music

joe jones: mechanical orchestra

ben vautier: secret room

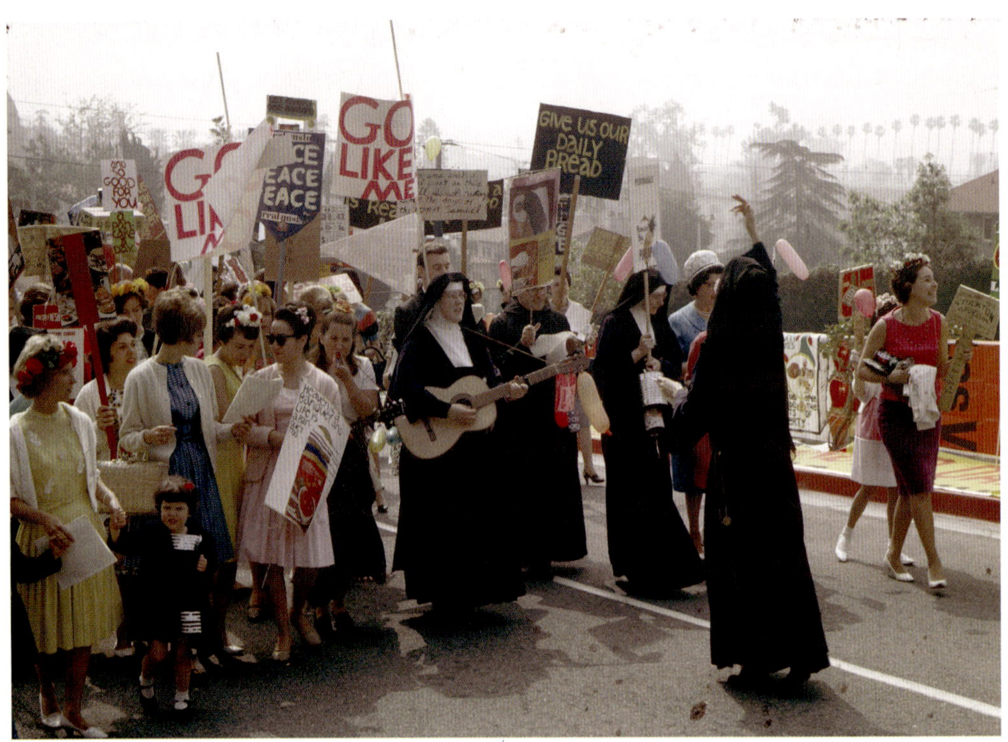

Sister Corita Kent leading
the Mary's Day Parade,
Los Angeles, 1964.

common enough when carried in celebrations, like those mounted by
Sister Corita Kent, photographed leading a Mary's Day Parade in 1964,
or in the protest marches of the late 1960s held on the broad boulevards
of Paris. But many of these works could be found indoors as well. Whether
in Cold War Warsaw or the Summer of Love in San Francisco, these new
posters came in from the streets, colonizing interior spaces and enabling
a breakdown between room and self. In many ways it was only natural
that posters should become more intimate, their messages reflecting
consciousness-raising sessions and private journals and diaries as much
as Madison Avenue ad campaigns. Launched into the public realm,
these new posters could imbue streets and pavements, coffee shops
and shop windows with private messages. In many ways, they fulfilled
Walter Benjamin's observation some 50 years earlier that 'the street
becomes room and the room becomes streets'. What was once outside
was now in, and what was once inside, now out.[4]

The history of posters in this period is a complicated thing,
however, since it straddles several different worlds. The great minds
of modernist design continued working, indeed luminaries like Josef
Müller-Brockmann and figures like Otl Aichler proved conclusively that
crisp, cleanly designed posters were well suited to the self-images of

large corporations and local governments. This line of thinking might be seen not just in corporate identification, but also in the countless poster designs for the Olympics, especially in Mexico City in 1968 and then Munich in 1972. At the same time, the ethos of Madison Avenue's New Advertising crept into magazine ads, but could also be found in subway posters; conjoining creative teams of copywriters and artists, the most progressive ad agencies favoured arresting images and concise headlines. The New Advertising created a series of iconic images for products like rye bread and the Volkswagen. But real innovation for posters was increasingly seen by outsiders to this system.

Plakatodrom: The Polish Poster School

It is no accident that Poland was a fulcrum for poster change. By 1947 some 80 per cent of Warsaw was destroyed from bombing campaigns; by war's end, its misery culminated in a planned demolition by the retreating Nazis. As poster artist Mieczysław Gorowski recalls: 'the streets were very empty at that time . . . It was a sad landscape'.[5] As the capital pulled together to rebuild, posters were welcome intruders. They quickly became a kind of colourful 'robe decorating the city'.[6] While many of these posters spewed the Marxist political rhetoric of the Soviet occupiers who pushed the Nazis out of Poland, the city also nurtured a more allusive form of poster. A 'Golden Age' of Polish posters ran from the 1950s to the early 1970s. With wide-spreading wings, it introduced a remarkably conceptual approach to poster-making. To some, Poland became what Roman Cieślewicz called the *plakatodrom*, a 'poster drome' or land of posters; to others, it fostered a 'grey zone' where posters made space for independent thought.

Of course, posters have never enjoyed a higher status than in communist countries. At its most restless stage, the Russian Revolution encouraged avant-garde artists to make visionary posters that sold change, not products; a better world was on the horizon, just out of reach but almost visible. Their job was to envisage and persuade others to see it. But, as Stalin rose to power, posters became more self-justifying, while also rejecting abstract values for a relatively realist style. Exhorting production goals and reinforcing collectivity, these so-called Socialist Realist posters tell us, with government permission, of society's new goals. Hard-pressed during the Second World War, posters stretched beyond the political, reaching deep into the Russian

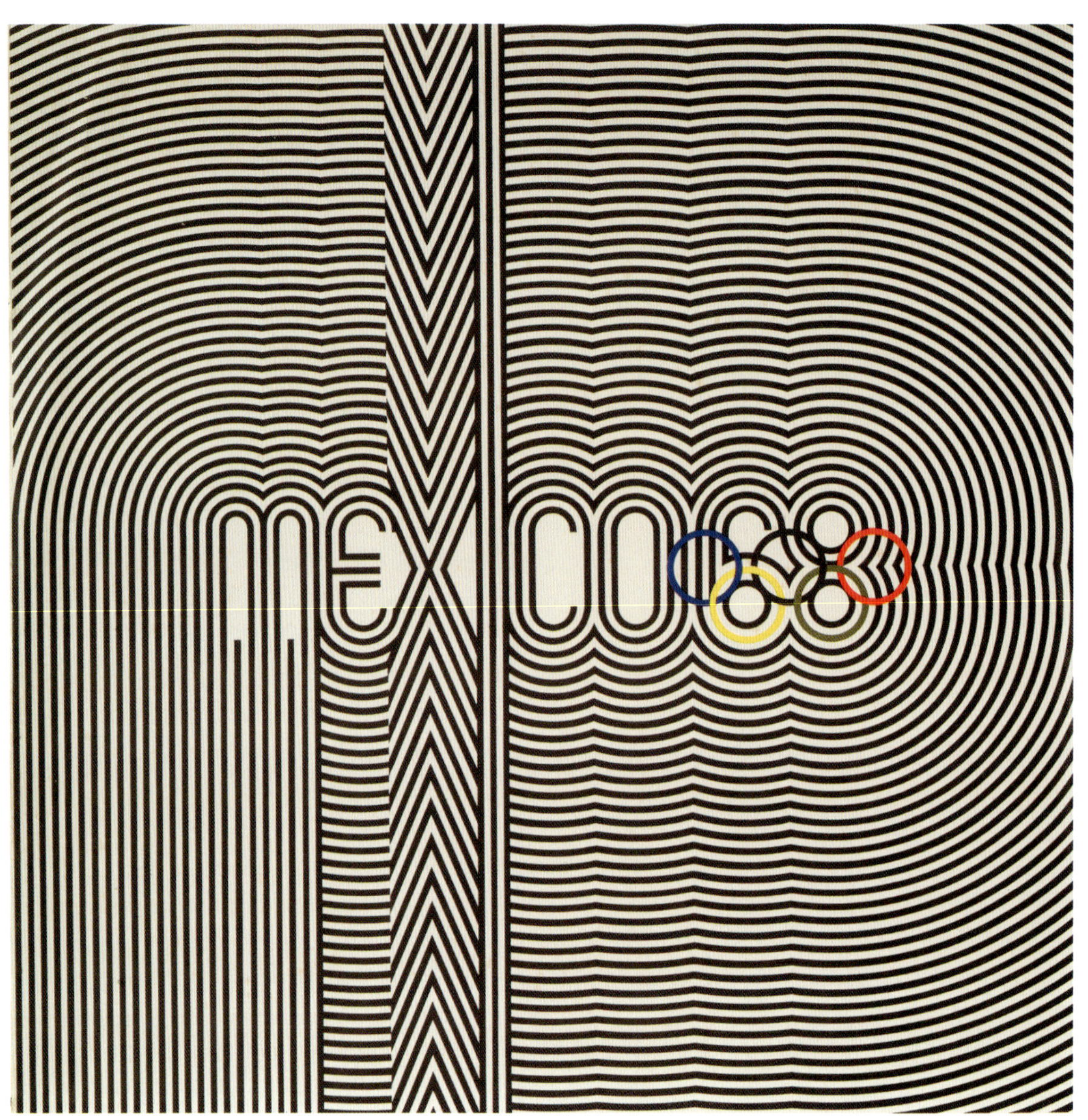

Eduardo Terrazas and Lance Wyman, 'Mexico 68', 1967.

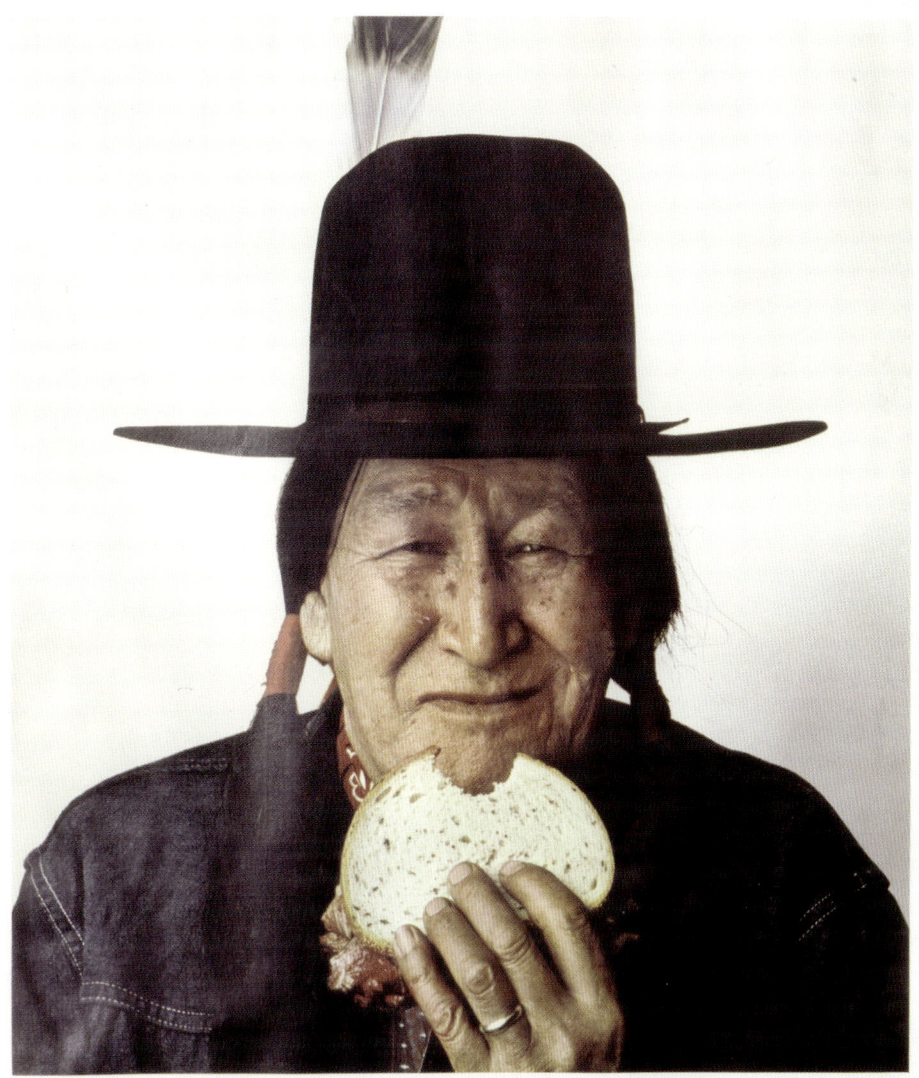

Howard Zieff, 'You Don't Have to be Jewish', 1967.

past and evoking patriots like Alexander Nevsky, Alexander Suvorov and Vasily Chapayev.

It is hardly accidental, however, that after the Second World War and the inevitable winding down of the war machine, Stalin called for a renewed 'class struggle'. In furious efforts to quash any 'subversive' elements that might have crept back into Russian society during the war, Stalin's grip on the aesthetic was renewed. By 1949 the earnest and eager Central Committee of the Soviet Communist Party adopted a resolution 'On the Shortcomings of and Measures to Improve Political Posters'.[7] Stressing the need for ideologically correct posters, artists were urged to 'cover all the aspects of home and international affairs, and answer the most vital questions of the time'. But for some years thereafter, they also held designers in a virtual stranglehold.

In the Soviet Union, posters were commonly placed in public spaces, portraits of political leaders embellishing May Day celebrations and marking important buildings. But they also lurked in factory and office hallways, village reading rooms and even dormitories for unmarried workers. Alternately feisty and grudging or brisk and cheery, these posters were anything but conceptual. Depicting

'Two Classes, Two Cultures', Soviet propaganda poster, 1934.

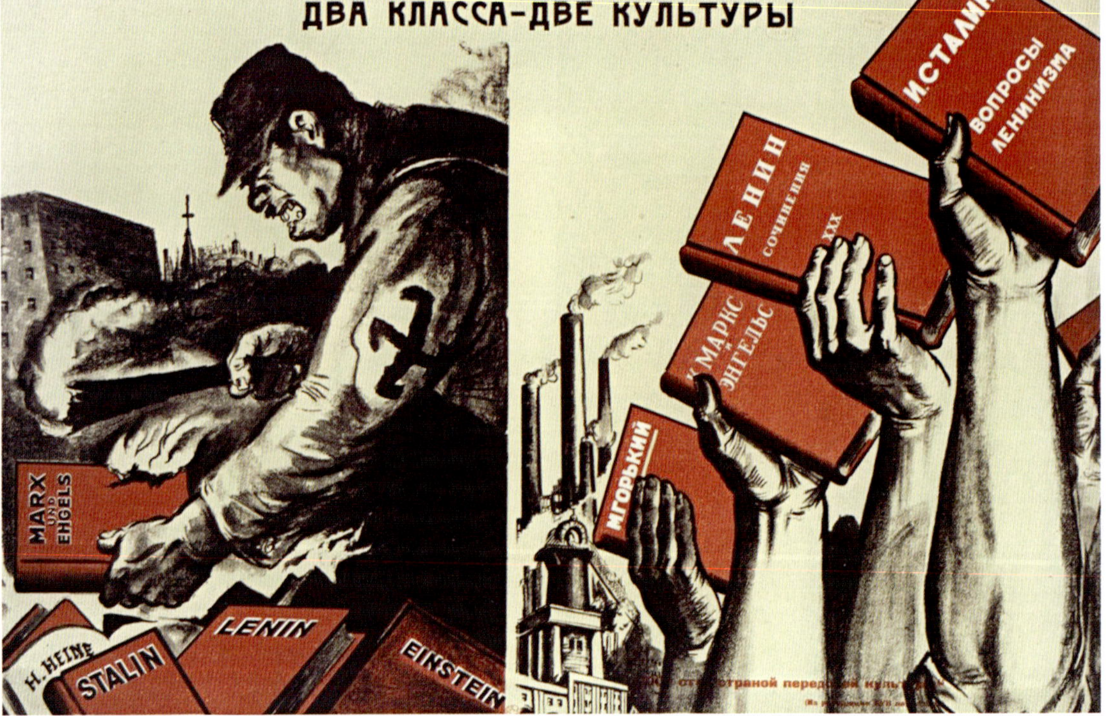

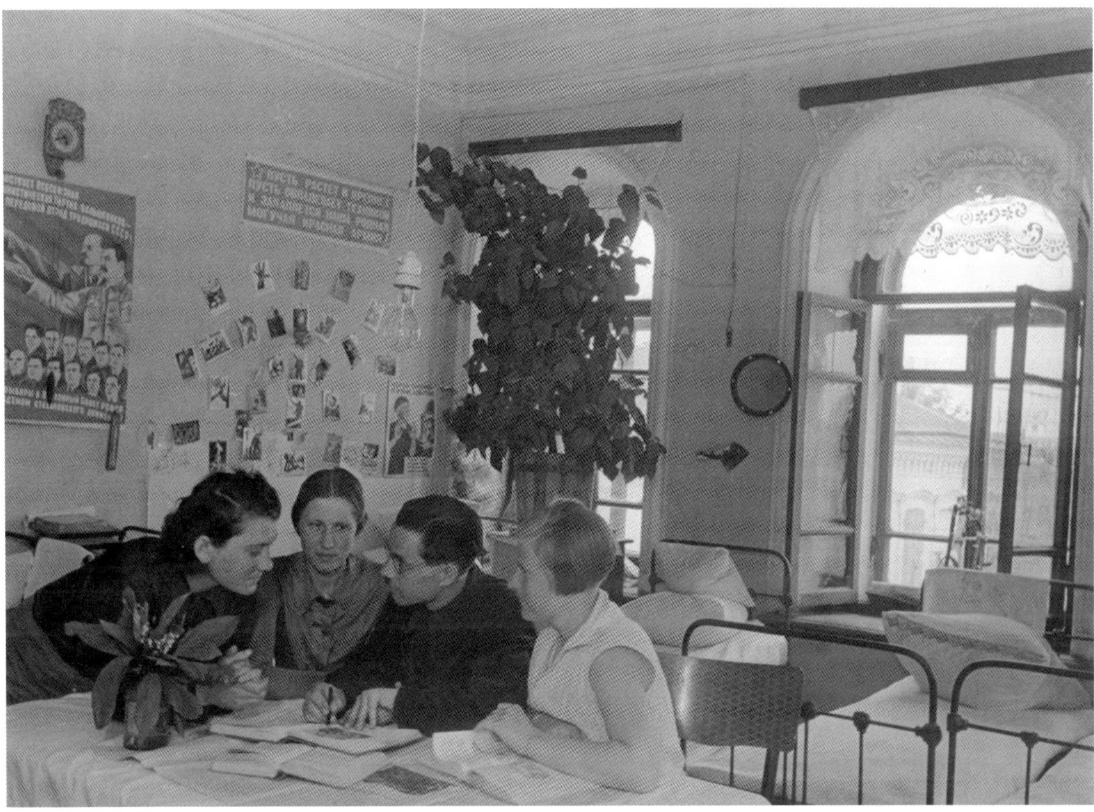

Students studying in a
Soviet dormitory, 1937.

friendly soldiers and relentlessly optimistic schoolgirls, their heavy,
rather ponderous messages tried to shape the behaviour and attitudes of people. Solemn exhortations and vigorous slogans urged
newer 'labour victories' and exhortations to 'strengthen the union
between hammer and sickle'.[8] For true believers, these depictions of
energetic factory workers and sturdy women driving tractors were
more real than any government book, report or statistic. But most
viewers understood that they represented a fantastical ideal in the
minds of their leaders and that their goals were aspirational rather
than real.

In the great fatigue that spread across Europe in the aftermath
of the Second World War, posters played a role in establishing a
new norm. In the Eastern bloc, where Soviet ideals were imported
wholesale, posters were part of sweeping, agonized change. In parts
of Eastern Europe, posters were entirely new; other regions, like
Czechoslovakia and Poland, had vital poster traditions that, for a
time at least, had proved fairly successful. In the latter, the post-war
pro-Soviet regime threw its full support behind the poster format,

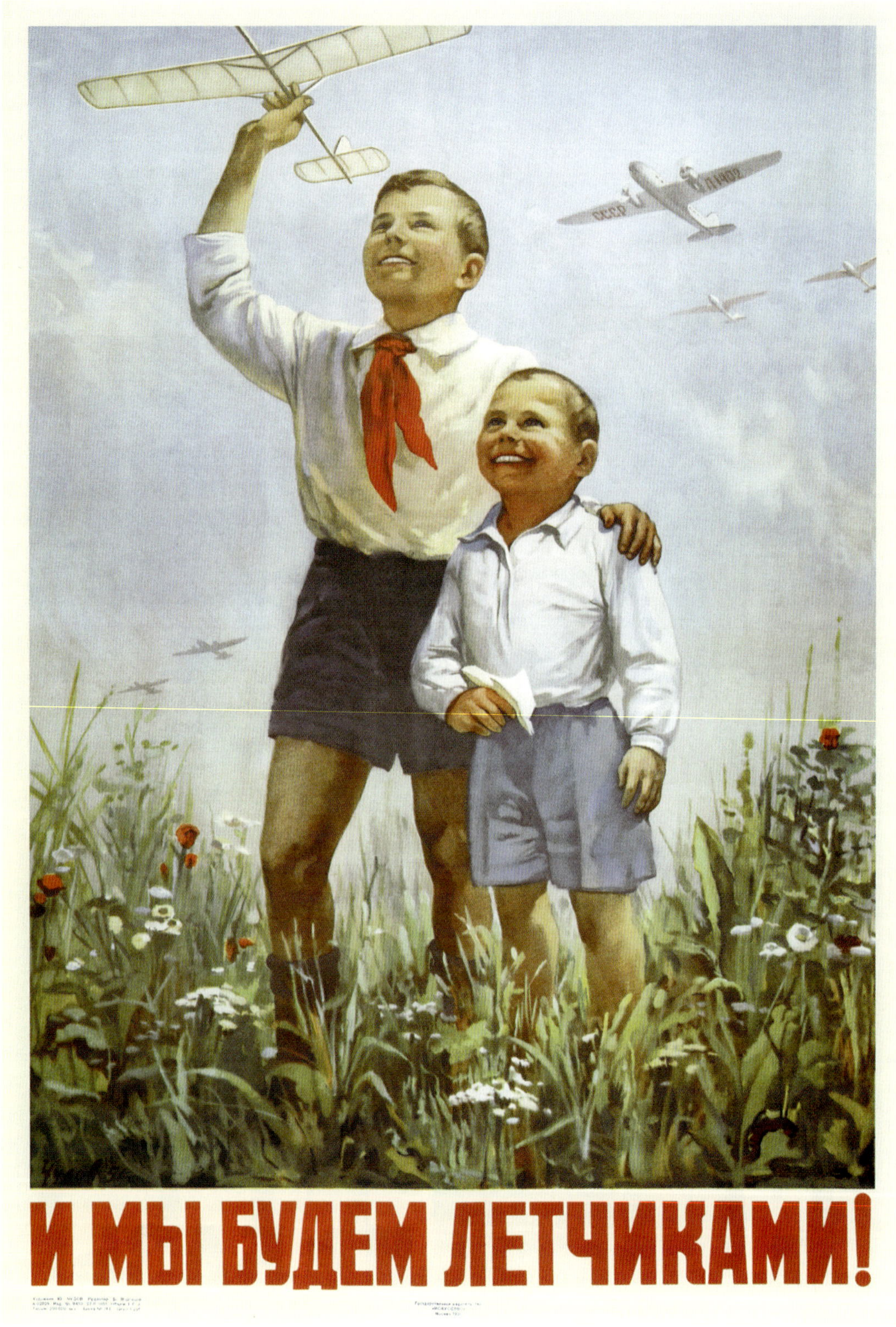

Yury Nikolaevich Chudov, 'We Will be Pilots, Too!', 1951.

but pragmatism often triumphed over political principles. And it is thus that artists like Włodzimierz Zakrzewski, a Pole who had studied in Moscow and whose posters were designed in the Socialist Realist tradition, came to direct the country's earliest post-war poster studio in Poznań. But Poland was not the USSR. Although partitioned between Austria, Prussia and Russia in the nineteenth century, the Poles had already fiercely and loyally used the poster format to hail their half-suppressed ethnic identity; even after their nation disappeared, they continued invoking clothing, historic motifs and nationalist imagery that flowed from Poland's past. After the First World War, when Warsaw became the capital of a newly independent Poland, it also became a fine proving ground for modern commerce and advertising. Here developed a hotbed of Expressionist, Cubist and Russian vanguard experimentation. This was suspended during the war years but left a lively and loose tradition of avant-gardism, even after the Soviets entered Poland at the end of the Second World

Poster pillar, Warsaw,
c. 1939.

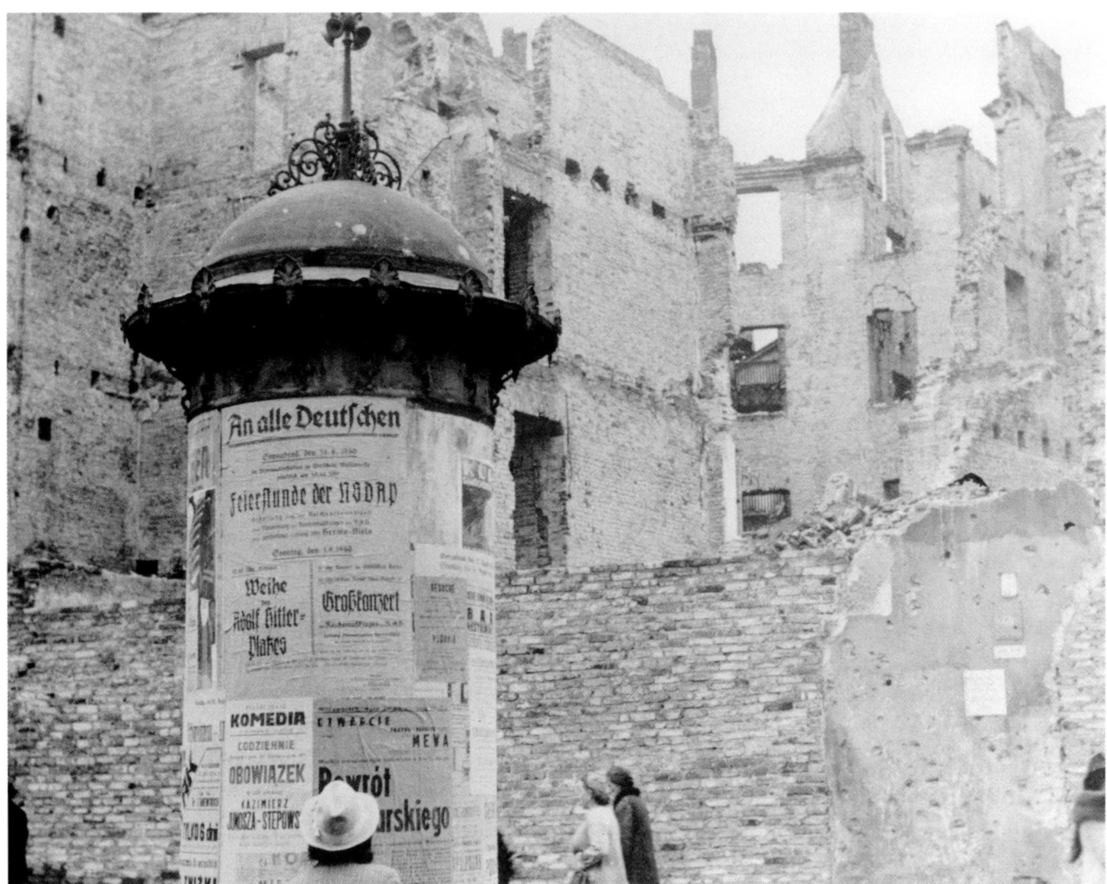

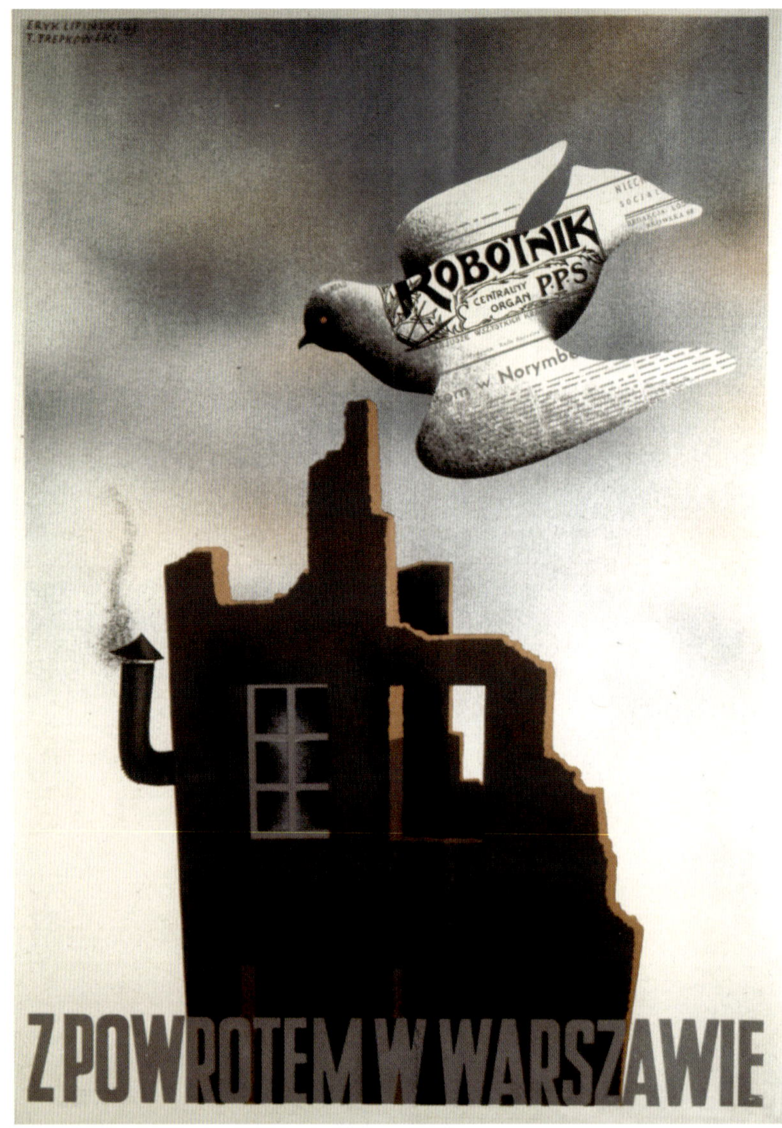

Eryk Lipiński and Tadeusz Trepkowski, the dove of peace and the ruins of Warsaw, *c*. 1945.

War. At that point, the grim and exhausted landscape was broken only by

> some elements of propaganda, red flags or red banners . . . But within that space were those round kiosks or fences with posters that were always referred to as flowers in the empty space.[9]

A shadow of its former self, Warsaw embraced its new posters, just as its leaders appreciated their political, if not decorative, applications. The government even took the unusual step of creating two separate

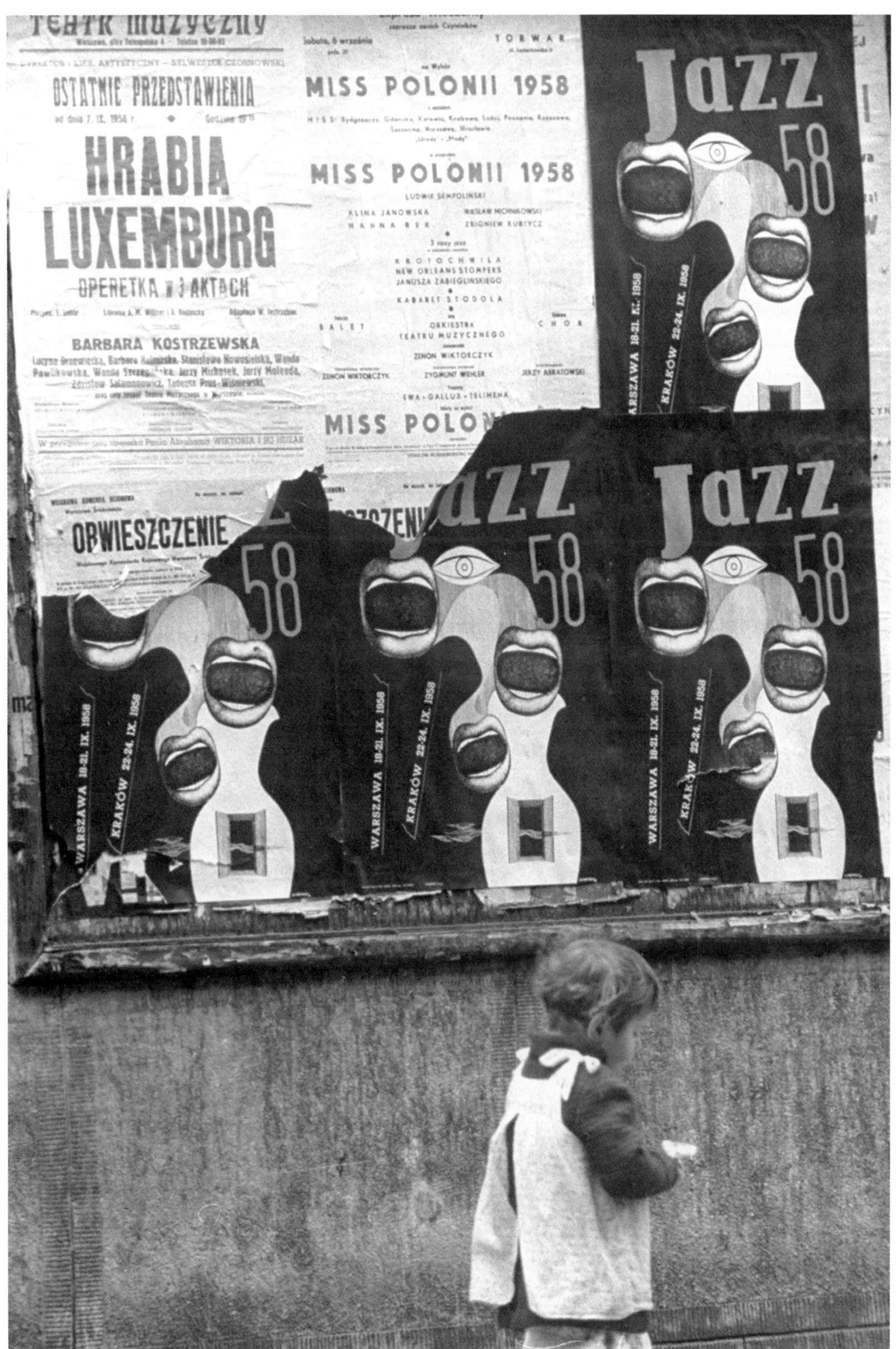

Mark Kauffmann, child walking past posters for a jazz festival, Warsaw, 1958.

chairs of poster design at the Academy of Fine Arts in Warsaw. There is no question that the professors, Józef Mroszczak and Henryk Tomaszewski, were given considerable support; poster design attracted many of the country's best art students. And yet, at a moment of phoenix-like vitality, the most successful Polish posters relied on a peculiar art of substitution, disguise and even trickery.

The Polish Poster School's elan may partially be traced to an unusual system that allowed its poster artists more space for allusive insinuation than many of their Eastern European contemporaries. Elsewhere, both openly and snoopingly, poster production was monitored, often by centralized committees as well as by cultural commissars. But in Poland there was no art police, no determination to censor consistently, no constant goal to restrict; most poster briefs came from unions of artists, so-called aesthetic committees that knew to perfection the whims and dislikes of their government. Moreover, these groups collected official commissions and doled them out to members. The main poster publisher, Wydawnictw Artystyczno-Graficzne (WAG), for example, employed a 'committee' of poster designers who could exclude posters from publication, amounting to what one critic called 'a kind of self-policing'.[10]

On the surface, these unions were created to protect their members, but they also served to guard and enforce the party line. Some commissioners were only loosely associated with the Communist Party. For instance, the Centralna Wynajmu Filmow (CWF), the state film distributor and another prolific commissioner of posters, did not insist on ideologically strict announcements of new films. Arguing that 'if the purpose of film is art, art should also be the aim of the poster', groups like the CWF claimed to side-step the fine points of propaganda and its platitudes, giving wider berth to the circumstances and accidents of creativity.[11] To be sure, these artists were still working within a system mapped along the lines of Marxist principles. To refuse a commission or create a poster critical of the government could mean, as one artist put it, 'the search for another job'.[12] But more often, as one scholar pointed out, 'designers were their own censors'.[13]

Under these circumstances, Polish posters contained a 'schizo-phrenic' tension between tangible promotion and ideological necessity. Roman Cieślewicz's poster of 1958 advertising the Polish release of the British film *The Fallen Idol* (*Stracone zludzenia*) shows the artist's talent for strange juxtapositions. A taut psychological thriller based on Graham

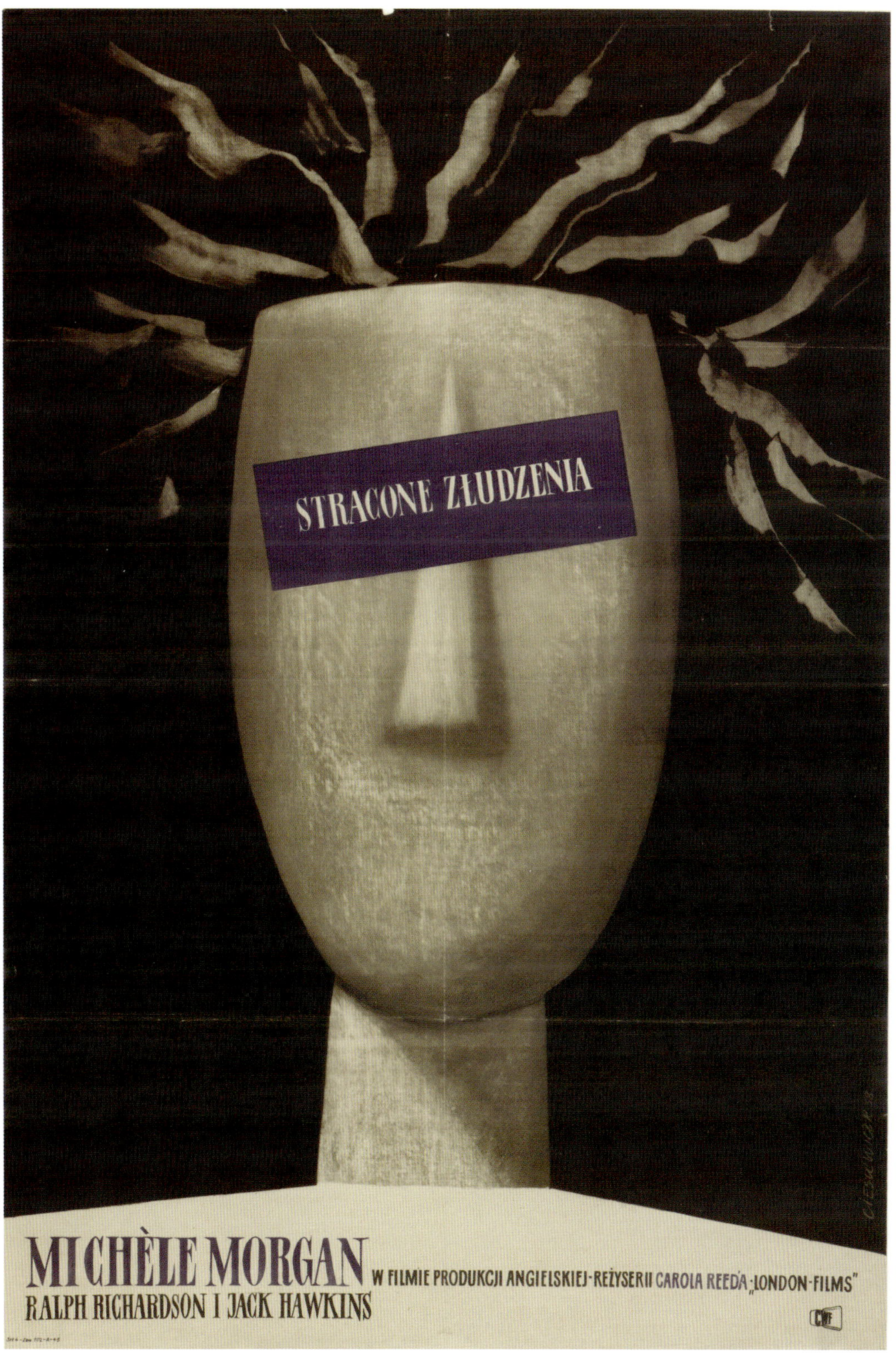

Roman Cieślewicz, poster for *The Fallen Idol* (*Stracone zludzenia*), 1958.

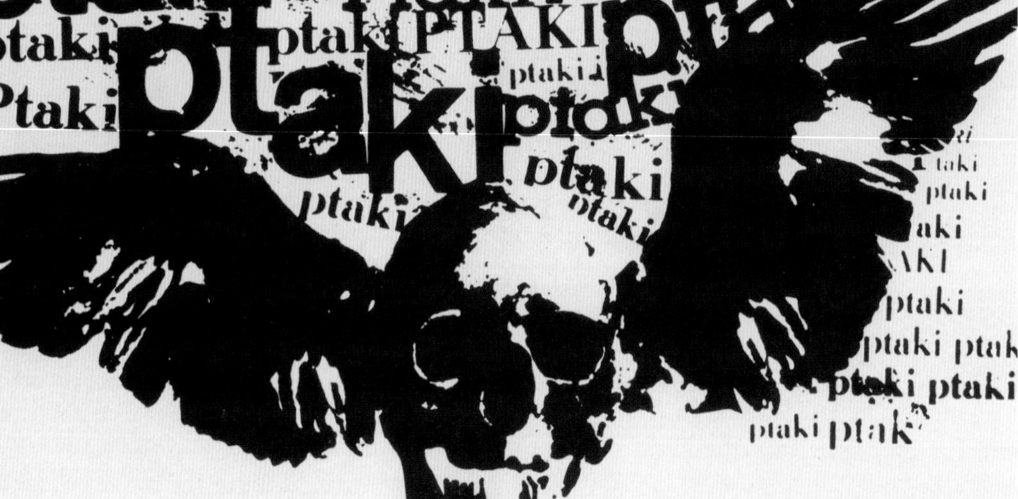

Bronisław Zelek, poster for *The Birds*, c. 1965.

Greene's novel about a boy who witnesses a murder perpetrated by the family's beloved butler, the film explores childhood disillusionment and the limits of human trust. Cieślewicz's poster, however, tells little of that story. Instead, it can be read as alluding to the circumstances of Polish artists, and Polish culture more broadly. Employing an agreeable austerity, the poster dominates with a blank bust, a half memory of some casually glimpsed Cycladic statue. But Cieślewicz's deity has no mouth or ears; mute and also blinded by the film's title, which appears on a small blue censor's bar haphazardly slapped over the figure's eyes, this fallen idol insinuates a half-forgotten truth; with the intensity and detachment of a powerful icon, it also eerily invokes the leader portraits that dotted the communist landscape. By no means is Cieślewicz's poster likely to cry foul or slander; even in a quick glance, we understand that it lives a restricted and sorely tongue-tied life.

With a kind of magic, *The Fallen Idol*, like many other Polish film posters, allows us to construct its message in our imagination. Visual metaphors, allusive images and surrealist wit push and pull these posters in different directions. But, as the artist Rafał Olbiński recalled, they played

> a double role. One role was to inform about something that was happening; another role for [the] viewer prepped [the viewer] for this to make fun, forbidden truth about something.[14]

Like moonbeams on a clear night, they slip between the real and the ethereal, mapping an interior visionary world in which familiar objects become transformed. Delicate teacups transform into scornful and sometimes violent human faces, while an elegant violin sprouts dangling arms and spindly legs. Eschewing the flashy headshots and lurid illustrations that characterized Western movie posters, Polish designers used a kind of surrealist patois, blending private symbolism with idiosyncratic wonderment. Bronisław Zelek's poster for Alfred Hitchcock's film *The Birds* (1963), for instance, presents a winged skull, trailed by a flock of words that rhythmically repeat the word *ptaki*, or 'birds'. Polish posters highlight 'intellectual labyrinths and games of hide-and-seek'; as ideas flow in, out and around them, viewers are challenged to reflect on the posters' range of messages. 'I think some of the artists wanted to react towards the system,' recalled one artist, 'and their only weapons were their brush, their pencil, their ink, their concepts and ideas.'[15]

At a certain point, the Polish School designers straddled Hollywood and communism, finding for themselves a third space, in between; joining a procession of intellectuals, scientists and other artists, they followed an ambiguous path that neither colluded with the Communist government nor objected to it. This led them to what has, in Eastern-bloc countries like Czechoslovakia, been called a 'grey zone'.[16] Located somewhere between the cultural and political bastions of the socialist establishment and the wider expanse of society as a whole, the 'grey zone' was largely inhabited by educated professionals. Many worked within state structures but were not part of the communist elite. For artists, writers and other cultural figures throughout Eastern Europe, 'readiness to serve' could be 'rewarded' both in the form of studio and apartment space, as well as fees and goods.[17] Those who accepted it found that the grey zone could be quite comfortable and was inhabited by a 'privileged technocracy'.[18] Explicitly anti-government messages were forbidden, but criticism, sometimes thinly veiled, was nevertheless tolerated. Many poster designers would agree with artist Jan Lenica, who believed that Polish posters might be a kind of 'Trojan Horse freely running in the streets and smuggling' ideas, not soldiers.[19] But the posters also proved that the grey zone existed not only in the imagination, but also in very real social spaces. These posters were sometimes placed in kiosks or theatres. But many were not. Socialist ideology assured commissions; every film released in Poland had official approval and, as government policy would have it, was accorded a poster. Furthermore, each poster was also ensured large print runs, typically with 40–100,000 copies commissioned annually. Yet sociologist Florian Zieliński observed a more common 'ambivalence' towards Polish film posters.[20] In Poland's command economy, the posters were produced 'independently of demand from cinema managers who rarely wanted them even though they were free of charge'; many were taken 'straight to the shredder'.[21] Others were simply put into storage and rediscovered only after the fall of the Iron Curtain. Increasingly, however, they began to infiltrate new spaces, moving off temporary fences and pavement kiosks or theatre windows into homes and museums.

Neither capitalist nor communist, yet participating in dialogue with each system, Polish posters slowly attracted attention in the West, arriving, as it were, from the far shores of another world; to many observers, they seemed inefficient, inadequate and utterly sublime. The poster's stature in the Soviet bloc drew both admiration and curiosity, but the bombastic tone of Socialist Realism did not appeal. Polish posters, however, seemed to map a new way for posters to hold relevance, like an infant born for a better world. Not encumbered with embarrassing practicalities like listings for theatre locations or dates of screenings, the Polish School of posters helped rekindle a broader illustrative tradition. In the West, where design was linked with the monotony of bombastic advertising, feckless promotion and clear-cut results, Polish posters seemed alien. Between slick, state-issued journals like *Poland* and *Projekt* and prestigious European journals like *Neue Grafik*, *Graphis* and *Gebrauchsgrafik*, Western designers believed that Polish posters inhabited a space unsullied by capitalism and profit. This space, that is, Cieślewicz's *plakatodrom*, was seen as if from the wrong end of a looking glass, its benefits clear and its flaws minimized. To be sure, admirers argued, the materials used to make these posters were not always good (both paper and ink could be second-rate),[22] but their conception and practice presented poster-making as an intimate act that should not be embarked on lightly. Seen in this way, many Western designers tried to 'learn' from the Polish experience.[23] As one Polish artist would later recall with some irony, the poster 'was one of our best export products, among the very few . . . like coal and the Polish School of Filmmaking'.[24]

Recognizing their rising popularity and hoping to score propaganda points, Polish authorities tiptoed gingerly towards acknowledging this peculiar school of posters, while overlooking their often-lush symbolism. They formed the International Poster Bienniale in Warsaw in 1966. Two years later, the Poster Museum, housed in an elegant carriage house attached to a baroque palace just outside the city, was created. The museum allowed the Polish government to present, as one historian put it, 'an apparently benign face to the world'.[25] It also proved that posters might decorate interiors as well as a well-furnished mind.

The Rise of the Pseudo-poster

Having just completed an ambitious world tour and producing a string of several best-selling albums, Bob Dylan was at the peak of his popularity in July 1966; possessing a spiritual skin that was abnormally thin, he suddenly vanished from public view for several protracted months. Later, Dylan would claim that he had crashed a motorcycle near his home in Woodstock, New York. After he withdrew from public life, fans and friends spoke of this period as 'The Accident'. Conspiracy theorists sometimes allude to the non-committal secrecy of this moment as 'the Bob Dylan Motorcycle-crash Mystery'. But the 'disappearing act' put Dylan's record label, Columbia Records, on edge. The company expected its artists to keep working, come what may. Rather than let a top-selling artist sink before the public eye, panicking executives decided to release a compendium of Dylan's music, an album of greatest hits. But Columbia's legendary art director John Berg proposed an even more radical scheme: pleased with Dylan's emerging cult status, he convinced Columbia to pack the Greatest Hits album with a large poster of the celebrated singer. Of course, the public greeted the entire project with a kind of ferocious enthusiasm. Released in March 1967, 6 million copies of the album were sold. The record was widely praised, but Milton Glaser's poster insert also gave shape to something larger; after the Bob Dylan poster exploded on the scene, it carried more cultural currency than virtually any commercial poster designed since the Second World War.

Glaser's poster should also be grouped with a wave of posters by new masters like Peter Max, Seymour Chwast and Tomi Ungerer, who took a very public art form and made it private. Whether casually hanging on a wall in Mick Jagger's luxurious hippy digs or a dorm room in Cleveland's Case Western University, posters became a creature of dark spaces, small rooms and stuffy psychedelic head shops. An icon for what one popular magazine called 'job-shifting, house-changing, marriage-altering youth', the Dylan poster announced the arrival of a new era as well as a new type of poster.[26] To be sure, it employed the kind of allusiveness normally associated with the Polish School. But Glaser's poster was more an exemplar of an 'art which is immediate, impermanent, expressive and neat' than any single poster from Warsaw. Although bitter critics sometimes likened its Pop aesthetic to the fizz of Coca-Cola, Glaser's eclectic designs bubble with mysterious energy. On the face of it, the poster makes a compelling graphic statement for youth and independence. But the poster's move indoors also marked the rise of what some critics call the 'pseudo-poster'.

This new type of poster has a complex genealogy. While Polish post-war posters stand out as a clear example of a more relaxed and intuitive approach, they were not alone. From 1936 to 1960, for instance,

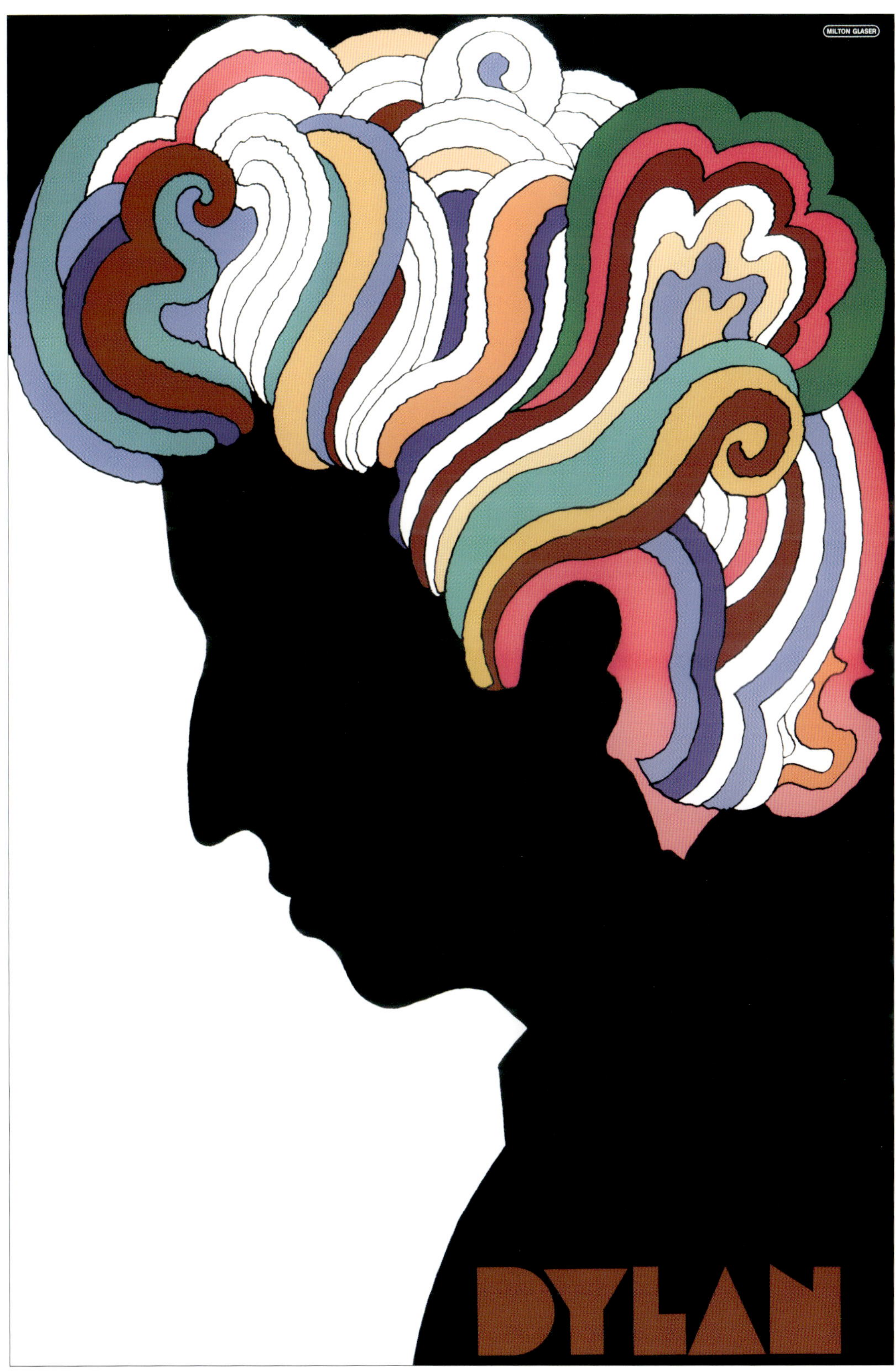

Milton Glaser, 'Dylan', 1967.

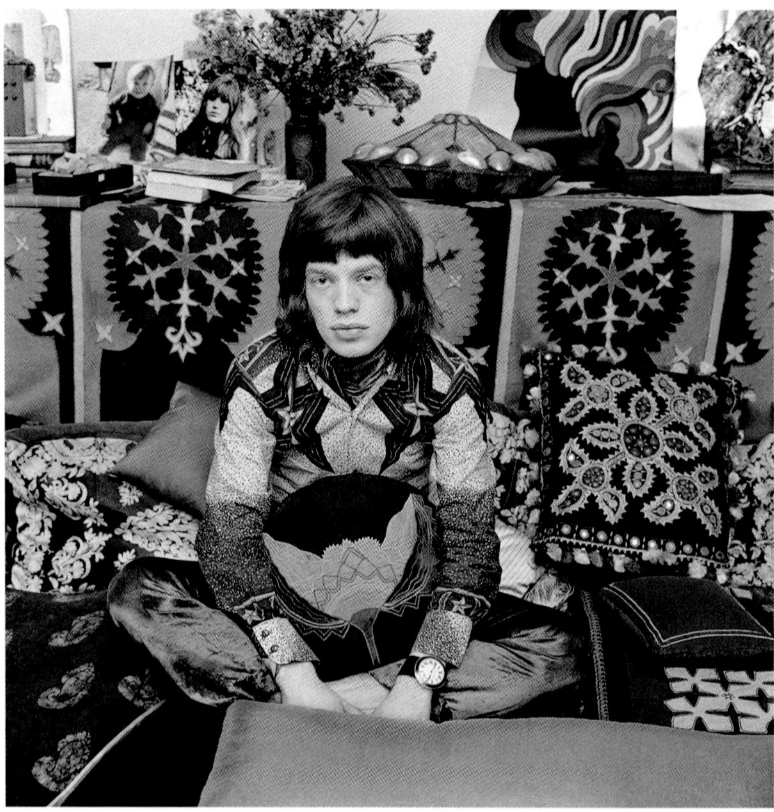

the Container Corporation of America hired vanguard artists and designers to make a poster series that focused on 'great ideas' of the Western tradition. Historians try to encompass new developments like the pseudo-poster by introducing terms like the 'Conceptual Image'.[27] Indeed, in the 1960s posters were not the only form to thrive as a new illustration style emerged, borrowing freely from Surrealism, Pop art and Expressionism. A number of new masters developed, including figures like Gunter Rambow of Germany, who used the poster format to remake familiar and traditional imagery.

First impressions may not be as important as is generally suggested, but more traditional critics found this rapid transformation of the poster shocking. Reporting the fad in a dispassionate tone, *Graphis* magazine's Manuel Glasser confirmed that 'true believers' began to feel 'estranged' from the 'cult' of the poster.[28] For Maurice Rickards, author of *The Rise and Fall of the Poster* (1971), this evolution spelled disaster. Not only did Rickards use the very title of his book to announce the poster's demise, but his text took aim at posters with no commercial purpose or social cause, being created entirely

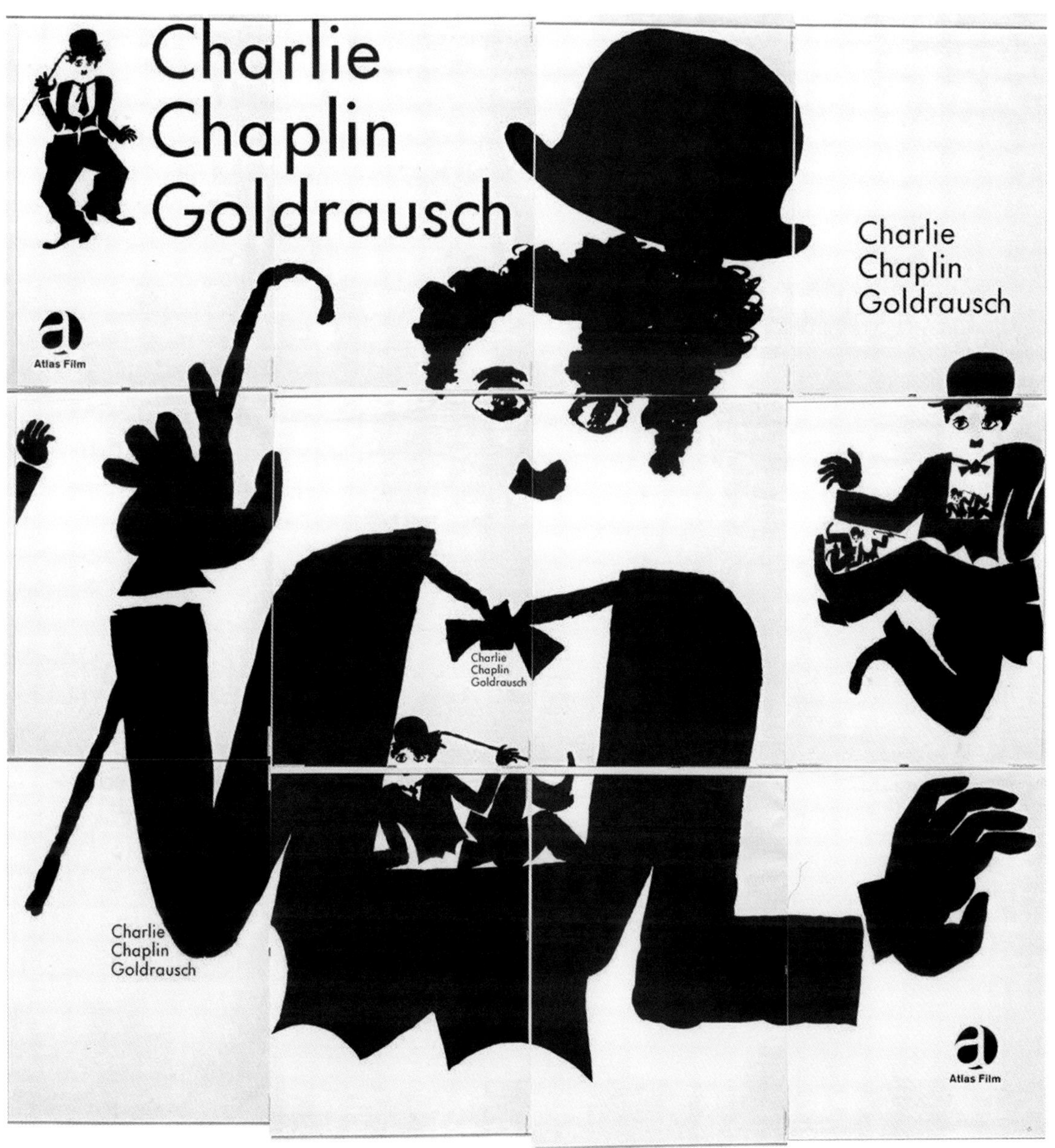

Gunter Rambow, 'Charlie Chaplin: Goldrausch', 1960.

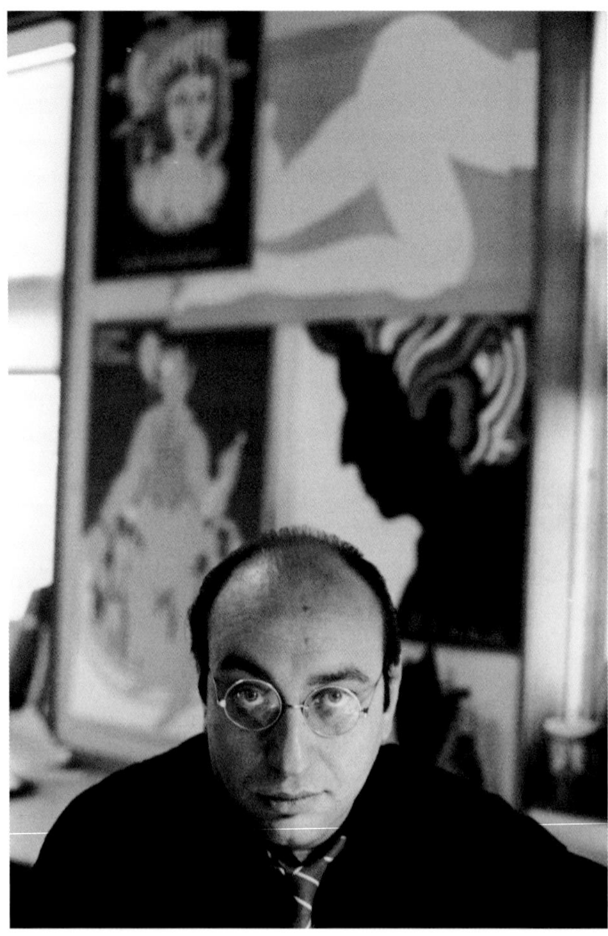

Bernard Gotfryd, 'Milton Glaser in his Studio', 1969.

for collectors. Dubbing these 'pseudo-posters',[29] he insisted that images like Glaser's Dylan were an example of shiftless and wanton irresponsibility. Real posters sold products. Pseudo-posters existed only to decorate or embellish spaces. Whereas real posters existed to exhort, educate or convince, the pseudo-poster was often little more than 'simple photo blow-ups', with little meaning.[30] With exasperation, by 1970 Susan Sontag took an equally dim view of developments, arguing that the poster 'aims to seduce, to exhort, to sell, to educate, to convince, to appeal'. In so doing, it 'presupposes the modern concept of the public'.[31] But, if a poster is made simply for decor, it leads a dull half life; these posters are clearly impoverished and can, another commentator stubbornly remarked, 'proclaim nothing except themselves'.[32]

On first glance, little about the Dylan poster marked it for greatness. To the best of John Berg's knowledge, no record company had ever given away a poster, even if it was part of a music album. Moreover, while Glaser would later display it proudly in his studio, the poster format was new to him, too. The Dylan insert, he recalled, 'was probably my third or fourth poster'.[33] The entire project was a gamble, 'cooked up', as Berg put it, because 'Dylan couldn't produce a new album'.[34] The gambit paid off, for Columbia Records and for the designer. In Glaser's case, he argued, 'it took a fresh view of what graphic material could look like'.[35]

Having mixed and fermented high and low culture for much of the previous decade, Glaser's own style was well known in design circles. After graduating from the Cooper Union and studying for two years in Italy under Giorgio Morandi, Glaser returned to New York in 1952. Taking Bologna's storied past in his stride, he 'suddenly realized that history was not the enemy'.[36] Nor should it be preserved untouched, like flies in amber. All this impinged on his spirits; when Glaser joined college friends to form the Push Pin Studios back in New York, the group also published *The Push Pin Almanack*. A kind of brochure, the publication changed names over the years but always showed flashes of clever excitement, reporting offbeat trivia and cheekily recycling older imagery. With an almost voluptuous pleasure, the group used Victoriana, Art Nouveau and Surrealism as generous springs for inspiration. They all flowed into the lake which was the 'Push Pin style'. By 1964, the *Push Pin Graphic* (the *Almanack*'s successor after a name and format change in 1956) demonstrated a large range of graphic styles, some scribbling and scratchy, others grandly mannered. Never quietly complacent, the Push Pin group established an eclectic aesthetic. Moreover, the Push Pin Group was not alone in using the poster format to challenge the design world's status quo. Robert Crumb, for example, designed posters as an extension of his irreverent and often risqué comic strips. Indeed, a new iconography of the marijuana leaf, a clenched fist and peace symbol also began to emerge.

Even so, when Glaser's colleague Seymour Chwast designed an ad for Booth's House of Lord's gin in 1964, he updated a brand that was slipping towards banality. The main ingredient for martinis, Booth's was the gin of James Bond (shaken, not stirred). Nevertheless, like the master spy, the brand found itself rapidly passing into irrelevance, at least for a younger generation; it was the antithesis of flower power and pot-smoking youth under 30. It was in need of a makeover. Chwast struck counter-cultural gold by designing a poster within a poster, his design self-consciously recalling gaudy street hangings from the nineteenth century. Flamboyantly announcing the Push Pin aesthetic, Booth's principal message, 'Protest against The Rising Tide of Conformity', is quietly captioned: 'Serve Booth's House of Lords, the Non-conformist gin from England'. Like Glaser, Chwast indulges in a vivid purple, yellow and green palette utterly inconsistent with nineteenth-century posters; needless to say, the poster's lettering imitates the hit-or-miss slapdashery of Victorian wood type. With a harmless drollery, the poster depicts a second poster. In so doing, it presents a subtle reversal of advertising law: the product is squeezed out, literally marginalized. Appearing almost like an awkward afterthought, an easily overlooked bottle of gin was shunted into the lower right-hand corner of the poster.

Dusting off and updating the stodgy, British-based brand, Chwast approached the past with clear eyes. In a masterstroke of coincidence, it unwittingly struck a memorable chord when the poster served as the background to an impromptu photograph of Dylan and his girlfriend, the folk singer Joan Baez, at Newark Airport in 1964. Amenable to every drift of meaning, the poster could immediately appeal to outliers everywhere. Like a person hiding a dirty secret, a photograph of Dylan and Baez from 1964 easily hides the gin bottle. Once the backbone of advertising, the poster instead dabbles with nonconformity; without a product to sell, even a commercial poster like this could join the ranks of the 'pseudo-poster'.

What was harder to emulate was Push Pin's quirky sensualism. Glaser built his depiction of Dylan on the musician's distinctive hawk-faced profile. With its layers of colour looking like frosting on a colourful wedding cake, the Dylan poster is a visual treat. It echoes the album's cover, a snapshot of Dylan captured by photographer Rowland Scherman. Taken during a concert, the photograph captures Dylan making music. Glaser's iconic image doesn't turn a deaf ear to Dylan's sound. Quoting a self-portrait by Marcel Duchamp from 1958, fashioned in silhouette, it relies on allusion. Duchamp's portrait itself mirrored an earlier tradition, the eighteenth-century passion for shadows cut from fathomless black card and mounted on crisp white backgrounds. Aside from the overt reference to Duchamp, Glaser also gives a nod to his own long-standing fascination with folk art silhouettes, which he began to collect after a trip to Poland in the early 1960s and published in an issue of *Push Pin Graphic*.[37] For all its quirks, the most striking aspect of the poster, though, are the syncopated tendrils of Dylan's curling mane. Resembling the colourful tentacles of a bewildered octopus, the highlighted strands repeat the backlit halo of hair captured by Scherman and published on the album's cover. Like an electric field of strange and swirling energy, the rainbow locks whirl around Dylan's head. Their vitality, Glaser would later claim, may be linked to the elegantly expressive arabesques of Islamic art. But they reminded others of 'a genie sprung from a Louis Tiffany lamp'.[38] In both style and form, Glaser may be paying homage to the golden age of posters. And yet, it is fundamentally different. Again, it advertises no specific product.

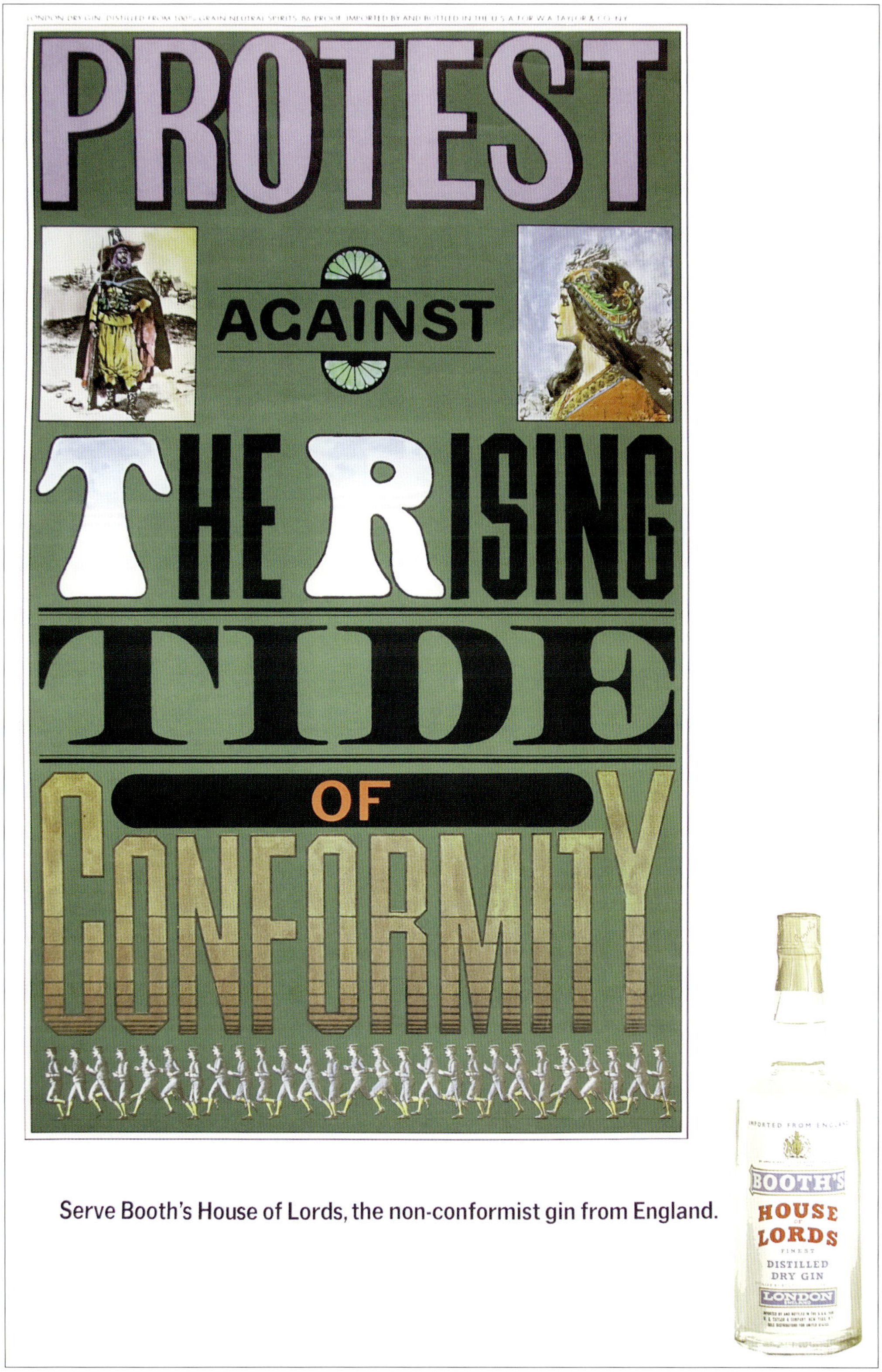

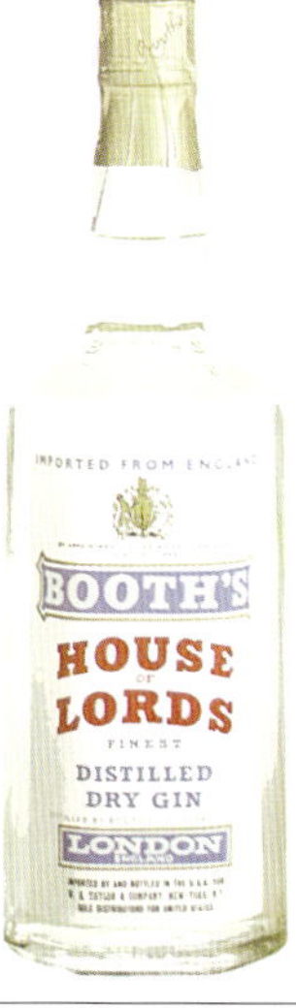

Seymour Chwast, advert for House of Lords gin, 1964.

Allusive and moody, Glaser's Dylan channels the wellsprings of
Polish School posters. The shadowy figure with tendrils of hair, which
suggest an emanation of colourful ideas swirling and dancing
around Dylan's head, echoes the cerebral illustrations found in
Poland. But designers like Chwast and Glaser gave illustration a
still-wider audience, nudging Polish subtlety into a world of popular
culture. By pulling weirdly phantasmagoric images into the dull
and repetitive world of mainstream American advertising, they also
stepped into the dominance of photography and the crisp, rational
design coming from Europe. Glaser's image is like the Chwast poster
for Booth's, which uses an illustrated poster literally to push a photograph of its product almost out of the picture frame. But Glaser's Dylan
poster uses a snapshot only as a point of departure; the outward
blandness of photography is sweetened and utterly transformed.

Glaser's striking poster was pinned to walls from Marrakesh
to New York. Years later, a French photographer described travelling
up the Amazon and stopping at an isolated Indian village. Entering
a hut, he waited a moment for his eyes to grow accustomed to the
darkness and then saw the Dylan poster on the wall.[39] Light years
from the Amazon, Mick Jagger displayed the Dylan poster in his
hippy digs. Jagger's poster was so new, it still shows the wrinkles
from its original album fold. Its presence only adds to the lush and
fantastical decor, almost rococo in its fantastic mingling of glass
lamps, appliquéd pillows and other cultural exotica, of his Marrakesh
redoubt. The brooding rock star joined the ranks of thousands of other
rebellious youths who used the poster as an aesthetic statement.

Old-timers like art critic Manuel Gasser may have identified the
emerging 'poster craze' as early as 1967. But Gasser, like many others,
was puzzled, asking readers of *Graphis*: 'What is there new about it?'
'After all,' he rationalized, 'people have been collecting posters, whether
historical or contemporary, for many years.' After reviewing it at some
length, he recounts, he slowly came to a realization. Indeed, 'something
was new: the scale.'[40]

Expanding Space: Instant Environments

Tongue conspicuously in cheek, in 1967 *Life* magazine observed:
'suddenly posters are the national hang-up'. Posters now, *Life* continued,
'serve as low-cost paintings, do-it-yourself wallpaper, comic Valentines

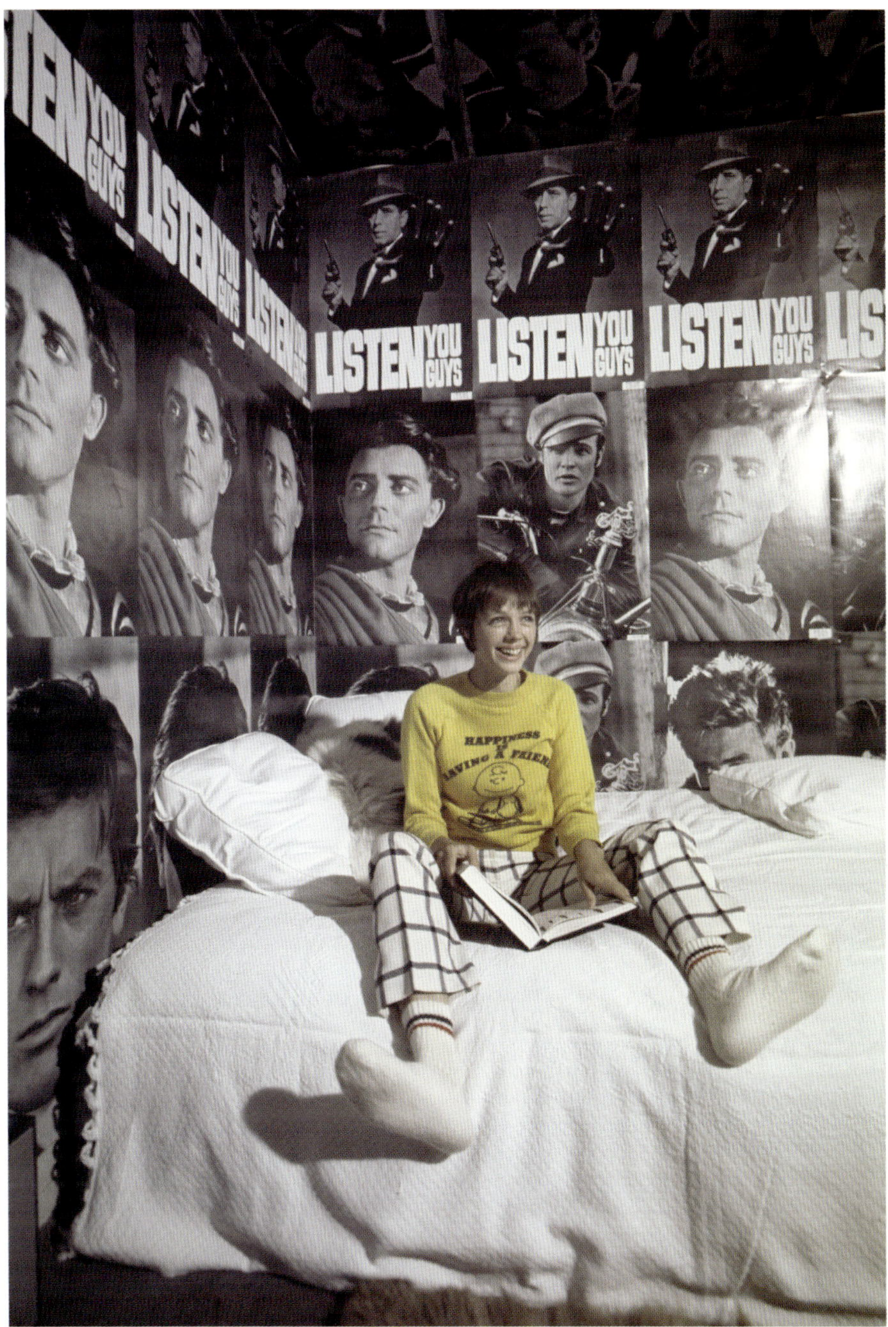

or propaganda for . . . Batman and rye bread'. What *Life* did not say was that posters were transforming empty space, as another writer at the time put it, into 'instant environments'.[41] *Time* magazine went further, calling these posters 'space expanding'.[42] This, of course, was a thin guise meant to describe hippies' fascination with mind-altering drugs

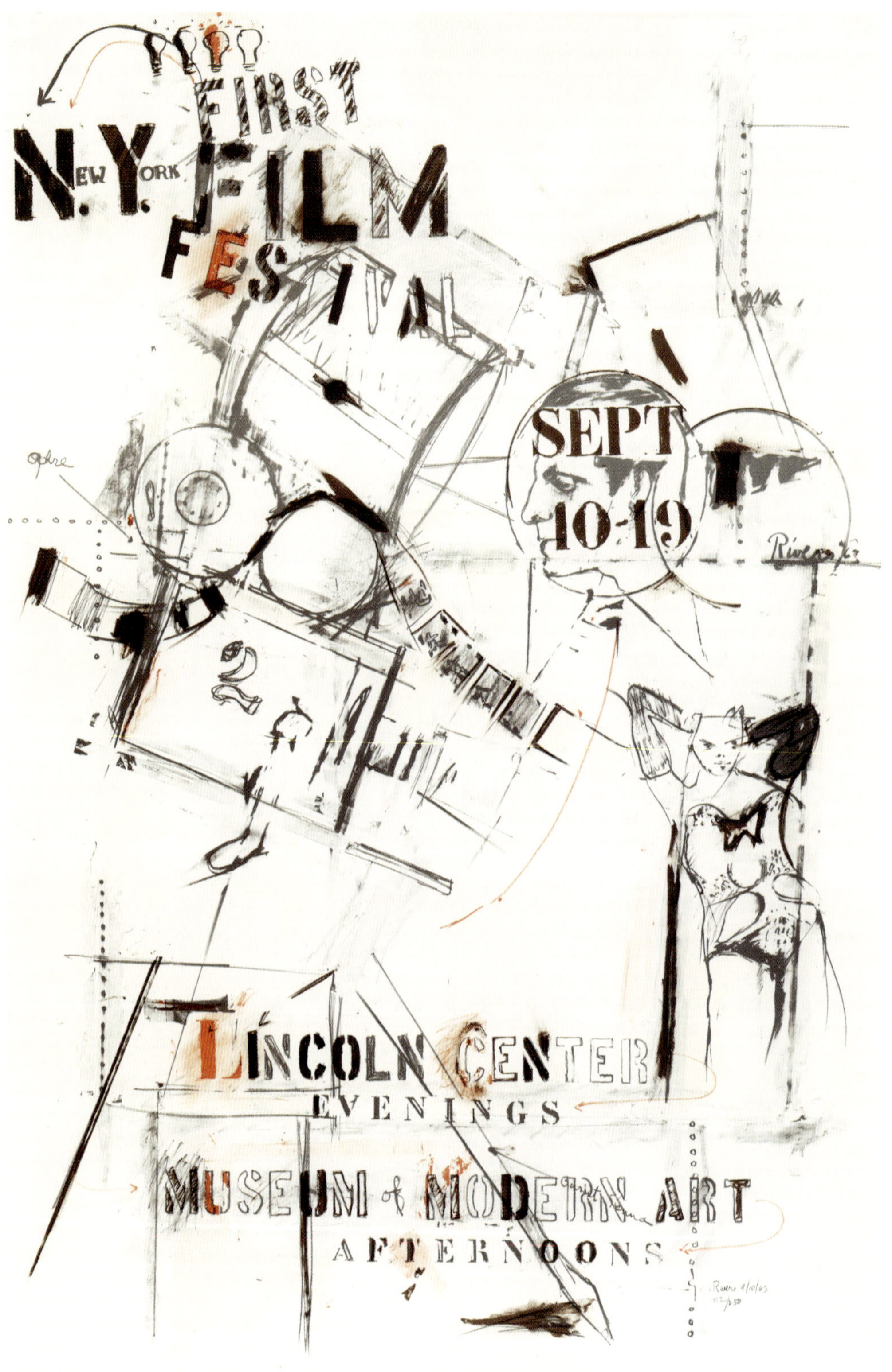

Larry Rivers, 'First New York Film Festival', 1963.

as much as posters' actual condition. Older observers believed that these posters pointed to a generational divide, representing some kind of glandular whip best tolerated as an expression of over-active hormones. But posters did begin to appear and thrive in interior spaces where youths gathered. The younger generation used wall space to share ideas and emotions, giving room to a special form of addiction based on paper and seemingly insatiable. Certainly, the scale of this fad was in itself quite new, but this also meant that the same posters could be found everywhere, not only in world capitals of art and commerce such as New York, Paris and London, like the first burst of postermania 70 years earlier.

At first glance, the lowly poster might seem to overturn the ferocious pecking order of high art. At its most compelling, the poster revival was an inversion of elitist values. Among students and left-leaning intellectuals in the 1960s, posters were intensely and even passionately esteemed because they 'carry not the slightest stigma of art'.[43] But the poster boom was also, in some ways, an extension of the comparative easiness of spirit that shaped Pop Art and its own embrace of 'low' forms like comics and billboards. Susan Sontag may have attacked Pop style as 'parasitic on commercial poster esthetics', but Pop artists like Robert Rauschenberg, James Rosenquist, Roy Lichtenstein, Andy Warhol and Larry Rivers were more often lauded for their slick, machine-made art. Moreover, many Pop artists even became poster designers themselves. Artist Larry Rivers not only made the poster for the first New York Film Festival, but also defied design conventions and hand-painted a billboard for the event.

Nevertheless, where artists like Villeglé ruthlessly stripped posters off walls, artists influenced by Pop began making posters themselves. By the late 1960s, designers feared the incursion of fine art on their own turf. Posters like the Lincoln Center design by Rivers struck design professionals as a 'misunderstanding of the nature of graphic design in general and the function of posters in particular'.[44] Calling these artists 'amateurs', *Print* magazine lashed out at the Center's well-funded List programme. Envisioned to support fine-art posters that would advertise the Center's burgeoning schedule of performances, the programme struck professional designers as utterly false, and even perniciously elitist: 'The fundamental assumption of the program is that fine artists give prestige to poster art, but that graphic designers do not.'[45]

This aestheticization of posters may also explain why Marshall McLuhan, author of the persuasive study *Understanding Media* (1964) and a leading commentator on media in the 1960s, utterly overlooked them in his sweeping theorization of contemporary communications. Not that McLuhan was a stranger to posters. In Woody Allen's deliberate self-dramatization in the film *Annie Hall* (1977), the Canadian academic makes a cameo appearance, stepping out from behind a film poster to explain and clarify his theories to an audience waiting in a cinema queue. Floating on a flood of academic attention, McLuhan himself was virtually blind to posters as a forum for expressing ideas. Instead, their theorization was left to observers of contemporary culture like Sontag. In her case, however, they were simply an extension of visual culture and she feared that the new boom was transforming posters into a privileged object; instead, she insisted, 'good posters cannot be an object of consumption by an elite'.[46]

When placed between four walls, even the most crowded or cluttered gatherings of posters implied, as *Horizon* magazine described it in 1967, 'a personal act of self definition'.[47] Posters were treated as 'a calling card, a manifesto and a banner', all in one. That same year, *Newsweek* suggested that 'what's important is not what the posters say but what collectors read into them'.[48] Simply displaying a poster – any kind of poster – was a mark of distinction, an end in itself. Students living in dorms where wall hangings were frowned on suddenly became resourceful, pinning posters to window curtains instead. Small lofts were deliberately crowded with blunt and sturdy messages, quickly turning living space into a swampland of printed slogans and images. Simply collecting and displaying them held a kind of status. As an early collector in the Bay Area put it: 'Poster collecting was something I did better than anyone. I was the king of my peer group.'[49] With no apparent saturation point, by 1967 the poster craze amounted to a hunger that was impossible to quench.

In bedrooms furnished with handmade quilts, small Chinese lanterns, patchouli incense and homemade portraits of John Lennon, posters became part of something bigger. Push Pin and Polish designers alike introduced the notion of an allusive poster, a cheap but expressive wall hanging that is a direct challenge to mundane ideas of functionality. To art and design purists, these new collecting and posting practices represented a failure of self-control; hypnotized like hens, they argued, buyers were too dazed to protest against the form. Gradually, they would

give in to wild cravings and start their own collections. In so doing, they
cast aside the rationalist ideas that had reined design in for at least half
a century. Although the popular press often likened the poster craze to
some kind of infection or 'virus', at its most extreme, this kind of poster
hanging was more like what Sontag called a 'mass addiction'; at its least
insidious, it presented the poster as a pointless form of embellishment.[50]
     Charged as guilty of being splashy and wasteful of space, blousy
and fulsome in its appearance, the form was also remarkably change-
able. Posters are confirmed vagabonds, ever-adaptable to a variety of
spaces. What is more, critic Jon Borgzinner observed in 1967, a poster
may be 'quick, and when its novelty has worn off, it can be replaced by
another just off the presses'.[51] Posters were promoted as expendable,
'the antidote to the boredom and certain pretentiousness of which
many paintings are guilty'.[52] For a marker of personal identity, posters
were remarkably 'demountable, disposable and replaceable at whim'.[53]
This shiftiness succumbed to a pattern of human ills, becoming a
metaphor for young people in general; with several years' perspective,
Print magazine intoned, 'what made the poster craze of the last six
years different was the emerging self-consciousness of youth as a
subculture'.[54] But to critics like Sontag, posters had become a

> cultural trophy . . . a code (for those who know it) by which the
> various members of a cultural subgroup announced themselves
> to each other and recognize each other.[55]

And yet, as rooms became alive with these posters, they
remade interior spaces into updated versions of the Art Nouveau
Gesamtkunstwerk – a total work of art. Hung on refrigerators and
over beds, appearing in hallways that doubled as 'galleries', posters
dominated many interiors. But, even more than a cheap form of wall
decoration, as posters advertising products or popular entertainment,
they also breeched breeding and good manners; they literally brought
public spectacle, however impermanent, into the home.
     In *The Society of the Spectacle*, the French Situationist philosopher
Guy Debord complained that the mass media was rendering the public
both passive and distracted. To walk through the streets of a city was to
become saturated with a world of alienating media, rendering passers-
by little more than sheepish consumers. Nowhere, he might have added,
was this distraction clearer than in cities like Paris. As posters began to fill

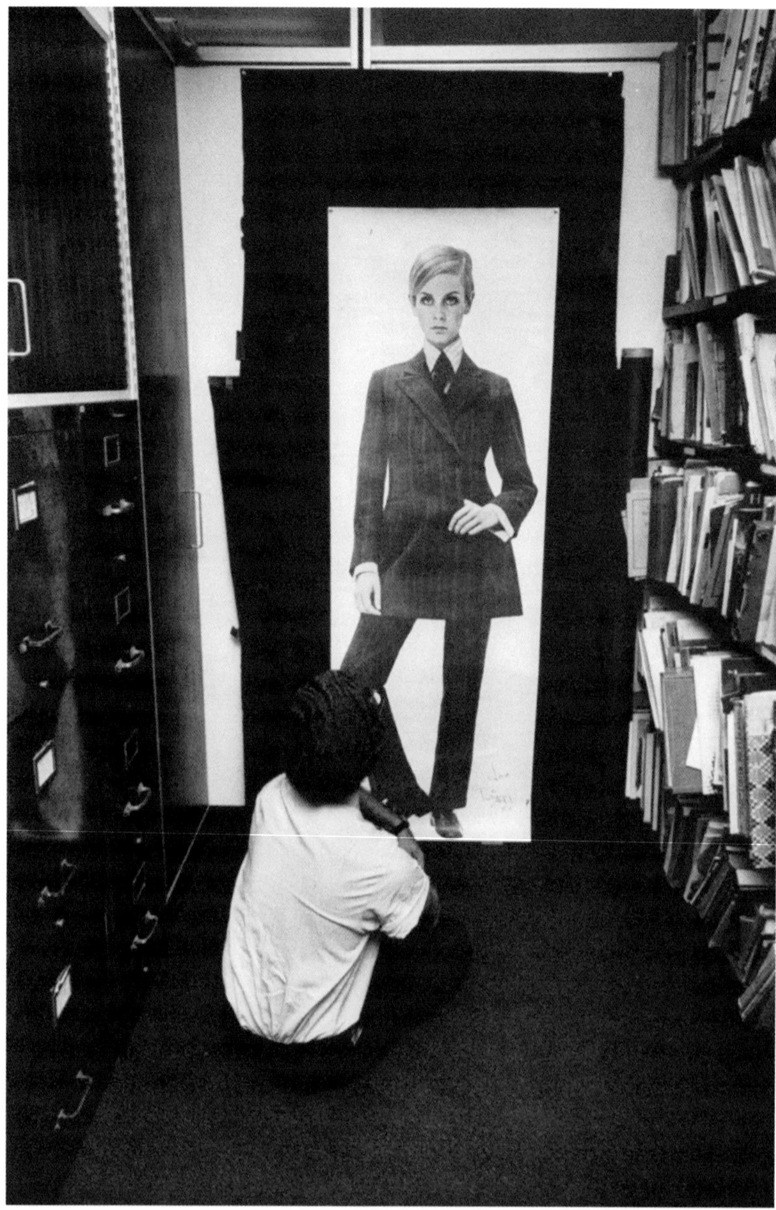

parlours and bedrooms with advertisements for gin and rock concerts, such alienation might seem complete.

In some ways, the site most emblematic of this mixing of puffability and individuality was a newcomer to hip shopping districts across the US and Europe: much of what was liked and disliked in this curious revival was embodied in the poster store. Some artist-designed posters were sold only at museums and galleries, but more social and worldly retailers, including the Psychedelic Shop in San Francisco, the

Print Mint in Berkeley and San Francisco, Poster Center in New York and Gear of Carnaby Street in London, were the prime vendors. Since the nineteenth century, when the first boom created a market for posters, dealers dealt with them like other works on paper. Offering posters for sale in the manner of Old Master prints, that is, crammed into portfolios, these were stocked in small galleries often situated in the bookish precincts of Paris and London. Collectors leafed through them slowly and delightedly, savouring the slow rewards of contemplation. But the nature of production and selling posters was changing. As Gasser said:

> Whereas in Europe a few hundred copies of a poster at most might find their way into the hands of collectors, in America they were soon being sold in thousands and tens of thousands.

What is more,

> certain types of posters, such as the giant pop photograph, have hit the very base of the popular mark, being available (gratis) at gas stations and hanging amidst all the other popular icons in the stands of the bouquinistes [booksellers] along the banks of the Seine.[56]

On both sides of the Atlantic, poster shops or even mail-order companies began to distribute posters on a vast scale.

To an entirely unprecedented degree, the poster shop modelled new ideas for display, packing in merchandise by covering walls with posters to an almost-hypnotic extent. Some posters were collaged onto floors and ceilings, while other shops even displayed posters made to fit corners – no spare space was left unpapered. Ambitious shop owners provided multiple environments for poster viewing, including small, walled-off, 'black-light' rooms painted in dark colours and displaying phosphorescent colours made visible by strobe lights. The closest retail equivalent, with what one observer called 'comparable degrees of crowding', were 'smaller avant-garde dress boutiques'.[57] Display racks were introduced, with posters attached to a central axis and swung or slid for display, much like trendy clothes. And, as at a dress shop, crowds wandered in and out, often stopping by simply to 'look'. Part community room, part hang-out, these stores also offered a sticky

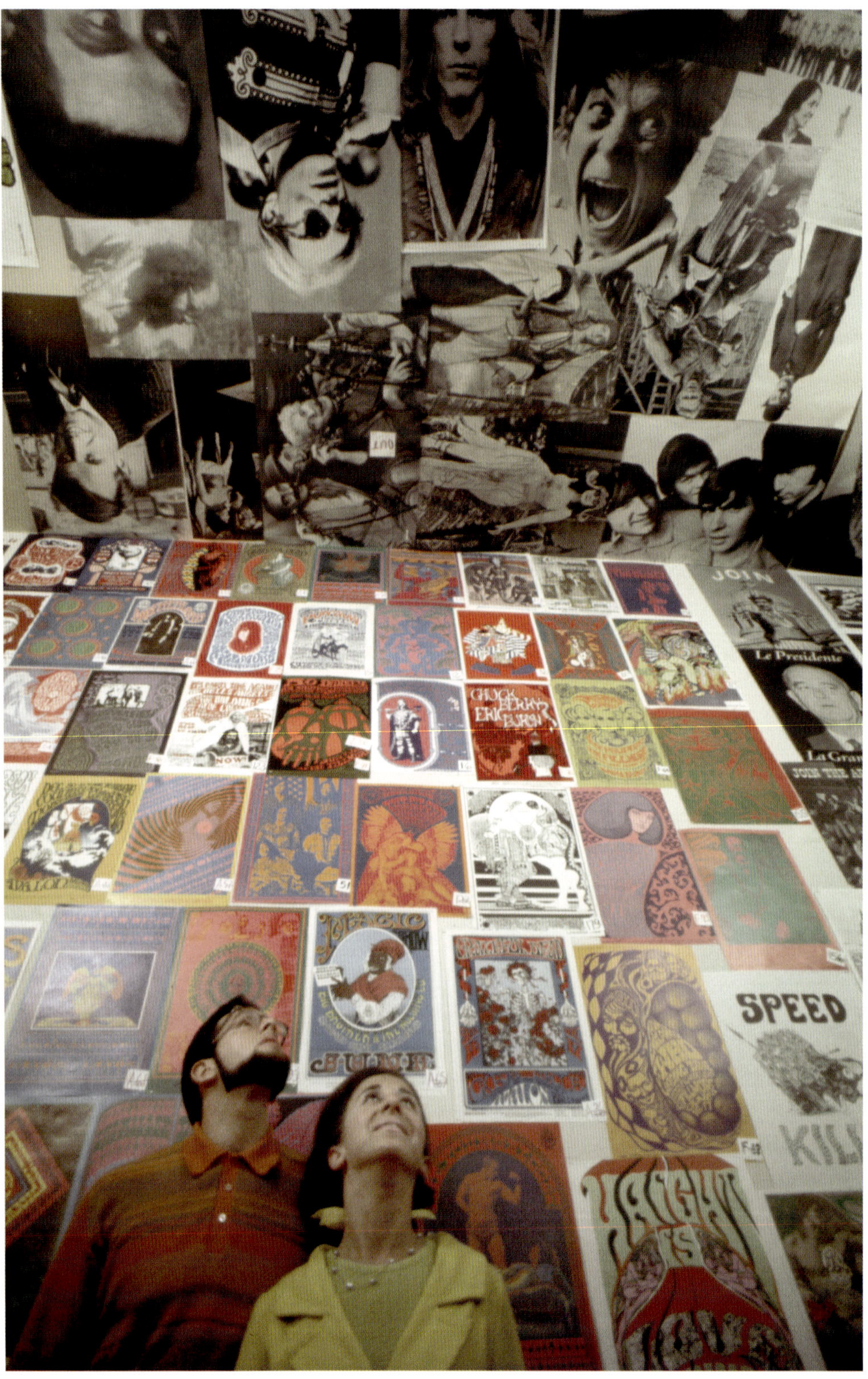

Ted Streshinsky, Print Mint poster shop, in the Haight-Ashbury district, San Francisco, 1967.

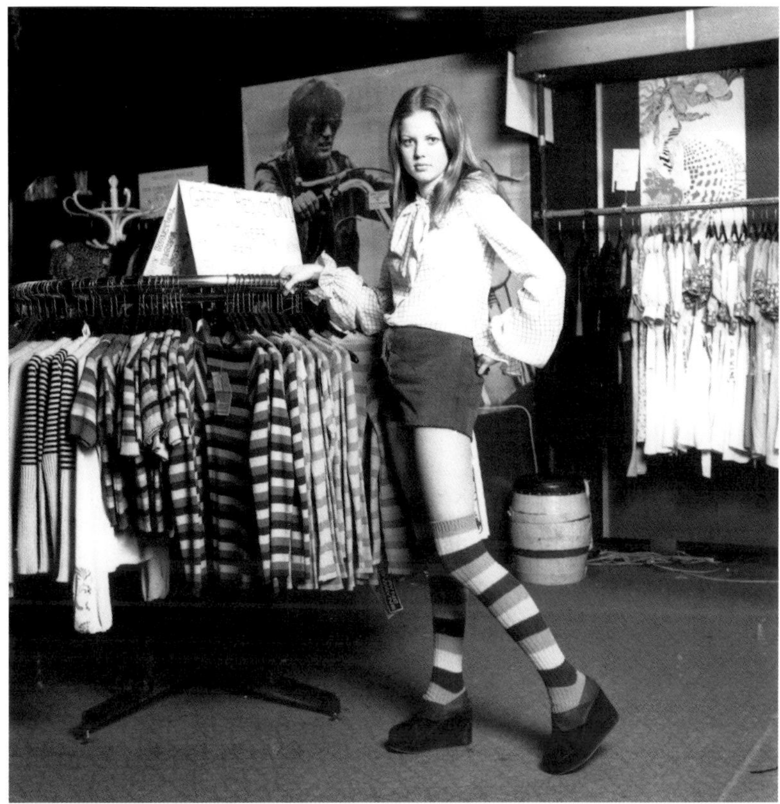

blend of commerce, entertainment and self-revelation. Nevertheless, as such shops developed, they began to include a wider range of work, too. Retailers gave pride of place to poster superstars like Peter Max, high priest of the poster revival whose career flourished at a New York advertising agency. By the mid-1960s he had shifted his work, becoming the author of hot-hued posters that announced little more than 'love'. But his graphic work was pervasive enough for *Life* to put him on its cover of 5 September 1969, introducing him as 'Peter Max: Portrait of the Artist as a Very Rich Man'.

For many years, the poster lived in a dull isolation, continuing to exist primarily on the walls of trains and army recruitment offices. But, although it was rapidly reinvented in the 1960s, not everyone embraced these developments. A hundred years earlier, posters had been called vulgar, dirty and immoral. The poster revival of the 1960s jogged a more nuanced critique. In an account from 1967 of the youth culture in San Francisco's Haight-Ashbury district, Joan Didion used posters as a backdrop for fecklessness and frivolity. Didion, for example, visited the district's main attractions, including one of the principal poster sellers at the time, the Psychedelic Shop. Looking for 'Deadeye', a friend of an acquaintance, she also made her way to a hippy apartment. When she finally tracked him down, he appeared to be living in a flat decorated with a huge poster of Allen Ginsberg. For Didion, the lifestyle and poster were part of something larger, a kind of rootless, shiftless lifestyle in which 'adolescents drifted from city to torn city, sloughing off both the past and the future as snakes shed their skins'.[58] Other commentators agreed with the art critic Hilton Kramer, who feared that, as the poster migrated indoors, it revealed a shallow fissure where a 'mass audience art . . . [has] been widely converted into private cultural pleasures – at times into private cults'.[59] To many more observers, however, the poster format was growing in its meaning, becoming an expression of lifestyle and even enlightenment.

The Acid Test on a Telephone Pole

While the poster revival was broad-based, it most closely coalesced in the hothouse atmosphere of the San Francisco Bay Area's music-and-dance scene of the mid-1960s; here posters blended cheap decoration and ear-deafening music, while gleefully tussling with the bounds of mind expansion. Combining sources in a way that would make a purist shudder in aesthetic horror, these posters showed bright hues from India jostling with references to Saturday-morning television cartoons, Art Nouveau publicity and Op Art optics. Initially, this sweeping if cluttered aesthetic was a patchwork attempt to meld advertising for dance concerts with spiritual enlightenment; they often looked as if Walt Disney had had a consciousness-raising session with Siddhartha, transcribed by the kindly ghost of Jules Chéret and art directed by the Push Pin group. The result was nothing, if not ambitious; in the words of one art dealer, these posters had to

> say everything. They couldn't just tell you the information about the show. They had to tell you what kind of people you might meet, what kind of far-out trip you might have or perhaps even reveal the mysteries of the universe. Wow. Quantum mechanics, visual mud wrestling, Acid Test pop quiz on a phone pole.[60]

Most psychedelic posters fused interior decor with internal soul-searching and enlightenment. But, truth be told, few actually hung

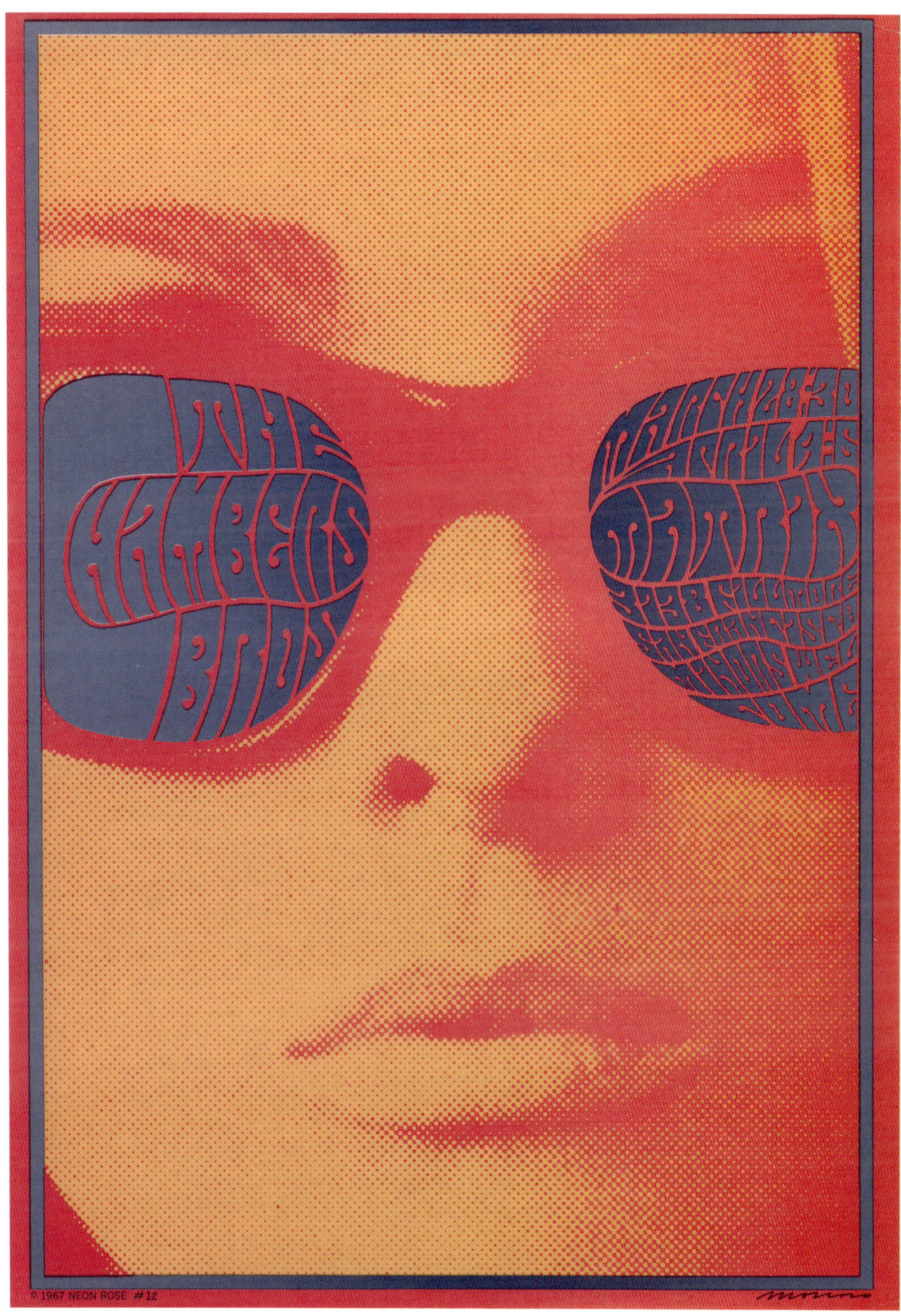

Victor Moscoso, 'The Chambers Brothers', 1967.

– at least for long – on the telephone poles and street fences of the Bay Area. As one rock promoter rather grudgingly recalled, an entire street could be canvassed, and then the billsticker might return a few minutes later to find that 90 per cent had been removed.[61] Describing a posting for the rock group Jefferson Airplane, *Print* magazine pointed out that 'almost as soon as it went up, eager hands tore it down'.[62] One poster disappeared from public view so quickly that, 'of the original edition of 300, only a few dozen were left at the end of the week'.[63] But even carefully placed posters like these were claimed by enthusiasts almost as rapidly as they were pasted up. As one Berkeley High School graduate recalled:

> every day, the moment school ended, we'd head to Telegraph Avenue, and then a whole ritual would begin. We would go into the store that had posters in their window and ask the proprietor if we could sign the back [with the collector's name, claiming it for later retrieval].

That said, he continued:

> You got to realize how intense this all was. The crowd that was into this collecting would catapult out from school, go screaming up the hill to be the first to sign the back.[64]

Posters arriving as free giveaways in music stores were in demand, but also anything posted outside was fair game.

Savvy promoters soon abandoned the cat-and-mouse game played out by distributors and music enthusiasts alike. Written and played by collectives with improbable names like Moby Grape, Quicksilver Messenger Service and the Grateful Dead, the music promoted by the earliest posters was performed in several dance halls around San Francisco, including the Avalon Ballroom and Fillmore Auditorium. Gradually, a kind of tight family ritual took place, lines rapidly forming as in-the-know collectors anticipated the weekly drop-off of the newest posters at music shops and other distribution centres around the region. Distributors would give out hundreds at a time. Collectors knew, for instance, to go to the Psychedelic Shop on Haight Street on Monday afternoons, waiting, as one collector would recall to a journalist years later, for 'the poster guy from the Fillmore or Avalon to walk in. He'd drop off a big stack on the counter, and I'd just grab like forty or fifty of them and split'.[65] Other fanatics would line up at the UC Berkeley campus knowing that music promoter Bill Graham's 'poster lady' would show up each Friday afternoon 'and the line of people waiting for her would be nearly down the block'. Anticipation could make the air tingle with a kind of decadent promise; but once begun, distribution moved so quickly, the same source remembered that one publicist had to wear 'gloves – she was handing out art so fast, the danger was getting paper cuts'.[66]

For an early collector in 1966, 'it was enough just to be obsessed with finding them and sticking them up where you lived',[67] but for many others, the posters were tempting because they described a form of psychic space. From his poster-stuffed headquarters in San Francisco, Bill Graham may have fretted that the psychedelic posters did not clearly convey significant performance details like date and location, but

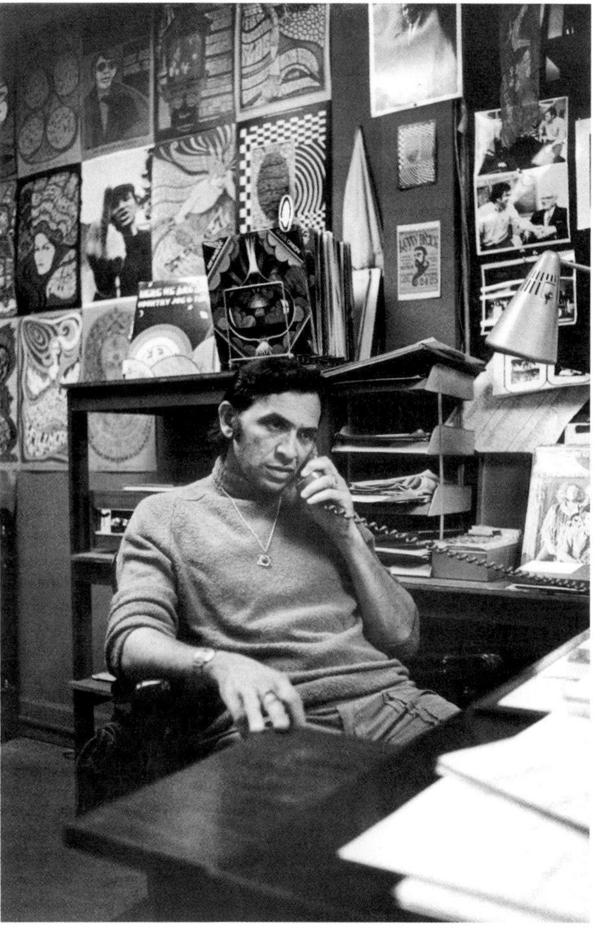

Jon Brenneis, Bill Graham in his office at the Fillmore West, 1969.

others would have agreed with Tom Wolfe, admitting that 'They know *where* it is, but they don't know *what* it is.'[68] These posters are preoccupied by sensory fantasies: the sound of the music, the accompanying light shows, the mingled smells of incense and marijuana and the pelting insights of LSD. As artist Stanley Mouse put it, these posters 'say more than "It's a dance."'[69] All were attempts to capture what one underground-press editor described as fleeting 'moments when the audience and the band fuse in a continuum of light, sound, and motion'.[70] But they also carry evidence of a kind of Promised Land; what's heard will sound good, and what follows might gain their viewers access to a kind of inner, psychic realm.

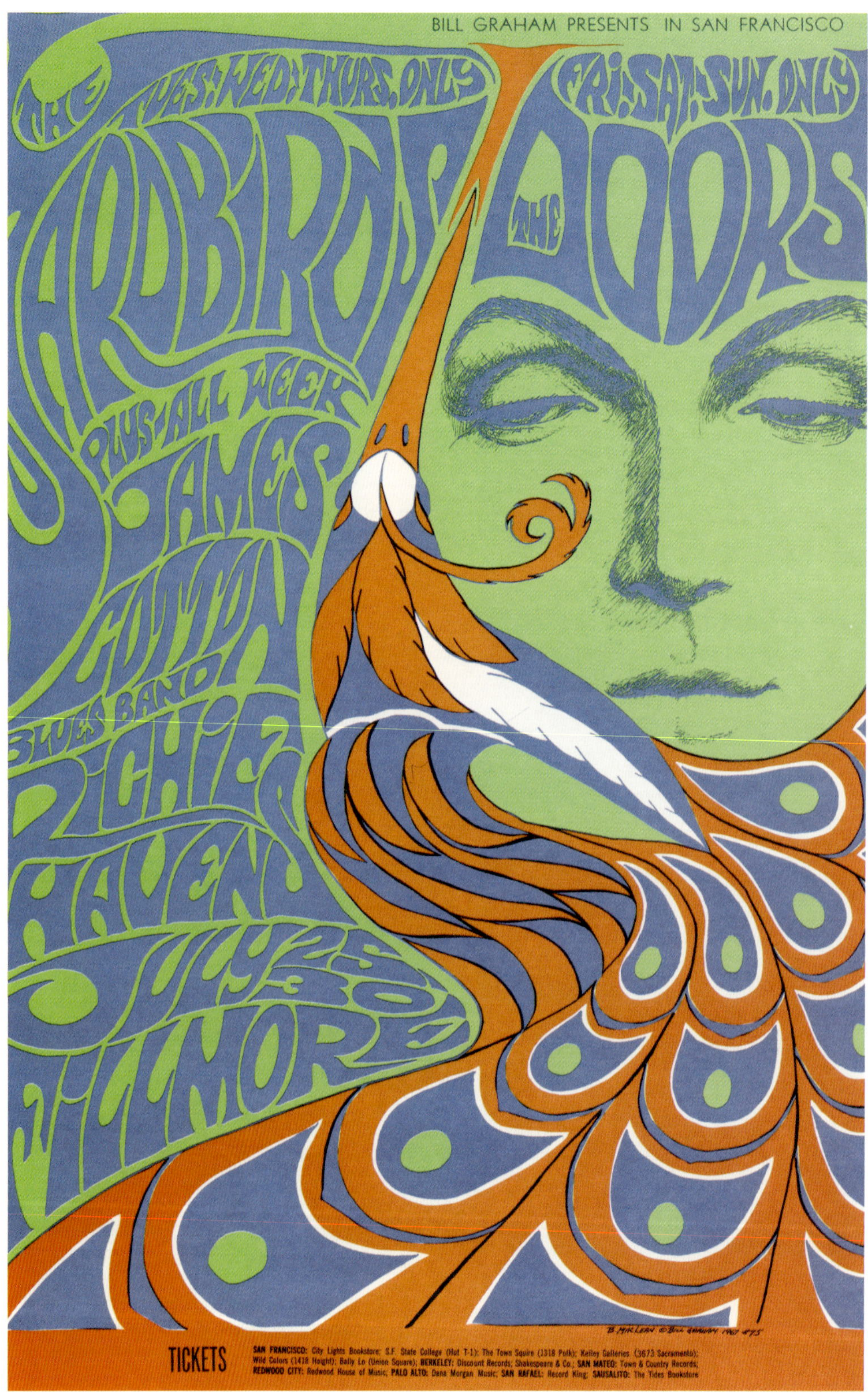

Bonnie MacLean, 'The Yardbirds at Fillmore Auditorium', 1967.

The effects that they amplified and mimicked were themselves difficult to create out of doors; this rather rarefied co-mingling of sound and vision again recalls the ideology of the *Gesamtkunstwerk*.[71] These experiences were duplicated in the flats and rooms in student halls where posters hung. Here, owners would 'drop' acid in living rooms cunningly pre-arranged, stocked with home-made biscuits, popsicles, fruit, psychedelic music, coloured lights and play toys like prism-lens glasses, reflecting mobiles and other airy trifles. And when the Haight-Ashbury Free Clinic opened a 'Calm Center' in 1966 for adventurers recovering from bad trips, an entire wall was collaged with psychedelic posters or cut-outs from them. Mirroring the anti-materialism of the hippy lifestyle, enthusiasts saw that posters 'often contain more meaning than meets the eye'.[72] Whether meant to evoke enlightenment or simply a tranquil ambiance, placed indoors these cheap and disposable items were part of more extensive decor that included candles and paisleys, fulsome joss sticks and rock music.

In 1969 San Francisco, with its deceptive sense of historicity, endless stream of runaways and truth-seekers as well as its surfeit of LSD, was not the only locus for psychedelic posters. Memoirs and anecdotes hotly debate the origins of the style. A burgeoning scene in London congealed around spots like the underground London club UFO (Unlimited Freak Out) and was promoted in posters by Nigel Weymouth and Michael English, who worked under the name Hapshash and the Coloured Coat. Whether situated in San Francisco or London, however, the posters evoked a state of inward-looking experience and served as a sort of cosmic initiation. This also happened to produce an 'in' crowd hewn together almost along 'tribal' lines.[73]

None of these early psychedelic posters was ever considered purely commercial but reverberated with a tint of cultism, uniting followers by expressing 'community ideas and spirit, which made them instantly identifiable'.[74] The proof of this lay in their loud and inaccessible messages. When Warren Hinckle III, editor of *Ramparts*, alluded to the size and style of these posters' print, he called it '36-point illegible'.[75] In 1967 *Time* magazine rather optimistically observed that 'at first glance, the calligraphy is totally unreadable', as if it were intended for an in-group. But they also noted that some 'people stop for a second glance'. After that, 'they are hooked'.[76]

Psychedelia's melding of text and image provided, as the artist Wes Wilson put it, 'something you can't say in words – only in line, color and feeling'.[77] Its posters were accessible, true believers claimed, only to those willing to take the time to 'decipher' the message. The mainstream press was an indifferent witness; at best, one reporter claimed, such posters were a 'cheerful' form of 'sadism'.[78] And yet, as one historian points out, these posters 'communicated well enough to fill auditoriums with the younger generation who deciphered, rather than read, the message'.[79] To understand them, you could not take them in while driving by, or even by glancing at them in passing. Just like the signs asking 'have you passed the acid test?', the posters emphasized in-group exclusivity. Most were best gazed at mazily, in a meditative way and with an undivided attention. Some devotees read this inwardly driven process as akin to an 'enlightenment' experience. However laid-back their rhetoric, these posters required a slow, voluptuous concentration that gradually allowed the viewer to fit together the pieces.[80] Indeed, followers would claim, these posters were never really shaped by aesthetic choice, existing as they did – for them – outside the humdrum world and in a psychic landscape open for charmed exploration.

Nevertheless, in the early autumn of 1967, just as the summer of love was fading and San Francisco's cool summer began to break, a curious march was enacted in the Haight-Ashbury district. Timed to coincide with the first anniversary of legislation making LSD illegal, a loose group gathered to announce the 'death of the hippie'. A mock funeral was held, and the community was in mourning. In the historical record, 1967 marks a moment when hippydom was seemingly growing, with events like Woodstock still on the horizon. But many residents of Haight-Ashbury took umbrage at their new reputation as a hippy mecca, as well as the media coverage, commercialization and tourism that came with it. An underground newspaper of the time called it a 'zoo', decrying how tourists came 'to see the captive animals'. But instead of accepting this new status, 'we growled fiercely behind the bars we accepted and now we are no longer hippies and never were and the City is ours to create from, and to be in'.[81] Half performance, half exorcism, the hippy funeral began with a wake at All Saint's church and continued with a parade the next morning. As some 100 people gathered for a makeshift ceremony, copies of underground newspapers, marijuana and psychedelic posters were gathered in a pile and burned. The group then carried a symbolic cardboard casket, 7.5 metres (25 ft) long and festooned with brightly coloured posters,

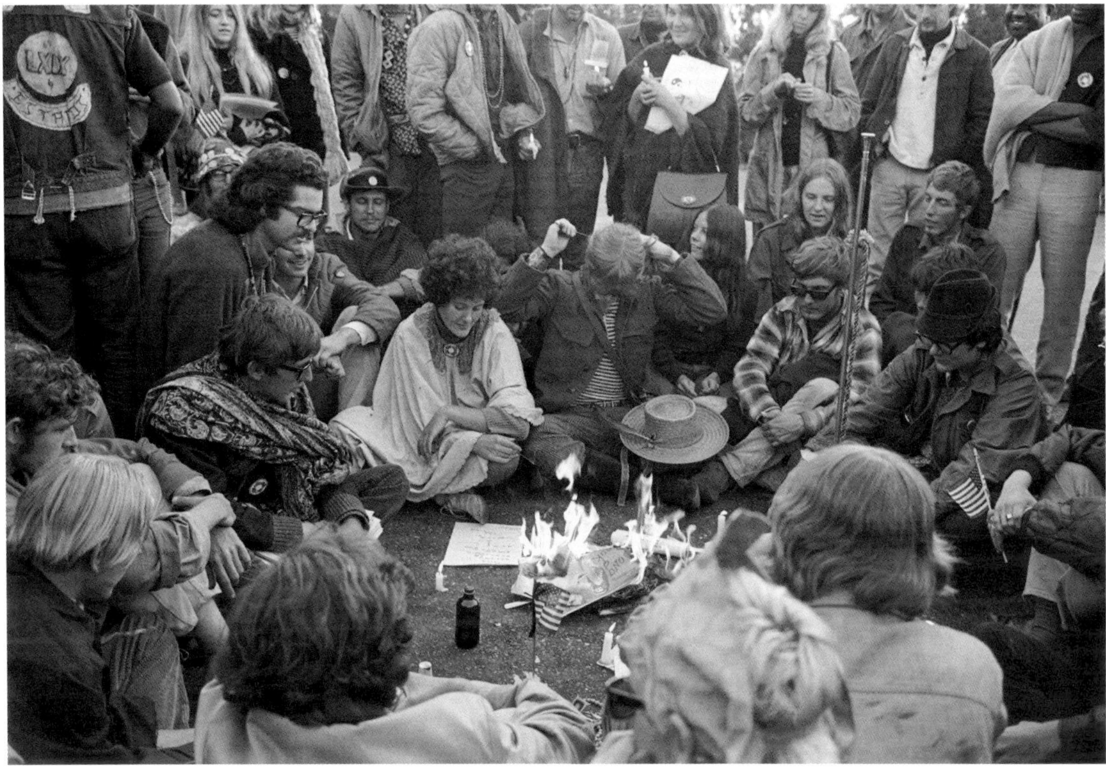

Ted Streshinsky,
hippies burning psychedelic
posters, 1967.

stopping near the recently closed Psychedelic Shop. The strange rite
of passage concluded as taps were played and the coffin was burned,
along with the psychedelic posters. The poster's death was announced
once again, but the poster revival and its near-explosive energy was,
in truth, only transformed.

The Feminist Poster and Value(s) of Pink

If hippydom began to reject the poster, the form only grew in stature
elsewhere. In 1974 the American Institute of Graphic Arts (AIGA) hoped
to increase a scholarship fund by asking 100 of its members, an
impressive array of artists, designers and photographers, to produce
a poster design that interpreted the word 'colour'. While many chose
to exploit the prismatic variety of hue, saturation and value, Sheila de
Bretteville, a young designer working in California, bucked the trend.
In keeping with the groundbreaking feminist education programme
she co-founded at the Woman's Building in Los Angeles, de Bretteville
not only chose a single colour, but was also the only designer to revel
in the oft-neglected shade pink. Using 36 squares of pink paper, she

solicited various women to shape, model and, to some minds, distort their reactions to this furtively fussy and feminine colour. The finished responses, pinned together in a rather rigid grid, ranged from highly nuanced handwriting and drawing to pale, bruised grey-pink photographs and collage. 'Pink is for babies', read one square; another tersely observes: 'Scratch pink and it bleeds.' The work appeared in a small AIGA exhibition at the group's headquarters in New York and was then published in *Color* (1974), a glossy, coffee-table book funded by Champion Papers. An admittedly spare and slightly rag-tag submission, de Bretteville's 'Pink' represented a curious encroachment on public space; it made public the simple and often intensely personal experience of colour and space.

Some months after its publication in the 'Color' exhibition catalogue, de Bretteville decided to summon the poster home and requested its return. The group organizer responded that 'Pink' was 'lost'; with no further explanation, the AIGA sent de Bretteville a photographic negative of her original work. Just what became of 'Pink'? Maybe it was misplaced. Perhaps it was stolen. Perhaps it had been damaged or thrown away. For all practical purposes, this neglect might be interpreted as a blunt hint; as de Bretteville saw it, the AIGA simply 'didn't care about it'.[82] With more astonishment than chagrin, she answered her own question – 'How could you just trash an original?'[83] – by making 'Pink' into a poster. Using the new printing presses at the Woman's Building in Los Angeles, not only did de Bretteville publish the poster herself, but she also deployed it as a piece of political theatre. Hanging 'Pink' herself around Los Angeles and then talking about it with passers-by, de Bretteville used the poster format as a vehicle for engagement and revelation. Leaving room on the poster for passers-by to write their own associations with pink, she urged casual pedestrians to call forth their own remembered feelings, associations and revelations; just as she had earlier asked friends and students at the Woman's Building to meditate on the somewhat-cloistered or even dingy conventions surrounding the colour, she now divulged them in public. Not ready to write the project off as a loss, de Bretteville not only resuscitated 'Pink', but also reconsidered the poster's format and function. If the poster 'renaissance' of the 1960s saw public messages being brought into private spaces, in the 1970s outliers like de Bretteville encouraged an entirely different phenomenon – pushing the private realm into public space.

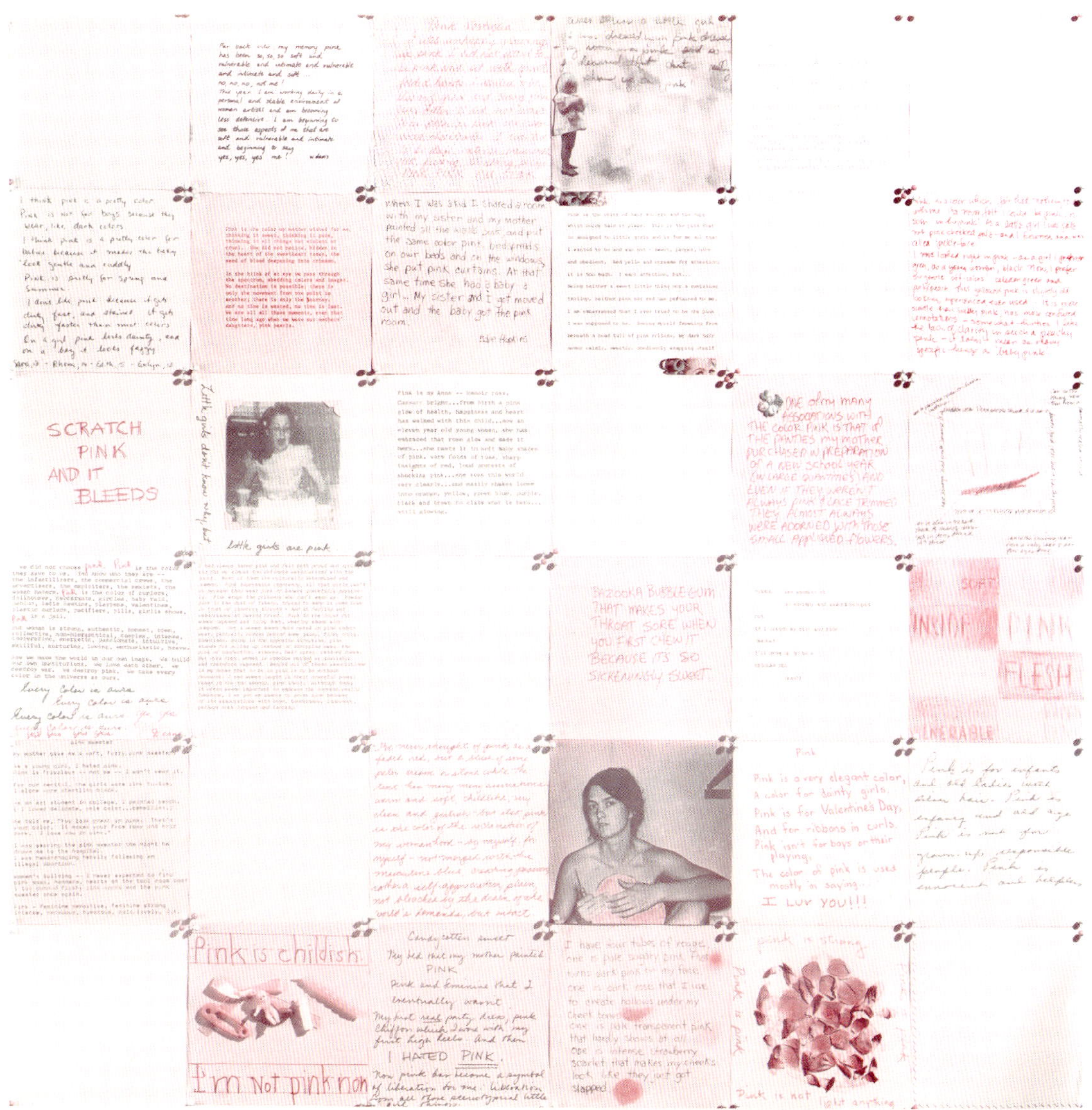

Sheila de Bretteville, 'Pink', 1974.

By the time Sheila de Bretteville began her 'Pink' project for the AIGA, posters had acquired the trappings of activism. Beginning in the 1960s, a large number of anti-establishment designers – amateur and professional – began to redeploy posters, using them as a vehicle of protest. Racism, classism, the Vietnam War, all took aim at the status quo. And still others, like de Bretteville, approached sexism. Nevertheless, even as they inundated student accommodation and living rooms alike, posters were often little more than a form of visual noise; many aped the allusiveness of the Polish School, or else mimicked the doughnut type and exuberant colours of psychedelic posters.

'Pink' was executed with one of the truest signs of fine art: a complete lack of caution. As small pink sheets were distributed to students in the Feminist Studio Workshop as well as de Bretteville's friends and acquaintances, each square was intended to carry the same truth-telling and often volatile revelations that concretized feminist theory and politics in this period. The format proved an apt metaphor for the movement's commitment to participatory democracy, with each 13-cm pink paper square constituting a system of equality. 'Pink' reflects notions of decentring and the revaluation

Sheila de Bretteville (in background) hanging 'Pink' on a Los Angeles street, 1974.

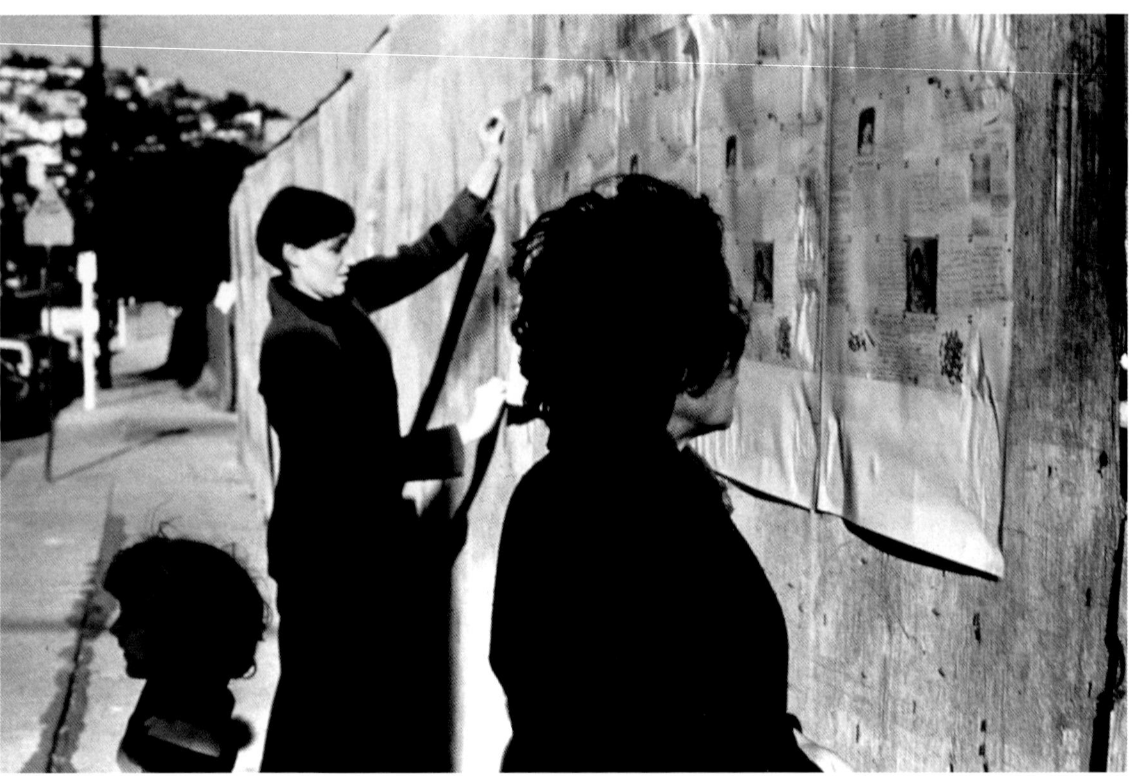

of traditional forms of women's creativity.[84] That same year, Patricia Mainardi published *Quilts: The Great American Art*, impertinently suggesting that quilting could and should be viewed as a creative act.[85] Replacing needle and thread with paper and ink, de Bretteville constructed a quilt of paper, relying on the grid to establish structure and embody ideas of community. Where traditional quilts often marked social rites of passage, for instance leaving home for marriage or a child's birth, 'Pink' suggested the coming of age of feminism itself.

As random as its messages appear, the entire 'Pink' project relied on a simple semiotic equation: intimate and refined or coarsely vital, each square acts as a marker, signifying a particular person revealing her feelings or memories. The vividly dissimilar and mismatched appearance of the 'quilt' was invested with heartfelt emotions; an entire generation's relationship to feminine identity could be wrapped in these small square pieces of paper. De Bretteville's patchwork of messages is messy and vibrant. 'Pink' remains an almost-magical essay in self-revelation, as it plumbs inner landscapes with a seriousness that recalls orderly religious rites. Magical or political, its author saw the project as 'one woman talking to another to make change'.[86]

Building on this idealistic basis, 'Pink' employs a sharp, crisp modernist grid, a prescribed rhythm. Some of 'Pink''s texts were written in neat, calligraphic scripts, some jittery and hastily scrawled in cursive handwriting, some typed mechanically. On display are original drawings, family photos or recent snapshots. Several contributors attached pink nappy pins, ribbons or birthday cake candles. Unravelling snippets of sensory recall, many of the contributors explored the colour's most evocative qualities. As one anonymous writer recalled: '[in] my memory pink has been so, so, so soft and vulnerable and intimate and soft'. Others equated the colour with a variety of tastes, including 'Candy cotton, sweet' or 'BAZOOKA BUBBLE-GUM THAT MAKES YOUR THROAT SORE WHEN YOU FIRST CHEW IT BECAUSE IT'S SO SICKENINGLY SWEET'.

Many associated pink with childhood, recalling children's dresses, stuffed animals and girlish bedroom decor. One contributor remembered: 'When I was a kid I shared a room with my sister and my mother painted all the walls pink, and put the same color pink bedspreads.' Others directly link the colour with infantilization; as one contributor insisted: 'Pink is childish. I'm not pink.' 'One of my many associations with the color pink', one woman wrote, 'is that of the panties my mother purchased in preparation of a new school year (in large quantities) and even if they weren't always pink and lace-trimmed they almost always were adorned with those small appliquéd flowers.' But others sought to subvert these very associations: 'My bed that mother painted / PINK / pink and feminine that I eventually wasn't My first real party dress, pink chiffon eventually wasn't'. Subversive or acquiescent in their associations, these squares are indexical, revealing the hand and physical traces of various makers; they present a melange of seemingly disconnected emotions and memories.

From de Bretteville's point of view, 'Pink' had a successful debut. Unable to attend the 'Color' exhibition's New York opening, she asked a student to attend the event and report back. 'I was curious what the reaction would be', she recalled, since it was 'not a modernist poster'. With varying degrees and reasons, the student recounted how 'there was a whole glut of people around it because everybody was reading' the poster.[87] When the AIGA later reported that the pink project had gone missing, de Bretteville observed that at least one other submission, an elegantly calligraphic design by Ivan Chermayeff, had recently been printed by the AIGA and sold as a poster for fundraising.

In the early 1970s the AIGA found itself facing a series of paradoxes. While its members reaped the benefits of professionalization, AIGA's designers generally had little acknowledgement or opportunity to exercise their artistic nature. Introducing the 'Color' catalogue, AIGA president Robert Bach reflected on these tensions. 'More than a simple professional association,' he insisted, 'the AIGA is a meeting place for ideas.' But geographically and intellectually locating this spot, this halcyon place where the group came to gather its 'ideas' is difficult. It certainly was not housed at 1059 Third Avenue, the organization's headquarters and a stone's throw from Madison Avenue. In some ways the AIGA was remarkably current with the push and pull of the times; in other ways, it remained fuzzy in its creative aspirations. Several contributors to the 'Color' project, for example, linked the theme of the project to the bleeding wound of race politics. Thus, Ron Mabey and Don Trousdell's *White Only* depicted a decaying segregation sign; conversely, Alan E. Cober's monochromatic line drawing portraying an African American man was titled *Colored*. As a whole, however, the group was vague and often skittish when addressing gnawing social and political issues. Although several women contributed to the 'Color' project, overtly or subliminally, de Bretteville was the only one to ponder and probe feminist themes.

As de Bretteville recalled, learning that 'Pink' had been lost was bewildering, but also a call to action: 'I said, I don't need you to print it. We can print it . . . at the Woman's Building.'[88] Indeed, when she, Judy Chicago and Arlene Raven helped found the Woman's Building as a non-profit teaching and community centre in 1973, one of their first priorities was to install professional-quality printing facilities. Student tuition helped pay for an offset press, a letterpress and printing workshops. They led, by a somewhat crooked path, to a consideration of the philosophies of Karl Marx and A. J. Liebling. De Bretteville maintained that one part of power is controlling the source of production; her workshops focused on 'making a lot of whatever you made and getting it into the hands of a lot of people'.[89] Almost inevitably, the 'Pink' poster claimed absolutely 'no preciosity', partly by stern design, partly by accident.[90] Its blurred images and uneven cropping result from the AIGA's return of a single, rather indifferent, negative. The aesthetic graces embraced by the design profession figured little here. What is more, the ad hoc nature of each contributor's works in some ways amplifies the rough shadows cast by map pins and a ragged left edge. But photographic quality aside, perhaps the most telling aspect of the poster was that it was not made for long-term outdoor exposure. The cheap paper and murky ink aged quickly, and its trademark pink colour faded disappointingly into an indeterminate greenish shade.

In some ways, 'Pink' was echoed a few years later by the avant-garde artist Jenny Holzer; nevertheless, de Bretteville's poster begs to be examined as part of a longer, more venerable tradition of public-service posters. But even these were beginning to change. Often invoking a blast of furious sarcasm, the New Advertising of the period trumpeted frank statements and arresting imagery. In this publicity-savvy climate, groups like Britain's Health Education Council embraced posters that assaulted viewers with shock value. Designed by Jeremy Sinclair, who worked for Cramer Saatchi, a forerunner of the global firm Saatchi & Saatchi, the 'pregnant man' poster of the 1970s was more than a simple attempt to get men to think about birth control; dissatisfied with public-service posters' typically bland and cursory treatments, the firm readdressed an issue previously considered pertinent only to women. Simple and to the point, the

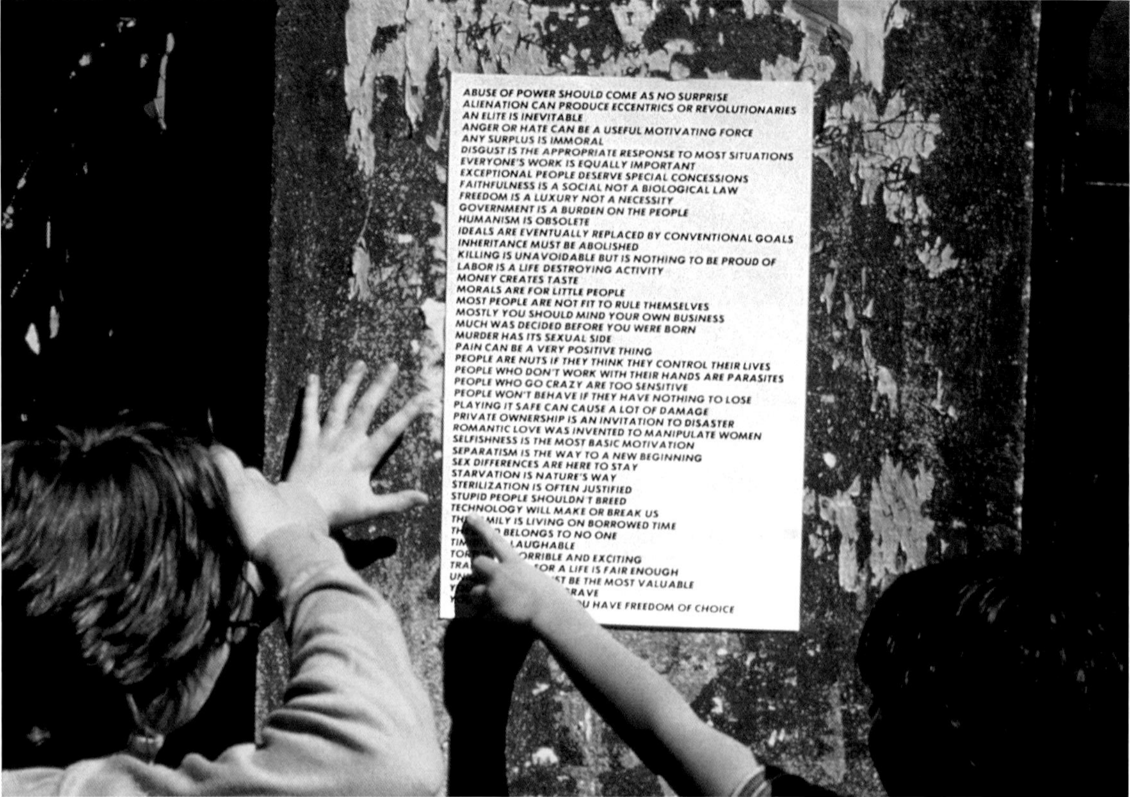

poster depicts a pensive man whose lusty past is now tempered by his swollen stomach. While he stares towards us dolefully, the simple caption reads: 'Would you be more careful if it was you that got pregnant?'

Of course, the question was rhetorical and the approach towards gender roles playful; the public took to the poster campaign with relish. The pregnant man was aped, copied and re-posed at office Christmas parties and family-planning rallies alike. When six 'pregnant' men attended a demonstration at the Queen's Road market in Stratford, London, in 1972, for example, they carried the original poster – as if the public needed a memory refresher; inhabiting their roles grudgingly, they seem to be doing penance for all male desire. As one Saatchi & Saatchi colleague would later opine: 'The pregnant man was more than just a piece of advertising.'[91] For a poster intended to be hung in doctors' waiting rooms, the pregnant man quickly moved into the national and international spotlight, as if it might act as a kind of purification for sins past. As a powerful symbol, the poster divulged topics previously whispered in private and aired them in public.

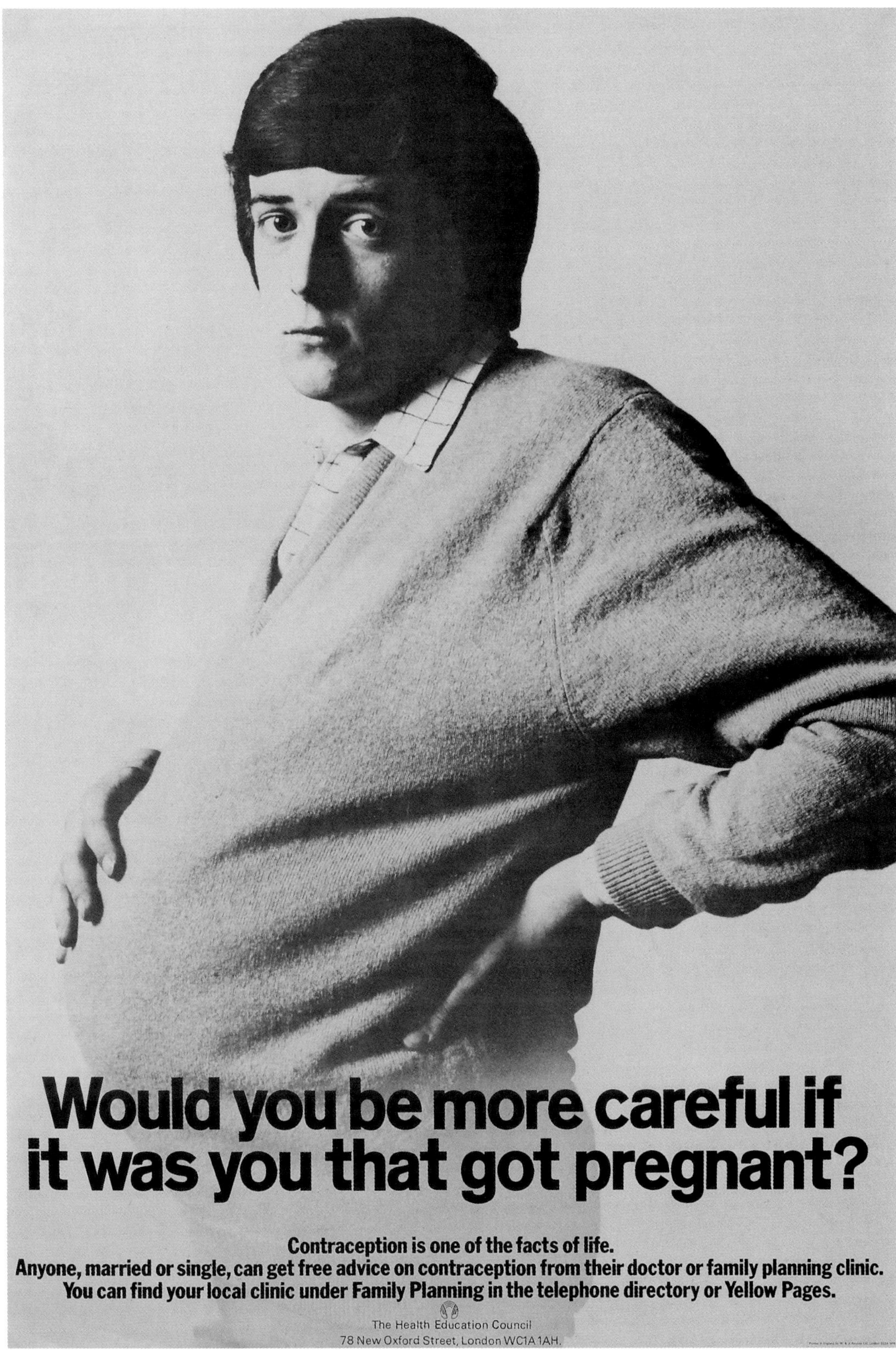

Jeremy Sinclair and Bill Atherton for Cramer Saatchi, 'Pregnant Man' advertisement for the Family Planning Association, 1970.

This slick advertising campaign may seem an odd bookend when juxtaposed with de Bretteville's 'Pink'. The pregnant man launched the creative reputation of Saatchi & Saatchi's advertising juggernaut, while de Bretteville's poster remains little remembered outside the women's movement. But each used the poster to lay bare social concerns, making the private public. Moreover, each poster was used to engage the public directly, in an almost performative manner. The real question, though, is how the poster began to transform not just in Europe and America, but also as a truly global form.

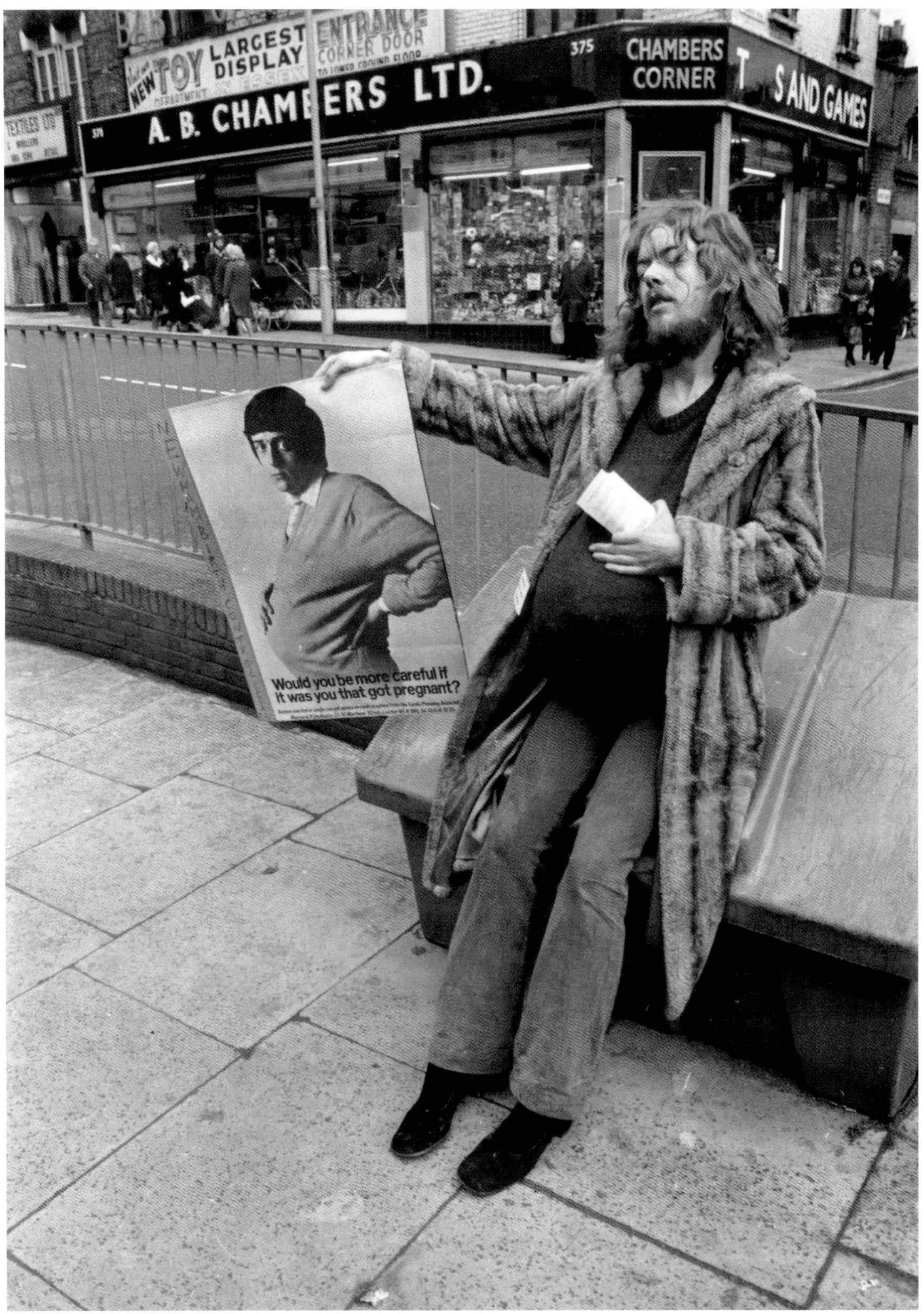

A man with a fake pregnancy bump holding the 'pregnant man' poster, 1972.

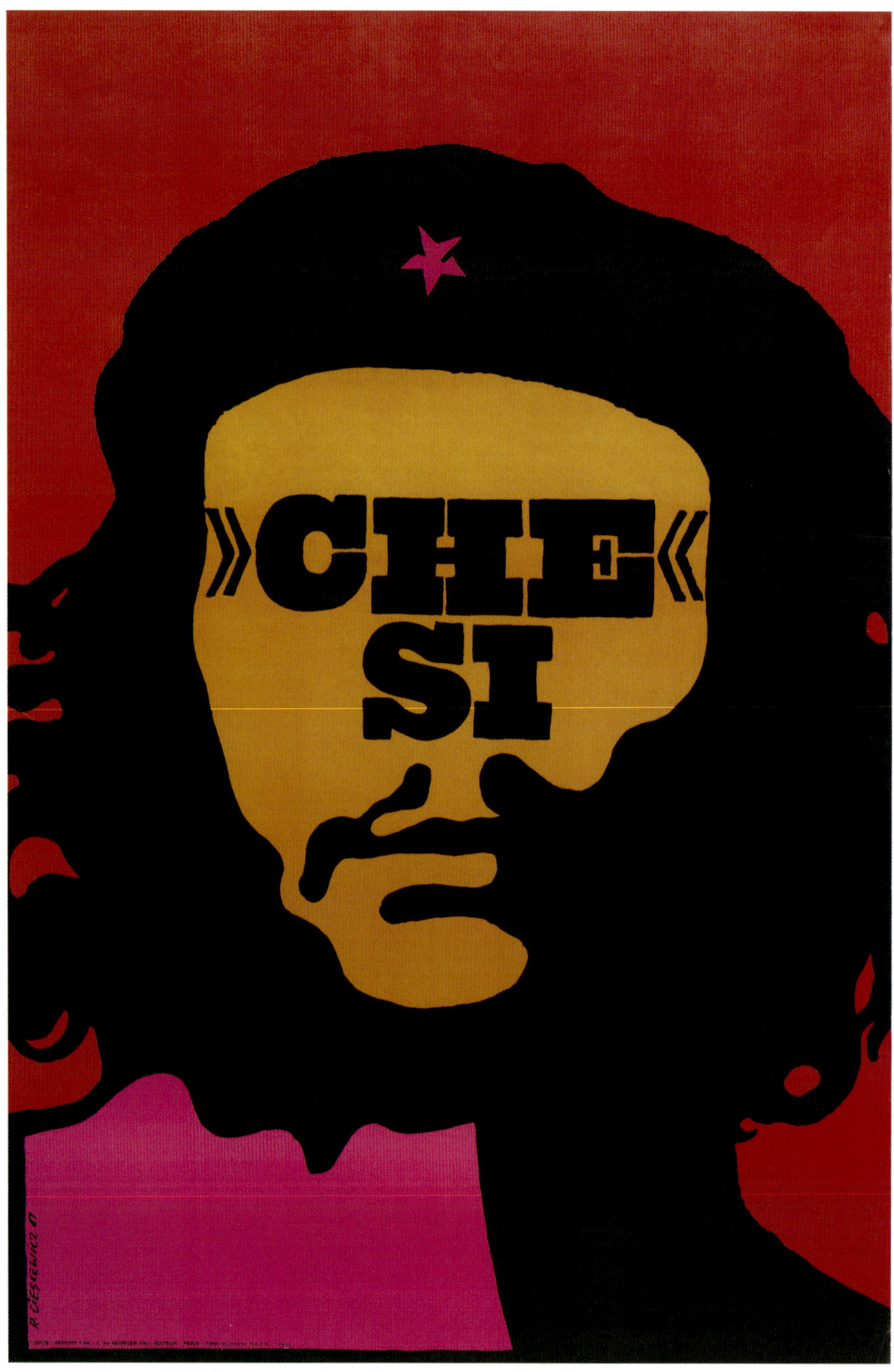

Roman Cieślewicz, 'Che Si', 1967–8.

4 FETISHISM AND THE GLOBAL POSTER: 1960–1980

When Cuban photographer Alberto Korda photographed Che Guevara in 1960, he never anticipated how this single image would change the visual culture of his period and the future. Korda was Fidel Castro's personal photographer, and his understandable assumption was that the now-famous picture, snapped at a memorial service for victims of a munitions explosion on the French freighter *La Coubre*, would be reprinted in the next day's copy of Havana's daily *Revolución* and then be done. Instead it went on to become an international icon, fetishized worldwide.

If this image floated to the top of a generation's pile of vaunting and preening posters, Korda's first takes were unimpressive. According to the photographer, Guevara appeared in view for a few seconds, and Korda managed to squeeze off two frames of him before the insurgent leader moved out of sight; one framed the famous guerrilla leader with a palm tree, while the other included the distracting presence of other mourners. Korda's editor rejected both, publishing only photographs of Castro, Jean-Paul Sartre and Simone de Beauvoir, who also attended the memorial service. The photographer later cropped the portrait and mounted it on his studio wall, occasionally giving copies to visitors but never assigning rights to anyone else. This cropped image was later 'discovered', arguably first by the leftist Italian publisher Giangiacomo Feltrinelli, who picked up the image while visiting Havana in 1967. It was later published by the French weekly *Paris Match*. The Irish designer Jim Fitzpatrick reworked it again, creating the most memorable and popular version by reducing the grey tones to black or white and isolating the head against a red background. Roman Cieślewicz's poster mixed revolutionary fervour with chic psychedelia: the chiselled chin, ruffled curls and familiar beret emerge amid hues of glaring persimmon, overripe cantaloupe and bubblegum pink. Less iconic

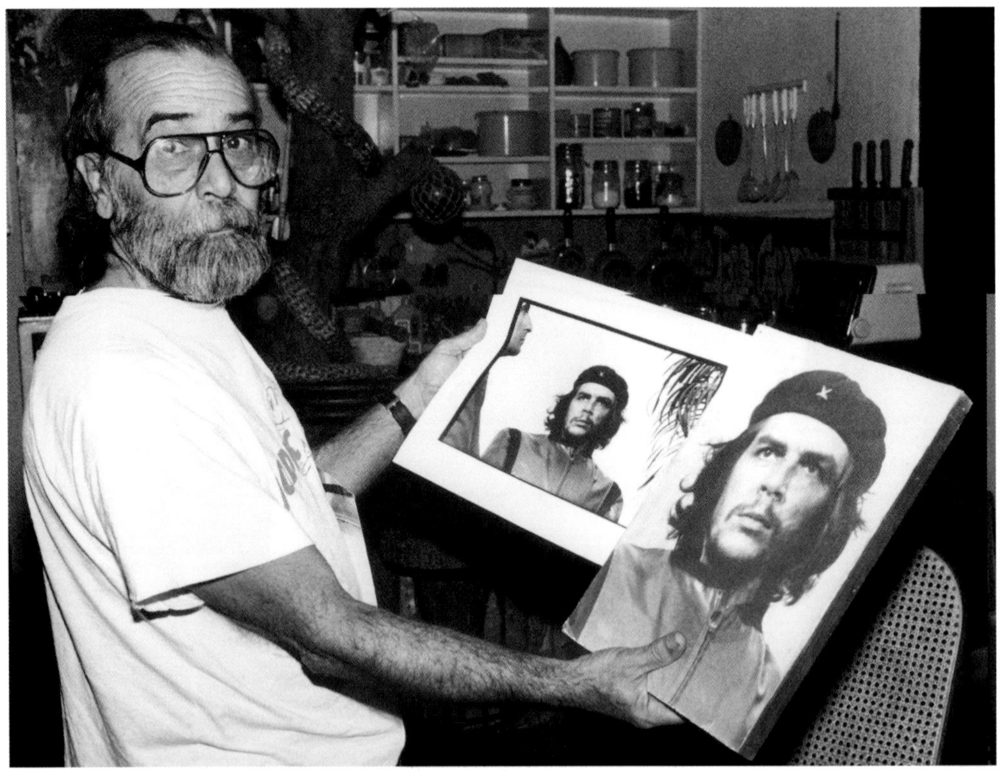

Alberto Korda and his portrait of Che Guevara, 1989.

but more complex, Cieślewicz's poster reflected his training in Poland and affinities with the Polish School, but also explained how that school's ideas were being reinvented in Paris, Havana and Beijing.

The turn to political posters is nothing new; they can be found in virtually every period traced in this book. The Russian avant-garde has long been credited with some of the most striking poster imagery in the twentieth century. Moreover, fascist posters often claimed a deep emotional hold on viewers. But coupling them with fetishism, an admittedly difficult word, is less common. Loosely speaking, fetishism describes an obsession. But Freud expanded this understanding with the notion of a sexual fetish – that is, arousal from an object or act. It can also, however, be seen in Marxist terms as referring to the pursuit of buying for no real need. But neither Marx nor Freud invented the word 'fetish'. The word originally described religious or mystical qualities that could be attributed to inanimate objects. The latter came from the Portuguese, who saw in West Africa how things they did not value were treated with reverence. Writer and scholar William Pietz proposes that the fetish is a hybrid, or is perceived in a hybrid manner, the product of intercultural spaces where people's ideas

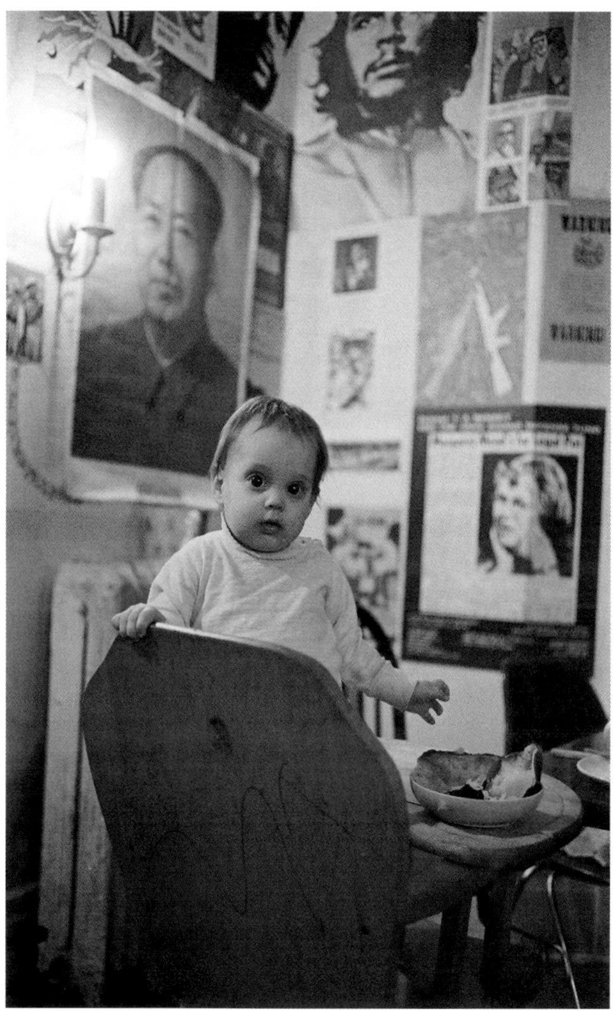

David Fenton, 'Lefty Baby', 1971.

of value clash.[1] The fetish draws our attention to the nature of conflicts of meaning within and between cultures. Today we see this differently, as a kind of culture clash, in which one group's cult object is another's fetish.

In the West, the poster boom of the 1960s may have encouraged critics to take aim at the 'pseudo-poster' – that is, a sheet with no meaning and used as empty decoration on college campuses and in homes. But, on a more global scale, posters were increasingly functioning as stand-ins for entire political systems as well as specific leaders; paper posters were endowed with almost magical powers. Whether they depicted China's Mao Zedong or Che Guevara, supporters saw these posters as a reflection of something larger, as assertions of identity and solidarity, but also to be hung and gazed upon.

At the same time, poster portraits from China and Cuba were hung in university students' housing in Ann Arbor, Michigan, and pasted on the walls of the Sorbonne, appearing there almost as quickly as they appeared in Beijing's Tiananmen Square. In the age of tear gas and tanks, these imported posters claimed an immediacy rarely seen in the last 100 years. This phenomenon is traced here only in a limited way. For every poster from Cuba, a series of others began in the 1960s and '70s to sprout in Nicaragua and Chile. The process of decolonization meant that revolutionary posters, like those of the Medu collective in Botswana outlined here, had eager counterparts in Namibia and Zimbabwe. To supporters, such imagery was greeted with revolutionary

zeal. It seemed to indicate a new political destiny, glimpsed on flashes
of paper that carried their own special power.

Making a Model Work in China

In July 1968 the Chinese photographer Li Zhensheng captured an
unusual flotilla crossing the Songhua river in Harbin. Snapped at the
height of the Cultural Revolution, he photographed swimmers marking
the anniversary of Mao Zedong's swim across the Yangtze in 1966. Mao's
original swim was calculated less to advertise his swimming abilities
per se than demonstrate how the 73-year-old leader was still filled
with youthful vigour. Through the whirling waters of upheaval and
discontent that characterized China at this time, it is hard to say which
is more curious, the fact that Mao's avid followers in Harbin followed
their leader into a local river, swimming and chanting in unison, with
their clenched fists bobbing in the air while they trod water, or that
they were carrying with them, through the choppy river waves,
over-life-size posters of the great leader.

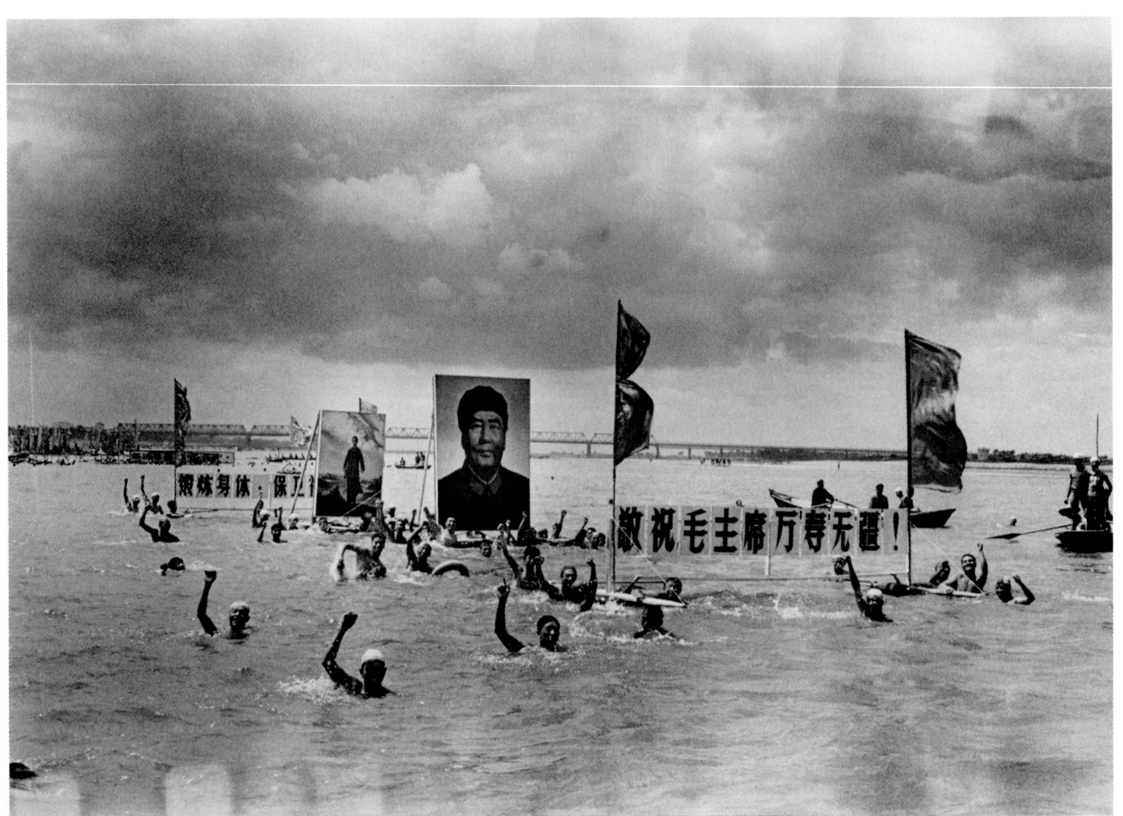

No one in Minneapolis or Leeds traversed great rivers while carrying posters of Lyndon Baines Johnson or Harold Wilson through the water, but the poster was a powerful visual form for powers such as China, where the nation was beginning to flex its political muscles like a giant emerging from a great sleep. It is true that the immediate catalyst for such imagery in China was the Central Committee's approval in August 1966 of the 'Decision Concerning the Great Proletarian Cultural Revolution'. Although the Cultural Revolution is often described with insularity as little more than a Maoist power grab, in the People's Republic of China it was represented as a granting of new rights that recast Chinese society profoundly. Mao urged China's artists and writers to 'go among the masses and serve the people'. Indeed, the edict set a tantalizingly high mark, urging the creative classes to 'work to discover and promote that revolutionary consciousness of the Chinese peasantry through all art and literary forms'. While many did just that, floating from city to villages across the country, Mao's best emissaries were not gung-ho revolutionary Red Guards or chastened intellectuals, but rather the millions of Mao poster portraits distributed during the Cultural Revolution; alternately blank and vivid, these became powerful objects that presented their subject not simply as a man, but also as an embodiment of the Chinese people.

Marxist regimes had long tried to use posters as a kind of glue, meant to dominate and consolidate with powerful, if often unstated, messages. The Soviets turned to the 'cult of personality', promoting a collective vision around poster portraits of omnipotent leaders. The ubiquitous poster portraits of Lenin, Stalin and other Communist leaders might strike some not as an example of good governance, but rather as nervous management of an uneasy political situation. Embellishing government buildings, factories, offices and schools, but also decorating temporary parade stands or carried during celebrations and in military or workers' parades, they filled semi-public spaces in Russia and its satellite states. Seen and remembered, they impressed themselves indelibly on several generations' subconscious; in a time and place where art museums were few, posters carried a special clout.

After the Revolution, Chinese artists began to produce a variety of poster types, including political news, advice on health, propaganda and tips on production; but the portraits of Mao were, in some ways, category-defying. Mao himself always claimed a fascination with the form. With guarded care, for instance, he used posters in his earliest

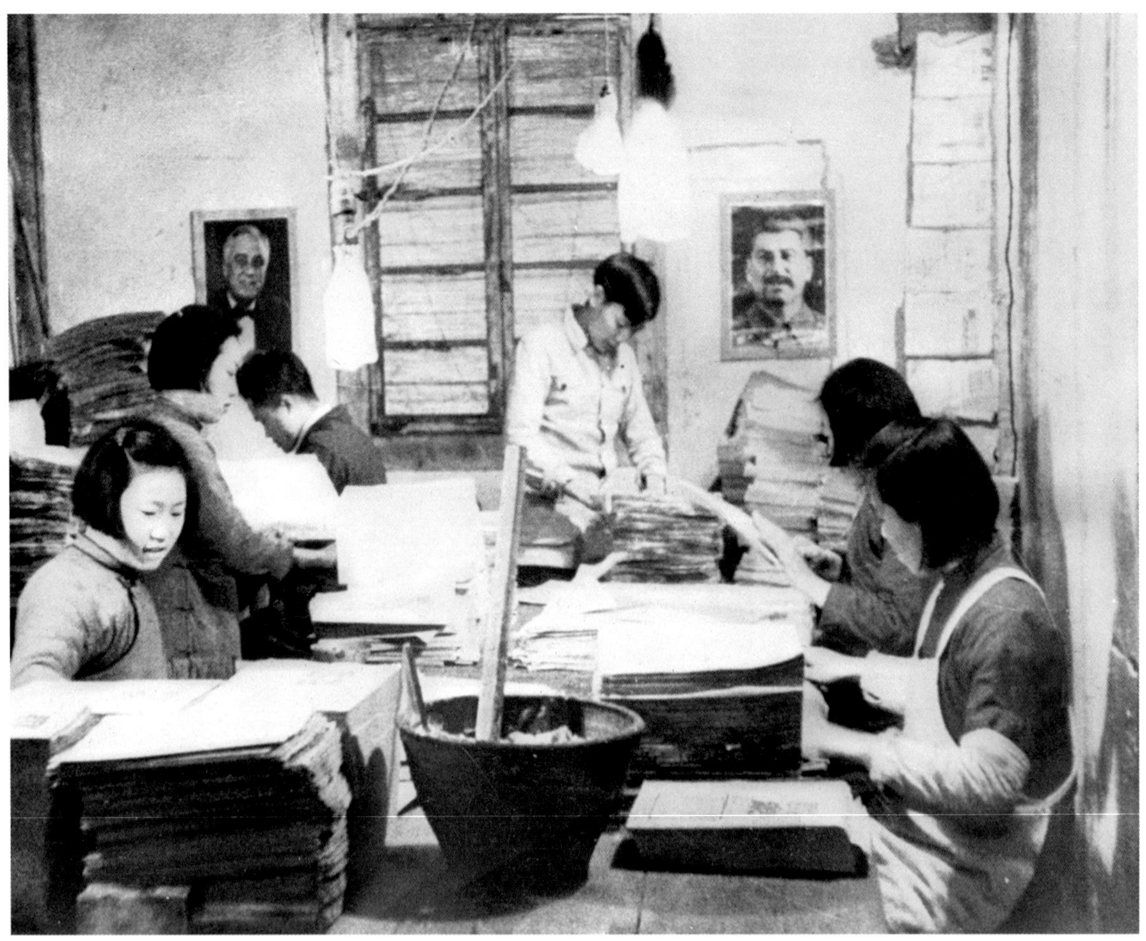

political actions to draw students to his workers' night school.[2] China's
large and illiterate rural population was already flush with 'readable'
visual images, for example, pictures in temples and banners displayed
at opera performances, as well as decorative calendars and posters
distributed at the beginning of the lunar New Year. The first published
portrait of Mao Zedong appeared in 1933, but is largely forgotten;
after decades of civil war, the web of a common political life had been
twisted and shaken almost to the point of breaking. As late as the
Second World War, as in one particular war-era printing plant run by
the Communists in northern China, portraits of wartime allies Josef Stalin
and Franklin Roosevelt were published with enthusiasm. Only when the
People's Republic of China was finally founded in 1949 were portraits of
Mao rapidly standardized by the Central Propaganda Department; these
were intended to weave together a new government that, in times of
great strain, could still hold this huge and wildly diverse country together.

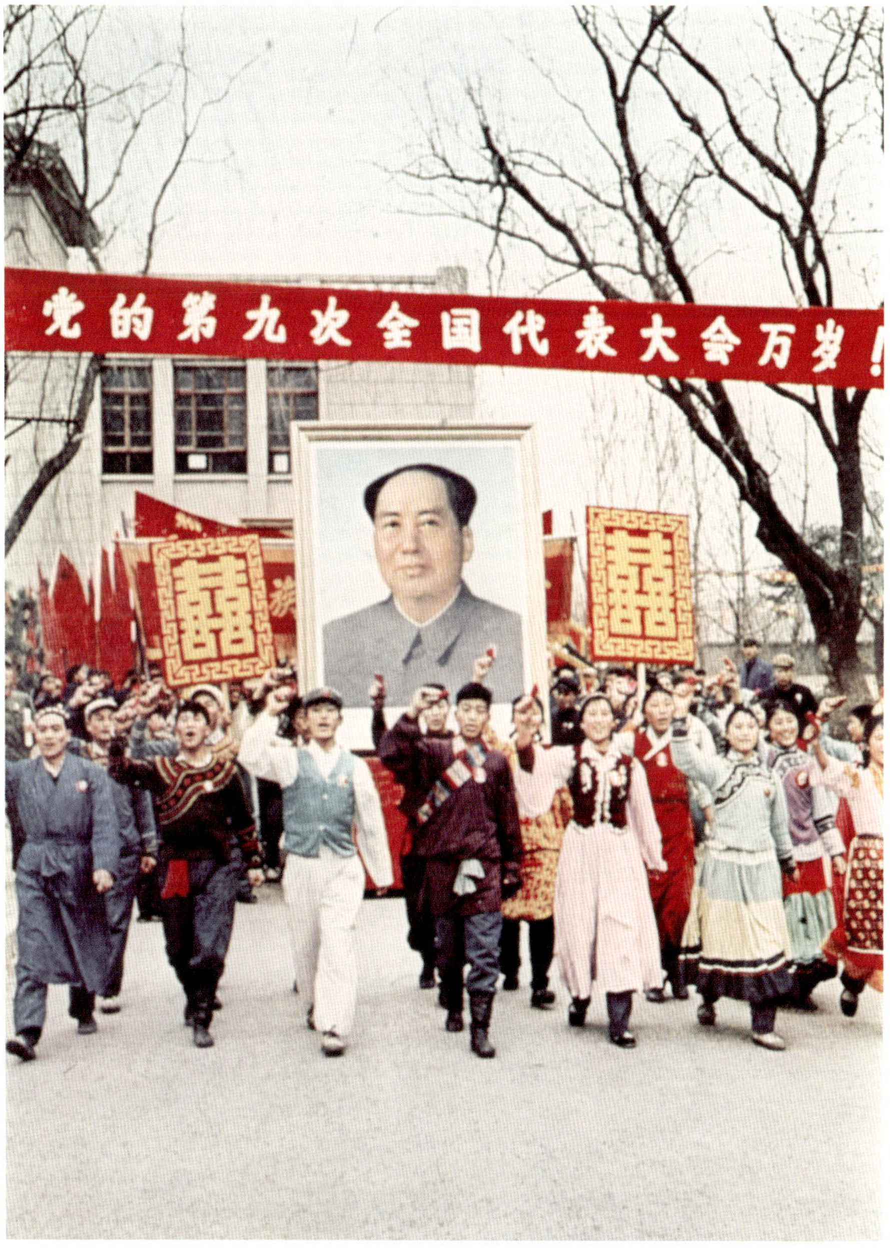

When the Cultural Revolution was officially launched in 1966,
it represented an internal power struggle, 'a revolution to touch
people' that jettisoned established structures of power and challenged
conventional social and political hierarchies. Mao's Yangtze swim may
have been calculated to win propaganda points, but the youth who
poured into the streets to march in traditional dress while shouting
slogans of Marxist unity and parade in public carrying giant portraits

felt differently. One group, captured in a photo from 1968, is dressed in the ceremonial wear typical of China's many ethnicities. Nevertheless, they march below Mao's portrait united. They, like Mao's swimming followers in Harbin, looked to the Chairman himself as a role model; indeed, their swimmer counterparts began their epic jaunt of 1968 across the Songhua River united, the participants lining up on the riverbank to read in unison from the 'Little Red Book' containing the compilation of Mao's quotations. The posters they dragged through the water were an ideological boost, the CCP (Chinese Communist Party) supplying its citizens with massive doses of posters that, like a supplementary vitamin, were intended to shake things up but also impart the sense of belonging to something bigger than themselves, driven, mighty and united. No longer did Mao share poster space with Stalin or Roosevelt; posters of Mao were becoming virulently monotonous but also presented a leader who embodied a vast and varied nation.

Mao, the man, had not always embodied the ideology of utopian socialism; neither had he necessarily sought to create a cult of personality that made him more elevated and powerful than a mortal man. Before the Cultural Revolution, in a stroke of creative luck, the American journalist Edgar Snow casually snapped the most widely used portrait of Mao to date. The Chinese leader would always claim Snow as a friend, and even borrowed the American's Red Army cap for the photo when he discovered he did not have his own at that moment. Taken just after the Long March, when the Communists left southern China for the far north in 1936, the image dispelled rumours; Chiang Kai-shek had reported Mao dead, and Snow's modest and seemingly effortless snapshot was quickly replicated in oil paintings, watercolours and photograph reprints. To a Western audience long familiar with the dark arts of photo manipulation, it can be hard to understand how ingenuously these images were received. Clipped and cropped, airbrushed and polished, it seems all the more remark-able today that these posters were seen and treated as the authentic eye and ear of the people. But the image's pretensions were modest and, compared with things to come, it circulated in a relatively limited fashion.

By the time of the Cultural Revolution, public imagery was changing, and Mao ascended onto a kind of crystalline, over-sized stage. In the earliest phase of the movement, ideologically driven

Mao Zedong, 1925.

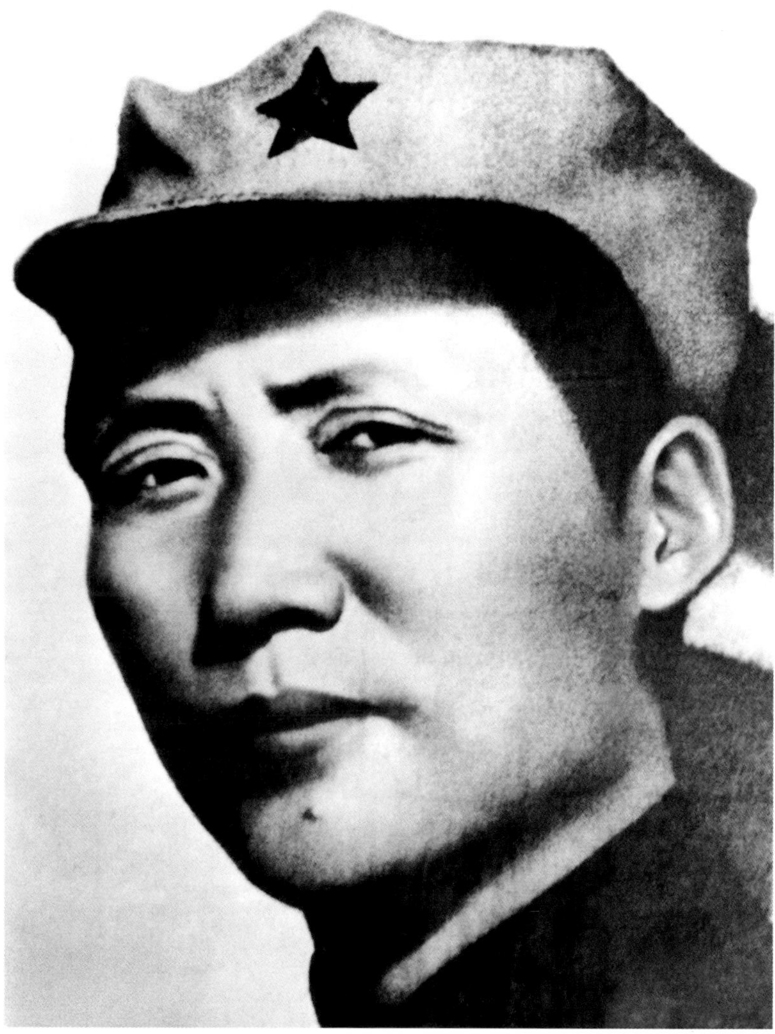

amateurs crafted quick, urgent images that relied on crudely effective
brushwork. Guidelines for depictions of Mao were confidently formalized in a small booklet published by the Red Guards of the Central
Academy of Fine Arts: *Long Live Chairman Mao*. As the Revolution
matured, however, more polished paintings and heavily retouched
photographs emerged as a new lingua franca.[3] The most ubiquitous
poster, approved personally by the Chairman in 1964, religiously and
righteously presented the leader with bright flashing eyes and skin
that was a hot-pink and waxy beige. It was rendered in the semi-
photographic style of Mao's official portraits, part of an emerging
canon of depiction whose strictures were rigorously reworked and
artfully calculated.[4] By this time, for instance, all Chinese artists were

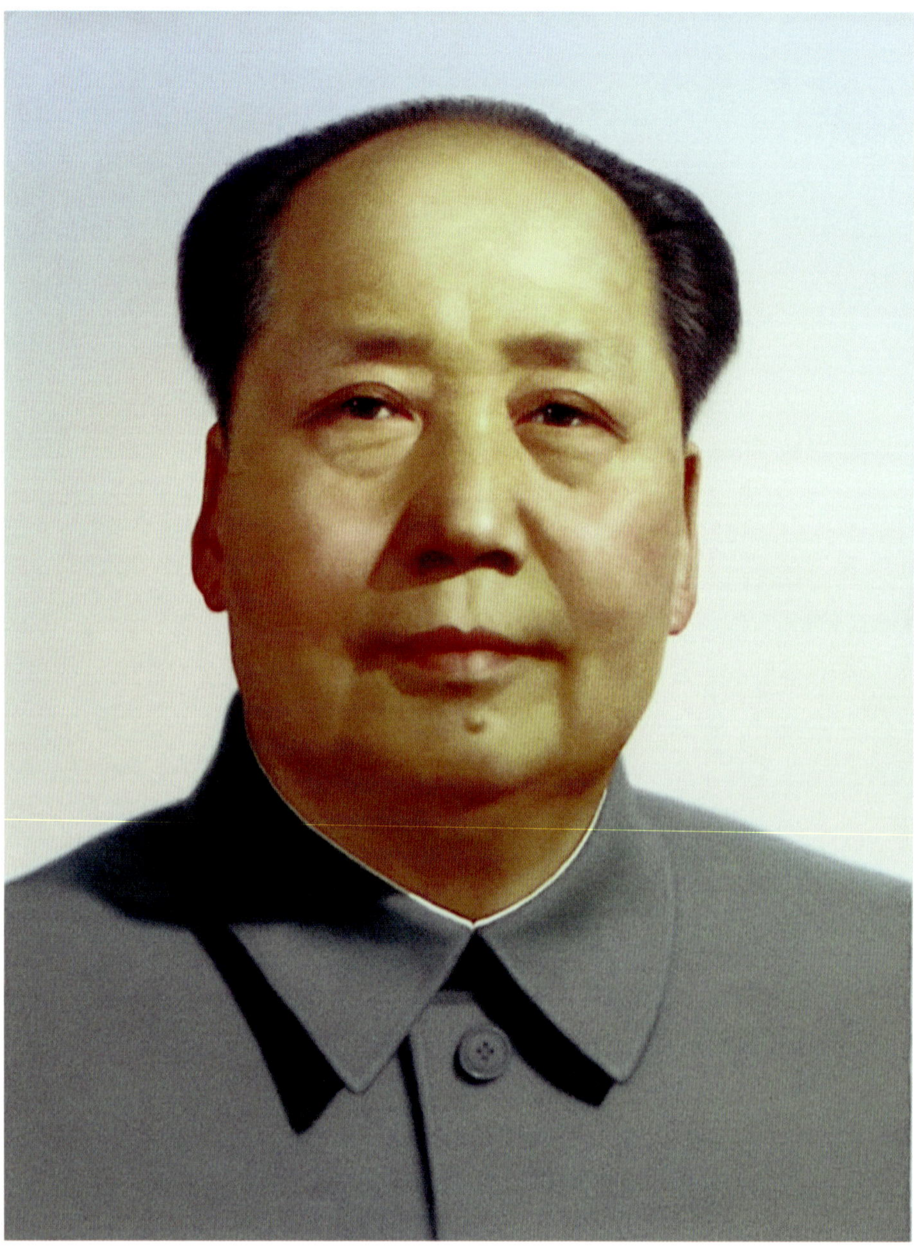

directed by Mao's wife, Jiang Qing, to depict their leader as 'red, bright, and shining'.[5] Cool colours were sidelined, as were any lighting effects that might detract from Mao's figure; ideally, the leader radiates an almost magical light. At institutions like the photographic department of the new China News Agency, this style typically had Mao surrounded by a haunting luminescence that seems to emanate from his body, making tangible propaganda slogans such as 'Mao is the sun in our heart.'[6] The size and turbulence of the revolution may have been accepted as inevitable in many quarters, but carefully calculated poster art played an undeniable role here.

Thus, even in a visual culture buoyed by the belief that everything the Chairman does, everything he thinks about and everything that happens to him is of general interest, Liu Chunhua's painting *The Chairman Mao Goes to Anyuan* stands out as a 'model image'. The piece depicted a young and vaguely poetic Mao as the leader on his way to Anyuan, where he would lead coal miners into the first significant union action organized exclusively by the Communists; this group would be one of the party's most stalwart sources of support before 1949 and the air practically tingles with a kind of expectant promise. Dressed as a scholar and pausing his determined stride, Mao stands above the clouds along a mountainous ridge.

The image struck the shining note that Mao's propagandists sought. Walking with visionary deportment, Mao is poised and forward looking, standing on the mountaintop far above the welter of passing events that take place in the real world below. The artist himself described how the image was planned so meticulously, bringing significance to every small detail. Reflecting on *The Chairman Mao Goes to Anyuan* years later, the artist explained how this seemingly simple image reflected revolutionary ideology. Thus, the Chairman appears 'tranquil, farsighted and advancing towards us like a Rising sun bringing hope to people'.[7] Small details, for example Mao's clenched fists, depict his 'revolutionary will, scorning all sacrifice, his determination to surmount every difficulty to emancipate China and mankind', while his 'hair grown long in a very busy life is blown by the autumn wind. His long plain gown, fluttering in the wind, is a harbinger of the approaching revolutionary storm'. The worn umbrella under his right arm 'demonstrates his hard-working style of travelling, in all weather over great distances, across the mountains and rivers, for the revolutionary cause'.[8] The composition was endorsed by Mao's inner circle. More than 900 million copies of Liu's original painting were distributed as stamps, prints and especially posters in a country whose population at the time was an estimated 700 million.[9]

Institutionalized as what the *China Pictorial* of 1968 described as 'an outstanding achievement implementing Chairman Mao's great thought', its true power was fixed only when the image was reproduced as a captioned poster.[10] Many read it at face value, holding it to the

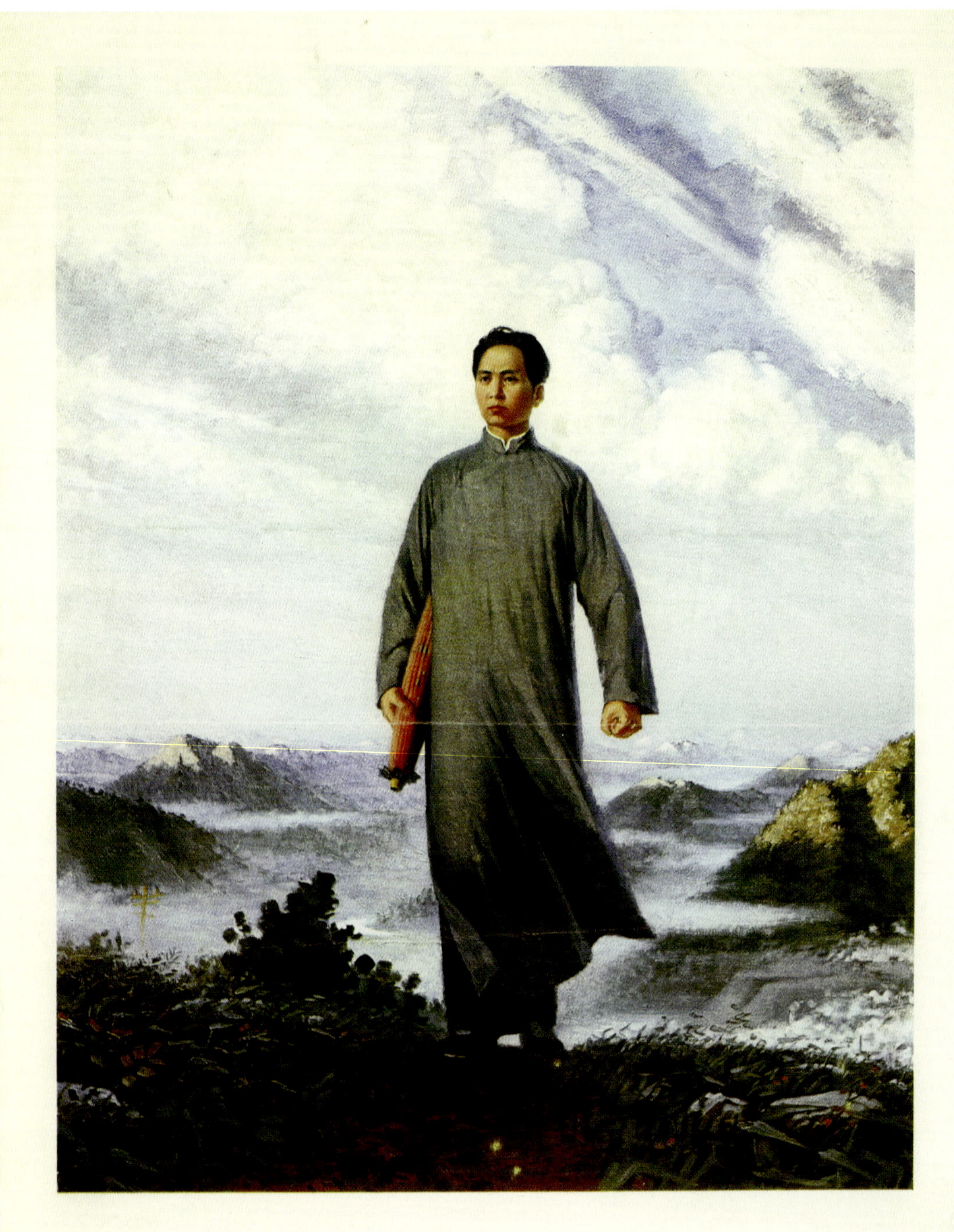

Liu Chunhua's painting *The Chairman Mao Goes to Anyuan*, 1968, was widely distributed in poster form across China.
The version shown here includes an English-language translation of the original Mandarin caption.

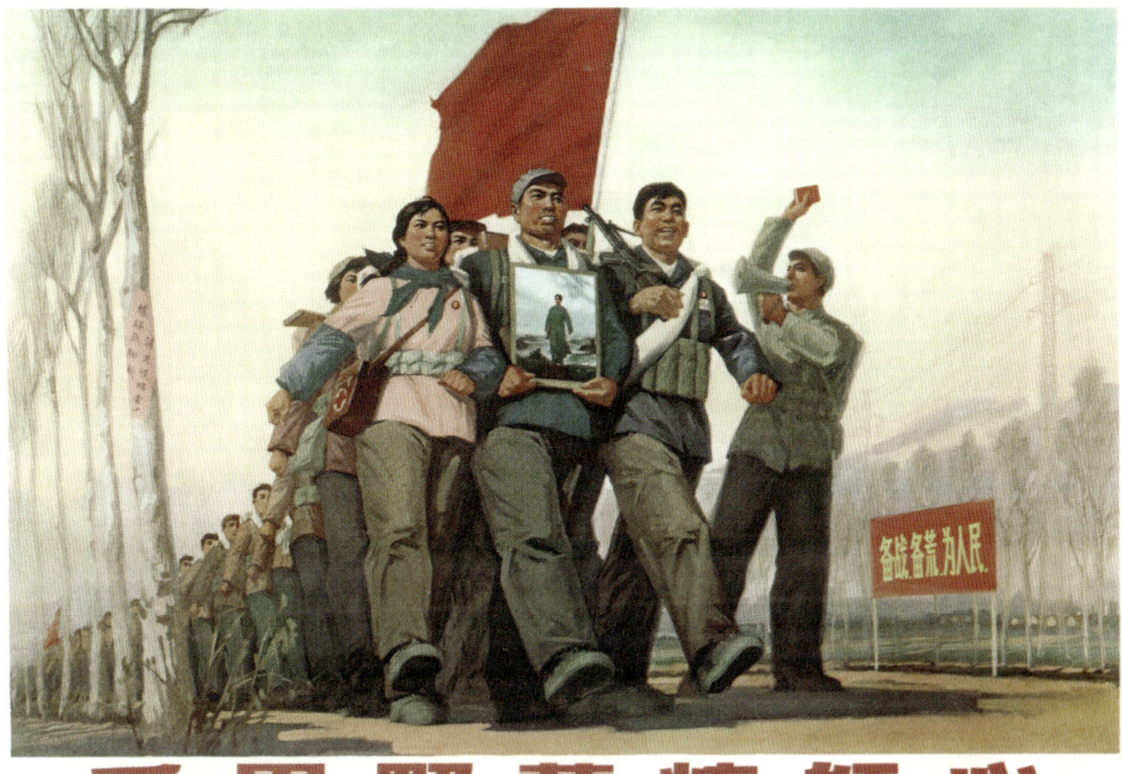

'To go on a Thousand *Li* March to Temper a Red Heart', 1971.

simple caption usually published along the bottom: 'In autumn 1921 our great leader Chairman Mao went to Anyuan and personally kindled the flame of revolution there.' Indeed, the image was endorsed by the miners of Anyuan; sure enough, in a discussion originally published in the periodical *Chinese Literature* in 1968, 'revolutionary miners and cadres of the Pinghsiang Mining Administration' affirmed that the image accurately captured 'the bright image of Chairman Mao, the red sun in our hearts . . . the way he came to our mine 47 years ago'.[11] Beyond such dubious generalities, however, if the poster was venerated by millions, it was because it radiated a form of visionary self-confidence. That is the basic ingredient.

But 'Mao Goes to Anyuan' also speaks volumes about posters' role in rendering the Chinese leader into a symbol. The original painting was an instant success when first displayed at the Beijing Museum of the Revolution in 1967. Rumour had it that Jiang Qing realized that the painting could score a propaganda coup similar to the 'model' operas and ballets that she had already begun to promote ardently. Thus, the

193

painting was quickly published and republished in the *People's Daily*
as well as other newspapers and journals across the nation. But the
composition found true immortality only in poster form.

The poster 'Mao Goes to Anyuan' soon swept Mao's followers
further, leading them into a kind of fever of unstoppable motion;
inescapable at party rallies, meetings and demonstrations throughout
the period, the poster was a feature of everyday life. Svetlana Boym
has described how, in Soviet Russia, a process that she calls mass
'culturalization' translated ideology through the widespread possession
of material objects.[12] Through lacquer boxes and miniatures decorated
with pictures of Vyacheslav Mikhaylovich Molotov and Stalin, revolutionary energy insinuated itself into the intimacies peculiar to private
life. Making a riff on the French *mission civilisatrice*, she sees this as
a kind of Soviet 'civilizing process'. The Cultural Revolution in China
spawned collectible Mao badges to be worn on clothes, clocks,
pen holders, teapots, mugs, flower vases and ceramic figures as
well as posters to fill homes, schools and the workplace.[13] Just as
Mao consolidated power, it can be argued, the image of the stalwart
and intellectual youth, wearing a shaggy haircut and carrying a
weather-beaten umbrella, had its own mission. More to the point
at that moment, the new fervent youth of the Red Guard saw an
idealized mirror of itself here. The image can be read as a metaphor
for Mao's efforts to send his followers out into the countryside.
Inspired by the Chairman's own youthful example of travelling to
Anyuan, hundreds of thousands of Chinese youth cheerfully carried
the image with them as they fanned out across rural China, pushing
aside the normal frustrations of daily life and dedicating their young
lives to revolution.

This furious fervour was amplified in a curious, though telling,
subset of Maoist posters that duplicate Liu Chunhua's original image,
but also describe various feats and episodes that it inspired in contemporaries. The poster 'To Go on a Thousand *Li* March to Temper
a Red Heart' (1971) depicts a cadre of youthful Red Guards marching
in unison. Parades of this sort were not unusual and groups of
workers or classes of children as young as eight or nine participated
in 'toughening-up rallies; marched out into the countryside, red flags
or scarves aflutter, they stood in columns whose leaders carried similar
posters'.[14] In the poster, a group moves forwards as the light thins and
runs a reddish-pink. The sunset does not daunt them; continuing their

march, they parade forward 1,000 *li* – roughly 500 km (310 miles). The group appears as if in a joyous trance; the poster gives us a worm's-eye view, emphasizing the unified cadence of the workers' trunk-like legs, stomping in unison as they proceed through an orderly landscape. Confidently following the exhortations of a barker, who carries a megaphone, their leader proudly holds a reproduction of Liu Chunhua's painting. Forming a seemingly endless column, the youths here march in solidarity; cheerfully marching forward, their destination is as clear to them as the goal set before the youthful Mao on his way to Anyuan decades earlier. Another poster, 'Tempering Red Hearts in the Vast World', from 1970, depicts a slightly different variation on this theme. Here a boy and a girl, both city dwellers, arrive happily in a rustic village. The earnest youths radiate an intense excitement that is echoed by the peasants who gather round them. Children run forward to take their luggage and greet them. The villagers, who have bedecked their homes with red flags and banners, carry a proclamation reading: 'It is necessary for educated youth to go to the countryside to receive re-education from the poor and lower middle peasants.' In their turn, the youth have arrived carrying a poster of 'Mao Goes to Anyuan'. Showing perfect unity, peasants and city dwellers mingle with a common goal.

Swept along with the changes of an *époque*, Liu's image and other posters of Mao were never mere decoration. They folded together a sometimes-volatile mix of personal aspiration and national identity. Moreover, their treatment and use was often prescribed. Red Guards and officials alike made a regular display of placing Mao posters in public buildings. But the national press also published stories of how ordinary people busied themselves with inventive use and reuse of this and similar posters. When the *People's Daily* reported how 'an old peasant had stuck thirty-two portraits of Mao on his bedroom walls "so that he can see Chairman Mao's face as soon as he opens his eyes, whatever direction he looks in"', students at one school 'covered the walls of our classroom with pictures of Mao's face beaming his most benign smile'. They hastily tore them down, however, when 'word circulated that the peasant had really used the pictures as wallpaper because Mao's portraits were printed on the best-quality paper and were free.' It was said that the 'reporter who had written up the story had been found to be a class enemy for advocating "abuse of Chairman Mao".[15] In the Red Army, Mao posters were treated with a reverence that, in the West, might be reserved for a national flag. For example,

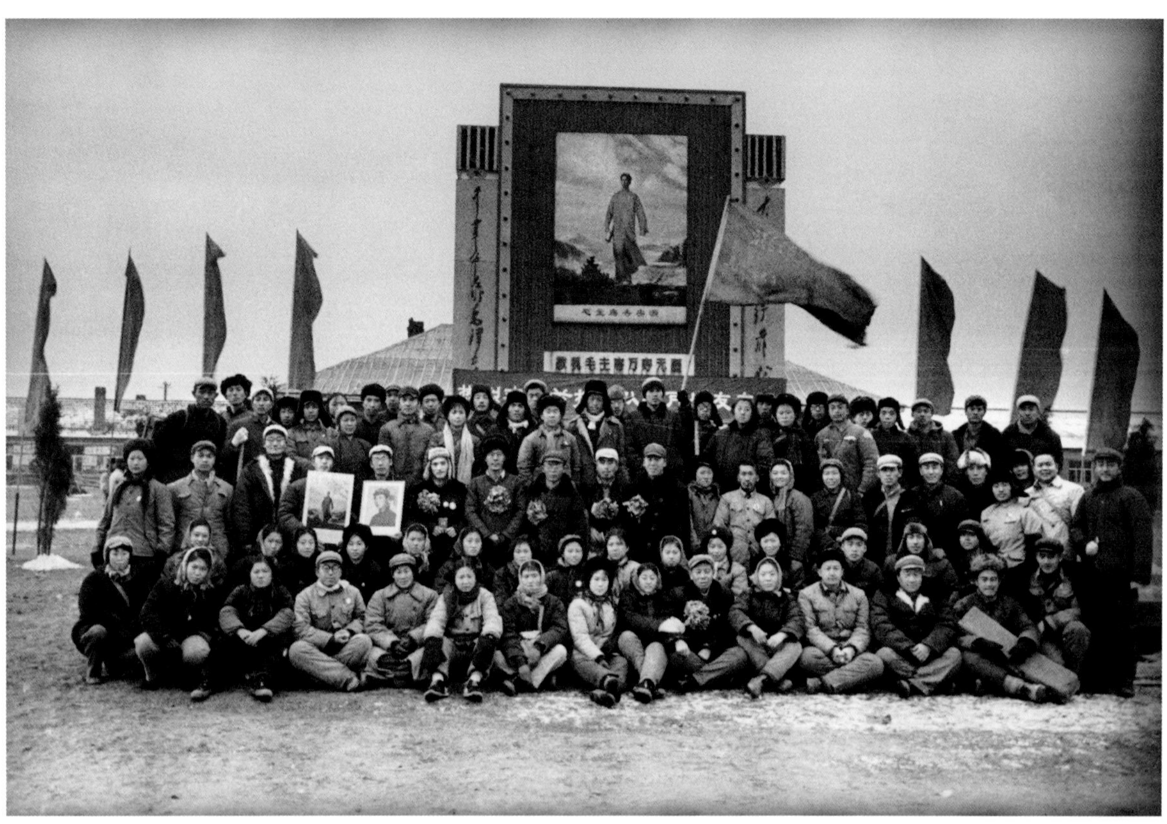

Li Zhensheng, 'Soldiers from the Liuhe May 7th Cadre School', 1969.

throughout the 1960s the Chinese and Indian governments skirmished repeatedly over conflicting claims along the Sikkim–Tibet border. One of the worst flare-ups occurred in 1967, when Chinese troops escalated the dispute by hanging a Mao poster on disputed land; the action resulted in a full-scale artillery and mortar attack on their positions by Indian troops.[16] But across the country, teenagers even saved pocket money to buy posters for their classrooms, hoping to earn their group collective honours such as 'five-distinctions class'.[17] Others, like the earnest members of the May 7th Cadre School, posed for a group portrait before a blow-up of the Anyuan poster; and as if this official poster, teetering on some kind of scaffold hidden behind the group, were not enough, one student announces his dedication by bringing along his own copy of the print. Not to be left behind, a comrade sits next to him, holding a copy of Snow's earlier Mao portrait. Little wonder that many adults and children alike saw in Mao a god-like omnipresence.

A culture in which the 'Little Red Book' was treated as a talismanic object and plaster sculptures of 'the great helmsman' became objects

Carl Mydans, customers
buying patriotic posters in
a Shanghai bookstore, 1978.

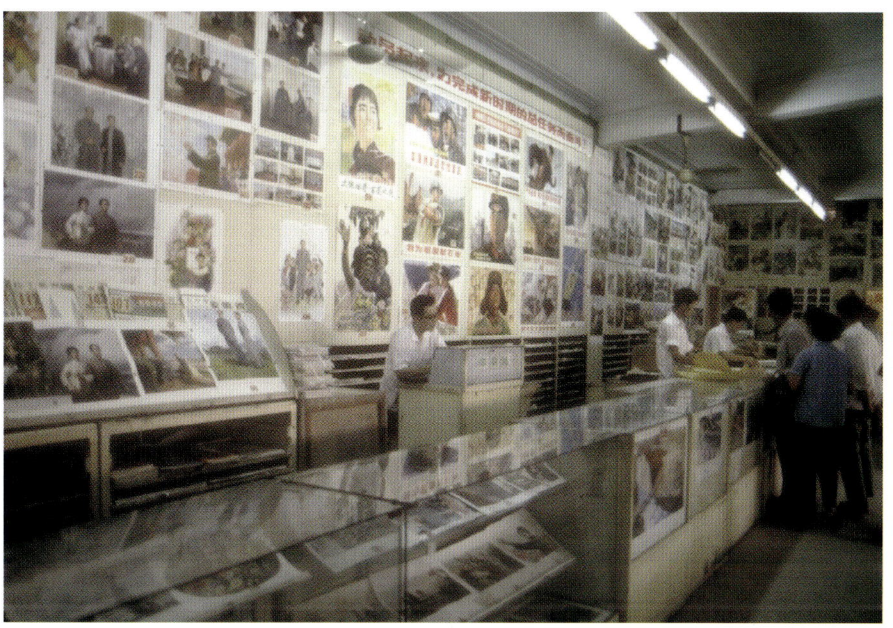

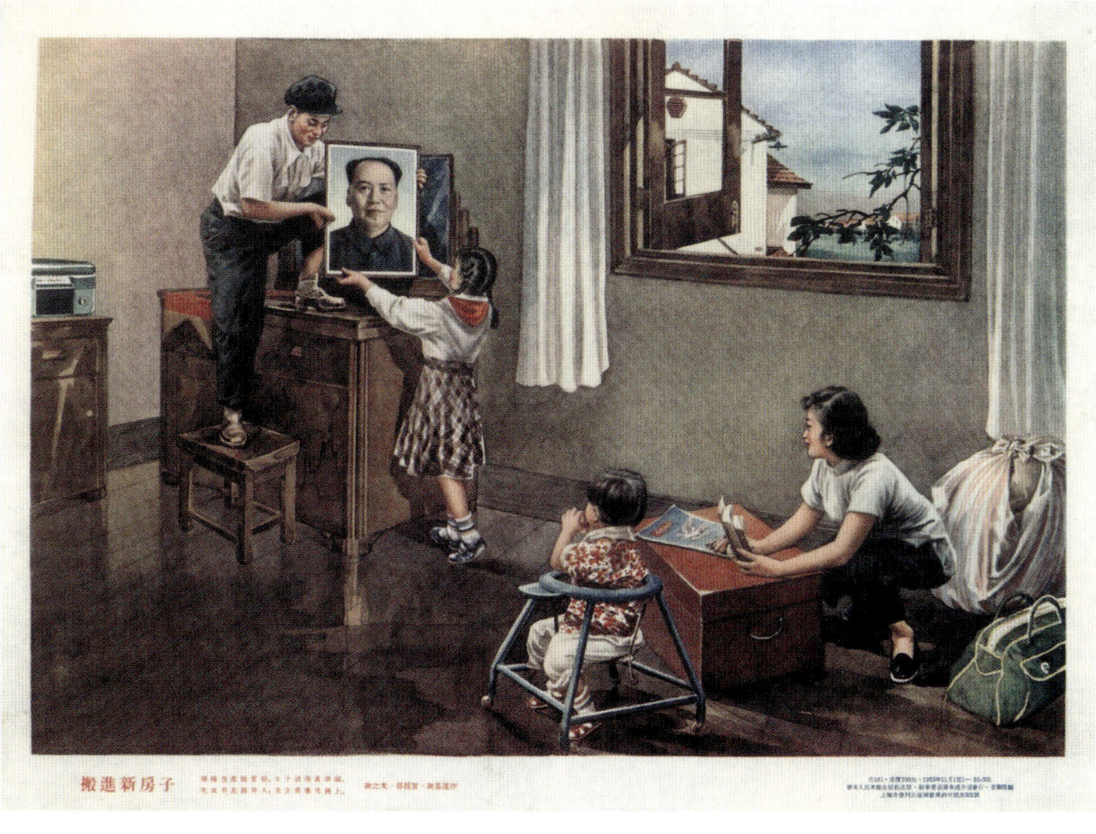

'Moving into a new house', 1953.

of reverence reminds us how much these depictions of the 'great leader' were fetishized. Enthusiasts busied themselves by making revolutionary culture common or mandatory through the widespread possession of material objects. But many poster owners felt a deep connection to these objects that stretched far beyond the rules of propaganda. On sale for the equivalent of a few pence or cents per copy, posters were dubbed 'proletarian art' and could be purchased in the state-run bookshops found in every town in this 'new' China.[18] These posters were never understood in China as fetishes. Indeed, Mao himself urged his followers to 'be self-reliant, work hard, and do away with all fetishes and superstitions and emancipate the mind'. But they were deployed with careful concern and often invested with remarkable power.

Most observers outside China did not know what to make of this enthusiasm; although contemporary with the poster craze that swept through San Francisco and London, Westerners approached the concurrent boom of poster imagery in China warily. Outside China, journalists wrote of these posters with amazement and tales of poster usage were retold with a strange foreboding. As Chinese relations with the Soviet Union soured in 1967, for instance, Red Guards harassed and even manhandled Soviet embassy dependents in Beijing. Evacuating Russian women were, by their own accounts, forced to crawl beneath giant posters of Mao.[19] In 1970 *Life* magazine sent a reporter to China, accompanying the thirteen-member US table-tennis team on its pioneering diplomatic tour. After *Life*'s seasoned reporter returned from this exercise in 'ping-pong diplomacy', he tried to make sense of what he saw: 'China is naked of signs and drab for want of color', he reported, except for posters and slogan boards. And those, he remarked, 'are everywhere. At the entrances to communes or factories' were portraits of Mao 'gazing into the middle distance; [Mao] pensively contemplated life in the cities from innumerable billboards or, caught in mid-stride, atop plinths surrounded by banks of flowering plants'.[20] Visiting China in 1972, the journalist, historian and old China hand Theodore White declared that posters had taken the place of venerated ancestors in shrines.[21]

Alone or in a crowd, Mao's admirers collected these posters in a fervent manner whose intensity seemed, to outsiders at least, to border on idolatry. As *Life*'s reporter observed in 1970, 'the trappings of Maoist ideology and the images of Mao himself are never out of sight or sound for long'. Not having a poster of Mao in a home or office was more than an embarrassment – it might be taken as a slight. Moreover, owning one required its own protocols and a thousand courtesies. The posters, for instance, had to be carefully placed. When hung on a wall, nothing could be placed higher than the portrait.[22] It was common, too, to place the poster above doors or other entryways in the home. Even the gesture used when holding the poster was carefully orchestrated. In both the school group portrait and the posters depicting groups carrying Liu Chunhua's 'Mao Goes to Anyuan', the portrait is treated gingerly and the young Maoists carry the poster in precisely the same manner: holding the bottom corners of the poster with both hands, the image is carried mincingly, in a notably awkward pose. The image always faces out, ready to be seen not by followers, but by the viewers whom they assume are watching them. As a former youth league member recalled, this was 'a culture where posters remember, talk back, and also constructed and reconstructed who I was and what was socially expected of me'.[23] In this way, the Mao poster cult diverged from the carnivalesque spirit in which contemporary posters were made and hung in places like San Francisco and London.

Here, suddenly, the contrast between poster boom and poster fetish was most evident in the hands of fine artists like Andy Warhol, who remade the poster portrait of Mao from 1964. The carefully airbrushed image now bears randomly drawn squiggles suggesting, as art historian Arthur Danto puts it, a form of 'mock impulsiveness'.[24] The original posters in China may have been as bare and bright as a cheap postcard, but they were carefully calculated to give the leader a warm, reddish glow. In Warhol's hands, they become archly vivid. Adding bright hues to Mao's skin colour and making over his lips as if they were coated with Technicolor lipstick, the silkscreen portraits that emerged from Warhol's Factory were an ambiguous parody. Just as Warhol made a point of taking on commonly fetishized icons like Campbell's Soup, he took the Chinese portraits to task. Consumerism and communism were equal grist for Warhol's Factory.

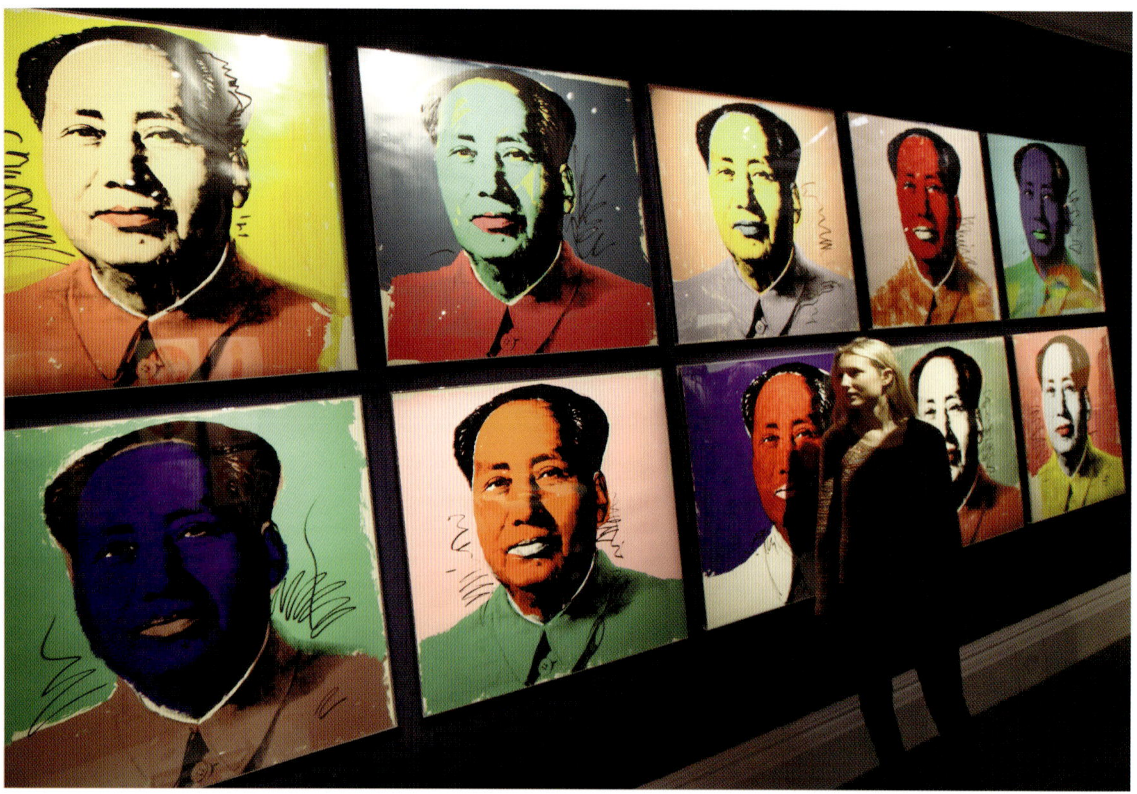

Andy Warhol, *Mao*, 1972, screenprints.

Portable Politics: Cuba's *Comandante en Jefe*, the *Guerrillero Heroico* and the Commodity Fetish

Mao may have worried about internal political threats, but in the West his only great rival, at least in the precincts of student protestors or their admirers, was the visual completion of the ubiquitous portrait of Che Guevara. And, while the Chinese embraced the notion of an entire nation rapt in the figure of a single leader, Cuban contemporaries used posters to search for a different expression of nationalism. Indeed, the face of international communism was shifting. Born two generations earlier, the heroic worker and rebellious peasants of Soviet posters were stagnating metaphors of revolution, but Cuba's fighting intellectual could claim political and economic difference from both China and the Soviets. Cuba was also a highly centralized political apparatus anxious to consolidate power. Calloused by years of indifference, the Cubans also shielded a dense and loyal community of artists filled with revolutionary fervour for a state that actively supported the arts. Both factors worked together to create a rich poster culture based on idealized notions of difference.

200

Embracing an aesthetic of difference, small Cuba is estimated to have printed about 5 million posters in 1972 alone. Dulled by the stupefying numbers of prints that circulated in China at this time, we might be deceived by this figure, but posters' ubiquity in infinitely smaller Cuba must also be considered. Indeed, Korda and Guevara were not responding to Mao's call for a global communist revolution under the Chinese banner; they were ready to introduce their own approach instead. Could Cuba find a visual idiom that would incite an enthusiasm to equal that of Mao's followers, who eagerly hoisted posters of their leader across the Yangtze river? Many Cuban artists were eager to try.

We have grown so used to the ubiquity of posters in Cuba that a photograph from 1963 of a man selling them in front of a line of students at the University of Havana is easily overlooked, and yet it suggests the beginnings of a different poster cult. His back to us, the vendor hawks watercolour portraits of both Lenin and Castro, cheaply reproduced as posters. But he has few takers. The iconic image of Cuba's guerrilla leader Guevara took time to develop and it both reflects and repudiates the traditions of post-war communism. Marx spoke strongly against the 'commodity fetish' (an ideological nicety overlooked by the street hawker here). But, while Cubans grappled with how to make good on Marxist revolutionary rhetoric, this celebration of the individual was its own kind of fetish. Marxist propaganda, however, only partially accounts for the image's popularity. Cuba became a

René Burri, 'A man selling posters of Lenin and Fidel Castro, in front of the University of Havana', 1963.

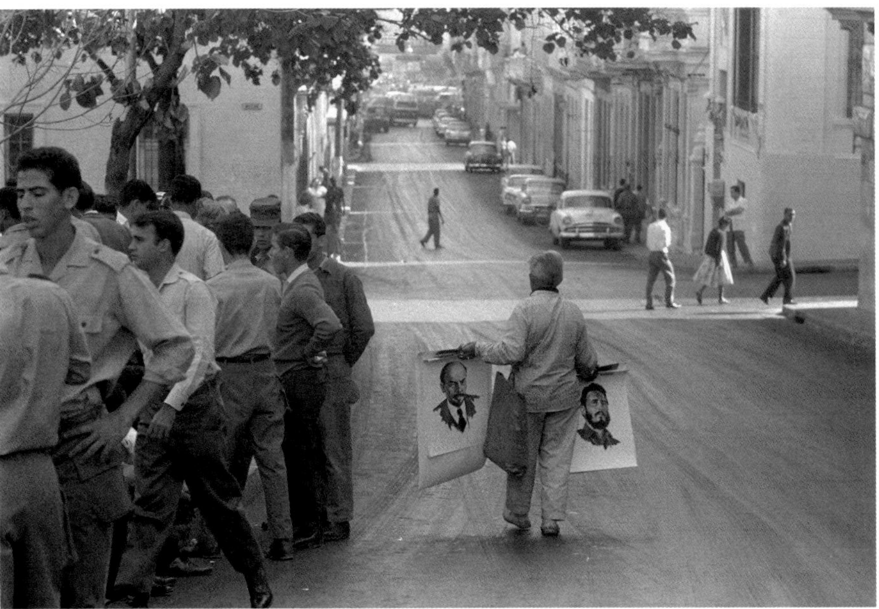

powerhouse for posters and their revival here was part of emerging global circuits of exchange. But it was not always so; as events and portents swirled around all their heads, Cuba's leaders in the early 1960s could hardly guess the power and sweep of their nation's earnest posters.

Although best known for his ubiquitous fatigues, Fidel Castro wore various guises of propaganda; not all have been a good fit. Only moderately interested in posters, Castro nevertheless made a point of encouraging poster-making; assuming power in 1959, and surrounded by adoring crowds, he could take time easily enough to sign a small hand-drawn poster thrust before him by an admirer. By this time, Cuba had a 100-year-old tradition of printing commercial lithographs. And Castro's march to power led past an already-booming visual culture. Indeed, posters advertising tourist events like Cuba's Grand Prix or the beaches and nightclubs of the 'Isle of the Tropics' thrived through the 1930s and '40s. Presenting Cuba as a travellers' paradise, airy dollops of brightly coloured posters promoted the country as a sun-favoured location whose lurid appeal included non-prohibition alcohol and hypnotically dancing women.

And yet Batista's regime took little notice of the political poster and it fell to Castro's Communists to capture imaginations with a

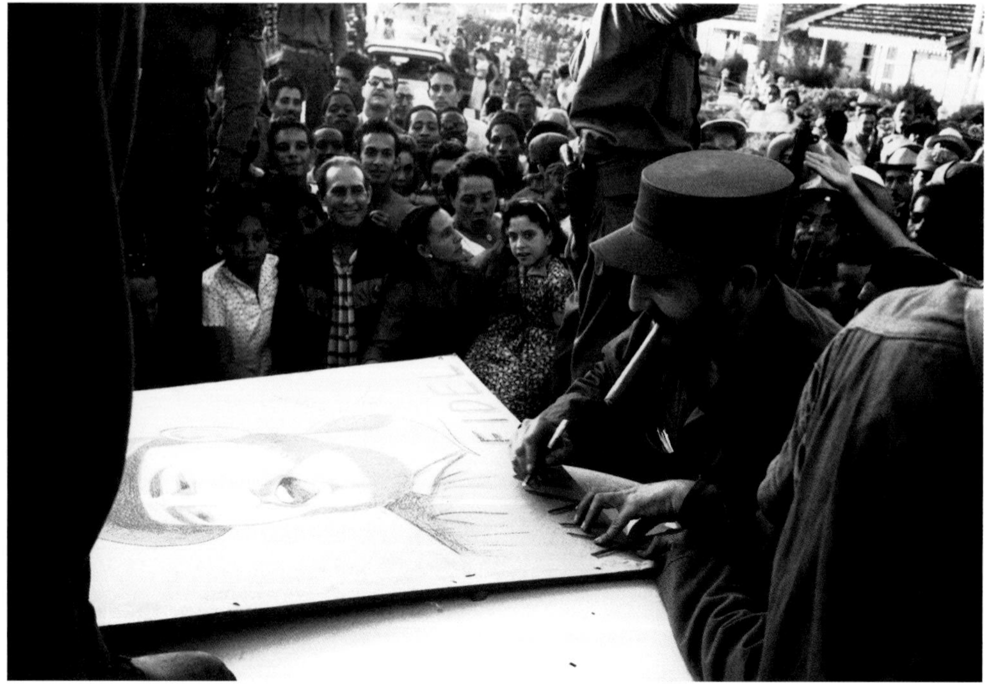

Burt Glinn, Fidel Castro signing a poster-portrait, 1959.

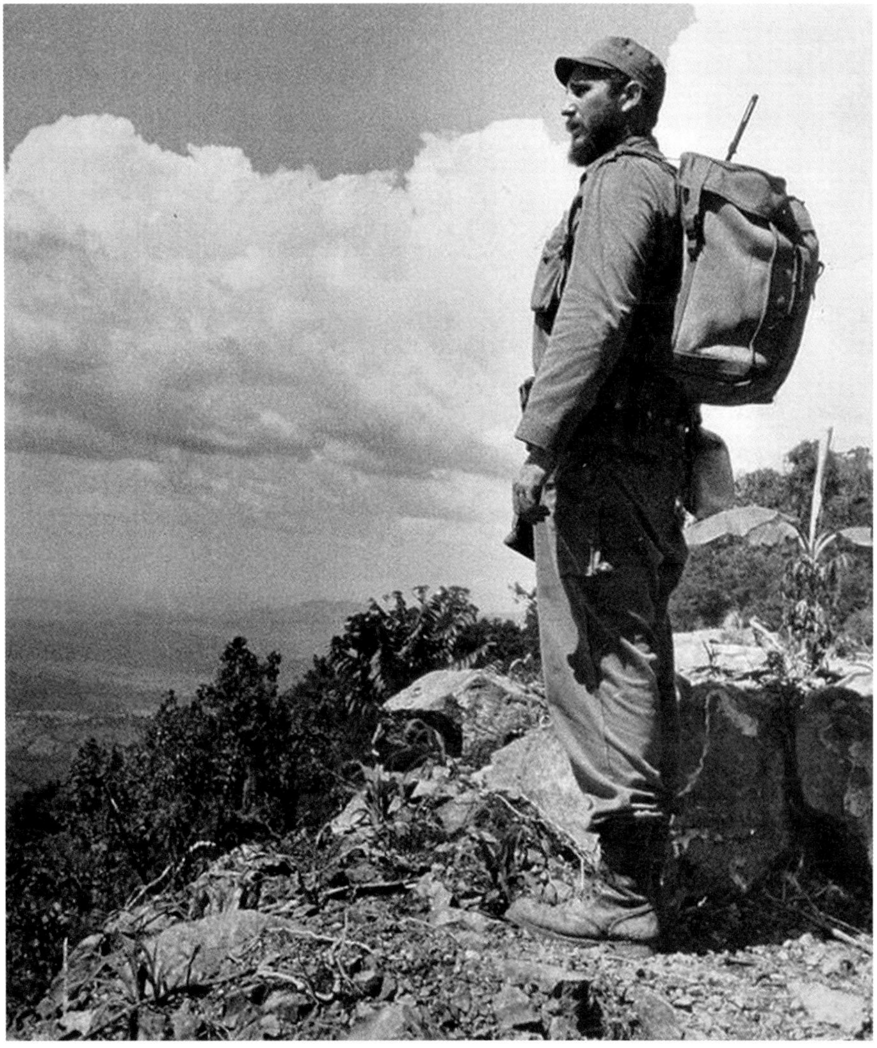

populist image. Well aware of the need for practical propaganda,
Cuba's new leaders began issuing images that could be pinned up
on humble sugar shacks as well as on the frozen custard facades
of Havana's most elegant buildings. Castro's strategists almost
inadvertently fell on the earliest of these images. 'Comandante en
Jefe' ('Commander-in-Chief') shows Castro standing above the Sierra
Maestra, the wild region of deep river valleys and steep mountains
that proved an ideal locale for launching his original guerrilla-led
rebellion. The imagery loosely recalls Liu Chunhua's depiction of Mao,
pausing along his mountainous path to Anyuan. But the differences
between the two images are profound. Mao is depicted in a painting,
while Castro has been photographed. Dreamlike and timeless, Liu's

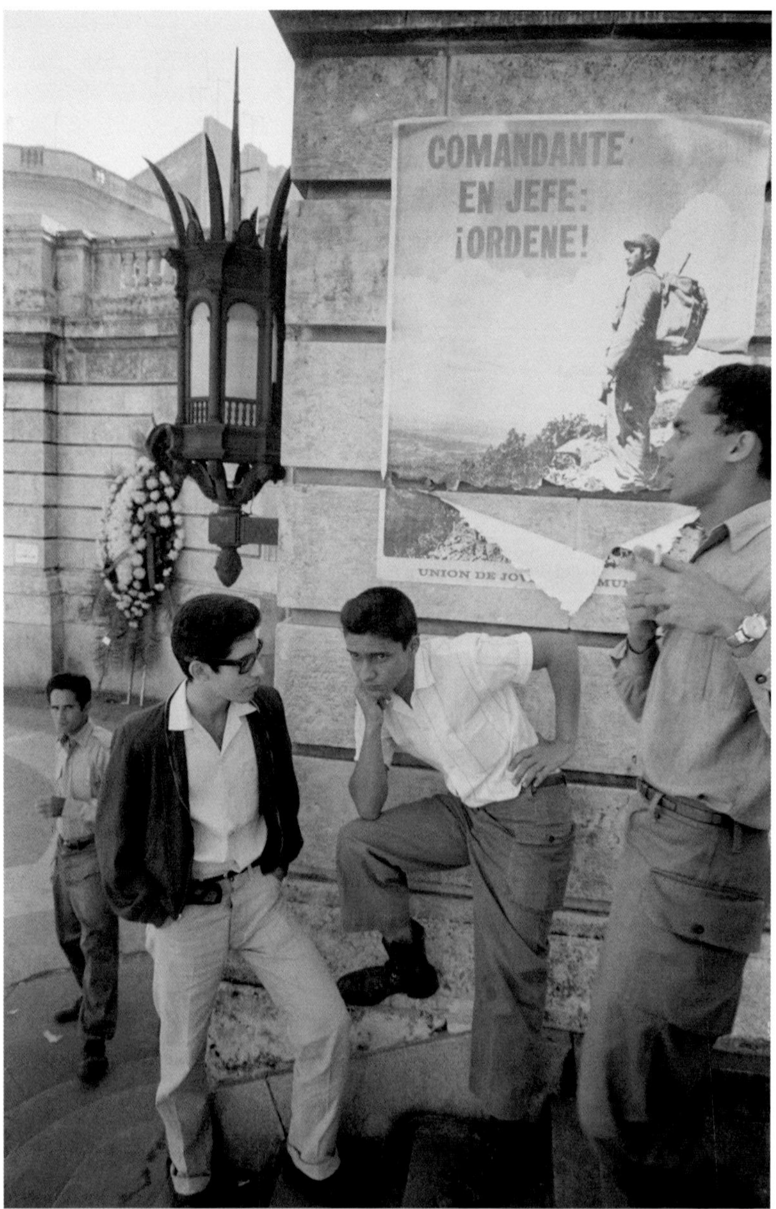

portrait almost makes Mao appear an effete philosopher who inadvertently wandered up the bare, bleak mountainside. Castro's expansive
stance, on the other hand, seems to prove that the road to a Marxist
Cuba was less cerebral, paved by soldiers who plugged doggedly
across muddy fields, over foot-worn paths and across the brambly
peaks of Cuba's mountains. Making it all seem almost too real, Castro
is dressed in army fatigues and carries a large backpack; he looks
every inch a guerrilla leader. The photograph was taken in 1962 by

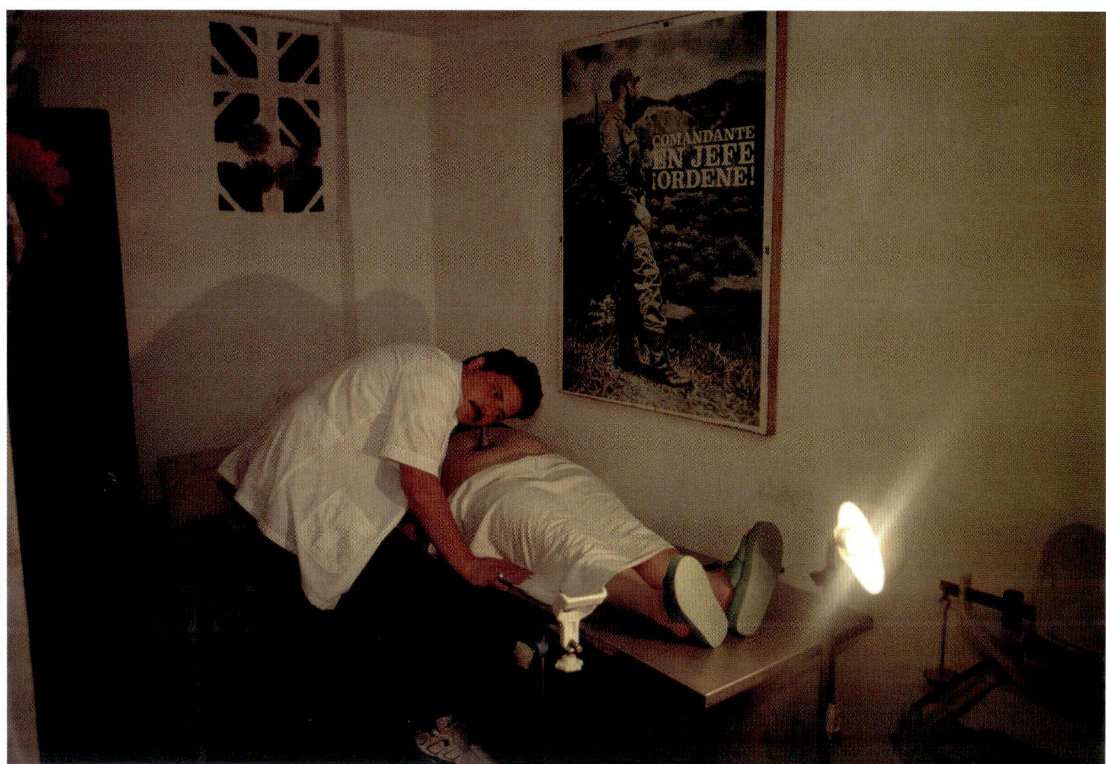

David Alan Harvey, a doctor examines a patient below a portrait of Castro, 1998.

his favourite photographer, Korda. With poise and aplomb, Korda accompanied Castro when he launched a very public trip to revisit some of the spots familiar from his decisive campaign several years earlier. Learning that Korda had just returned from the Sierra Maestra, the coordinator of the Union de Jovenes Comunistas (Communist Youth), Juan Ayús García, snatched up the image with deep satisfaction. García and Korda had worked together earlier as advertising specialists in the flush days of Batista's regime. In less than 24 hours, García dashed out the heroic image, investing it with revolutionary brio. Intended to give the country a rallying point in the tense days of the missile crisis, the poster bristled with solidarity, its bright red slogan in the upper-left corner of the photograph, all in capitals, sharply saluting: 'Commander-in-Chief: Give us your orders!' Here was a firmly presented image of revolution that was equally at home on the University of Havana campus and in a doctor's rural examination room. There are kindlier and even more restorative images of Castro; this poster, however, marked a turning point in his rule, appearing just as he shifted from self-styled guerrilla leader towards becoming a plausible head of state capable of standing up to foreign powers like the US.[25] But the image itself was for internal consumption; depending upon one's ability to accept Castro's rule, it defined for Cubans a particular moment in the revolution. But it lacked the brio of the Che Guevara posters that would blossom not simply across Cuba, but also the globe, several years later.

Even when first scaling the Sierra Maestra, Castro must have had moments when he puzzled over how to hold his small but variegated country together. Where some commentators saw its fate in flux, Castro conceived the contours of a Marxist country that emphasized cultural diversity, not uniformity, as a kind of spiritual accumulation. Almost as puzzling were contemporaries' attempts firmly and coherently to find an immediate visual equivalent to this vision. Very different from China, with its millennia-long history and strong Han identity, Cuba had been settled by waves of indigenous peoples, then Spaniards and the French, Africans and Chinese; many had been ripped from their original homelands by force, politics or hunger. Cuba's unique cultural and racial heritage was often suppressed, even when José Martí and Fernando Ortiz fought to create a 'nation for all'.[26] But, after the revolution, a multiplicity of styles – or what art critic Gerardo Mosquera calls Cuba's 'cultural and artistic pluralism' – emerged.[27] And a liability changed to an advantage. To many left-leaning intellectuals in western Europe and America, this approach seemed respectful of artists, as well as pragmatic. As Susan Sontag put it: 'What is impressive, and heartening, is the Cuban solution; not to come to any particular solution, not to put great pressure on the artist.'[28] Papering posters all over the country, Cuba's revolutionaries embraced multiplicity and individuality as an official style but also a new type of poster.

The sharp immediacy of Castro's 'Comandante en Jefe' of 1963 differed from the typical communist portrait poster. By the late 1920s, of course, the Soviet establishment turned its back on the squiggles and squares of Revolutionary avant-garde design, leaving behind its furious abstractions and settling for more conventional poster depictions of Lenin, Stalin and other leaders. The high priests of political culture in China after the Revolution also eschewed experimentation; the hunger and shame of a century's sufferings had been half forgotten by the new generation, who also opted for seemingly fresh and new realist painting styles. But the Cubans found inspiration elsewhere. Above all, their glance fell on cinema pictures.

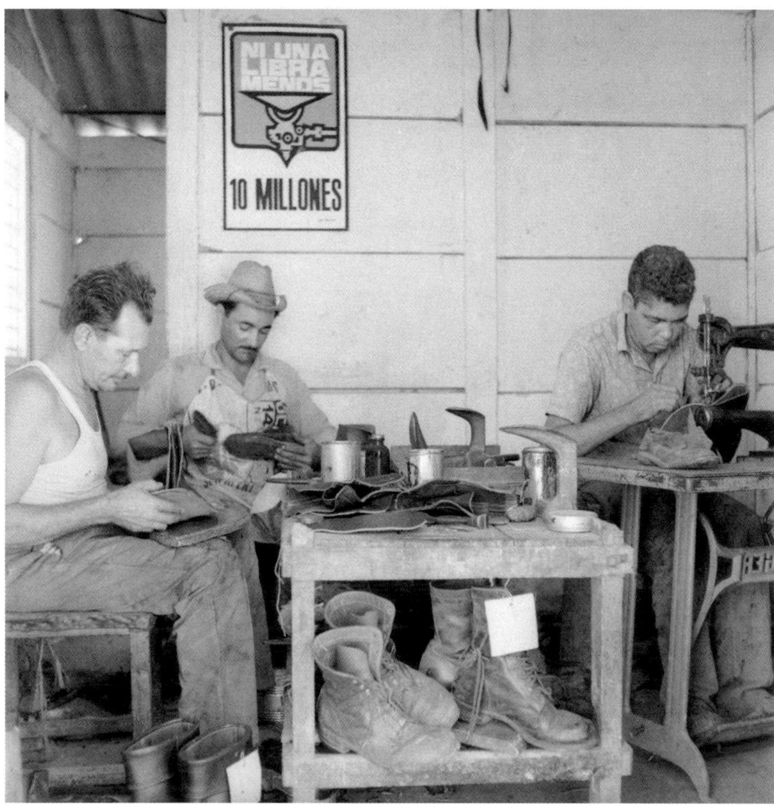

A fledgling film industry had existed under Batista and its flavour penetrated the public's consciousness in the 1940s and 1950s; Cuba was known for a spirit of luminous gaiety in its music, and some of this ran through early Cuban cinema. In the early 1960s, after the Revolution, the film industry began to get more serious. The ICAIC (Cuban Institute of Cinematic Art and Industry, more commonly known in English as the Cuban Film Institute) was organized just three months after Castro came to power. From production to distribution, Cuban film-making had only recently been nationalized and sought to evoke the rich weightiness of the political moment, depicting a corrupt past and powerful future. Subsidized by the government, and offering virtually free admission to the cinema, Cuba's film industry began to flourish.

Cubans hoped to create a body of films worthy of their revolution. And, lest their work feel unreal, it was vigorously promoted abroad. In so doing, they broadened their vision and an industry of film posters ground into action. It might seem natural that such posters would have adopted the vocabulary of Pop art, psychedelia, Op art, minimalism,

Abstract Expressionism, conceptualism, Cubist collage, Constructivist montage and Surrealism, but Cuban poster artists appeared then to be radically eclectic in their sources; rather than explicitly expressing a plot or profiling stars, they aimed to explore solemn truths and heady revelations only hinted at in the films that they promoted. Moreover, the Cubans drank deeply from the Poles' conceptual poster binge. As Alfredo Rostgaard, a poster designer who served the Cuban government as an artistic adviser for many years, put it:

> The Polish artists showed that we could make completely political posters for 1 May or the anniversary of the October Revolution, with poetry, with beauty, with an indirect language.[29]

The Cubans took to the Polish model with relish; not only was there room for intellectual expansiveness, but they also made space for a kind of spirited eclecticism expressing the *mestizaje* of Cuban culture, drawing from the country's indigenous as well as Afro-Cuban, Euro-Cuban and Asian-Cuban heritage.[30] Cuba's poster makers felt a peculiar duty within the new Cuban society: using 'traditional' forms of African and Latin American sculpture such as masks and carved reliefs, they mixed and matched their sources with avant-garde European aesthetics, echoing the noisy and sometimes confused communist cause touted by Castro. They took an expansive and generous view of the Revolution, one that quietly ignored its worst mistakes and softened the hard ideological contours that drove so many to leave the island during these years.

Tailored and trimmed of its colonial associations, in the hands of artists like René Portocarrero the Cuban poster revisited older pictorial traditions. In the 1940s the Mexican Communist Party had attempted a different approach, but this was quite unusual.

Stirring up tradition and stealing from the Polish rulebook might seem a dangerous thing for the Cubans to do. Certainly, abandoning the official Marxist hierarchies of art and style advocated by the Soviet Union, one of Castro's strongest supporters, was unusual. Seeing the poster format as a sort of spiritual vindication, the Cubans quickly latched onto the Polish School of posters as a model. But this was part of a larger policy based on energy and aesthetic verve.[31] The Cuban government believed that art is recognizable in embryo, or at least to those in the know, and it was not worth arguing over its aesthetic pedigree. As Castro would later put it: 'Our enemies are capitalists and imperialists not abstract art.'[32] Posters helped give shape and form to embryonic ideas of Cuba as a progressive and a variegated, though still Marxist, state. Dramatizing the less than glamorous and adopting subjects ranging from occupational health, glass recycling or the proclaimed goal of producing 10 million tons of sugar, these posters, and their vanguard look, spread across the country.

But Cuban posters soon became something more, rapidly transmuting into an international phenomenon. When Susan Sontag wrote about them in 1971 they were at the height of their influence and fast becoming a fashionable accessory for leftist interiors. In her view, Westerners fetishized Cuban posters, collecting them as a substitute for the real experience of revolutionary ardour. But Sontag is less clear about the Cubans themselves, who today at least seem complicit in this publicity; if their posters were well known, the government worked to make them so. Unlike the Chinese, for whom Western poster audiences were a hasty afterthought, the Cubans boldly chose to internationalize their poster efforts with the founding in 1966 of OSPAAAL, a Cuban organization of solidarity with the people of Asia, Africa and Latin America. With its creation, Cuban posters infinitely expanded their reach. Under the direction of Alfredo Rostgaard, OSPAAAL was meant to fill the rather mysterious void created by the political break between China and the Soviet Union. They would not propagandize for either faction, but also refused to leave the Marxist poster tradition unmoored. OSPAAAL artists advocated for broad themes of liberation and peace, as well as establishing Cuban 'solidarity' with revolutionaries worldwide. With Rostgaard at the helm, they moved their campaign beyond the smaller and somewhat dirtier here and now of actual revolution, leaping ahead of themselves in order to make key propaganda points. Acting as if the socialist realists of China and Russia sapped creativity one from the other, Cuban artists challenged the aesthetic focus of the revolutionary poster.

But the rush of remarkable images that appeared in the months after Che Guevara's demise in October 1967 operated both inside and outside the Cuban system. As news of Che's death in a remote Andes hamlet spread, a myth was launched – some would say catapulted – into world view. José Gómez Fresquet, a renowned

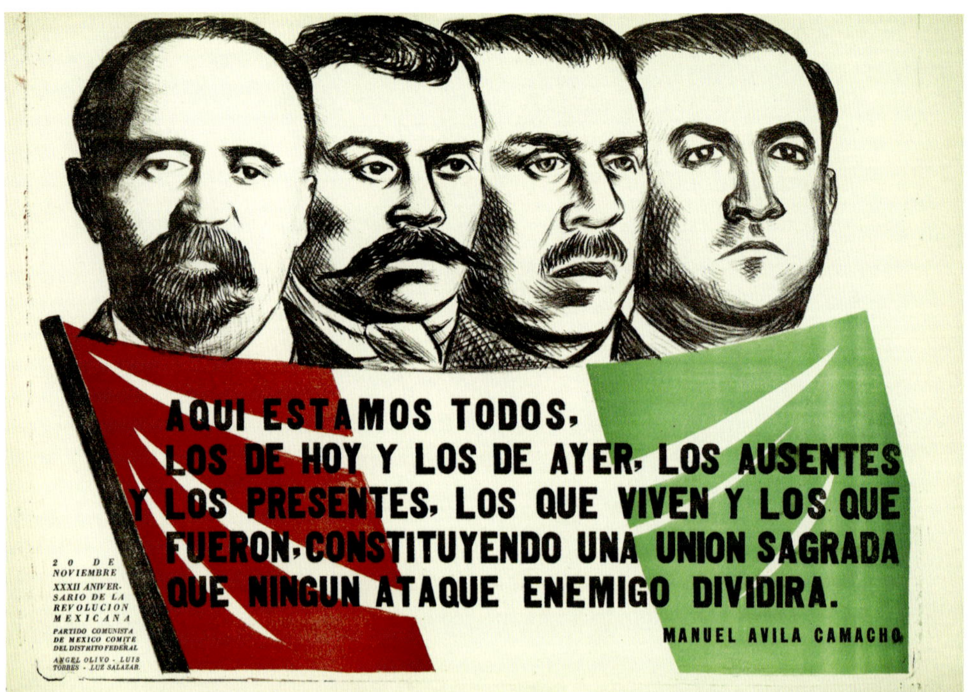

Taller de Gráfica Popular, 'We are Here Together', 1942.

Cuban poster maker and graphic artist, recalls how, on hearing the news of Guevara's death, he immediately worked all night producing the poster to be used at the rally honouring him the next day. However, it took, at most, several months after the news reached Europe for the Irish designer Jim Fitzpatrick to be given the image and make his own poster (arguably the best-known version today), enveloping the leader in a red background. A year later, Cieślewicz erased the revolutionary's eyes and nose while reducing the image to a series of flat, colourful abstract signs.

Certainly in Cuba, as well as in Europe and America, Che's personality – that is, his location and characterization as an individual – began to disappear. By 1968 OSPAAAL brought its now considerable stature to bear and became involved with its own brand of mythic solidarity. When 8 October 1968, the first anniversary of Guevara's death, was declared the Day of the Heroic Guerrilla in Cuba, the group commissioned a poster from designer Elena Serrano. Centring Guevara's portrait in Bolivia, the heart of South America and also where Guevara died, the image dazzles with radiating frames that echo and refract the original picture, causing it to spread out across the whole continent and beyond. Meant as a metaphor for revolutionary zeitgeist, and therefore a play of human wit, the image does

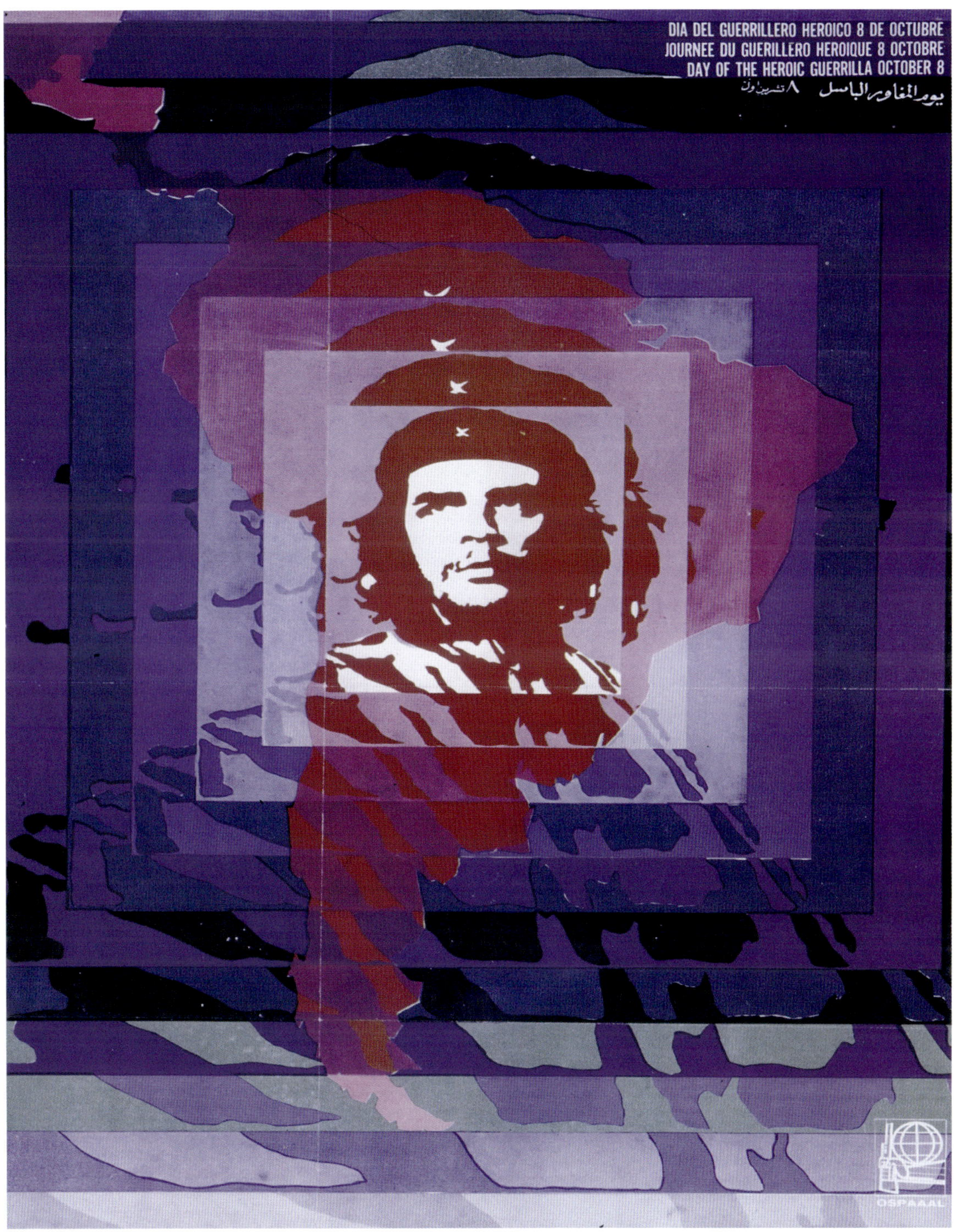

Elena Serrano, 'Day of the Heroic Guerrilla', 1968.

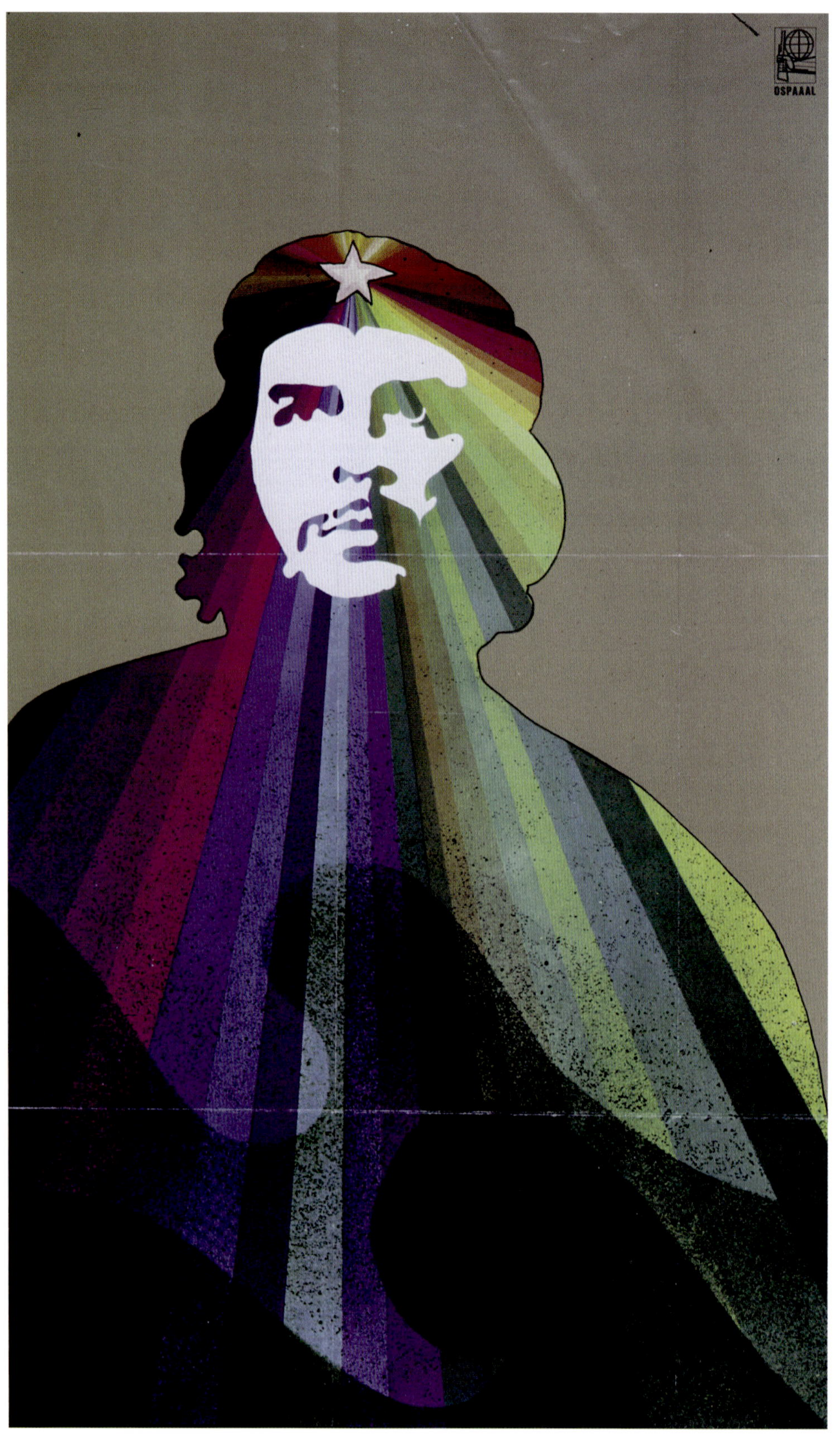

Alfredo Rostgaard, 'Che', 1967.

something more substantial than the simpler red-and-black posters already circulating in fashionable circles in western Europe and America. Che is also more than a *comandante en jefe*. Intended as a beacon to decolonizing nations in Africa, Asia and Latin America, like other OSPAAAL posters Serrano tries to balance free-thinking and hipness. But her image fundamentally changes Che's very being; his refracted image is the objectification of an idea, an emanation from a much more directed and deliberate philosophy.

Produced for display both within and outside Cuba, and echoing their internationalist stance, OSPAAAL's posters were widely distributed through the group's *Tricontinental* magazine, which reached audiences far beyond its intended readership in Africa, Asia and Latin America. Tens of thousands of copies were printed, and OSPAAAL's message was delivered in French, Spanish, English and Arabic. This spirit infuses Rostgaard's own Che poster for OSPAAAL. More mystical than the one by Serrano, the hero's face is frozen into a white mask and a prismatic rainbow shines from the star on his head, shifting the image from the

A revolving series of poster portraits of Che Guevara was installed at the 1970 'Third World' exhibition in Havana.

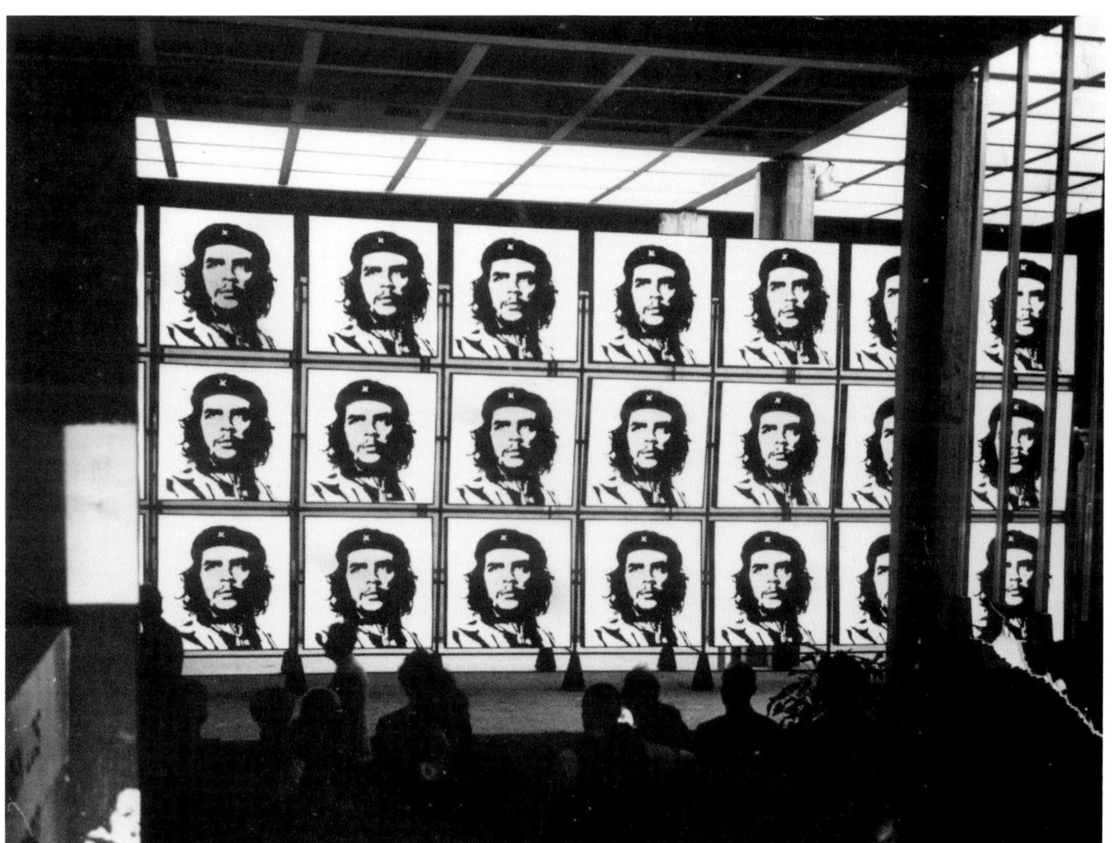

political realm to the spiritual. It aspires less to hipness than to spiritual transcendence.

In Cuba, the Che image was mounted in rotating displays as repeated series, presented in special poster stands which were periodically changed, reproduced in books as well as in magazines and posted on a monumental scale on billboards, all as if to prove that no place could have too many pictures of the *Guerillica Heroica*. But it was through the cheap and ubiquitous silkscreened poster that most people encountered the image. In the island nation itself, many ended up in union halls, community centres, schools and private residences; and others were simply posted on street walls. Each carried its own small cargo of emotions.

Abroad, the Che poster functioned differently from its Maoist or Soviet bloc counterparts. It was quite unlike the communist leaders usually depicted in official poster portraits, their chests weighed down with colourful tags and medals and their artistic treatment claiming a bland immunity to hipness. In Korda's original image, the guerrilla leader wears no ornament beyond the small red star emblazoned on the crest of his beret. On the other hand, the posters of Cuba's hero were never carefully positioned and treated gingerly like the poster portraits of Mao in China. At home and abroad, posters of Guevara mixed with the trivial, everyday ephemera of life. Noting the ubiquity of Che posters by 1970, one left-leaning journalist remarked: 'Che is dead, but his spirit lives. His name and his portrait appear on placards carried by demonstrators in scores of countries.' But he also noted, more ominously, that Guevara 'has become a fetish, a cult in New York and San Francisco, in Algeria, Tanzania, Nigeria, and Guinea.'[33] Of course, the notion of poster as fetish can be linked to a much longer tradition still. But Guevara's reinvention into a leftist fetish was both unexpected and understandable. He put a face to an entire sensibility, and the poster format was constitutionally fitted for its success. For his part, Alberto Korda was flummoxed by the international attention. Certainly nothing like this had happened to his earlier image of Castro in the Sierra Maestra. Of the Che image he would later say: 'I am not averse to its reproduction by those who wish to propagate his memory and the cause of social justice throughout the world.'[34] After a vodka company used his wandering photograph of Guevara for its advertising, however, Korda filed suit and won an out-of-court settlement. But the leader who called on Marxists to reject capitalism's fetishes has himself continued to be fetishized.

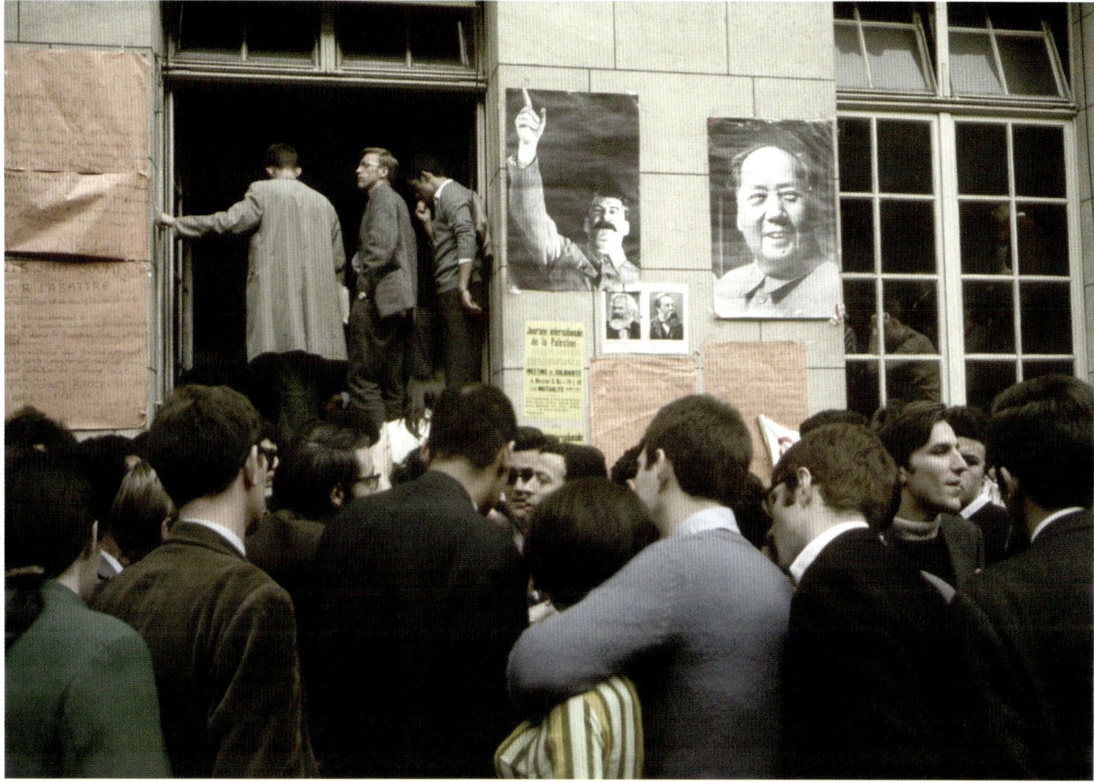

Jonathan Blair, students protesting in the Latin Quarter, Paris, 1968.

The Anti-poster and 1968

There is a mistaken idea that portrait posters can be effective only in authoritarian or totalitarian regimes. Che Guevara and Mao aside, the transformation of the poster in the 1960s was most profound in France, where the genre first flowered. Put most simply, making a poster in 1968 was very different from making one in 1868. Posters of leaders, radical or conservative, have been fetishized at least since the days of Mussolini and Hitler, but for the first time a variant of the traditional poster began to emerge. This was so different, it can best be termed the 'anti-poster'. Like the Italian 'anti-design' movement of the late 1960s, French leftists used a conventional design form – the poster – to critique society. Posters of Mao and Che, as well as Marx and Stalin, graced the walls of student precincts in Paris in 1968. But these protestors also developed a new type of poster, one that stood as the opposite of virtually everything that the poster had been and would become. Superbly convinced of its own rectitude, the French anti-poster emerged as an appraisal not only of the poster boom of the 1960s, but also of the poster fetish.

215

By May 1968, things were neither simple nor straightforward.
As part of the anti-Gaullist May revolution of 1968, a mixed group
of students and a cadre of left-leaning intellectuals occupied several
schools and universities. They were influenced by the Situationists,
the loosely framed group who critiqued capitalism and the media in
the post-war period. But, in the balmy first days of spring 1968, these
radicals faced a curious poster legacy. Posters occupied a shadowy
place in French public life. Of course, Nazi propaganda had been
widely posted during the war. Afterwards, the rapid acceptance of
magazines, radio and television, which ran through France in torrential
secession, eclipsed the advertising poster in the post-war years. Except
for limited electoral campaigns in the 1950s, posters lived in the French
imagination as a murky backwater of communications, a sideshow to
strikes and riots and general political uncertainty.[35] Posters still filled
designated advertising spaces on French streets and subways, and
they continued to inhabit alleyways and overlooked fences. However,
they were so obscured by flashier forms of mass media that, as it
seemed to the radical young poster makers in 1968, the older form
simply got lost in the melee.[36]

All this surmising, however, does not explain why the poster
burst back into view in Paris that May of 1968. Posters would become
a key factor in arguments for social and economic reform. Posters
were cheap, sidestepped conventional channels of communication
and could be effective in densely populated settings. Moreover,
what Paris's youthful radicals lacked in money they made up for in
temperament or, perhaps, nerve. As Paris's schools and universities
became hubs of radical activities, a number of groups put up posters
around the city, but especially in the Left Bank. The best-known art
schools, the Ecole des Beaux-Arts and Ecole des Arts Décoratifs, were
overrun and quickly occupied; once established there, protestors
congealed into activist art *ateliers* (workshops). The most prolific of
these, the self-styled Atelier Populaire, set up shop in the venerable
Beaux-Arts, producing somewhere between 350 and 500 poster
designs and 120,000 to 150,000 total posters over the course of two
months.[37] Founded on 8 May 1968, this group of former graduates,
current students and local artists dominated the school's quarters,
making it into a hub of radical activity. Inside its hallowed halls,
protestors transformed its staid decor into a revolutionary hub;
even its most workaday halls and rooms were filled with fresh

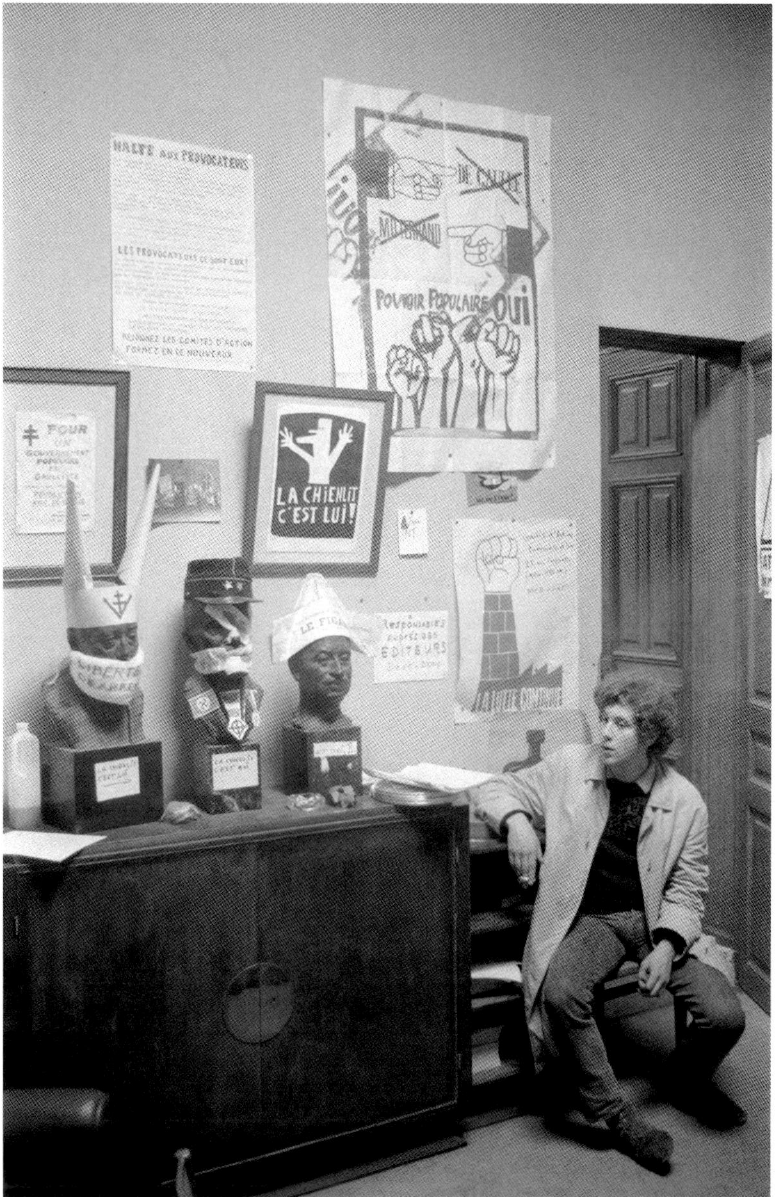

posters, its most venerable busts and bronzes consecrated with
childish paper hats and picture frames stuffed with newly made
posters. But they were not content to leave it at this. Like hothouse
flowers suddenly allowed to bloom outside, in student quarters and
factories on strike, these posters flourished across the country. But
these were not ordinary posters; claiming them as 'weapons in the
service of the struggle', their makers claimed that they were 'an
inseparable part' of their cause.[38]

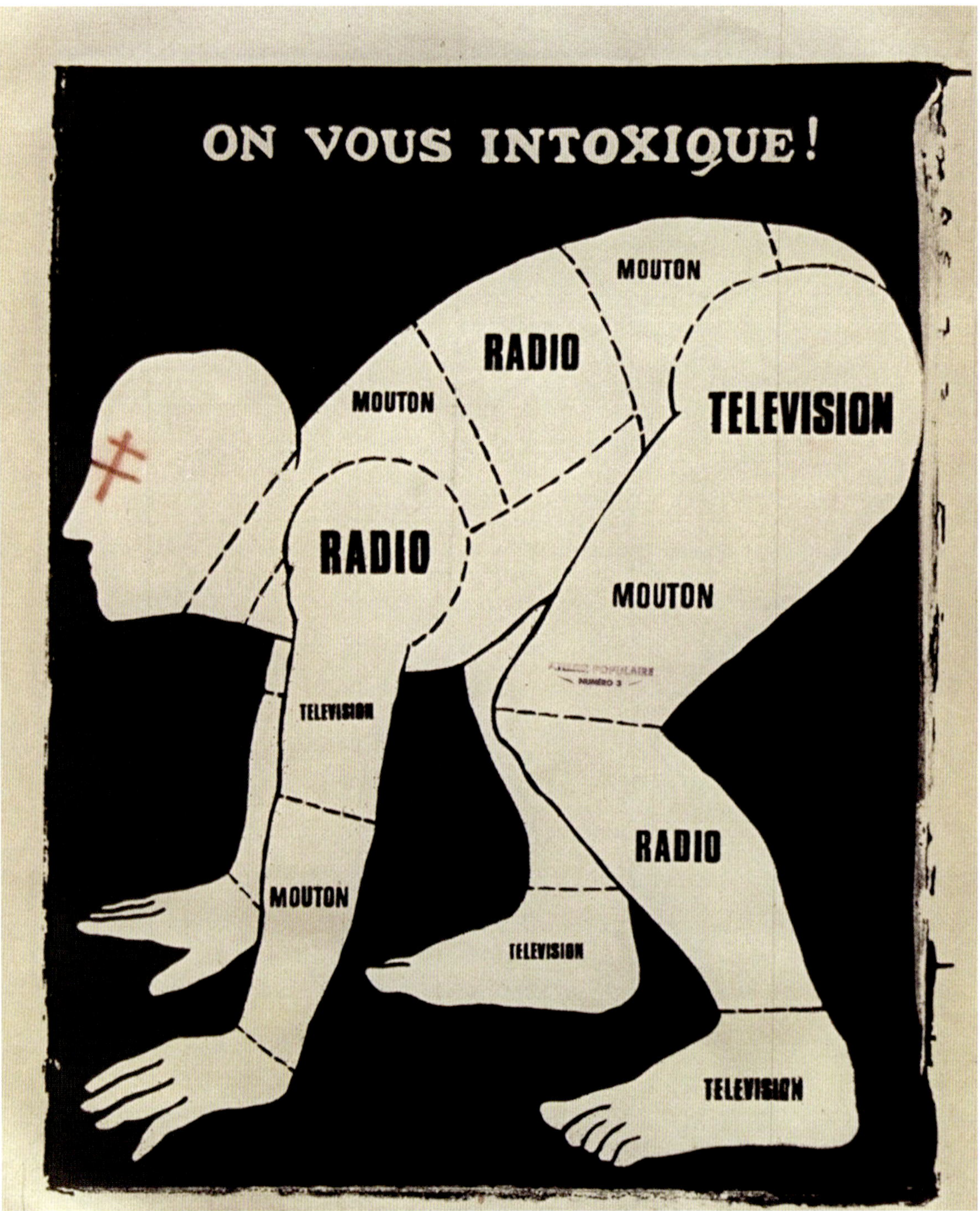

Atelier Populaire, 'On vous intoxique!', 1968.

These committed leftists both loved and hated posters with a ferocity that may seem perplexing today; the term 'anti-poster' encompasses some of this rich and sometimes confusing heresy, but it still fails to do full justice to the way in which they nourished a faith in the poster itself. Contrarian by nature, the anti-poster takes the form of the conventional poster, but its context and treatment are diametrically opposed to the happy pretences of mainstream poster traditions. Atelier Populaire posters in France echo in some ways the contemporary Italian anti-design movement and may be loosely aligned with anarchic design groups like Archigram and Superstudio in Florence. These claimed radical doctrines by attacking the sacred cows of art, design and architecture, but their production focused on writing, not making. In France, the political situation was more diffuse, but the critique was also more pointed. For at least the previous decade a group of radical thinkers affiliated themselves with Situationism, and one of its principal targets was the mainstream media. Drawing from the writings of Guy Debord and Raoul Vaneigem, as well as influential works published in the journal *Situationist International*, the group critiqued the banalities of mass-market newspapers, television's mesmerizing screen, the buzz on radio airwaves and the droning cinema. These newer media so twisted and turned mass communications, they argued, that the public was rendered indefinitely passive and distracted. They might stake out these positions, positing that free information was blindfolded – invisible, unjudged and mostly unarticulated – and that the average citizen was poisoned into a sheep-like state of docility; intentionally or not, it was increasingly difficult to tell the difference between news and ads. Long looked upon by advertisers as some kind of leftover from an earlier age, these French radicals used posters to plunge into a larger dialogue.

From Mao to Castro, leaders outside the West often used the poster to evoke a vision of strict ideological purity or a dream of a better society; but in 1968 the posters produced by the French Left were markedly different. Their message flashed over France, filling streets and buildings around schools and universities or embellishing the gates to factories where workers were on strike; radical students, sympathizers and workers were pushed and cajoled by messages that were both seemingly casual and also highly cerebral. Some of the most philosophical were devised by a loose-knit group of artists and activists calling themselves the Figuration Narrative ('Narrative

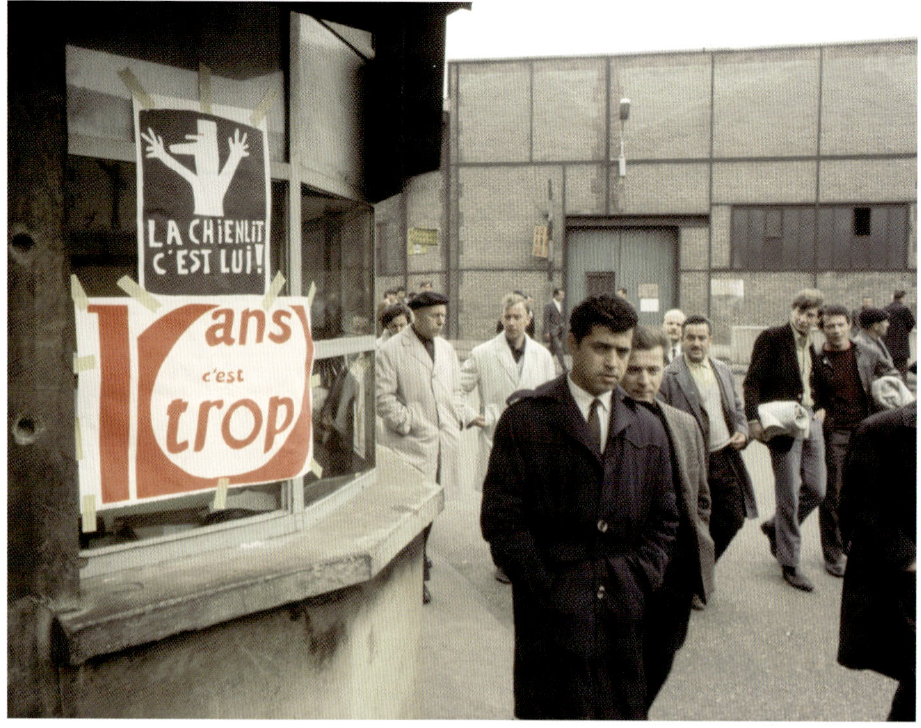

Figuration').[39] Their most radical arm, the Jeune Peinture ('Young Painters') group, commandeered the school's print shop. Many were recent graduates from Paris's art schools; joining together, they committed to making politically themed work and exhibited together leaving individual works unsigned. Ideologically committed and trying to live outside the clutter of everyday life, as one member recalls: 'We had worked in groups and had thought up treatises and questions, and discussed political subjects together.'[40] Reincarnated as a poster-making protest movement in May 1968, their ranks swelled and the fundamental nature of their work changed.

There is no doubt that in the few short months during which they operated in Paris, the Atelier Populaire and its leftist comrades developed a barebones style, both shabby and unpromising for a poster form, but quite right for the new anti-poster. Although made by well-trained artists, the anti-poster aspired to a kind of 'non style', and attributes like skill and practice were devalued in exchange for emotion and commitment. Unwinding at least 50 years of processes intended to sharpen photographic imagery, carefully planned letter spacing and well-honed standardized type, these anti-posters aspired to a rough-and-ready functionality that harked back to the urgent political handbills of the previous century. These posters combined a fervent call for action with a visceral, raw crudity. Other protest posters of the period, for example the Art Workers' Coalition's 'And Babies?', which memorializes the My Lai massacre, deploy a similar technique. Using a simple typewriter script magnified to the point that the rough edges of letters almost break apart, this iconic poster simply enlarges a photograph taken at the scene, letting the image's painful subject speak for itself.

However, the occupiers at the Ecole des Beaux-Arts pushed this aesthetic further. They first turned to the art school's old-fashioned lithographic presses, but these could not meet the demands of the twentieth century's intensely mediated world. As one maker remembered: 'We couldn't produce enough . . . People said, "Wonderful! We need to make more!" And we said: "Make more? That's impossible."'[41] By necessity, they turned to silkscreening, a technique well known to American advertisers but less familiar in France. Although this was 'a new idea', they were able to make large runs, as many as '2,000 posters in one night, sometimes more'. Not only could you 'find them everywhere in France', but they even 'went out quick, quick, quick'. In spite

Art Workers' Coalition, 'Q. And babies? A. And babies.', 1970.

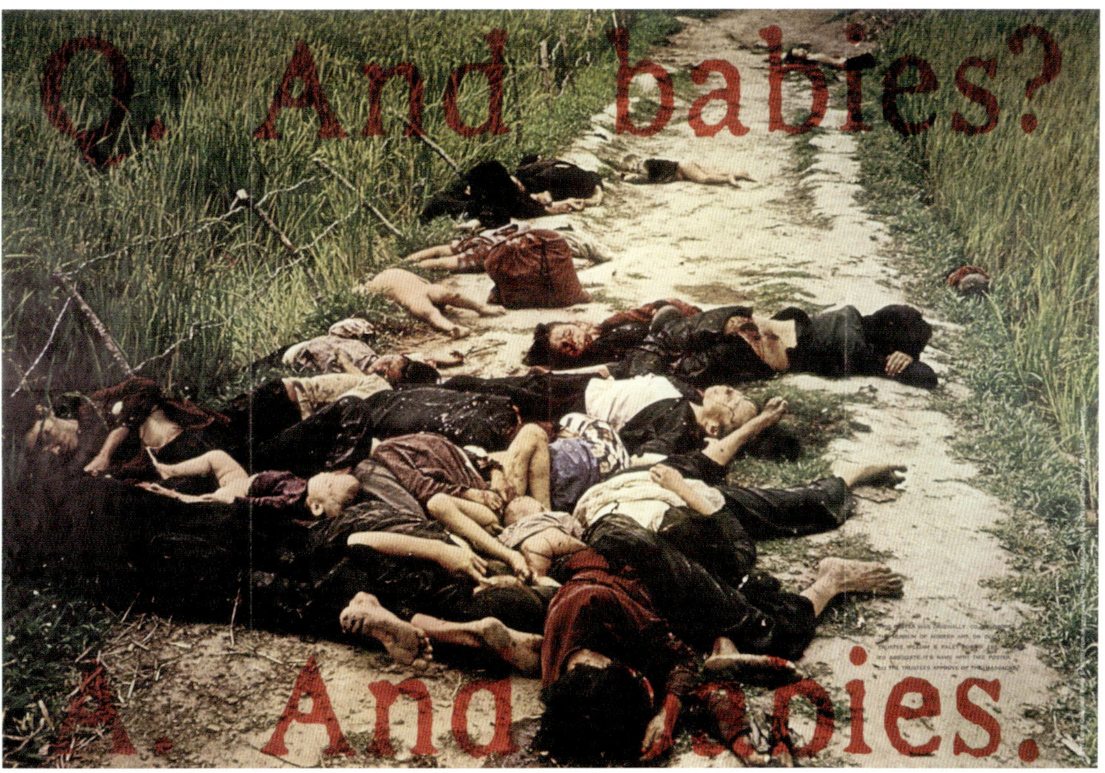

of their adoption of mass-media processes, the protestors kept their signature, primitive look as a sign of urgency. Recalling the ad hoc nature of their work, the workshop artists 'were in the pre-history of silk-screening'.[42] The tables they printed on, for example, were not designed for silkscreening and were not smooth.[43] The pace of the printing was so fast, and the paper so light, that the posters were rough and full of imperfections. They were mass-produced in a similarly ad hoc manner. Some appeared only in limited runs but others, usually those deemed especially successful, were given to striking printers who offered to reproduce compositions in larger amounts for free.

At first, rather like children allowed to play with dangerous toys in order that they learn to use them properly, France's government tolerated these activities. Soon, however, officials, and especially France's militaristic leader Charles de Gaulle, lost patience. He attempted to control them partly by mobilizing mainstream radio and television, while the radicals played cat and mouse between official media and the unofficial poster. Indeed, as newspaper, radio and television workers went on strike, the conventional media was increasingly deemed unreliable. Instead, the crude-looking posters not only attacked the French political system, but also provided a form of unofficial and general communication. Rather, theirs was a curiously unconventional version of the leader portrait. Indeed, these French radicals were happy to hang posters of Mao and Che, but their own portraits of leaders like de Gaulle were equally radical caricatures.

In posters like 'La Chienlit', General de Gaulle is recognizable from his kepi cap and exaggeratedly long nose. But, rather than identify him by name, he is accused of representing *La Chienlit* – that is, a form of disorder. De Gaulle, however, had already spoken of the student protests in Paris as a *chienlit*, using the word's dual meaning – 'chaos', but also a pun on *chie-en-lit*, or 'shit-in-bed' – in a speech, stating: '*La réforme, oui; la chienlit, non*', or 'Reform, yes, shit-in-bed, no.' As much as his ministers tried to soften the term, referring to it in the French media as a 'masquerade' or 'chaos', de Gaulle continued unrepentant in his use of the abrasive word, both privately but also in a high-visibility interview on national television. Delivered with a note of almost delirious maladroitness, the words were hardly out of his mouth before the protestors began to prepare a new poster.

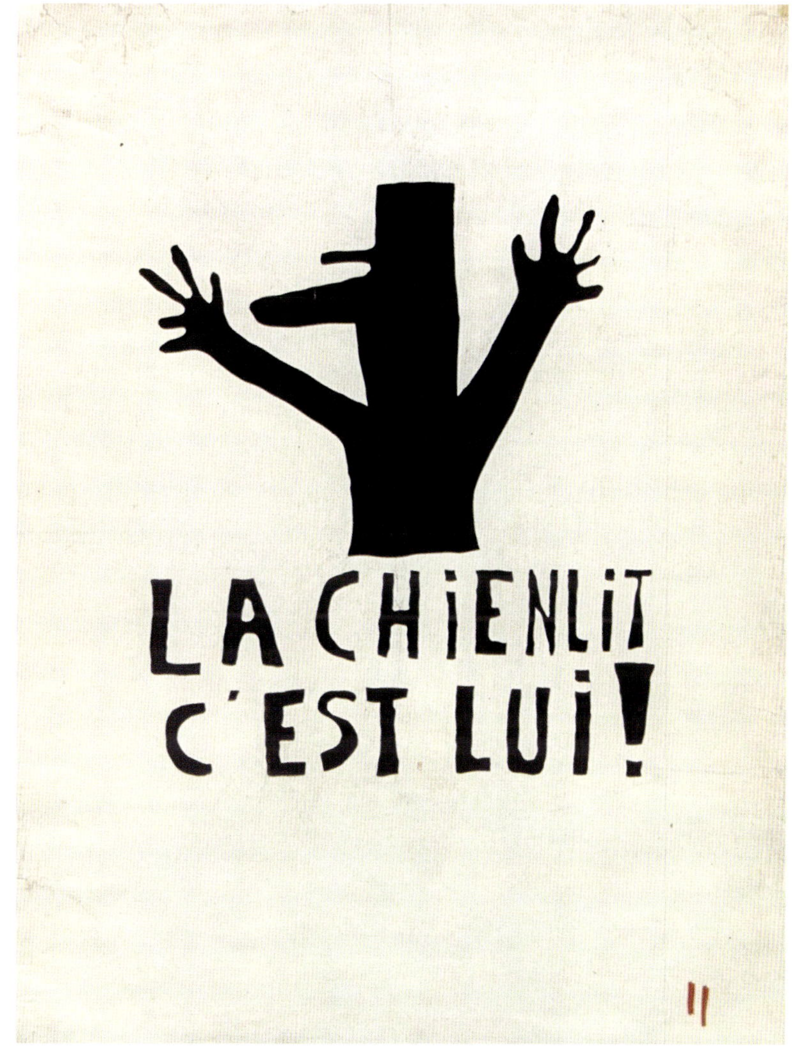

Subsequently, the students reused the expression on their own terms – namely on leaflets and posters, where the silhouette of de Gaulle was accompanied by the slogans '*La chienlit, c'est lui!*' (The *chienlit*, it is him!) and '*La chienlit, c'est encore lui!*' (The *chienlit*, it is still him!). In effect, the posters were in dialogue with newer media like the television, providing an unexpectedly quick and nimble responsiveness in the creaky old poster form.

If de Gaulle saw the movement as an expression of wild disorder, he missed the consistency of its underlying logic. The Beaux-Arts' *chienlit* pulsed with energy and daring, but also grew, as one protestor recalled, into a relatively efficient machine for propaganda. It was, one youthful protestor recalled, 'like being in

223

a factory, working 24 hours a day'.[44] But this factory was different
from those occupied by their working-class allies in the aircraft
and car-manufacturing plants outside the city. Nor was it like Andy
Warhol's self-styled 'Factory' – that is, a free-floating party masquer-
ading as an art studio in New York. The Paris student factory churned
out ideas in the form of posters. More than any other group at this
time, they approached production strictly as an expression of ideology.
The artists of the Atelier Populaire, for example, dismissed posters
made for mere 'decorative purposes'. Nor did they support any
opportunity 'to display them in bourgeois places of culture or to
consider them as objects of aesthetic interest'. Either use would,
simply put, 'impair both their function and their effect'.[45]

Such as it was, the plan was for artists to draw approved
themes in the afternoon, and then these would be printed at night.
Some veterans from the Jeune Peinture group initially assumed
that the posters would be sent to galleries or sold, earning money
for the cause. The painter Gérard Fromanger, who helped print
the earliest lithographs, remembers this basic, though telling,
misunderstanding. When Fromanger had just finished work on
the poster 'Usines, Universités, Union' (Factories, Universities,
Union), an early and seminal statement of ideological solidarity,
he recalled an ensuing moment of confusion: 'I was among those
who were supposed to take these lithographs to galleries to sell
them. We didn't think of them as posters at all.' Instead, he believed
that they would follow

> our usual practice [at the Jeune Peinture]. We made lithographs,
> or drawings, for such-and-such group, or cause, or whatever, all
> the time . . . So we were used to it and we were just continuing . . .
> We were going to donate profits to the workers and high school
> students on strike . . . So I [went downstairs to] the courtyard with
> my stack – and so did two or three others – but before we even
> got to the street, students took my posters – I mean, my lithogra-
> phies! And I say, 'Hey, wait! They're for . . . Oh, you suck!' And, bam,
> they glued them to the wall . . . And everyone was delighted to
> see 'U.U.U.' They said, 'Oh, yes, wonderful!' It was like an echo of
> what had happened during the day – of what had been said
> during the protests, and now it was written on the walls.[46]

Two generations earlier, no one would have questioned the duties and responsibilities of a poster: it was a messaging device meant for display on the streets and walls of cities like Paris. But if some of these young radicals found it difficult to imagine posting bills in public, it was because the poster's calling had radically changed.

A sign above the entrance to the Atelier Populaire may have read:

> to work at the Atelier Populaire is to give concrete support to the great movement of the workers on strike who are occupying their factories . . . by placing all his skills at the service of the worker's struggle,

but collectors had other ideas.[47] If, like Fromanger, some of the group's most ardent artists were unsure of the posters' purpose, this would change. Indeed, many began to prefer that the posters be posted exclusively on city walls, thus avoiding the capitalist fetishes of buying and consumption. Even as the revolution unfolded, however, word filtered back to Paris that posters from the Atelier Populaire were being sold as art in London and New York. An Air France flight steward reportedly whisked them to foreign capitals almost as soon as they left the presses in the Left Bank.[48] Their makers took umbrage. Any attempt to save the posters for posterity, including the efforts of a Bibliothèque Nationale's print curator who had begun ripping them off walls and archiving, were scorned. Any non-revolutionary use, the Atelier insisted,

> Even to keep them as historical evidence of a certain stage in the struggle, is a betrayal, for the struggle itself is of such primary importance that the position of an 'outside' observer is a fiction which inevitably plays into the hands of the Ruling Class.[49]

And yet, they were fighting a losing battle. In the end, the whole enterprise in May 1968 was so wild, so riotous and so complex that it is unsurprising to find that the protestors' initial efforts were subsumed. And so it was with the anti-posters as well. Try as they might, it was nearly impossible to sidestep the fetish-like collecting that already engulfed Chinese and Cuban posters of Mao and Che Guevara.

The Silkscreen Workshop in a Suitcase

As the movement of 1968 withered and the government retook
control of the schools later that summer, several members of the
Atelier Populaire, as well as their collaborators, regrouped and
formed the plucky design studio Grapus. Founded in 1970, the
group announced their unconventional attitude by adopting a name
that contracts *crapules staliniennes*, or Stalinist scum, an expression of
mockery directed by conservatives at anyone considered a left-wing
intellectual, and *graphisme* (graphics). Grapus took an anything-goes
approach towards graphic design, focusing on collaboration and
working for progressive cultural and political groups. But the Atelier
Populaire's anti-poster had a number of imitators. Within a year in
London, the Poster Workshop began producing similarly rough and
topical posters. But the legacy of the cheap and spirited posters of
1968 also took shape less literally, offering inspiration to many others.
By 1969, the Black Panther movement in America began issuing rough,
silkscreen posters that read 'Free the Panther' from their New Haven
shopfront.

    There is no point in trying to establish a careful chronology of
the impact of French protest posters, but one of the best examples of
its influence might be traced to southern Africa's Medu Art Ensemble,

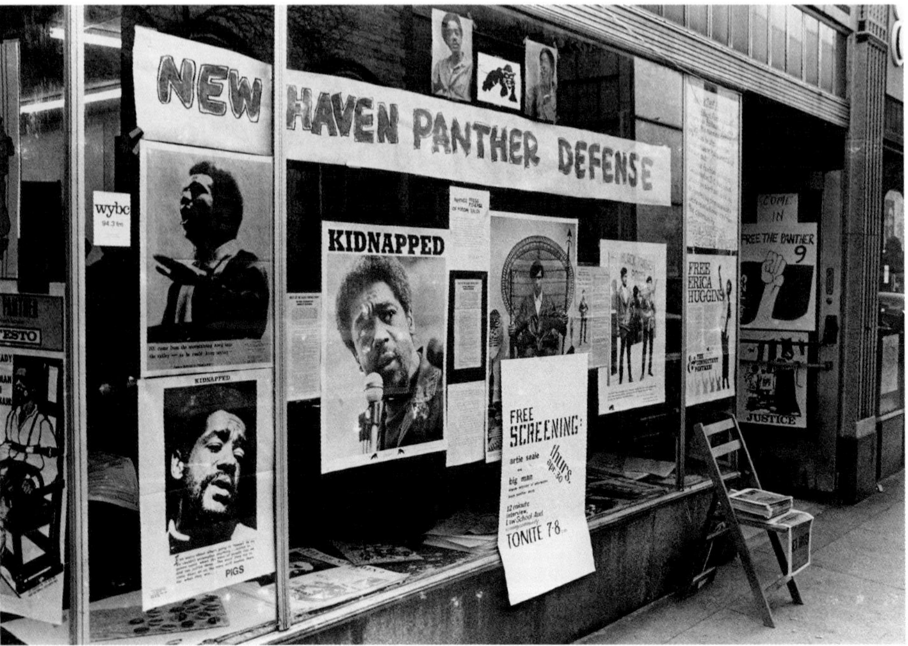

David Fenton, 'View
of the Black Panther Party
Headquarters, New Haven,
CT', 1970.

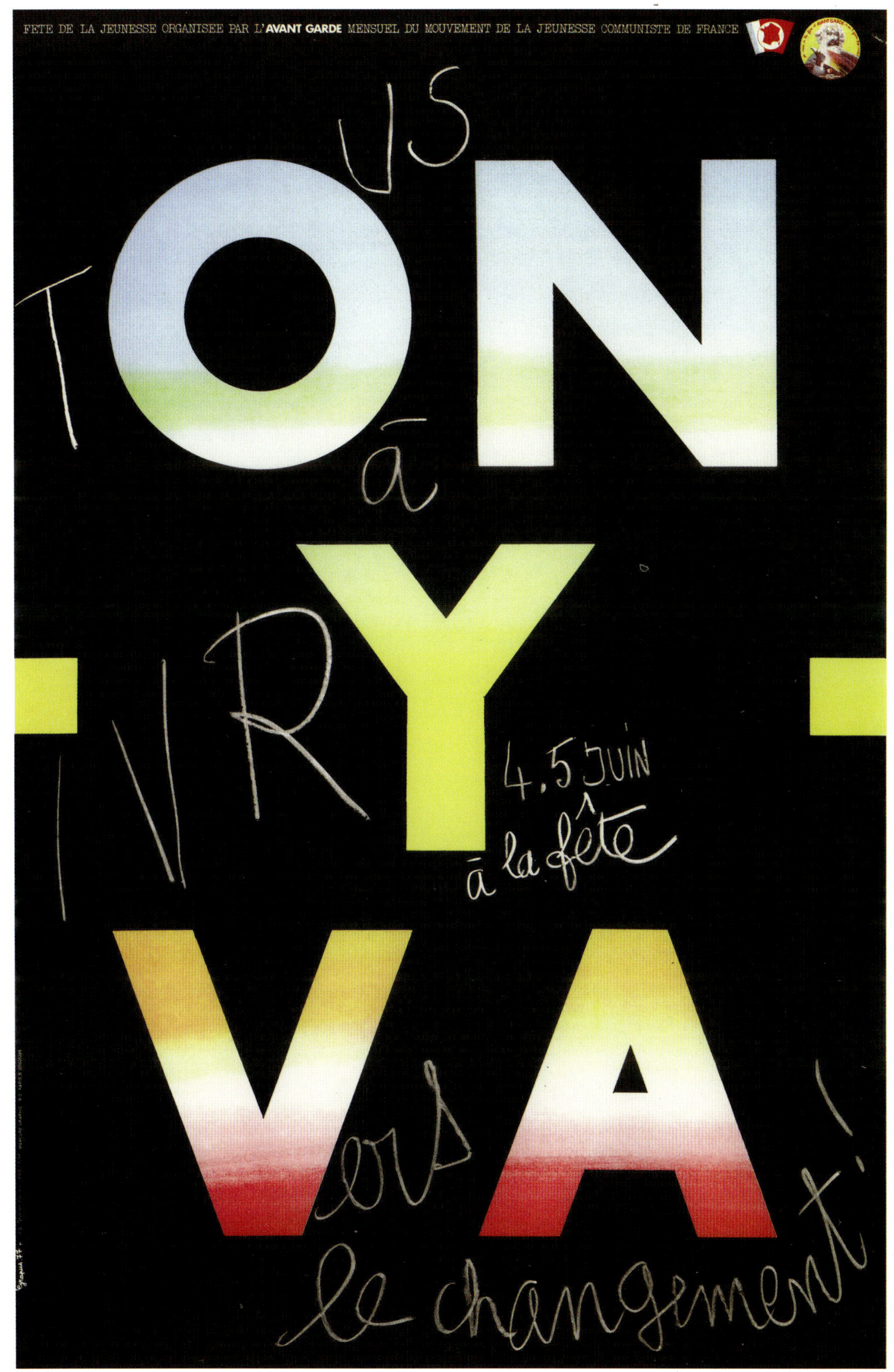

Grapus, 'On y va', 1977.

adopting but also altering its example; indeed, their approach recalled 1968 in its aesthetics, but presaged the twenty-first century in its tactics. A cultural collaboration dedicated to ending apartheid, in the late 1970s Medu was based just over the border from South Africa in Gaborone, Botswana, and toyed with the South African government, teasing with its close proximity. Taking its name from a gentle word in the local Sepedi language that means 'roots', the group would ultimately be absorbed into the African National Congress. They began as a cheeky, grass-roots organization and called themselves 'cultural workers' rather than artists (a term considered elitist if not odious by many of its members). Medu organized specialized 'units' that included theatre groups and a photography section as well as the Graphic Unit. The latter favoured silkscreen posters as cheap, fast and practical, and their methods still resonate as a simple how-to medium for untrained art workers. If the posters of Paris in 1968 were an inspiration, Medu copied their approach by creating posters on the fly, but also offering an immediacy with events-based urgency. From anti-apartheid cultural boycotts to frequent South African intervention in 'front-line' states like Angola and Lesotho, their messages were pointed. Coming all the way from France and landing on this strip of sunny African land, it may seem odd to find the highly intellectual French approach to poster-making resurface at this time and place. But Medu's posters continued a similar vision, and perhaps more successfully opposed poster fetishism.

Medu produced some 50 posters in the late 1970s and early 1980s. In addition to their spiky and rough style, they adopted many of the formats and themes typical of their radical predecessors, peppering their visual references with Russian and other revolutionary sources as well. But they also highlighted the goals of the process of poster-making from 1968. Indeed, while emulating the collective working method of the Atelier Populaire, Medu's wide-eyed, striking use of silkscreening was a populist approach. Like the Paris posters, the richness of their designs lies in the plainness of their aesthetic. But Medu also produced a fresh, new vision for making posters, what they called a 'silkscreen workshop in a suitcase'.[50] In so doing, they aimed to create an 'all-in-one portable container', which would hold a silkscreen, ink, squeegee and stencil-making material. Sized to fit a conveniently portable box some 50 x 75 x 15 cm (20 x 30 x 6 in), the kit was indeed small enough to sit in a suitcase, but large enough

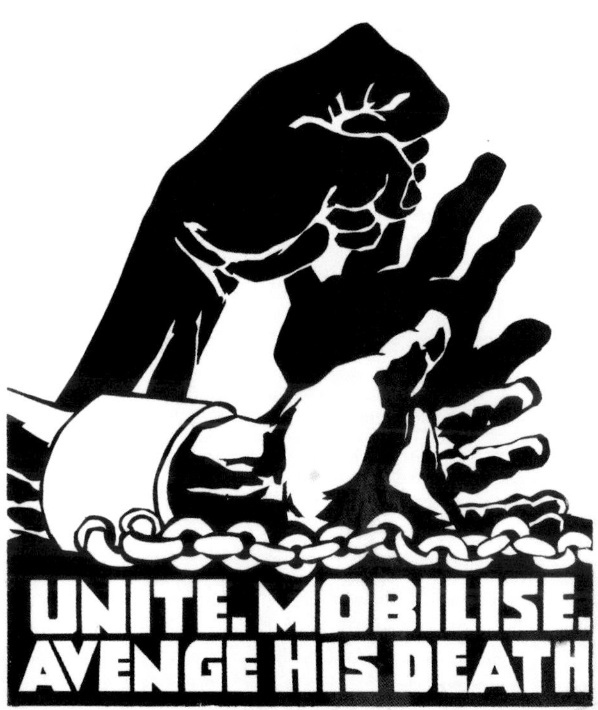

Medu Art Ensemble,
'Dr Neil Aggett: Unite.
Mobilise. Avenge His
Death', 1982.

to produce standard-size posters. It was also large enough to be effective, and yet small enough to avoid scrutiny. Dutch donors outfitted Medu with several suitcases, but the project was dealt a fatal blow when Medu's Gaborone base was struck in 1985 by a South African Army border raid; eight members were killed and the remaining supporters went underground.

The group remained inspirational, however, and not only for grass-roots activists in South Africa, including the Screen Training Project in Johannesburg and Community Arts Project in Cape Town; there was also something in Medu's larger vision, the very idea of a portable printing workshop small enough to fit in a suitcase that was prophetic as well. Their artists were largely untrained, but they were using the silkscreen poster in a way that takes the promise of 1968 into a new realm. The silkscreen in a suitcase not only envisioned poster-making on the fly. Little known and rarely collected, these were not precious objects, nor were they fetishized. Instead, Medu aimed to put cultural production in the hands of the people. Whether in China or Cuba, Paris or Botswana, a variety of poster artists working at this time saw themselves on the cusp of realizing a new world in which posters would lead the way.

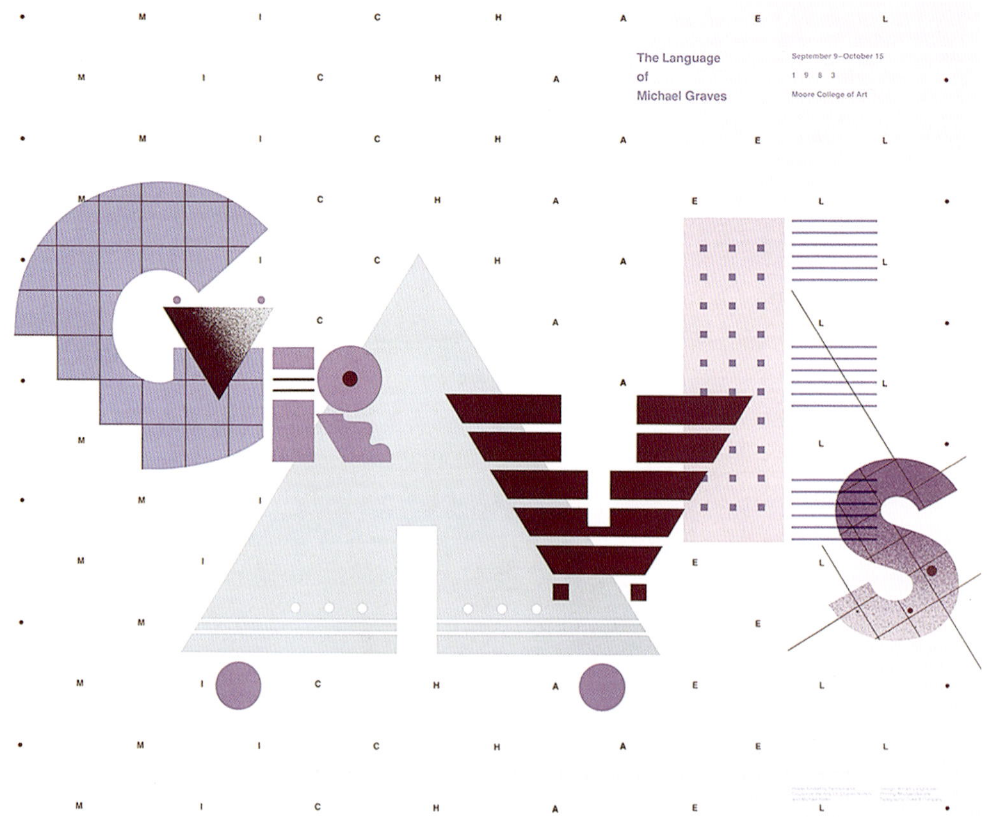
The Language
of
Michael Graves
September 9–October 15
1 9 8 3
Moore College of Art

The Language
of
Michael Graves

5 A NEW GOLDEN AGE – DIGITAL ENCHANTMENT: 1980–2014

Not since the development of chromolithography has the poster seen a bigger revolution than the present digital one; more than any other factor, cheap and relatively accessible technology has fostered the poster's present golden age. The current digital revolution has shaped the work of a generation of professionally trained graphic artists, but the personal computer has also opened up design and production to non-professionals. Medu's silkscreen workshop in a suitcase, the Atelier Populaire's anti-poster, and even the networks of poster exchange established by Chinese and Cuban propagandists were only a faint rumble in the revolution that was to come.

The twenty-first century has been good to the poster, but it still attracts little attention in the more conventional surveys of this period. As the revolutionary airs of posters from China and Cuba have faded, and the International Style began to lose energy in the 1970s and 1980s, posters have evolved away from cold formulae and dogmatism. In Switzerland, long associated with simple, spare modernist design, things were beginning to change. Here Wolfgang Weingart made experimental posters appear complex and chaotic, playful and spontaneous.

The poster has fundamentally changed. From hand-painted signboards by Indian graphics-wallahs to wall-mural advertisements by itinerant painters in Ghana, artisanal modes of communication are rapidly being replaced by digitally designed posters; moreover, they can now be produced in large numbers at the business communications shops that today are as likely to be found in urban parts of sub-Saharan Africa as in New York, Paris and London. Furthermore, new forms of communication like the Palestinian martyr poster or the West African street poster, work in ways very different from those of Paris in the 1800s. The global poster in its current form has changed the rules by introducing new materials, swapping paper for vinyl, for example, and

William Longhauser, 'The Language of Michael Graves', exhibition poster, 1983.

William Longhauser, draft for 'The Language of Michael Graves' exhibition poster, 1983.

by working with transcultural networks. Dominating such networks
is the Internet, meaning that a designer or publisher in an African city
can use a computer to download images and produce a poster that
talks about anything from war to fashion, and then distribute the
poster via networks including hawkers and small shop owners over
a wide area. The proprietor of a barber shop in Burundi, for instance,
may choose to buy a digitally produced poster of new hairstyles to
tempt his customers, where once a painted poster hung.

Such digitally made posters are part of an information network
that spreads news with alarming speed, but they also tap into broader
cultures of technology and enchantment. Unlike sneezing when we
breathe in dirt or catching hiccoughs when we laugh too much, we
have no automatic behaviour in the face of enchantment; it can be
hard to discern even when we are confronted with it. In his essay 'The
Technology of Enchantment and the Enchantment of Technology',
anthropologist Alfred Gell attempted to understand the almost
mystical, hard-to-define qualities that set fine art apart from other
objects. By way of explanation, Gell pointed to the technological
processes that lead to the creation of a work of art. Displays of
technical virtuosity, he tells us, can enchant beholders, creating
a kind of 'technology of enchantment'.[1] Magic is brought into being
through the technological process itself, provoking a profound sense
of awe in unskilled viewers. Others have reflected further on enchantment, seeing it as a way to understand post-modernity. Zygmunt
Bauman believes that the sense of magic is essential to understanding
the world today. But it is also the outcome of a network that wraps
together a maker or conjuror, the enchanting object and the people
who will be enchanted by this object.

Over the last century and a half, the poster has been confronted
with a variety of rival technologies of communication. But the advent
of the computer is different from the coming of radio and television
– neither were themselves instruments for further making. If the
computer was both a threat and a tool, we must remember that the
digital revolution was preceded by significant changes in production
during the previous two decades. By the late 1960s, photographic
typesetting and composition were commonplace, but the design
process – from typography to layout to photo manipulation and
collage – was still complex. In the year before the Mac was introduced,
William Longhauser's poster of 1983 for an exhibition of the work of

architect Michael Graves was assembled through an arduous process of ideation and production. From the multiple drawings that kicked off the process to its actual printing, its author recalled, 'the process was quite risky and nerve-racking'.[2] In Longhauser's case, fixing the right colour was especially vexing. But the larger undertaking was slow and protracted and required a remarkable degree of expertise and training.

Little wonder that the advent of the personal computer would soon seem close to miraculous. While histories of design often point to pioneers like April Greiman as early adopters, we forget that her early use of this technology anticipated a vast reimagining of a working process virtually unaltered since Gutenberg. The earliest pioneers, including Zuzana Licko and Rudy VanderLans, reapproached typography. But, as the age of desktop publishing began, no form was more transformed than the poster. In some ways, desktop publishing effected most fully the vision of a 'silkscreen workshop in a suitcase', conceptualized but left unrealized by Botswana's anti-apartheid collective, Medu, as well as the populist poster politics of the Atelier Populaire. But the digital revolution was much more. As Greiman soon discovered, the computer folds many previously complex design processes – typography, layout, photo manipulation, collage – into a single, easy-to-use interface. Computer technology not only enables these formats, but was also initially a form of creative inspiration. Essentially, building on this new technological wonder, digitally produced posters made a new kind of sense.

The Desktop Poster: Does It Make Sense?

In the autumn of 1986, subscribers to the venerable *Design Quarterly* (*DQ*) received a copy of the magazine unlike any other. A carefully printed slipcase arrived, looking like a rare book. The slipcase was a simple off-white, its cover embellished only with a black band of text that read: 'Does It Make Sense?' As readers unfolded the contents, and then unfolded again, they discovered that issue 133 was in fact a poster – 1.8 metres (6 ft) long – of a nude woman, printed in a grainy, blue-black ink. Eyes closed and set among a rough grid of celestial symbols, prehistoric drawings and a photograph of a human brain, the long-haired woman might be a latter-day Pre-Raphaelite Ophelia, enchanted while in a state of near-sleep. By its very nature, enchantment is not easy to communicate; its magic is universal and complex. Perusing the lattice

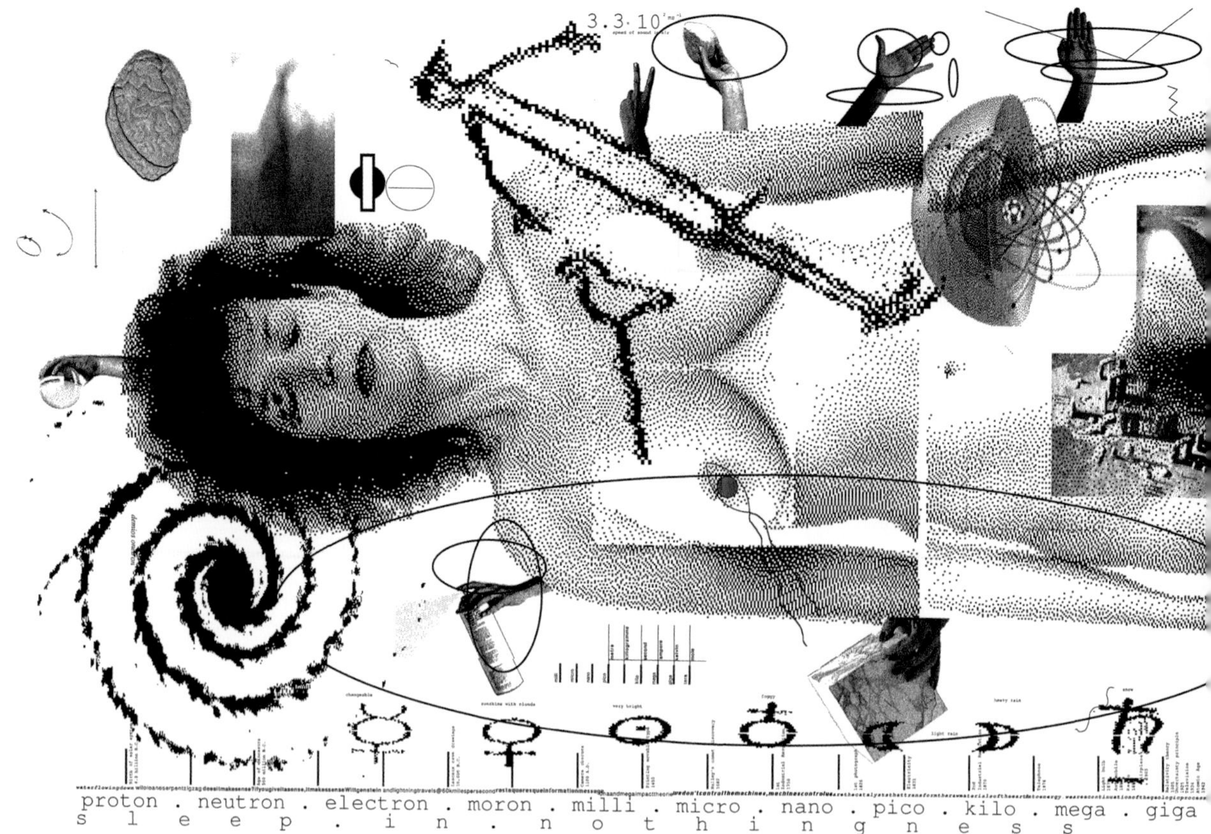

of images, along with texts that advised 'sleep in nothingness', regular
readers may well have found themselves puzzled. Following the
question printed on the cover and repeated on the poster, some
critics re-read the title 'Does It Make Sense?', answering with an
emphatic 'No'. But this life-size, digitized and nude self-portrait of
designer April Greiman from 1986 announced a new chapter in the
history of the poster. On closer view, out of its seemingly wild disorder,
a kind of nothingness comes to order. For Greiman the computer
offered its own justifications for making, presenting an utterly new
process that could be a 'magic slate'.

The development of the Mac was dominated by its own lore
and legend; early adopters had many theories about how to harness
the powerful computer's uses, but others were less convinced. As
designer Paul Rand would later remark, the computer offered speed,
but also produced showy effects 'without substance. Form without
relevant content, or content without meaningful form'.[3] Milton Glaser,
himself the author of the 'Dylan' poster from 1967, famously dismissed

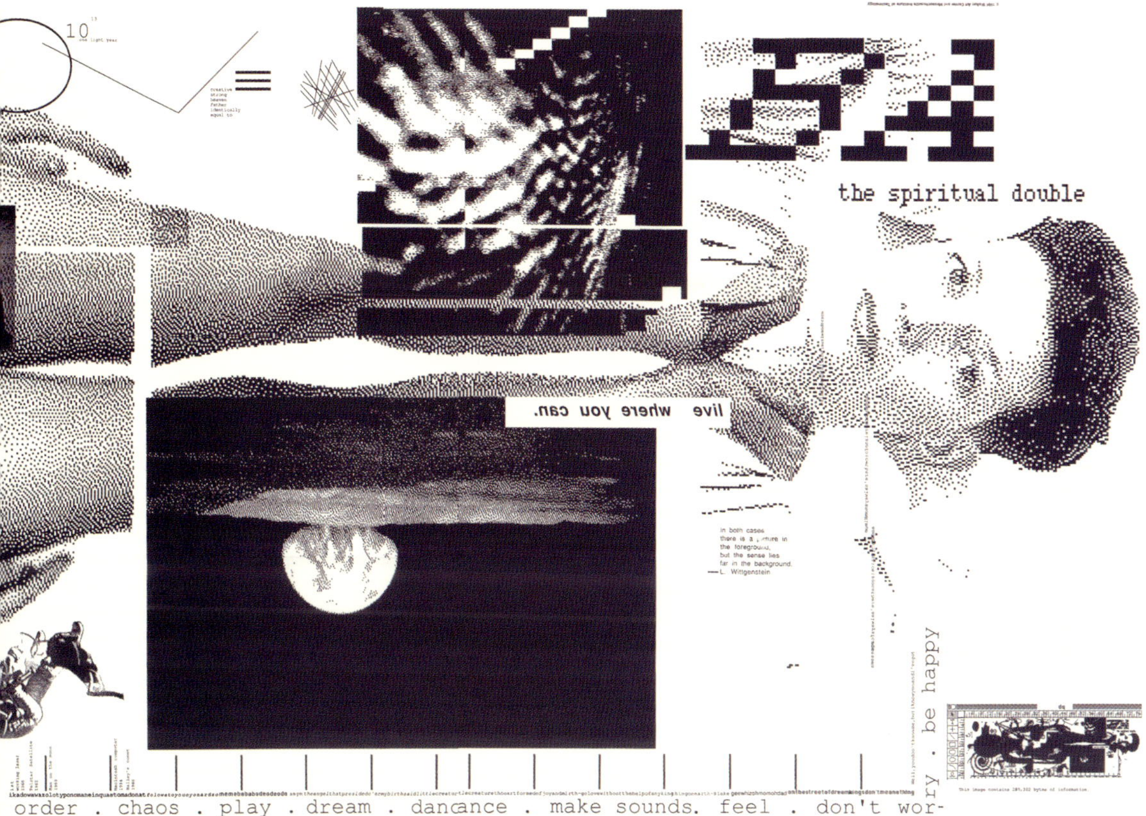

the computer because it sped the design process up 'too quickly'.
Moving to a cooking analogy, Glaser pointed to another new time-
saving device and argued that 'the computer is like a microwave'.[4]
But, for those who chose to use it, the computer could also hold
great potential.

When Alfred Gell wrote about 'the technology of enchantment',
he described art as producing an 'aesthetic awe bordering on the
religious'. But, in trying to understand this awe, he identified the
skilled use of tools or 'technology' as essential to producing this magic.
Whether the knives used by Trobriand woodcarvers on the prow-boards
of canoes or the hammers and chisels that hewed the Medici tombs,
tools are an integral part of this process. Magic is derived from their
skilful use. At a time when many established artists and designers
dismissed the computer as hampering creativity, Greiman used her
poster to recast the computer as a powerful tool. *DQ* issue number
133 is not just a fundamental rethinking of the poster; it also signals
a fundamentally new way of working in communications design.

Greiman's studies with Wolfgang Weingart in Switzerland in the early 1970s are significant. But re-evaluation of the poster occurred even before the desktop computer was widely introduced. Postmodernist designers favoured the poster, using its rectangular shape to play with narrative and type alike. At its height, the movement displayed a range of important computer-produced posters, including the work of Americans like Katherine McCoy and Paula Scher, and a number of Dutch design groups, including Studio Dumbar, Hard Werken and Wild Plakken. But Greiman was an early and enthusiastic adopter; indeed, for her and her generation, the computer was a powerful tool, best understood intuitively, through a language of enchantment.

Folded and fitting snugly into its slipcase, the *DQ* special issue announced its radicalism in its very format. It imitates a book, with its title printed on the spine so it could be shelved in libraries. But, as it is taken out of its cocoon, the poster must be carefully unfolded three times across, nine times down, to reveal the grainy, life-size image of the designer. Although Greiman fills the poster with prehistoric and contemporary symbolism that alludes to a kind of supernatural mysteriousness, the real magic of the work was the fact that she created it using a computer. Through the mystical alchemy of Apple's newly introduced Macintosh, Greiman's self-portrait was more than a life-size fold-out; with her imagery digitized and electronically assembled into a delicate haze of blue pixels, the daring poster served as a clarion call to an industry (the late twentieth-century fascination with computers and their alchemy has been discussed elsewhere[5]). If Greiman looks like a sleeping beauty, she also exists in a computer-made universe of her own devising; Greiman is not just enchanted, but also an enchantress, and she uses the poster to dazzle us with her newfound technological prowess.

From the outset, Greiman insisted of 'Does It Make Sense?' that 'It's a magazine which is a poster which is an object.'[6] Indeed, Greiman's magical keystrokes appear all the more remarkable considering the standard format of the magazine in which it appeared. Originally beginning publication as *Everyday Art Quarterly* in 1946, the magazine may have been reorganized and renamed *Design Quarterly* in 1954, but it kept to fairly conventional formats. Indeed, what really provides a sense of enchantment in Greiman's work is not her subject matter or even her style, but rather her mastery of digital techniques at a time when few, if any, other graphic designers even knew how to use a computer. Revealing Greiman physically and emotionally, literally placing her at the centre of her own design, 'Does It Make Sense?' broke new ground for designers, suggesting an utter reconceptualization of the design process, and of posters themselves.

Aware of how unusual it was to be designing a poster electronically, Greiman nudges viewers, through both the poster's text and imagery, to think of the poster as something 'made' via the new computer-enabled design process; it represents a huge leap in 'back-end' production – that is, the conceptualization and execution of the poster. Many of the words and inscriptions covering the poster allude to applied science and technology. Around her inert, nude body icons from prehistoric art, including Stonehenge and petroglyphs, jostle with images of astronauts, a view of the Earth from space and other motifs of space exploration. Like a latter-day Shiva,[7] Greiman is herself surrounded by a series of hands whose gestures are charted with lines. While some make universally understood signals, like the peace or victory sign, others indicate a variety of mark-making practices, including a hand carrying a can of spray paint and a slip of paper. But a number make motions that look like a mystical pantomime. Just as Greiman used a computer to compose this image, she also encoded in it an idiosyncratic history of personal computing. Running along one side of the poster is a timeline highlighting moments in the history of science and technology, including the Big Bang, the 'age of the dinosaurs', the discovery of Halley's Comet and the invention of photography; the timeline ends with the introduction of the Mac itself.

While she may have first used the Mac after learning of it at the first TED (Technology, Entertainment, Design) conference in Northern California, Greiman introduces an allusive vocabulary that mixes the techno-culture of Pasadena's Jet Propulsion Laboratory and a philosophical bent more at home in a Topanga commune. Together, these aspects let Greiman build an evocative portrait of the Mac, describing it as an enchanted machine for making. Deploying a series of ideas that flourished in California in the decades after the 1960s counter-culture, Greiman enlisted a vocabulary of fairytale imagery, Zen Buddhism and a Jungian cosmology that is sometimes dismissively claimed as California 'New Age' spiritualism. At times, her blend of utopianism and an eager elevation of consciousness makes the designer seem more like an alchemist than technician, but notions of enchanted technology appealed to Silicon Valley entrepreneurs like Steve Jobs

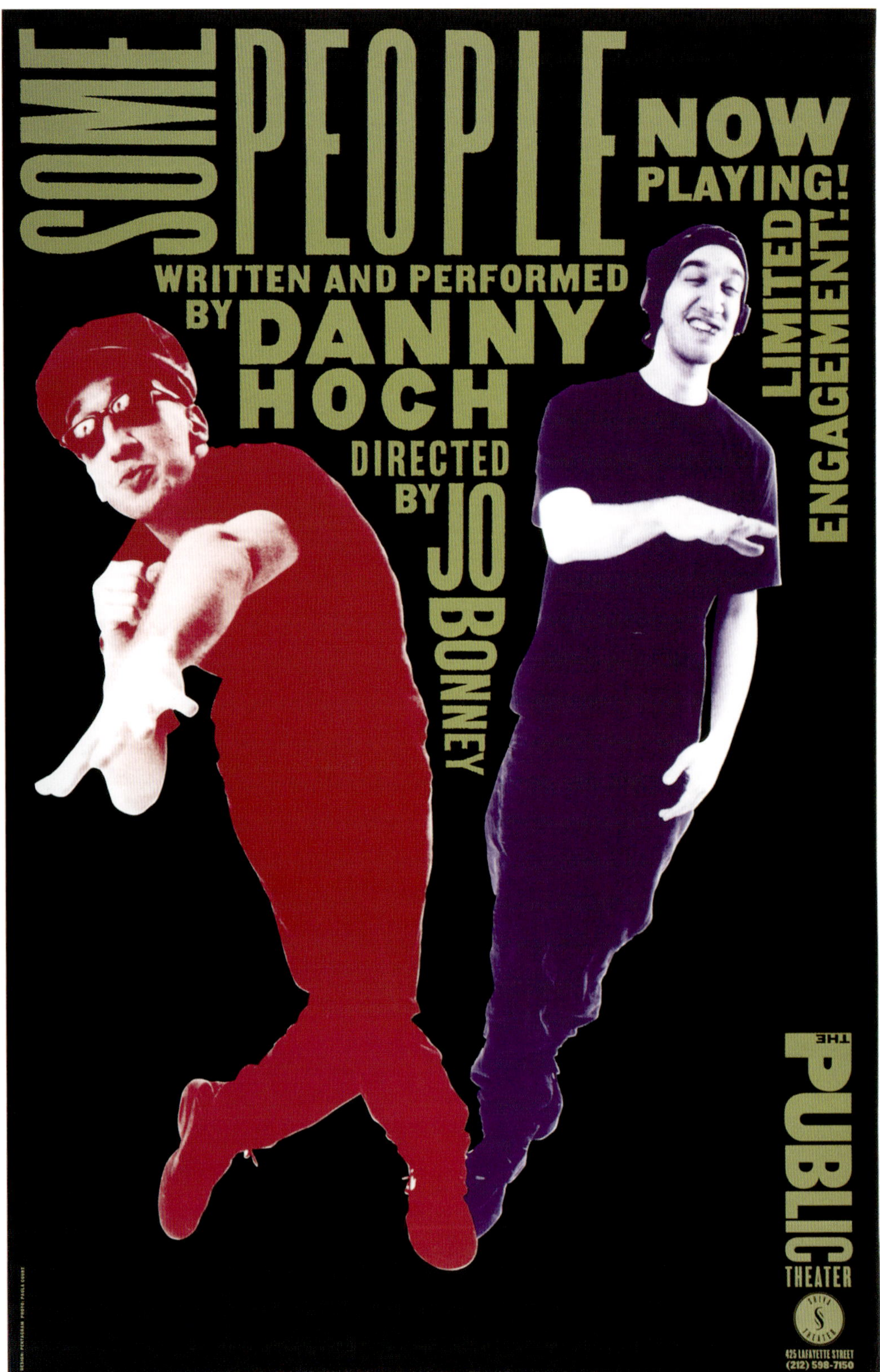

Paula Scher, 'Some People', 1994.

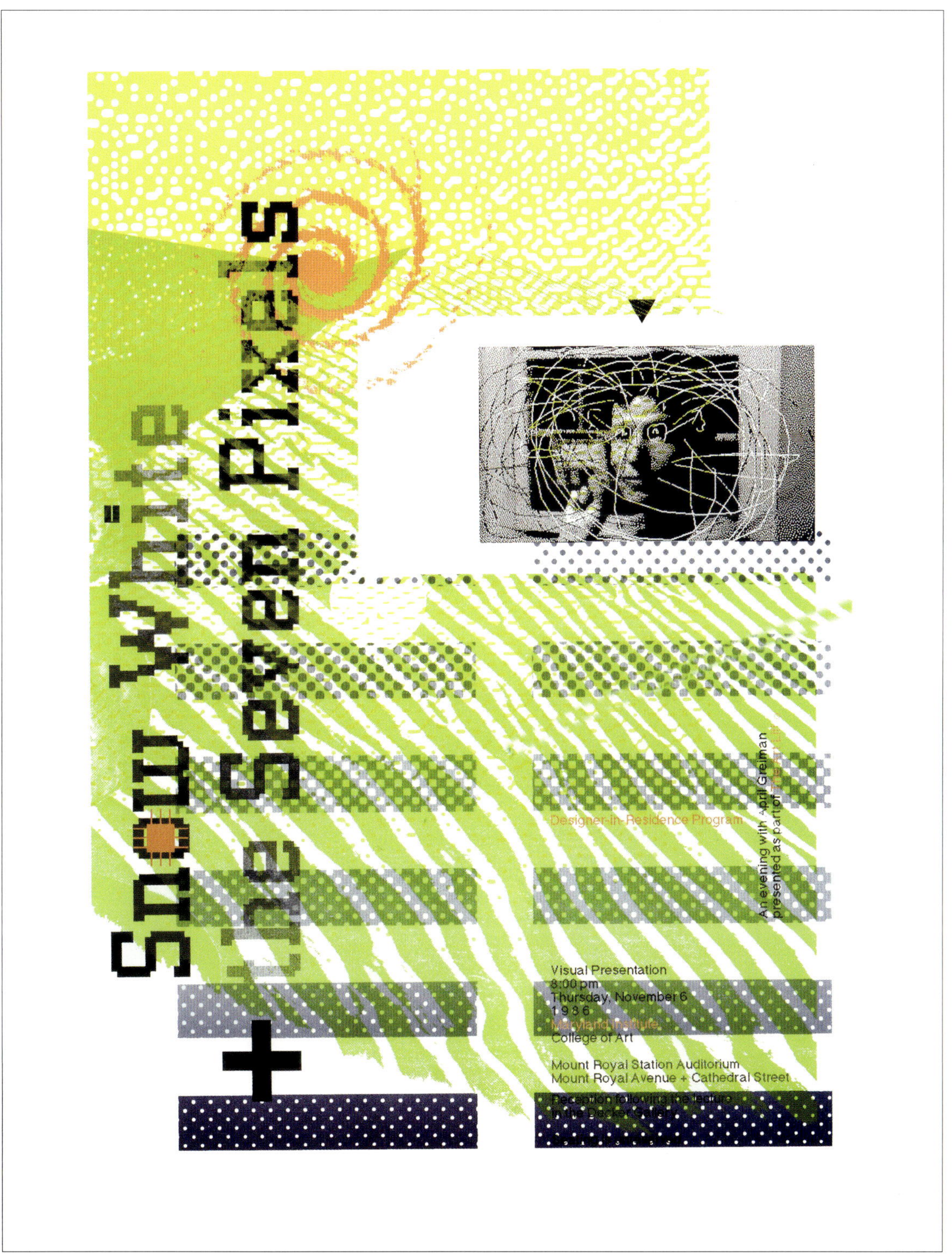

April Greiman, 'Snow White + the Seven Pixels, an Evening with April Greiman', 1986.

as much as mystically inclined creatives. Moreover, Greiman's poster also describes how this consciousness coexists within an uneasy narrative of scientific rationalism. This quiet tension is highlighted in the various chunks and shards of text in the poster; Greiman's fundamental question, 'Does It Make Sense?', introduces the thinking of Ludwig Wittgenstein. On the poster, Greiman answers with Wittgenstein's rejoinder: 'If you give it a sense, it makes sense.' The German philosopher's flexible brand of rationalism also reveals the logic that is sometimes associated with the birth of the computer. Indeed, Wittgenstein's thought may be seen as part of the philosophical scaffolding that anticipates computer-programming language. As he grappled with ideas of chaos and rationality in his work, Greiman's approach towards his ideas can in itself seem garbled and chaotic as well. Using the model of raw data output, for instance, she poses Wittgenstein's question as 'doesitmakesense?' but also notes the philosopher's answer as 'Ifyougiveitasense,itmakessense.'

Indeed, her poster is often touted as a photomontage; no doubt, the Russian and Dada artists who developed this style some 60 years earlier employed photos and text in a similar manner. Greiman updated this technique while acknowledging the poster's digital nature. In semiotic terms, the pixels in 'Does It Make Sense?' are generally the index of that process. A close look at the poster inevitably exposes its pixelated nature. Greiman revelled in the Mac's low-resolution textures, magnifying its 'flaws' (that is, the rough square shapes, her use of pixels to suggest greyscale and other features that some might call liabilities) so that they can function symbolically. If the subject of the poster is technology, then these re-enforce its message as magic.

Greiman was not alone in this enchanted journey; while some designers used the computer to extend their already-established practice, Greiman was part of a small cohort who saw the computer as a game-changer. Rudy VanderLans and Zuzana Licko, editor and designer respectively of *Emigre* magazine, embraced the Mac as well. Indeed, noting the computer's limitations, they pronounced themselves 'The New Primitives'.[8] Buying their first computer in 1985, they revelled in coarse, bitmapped type and unusual layouts composed in MacPaint. These make clear that the image is digital in nature. These digital pioneers also shared a similar format – the magazine. Although little discussed, before the World Wide Web, the magazine or journal format was the best way to distribute new ideas among designers. When, years later, he was asked to describe why he chose the magazine format for his new design ideas, *Emigre* editor VanderLans insisted that there was 'an infrastructure in place to distribute it – magazine distributors, newsstands, special US postal mailing rates – to print it, and to sell advertising'. Indeed, VanderLans and Licko, as well as Greiman, capitalized on the networking potential of print magazines. Nevertheless, as Vanderlans later noted: 'These infrastructures can also be very constricting, which is why most magazines look alike.'[9] Greiman's use of the computer allowed her to create a special issue of *Design Quarterly* that would resemble no other. Few believed that the computer could elevate the mind and soul.

In pursuing this integration, Greiman turned to the theories of the Swiss psychoanalyst Carl Jung. His *Memories, Dreams, Reflections*, she recalls,

> was totally pivotal in my life. Jung talks about his travels, immersing himself in various cultures, and his first exposure to Native Americans when he was taught not to think with just his head, but also with his heart.[10]

Greiman's introduction of the 'spirit double' furthers the poster's Jungian orientation; placed squarely at the feet of her closed-eyed, nude self is a portrait image of an open-eyed, short-haired person with the phrase 'the spiritual double' hovering above it. Greiman's relation to this image, which is indeed another depiction of herself, is complex. She later told interviewers that, shortly after completing the poster, she added this image as an afterthought. She claimed that she had recently cut her hair and wanted somehow to include her new short, punk-inspired style into the larger portrait. Within Jungian tradition, the spirit double suggests a holistic view of a person, providing a synergist duality between the physical and the spiritual. Figuring as an inverse of one's self, Western mythology and fairy tales are suffused with figures like Snow White in the crystal casket, whose double might be the evil witch who consults an occult spirit using a dark mirror, or a troll hiding under a bridge. Indeed, Greiman's notion of fairy-tale enchantment and its relation to technology was clearly signalled in her talk in 1986 on 'Snow White + the Seven Pixels' at the Maryland Institute of Contemporary Art. Greiman's engagement with mythological enchantment was clear; sizing up the two figures in 'Does It Make Sense?' for a visitor to her studio, she described them as a 'double-headed monster'.[11]

Shortly after 'Does It Make Sense?' was produced, Greiman called the computer a 'new paradigm', a conceptual 'magic slate' opening up a new era of opportunity for graphic artists.[12] As one of the earliest designers to use a computer, at times Greiman clearly struggled to articulate the new digital design landscape unfolding before her. In her design, she consciously tried to straddle what she saw as two realms, admitting that 'I've always been a science-friendly person, but also fascinated with magic.'[13] If the computer itself was a 'magic slate', of the mouse, she said: 'It's a miracle!' Harry Marks, the person who introduced her to the Mac, was 'my early tech-guruwawapal'. While dealing with the design process, which initially pushed the Mac to the limits of its potential, we can say that she found its uses 'wandering' and erratic, but also magical. The poster became a mythic beast:

> Meanwhile, System Errors were occurring – stretched images were printing with white scan lines due to incompatible software between the Mac and the LaserWriter – entire days are devoted to trying to figure out how to print the monster.[14]

In spite of such setbacks, Greiman dazzled with her growing mastery of the Mac's strange new powers.

As Greiman soon discovered, the computer brings together a series of complex design processes, folding them into a single, easy-to-use interface. However, computer usage and the growth of the Internet during the 1990s not only provided new markets for makers but also globalized the media. The personal computer also increasingly enabled non-professionals to prepare complex designs quickly. But these new forms had their own logic. They carried new meanings and wonderment, continuing to make a new kind of sense.

Making Martyrs in the Age of Photoshop

When anthropologist Lotte Buch visited the house of a young widow living just outside Nablus on the West Bank, she entered the living room and noted that plush sofas and grandiose chairs of black, cream and gold were all overwhelmed by a single poster. Fitted in a gold frame, the huge image of a young man in profile holding an AK-47 dominated the room. The man pictured in the poster is Nadia's first husband; killed by Israeli soldiers, he is deemed a *šahīd* – a martyr.[15] Palestinian photographer Ahlam Shibli has documented similar scenes. Part of a larger series that she titled 'Death', her *Untitled (Death, No. 32)* shows the sister of one such martyr, Khalil Marshoud, in his family's living room, dusting his framed poster. As the culture of martyrdom overshadowed Palestinian society, posters became a crucial means of communicating this.

Palestinian martyr posters were one of the earliest examples of the desktop computer's global reach, but, as already noted, they also proved its potential for spawning poster forms utterly inconceivable in nineteenth-century Paris or New York. In a few short years after April Greiman began to explore the Mac's creative potential, change began to spread. Indeed, the rapid march towards computer design and production, and the amateurization of poster-making, is usually chronicled as a series of baby steps. Photocopiers enabled punk posters, then there was rub-off transfer lettering, then the opening of access to clip-art inventories allowed embellishments. By the time that the computer was introduced, the field of design had begun to crack open. Before, days or even weeks could be spent communicating with the typesetter, layout artist or printer. Indeed, as designer Richard

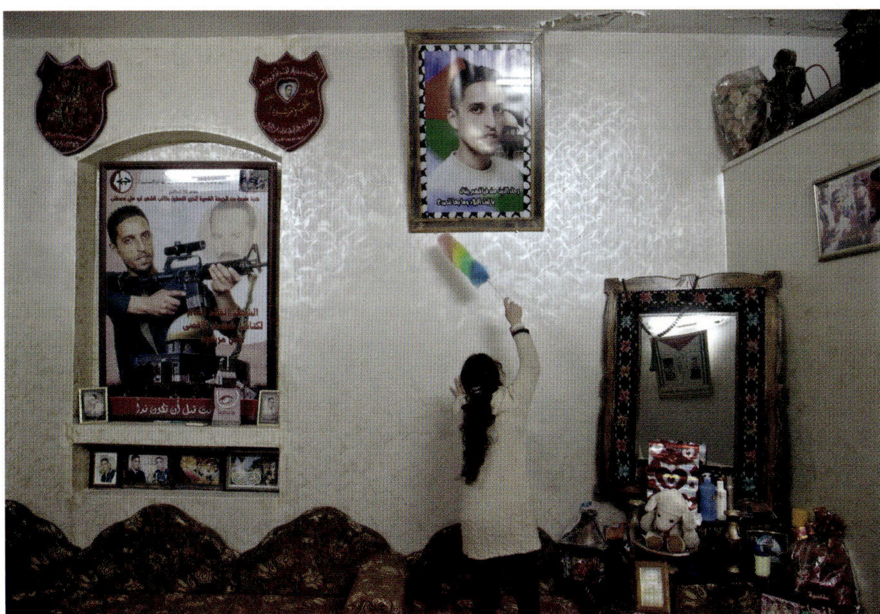

Ahlam Shibli, *Untitled (Death, No. 32)*, 2012.

Hollis recalled: 'My generation went from hot metal to photosetting to digital. Computers have changed everything, bringing total control to the designer.'[16] Very rapidly, computers were used by anyone who owned a PC or Mac. Some, like Greiman, were trained designers. But casual users often simply wanted to post lost-pet ads and announcements of office Christmas parties. In our myopic gaze, however, it is easy to overlook such developments and fail to see that larger forces were at work. Not only was Gutenberg's system supplanted, but so too was the control of Western technologies.

Through the 1990s, as desktop computers became more and more ubiquitous globally, they were hard-working, commonplace and also vaguely magical. There was no single mind or political entity behind the spread of computers, nor was there a single person who urged creation of Palestinian martyr posters. Moreover, saying that these posters were magical is not to imply that their makers intended, like Greiman, to cultivate enchantment. But it does help to explain the mechanisms that make pieces of printed paper into magical objects. Indeed, just as Elias Khoury's story *The White Masks* describes the insistent presence of these posters in the Beirut of 1980, and very like Joana Hadjithomas and Khalil Joreige's art series *Faces*, the posters have a haunting presence. As Gell would have it, the poster of Nadia's husband represents more. Gell, of course, is most interested in how art is invested with magic and looks to understand it as part of a system, or network, that submerges individual creators and objects. This system, he says, is a collaboration; it is the nuts and bolts of what he calls 'the technology of enchantment'. Within a broader system, or set of beliefs, the poster becomes enchanted, 'casting a spell over us so that we see the real world in an enchanted form'. Writing elsewhere, other scholars have claimed the martyr poster to be part of an 'enchanted modernity'. Technology and wonderment are seamlessly folded into the poster format.

Indeed, these posters were not born in Silicon Valley; the Lebanese Civil War was the crucible that shaped them, and Beirut became 'a factory for making posters'.[17] By the mid-1970s, as Lebanon's multiple political parties expanded, posters were deployed as political weapons. But posters marking the birth or death of Arab leaders were also increasingly common. In Lebanon during the 1970s, the anniversaries of the deaths of pan-Arab leaders like Egypt's Gamal Abdel Nasser or Lebanese resistance leader Antoun Saadeh were marked by small posters that were distributed publicly, carrying deep cultural significance and reminding Arabs of their shared cultural identity. But, by the early 1980s, Arab factions in Lebanon began to use hand-painted posters as a way to acknowledge dead fighters publicly. Painted by local artists and reproduced in print shops affiliated with various warring political parties, however, they were time-consuming and expensive to produce; only the posters of well-known politicians and commanders were copied and distributed widely.

In Muslim and especially Shiite culture, faith-based martyrdom is deeply honoured as a form of religious sacrifice as well as serving as an accounting for the deceased's absence from this world; but it also expresses shared social values and weaves communities into a lasting social fabric. Palestinian culture hinges on tales of struggle and sacrifice. But these ideas can be grafted onto larger political struggles. In Lebanon and Palestine, maps are dotted with roads called 'Martyrs' Passing' or 'Martyr Street'. In villages and cities, martyrs' families are widely respected and receive special privileges, including monetary stipends. In Khoury's novel, Khalil Ahmad Jabir, the crazed father of one such martyr, turns against these kinds of conventions when he begins to tear his son's posters down.

If such posters tap into a long tradition of martyrdom, whose interpretations have been socially agreed upon, their visual iconography is also relatively fixed. In addition to a photograph of the deceased, sometimes edged with whitened or colourized borders, the posters almost always feature the name of the deceased and the circumstances and date of death, as well as Quranic quotes in Arabic script. The Palestinian flag, maps of Palestine and insignia of political groups or movements, such as Hezbollah's yellow flag or Fatah's crest of hands crossing rifles, frequently appear. Popular background images include the Dome of the Rock in Jerusalem, flames or cloud-dappled skies. Red flowers, a printer in Gaza explained to a visiting reporter, can 'represent martyrdom. The blood that falls onto the ground will grow flowers'.[18] The template is generally repeated, with variations developing in Egypt and Syria to commemorate protestors and rebels killed during the Arab Spring.

Crucial to these posters is the image, sometimes heroic and sometimes mundane, but now always deceased. Some of these photo portraits are taken specifically for use on a poster, with gunmen or bombers supplying the designer with their favourite images just prior

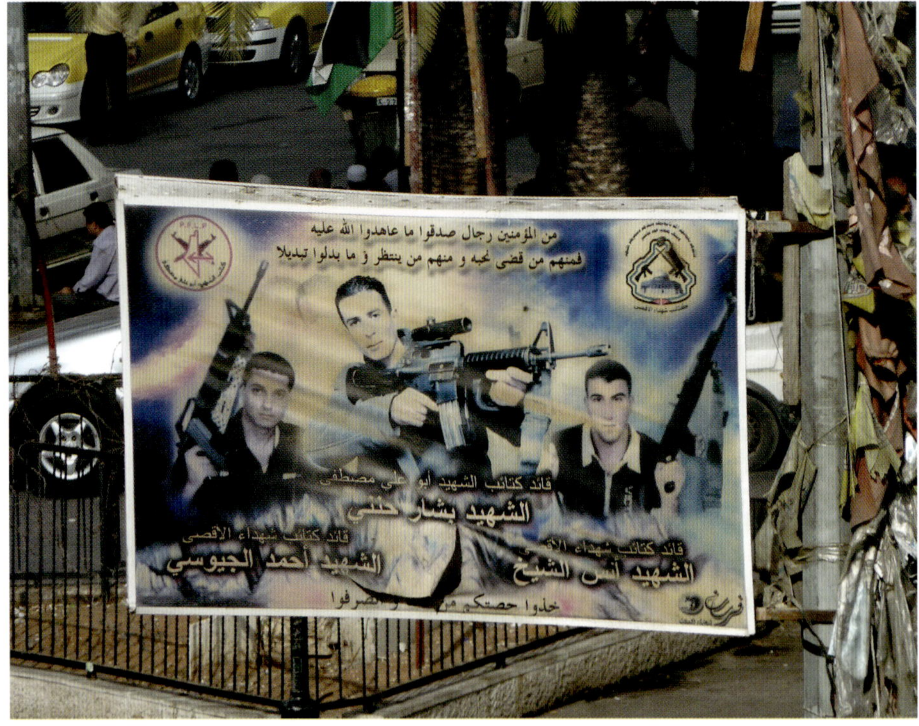

to undertaking an 'operation'. Others, often documenting civilians killed in bombings or shot during crossfire, are scanned from photos found in family albums or school class pictures. Images are accompanied by quotations from the Quran, the snippets haltingly expressing their sacred tenor: 'You must not think that those who were slain in the cause of Allah are dead. They are alive and well provided for by their Lord' (3:169). In this and other ways, martyr posters tell the simple story of entire lives. Nevertheless, many attempt to strike a balance between modernity and piety.

Nevertheless, if digitally produced martyr posters flourish, it has been because they are very quick and easy to produce. Moreover, they require no skill beyond the simple cut-and-paste actions found in basic computer software. Through history, printers have often functioned as de facto designers; indeed, there is nothing accidental about this pairing: graphic design grew out of the printing industry. Simple to make and following clear and efficient formulae, whether produced by teenage freelancers or designers employed by large-scale printers who use designs approved by the Palestinian Authority's Central Media Department, these digitally composed posters follow an uncomplicated script of digitized protocols. Trained or untrained, the

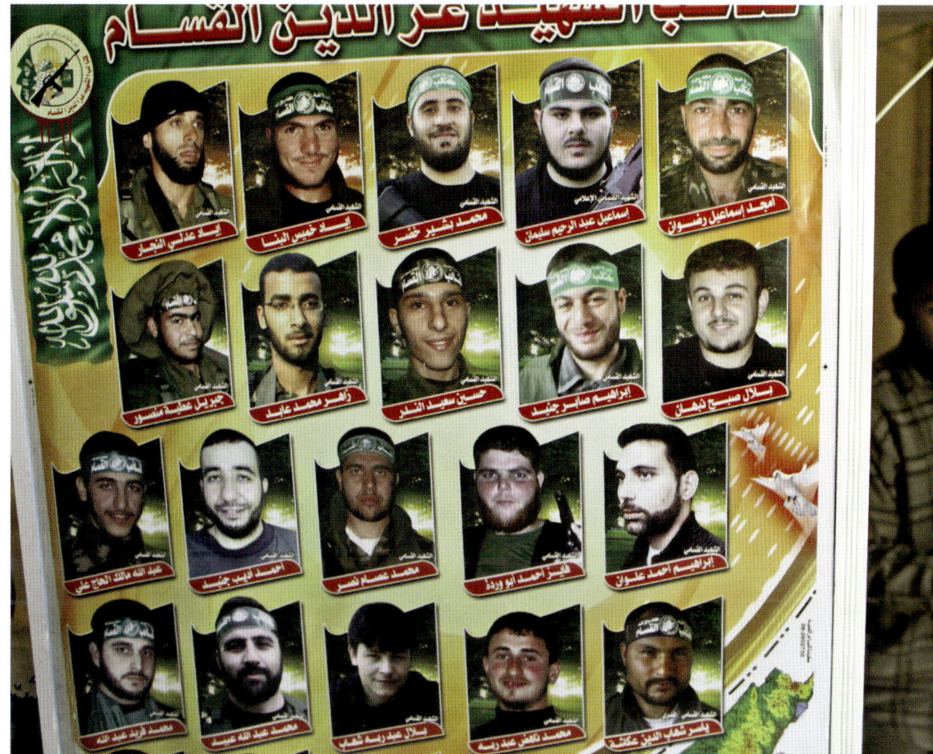
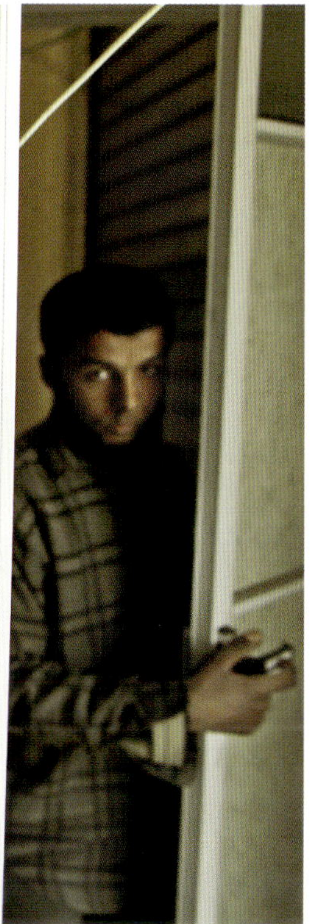

Print shop displays a poster showing militants who have died, 2009.

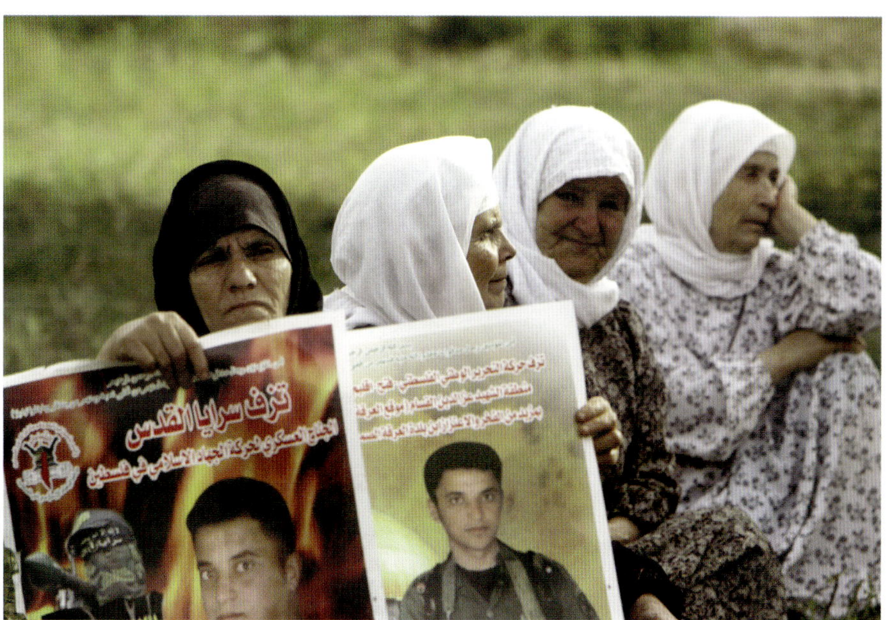

Palestinian women hold martyr posters, 2006.

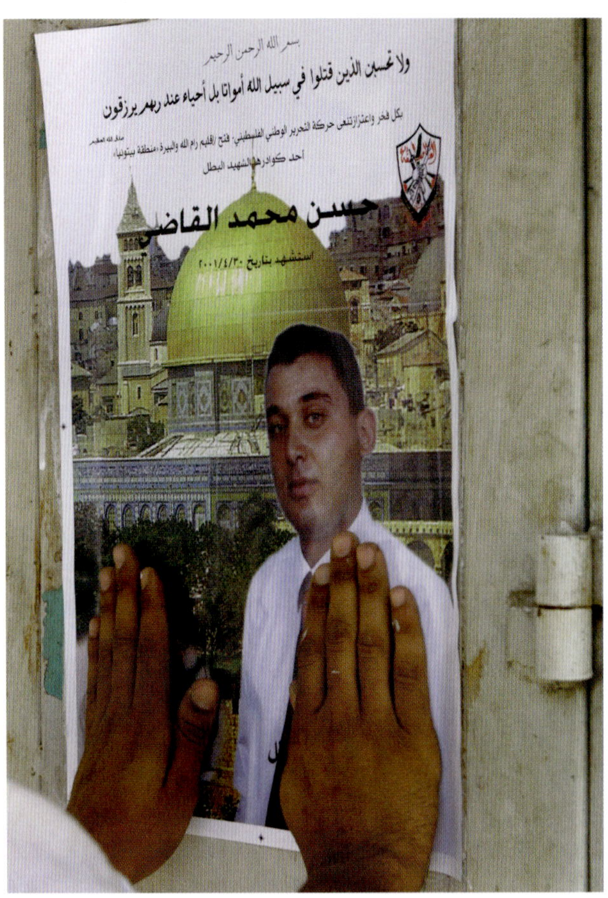

David Silverman,
'A Palestinian pastes up
a martyr poster', 2001.

designer first scans a photo of the person or uses a digital file. Then, using a software program, he or she edits the photograph for size, brightness and other factors and superimposes it on a scenic background. Finally, some information about the death and a verse from the Quran are usually added. In all, the process can take as little as ten minutes, ending with the production of a file on a disk or thumb drive.[19]

Taken superficially, the numbers of martyr posters are sometimes used by journalists and relief organizations in an unnatural calculus that tracks the death toll in long-running military operations; but it would be a mistake to see these posters only as a spectacle of deepening catastrophe. If such posters commemorate the dead, these inexpensive and widely distributed bills also mark physical space, spread ideas of heroism and help move their subjects from the world of the living into what has been called an 'enchanted' existence.[20] Combining text and verse, computer software transforms ordinary images into something magical. The secret lies in the way in which these computer-made images collage the banal together, following a rather strict template, but framing these oddments of daily life within a cosmos of politics and spirit. Whether killed in suicidal 'operations' or catching a random bullet, the poster subjects gain a kind of agency and seem actively involved in their own deaths. The head from a graduation portrait of a teenager may be superimposed on variations of a combat-clad, Rambo-styled body; balancing fierce modesty with military swagger, the dedicated student now carries a Kalashnikov rifle. Those already dressed as warriors are redeployed to lush fields of red tulips, an orange setting sun behind. No matter how common its digitized parts, the computer collage transforms them. As Mahmoud Hashhash noted:

> Images of the dead while still in this life are collaged . . . Stripped of their actual life context and redirected to inhabit another symbolic realm.[21]

Martyr posters today may be made with the help of desktop technology, but their evocation of the dead, their use of Arabic text and quotes from the Quran and the manner in which they bridge the chasm between life and death, summon a kind of magical recognition of the void left by death. Transcending their mystique, however, the sheer ubiquity of these inexpensive, easily distributed posters means that they are a backdrop to everyday life. Moreover, however personal the pictures, whichever background and symbols are chosen, the strict software templates produce a new kind of icon.[22] To an outsider, they may present a tedium of death and the unremarkable nature of violence.[23] Indeed, visual anthropologists argue that the computer templates create a uniformity that is so repetitive as to render the individual martyrs faceless; they may facilitate mourning on a communal level.[24]

The advent of digitally created martyr posters, however, is relatively recent. Back in the war-torn Beirut of the 1980s, Hezbollah's favoured artists found such a ready market for martyr paintings that they acquired 'schools' of followers and assistants.[25] These 'masters' built their reputations on lifelike realism and photographic clarity; as one painter told a journalist in 1998:

> Any picture you give us – a snapshot even – and we'll be able to paint an exact copy, life-like. We will reproduce the minutest details of the photograph.[26]

In these workmanlike environments, originality was of little import-ance.[27] But, by the late 1990s, as desktop publishing technology replaced earlier imagery, computer templates were formatted to imitate a set of preconceived expectations. Like the rigid stylistic formats expected in classical Indian sculpture, Buddhist canonic depictions of saints or formulae followed to sculpt Gothic statuary, these templates provide a venerable approach often expected in depictions of the sacred. In one sense we can agree with anthropologist Lori Allen, who indicates that 'in the standard regularity of their design, posters implied the homogeneity of martyrdom as a general category, and the democracy of death'.[28] But their strictly precise formats also remind us that enchantment is evoked through socially agreed-on norms, expressing the collective nature of shared values and wonderment.

It may be that such posters, while presenting a constant backdrop to everyday life, fill a void, marking an absence. Indeed, from Sofia to Accra, funerary or obituary posters have flourished in the wake of the personal computer. Hoardings just outside the Romanian capital, for example, present digitally produced posters that announce deaths and invite mourners to come to wakes, funerals and feasts. But, as Mahmoud Hashhash noted of the Palestinian works, these posters fill a void created by war and death.[29] Thus, they also commemorate less a personal loss than a collective marking of bereavement. Their ultimate efficacy, of course, stems not from computers, but from a cultural and religious context. Indeed, this form of enchantment reinforces social templates as well, weaving diverse Palestinian and Lebanese Muslims into a cohesive social unit. Displayed in relatives'

Nikolay Doychinov, wall covered in obituary notices in village of Vrajdebna near Sofia, 2011.

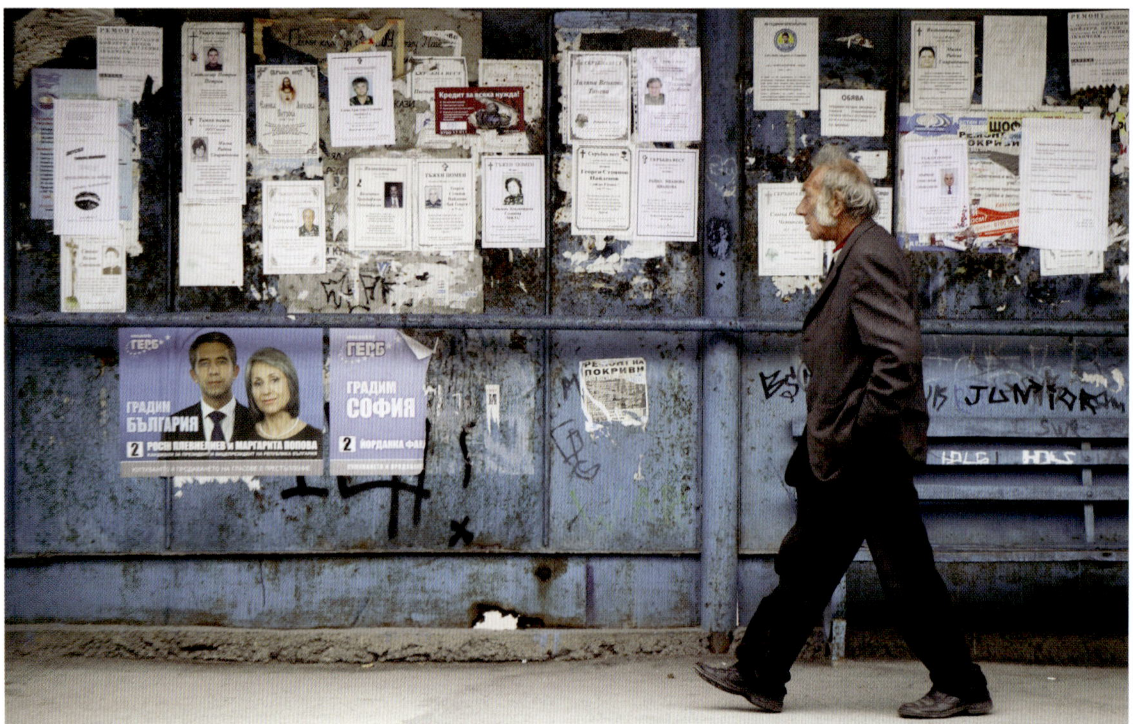

homes, they are a social fact 'thrust into the open by these posters'. In their wake, their posting triggers a series of behaviours, including 'the stories they occasioned, the visits they obliged'.[30] Hung at home, such posters grace the parlours where their subjects once sat, the bedrooms where they slept. On the street, these two-dimensional faces, as Buch noted, 'frame' the absence of people who could have been in the room or walking down the road.[31]

Lotte Buch's visit to the widow whose dead husband is memorialized with a poster is telling; her dead spouse is commemorated, but her second husband, who was incarcerated by the Israelis, is recalled only by a small snapshot photograph. Palestinian society has found a way to recognize loss from martyrdom, but is less successful in noting long absence and imprisonment. Martyr posters not only valorize the dead, but in some ways also overshadow the living. The intimation of mortality is everywhere now.

The Digital Interloper

Under scrutiny, the idea of wonderment withers and the results are almost always discouraging. For similar reasons, many critics quickly point to digitally made posters as the born enemy of enchantment. Posters made on a computer are often presented as a kind of visual auto-da-fé. Bewitched by technology, the argument goes, poster-makers have tossed aside skills honed over a lifetime. Some makers even attempt to imitate the crisp clarity of computer-imaging software with painting by hand.[32] The martyr posters of the Lebanese Civil War were so quickly exchanged with Palestinian desktop posters that we forget that their earliest models were made with brush and paint. Sometimes haphazardly, sometimes with a certain malicious pleasure, and sometimes with a clear consciousness of their own efficacy, digital posters had begun – by the late 1990s – in a serious way to displace older forms of poster-making. Indeed, on a global scale, the posters made on computers are accused of pushing aside traditions of art, storytelling and other long-held skills. But in countries like India and Nigeria, the story is more complex; if the digital age has led to a new poster renaissance, it also forces us to examine reactions against digitized posters (and why we have been slow to recognize this).

In India, for example, the conflict is cast in fundamental terms. Posters there were long-ago established not only for advertising,

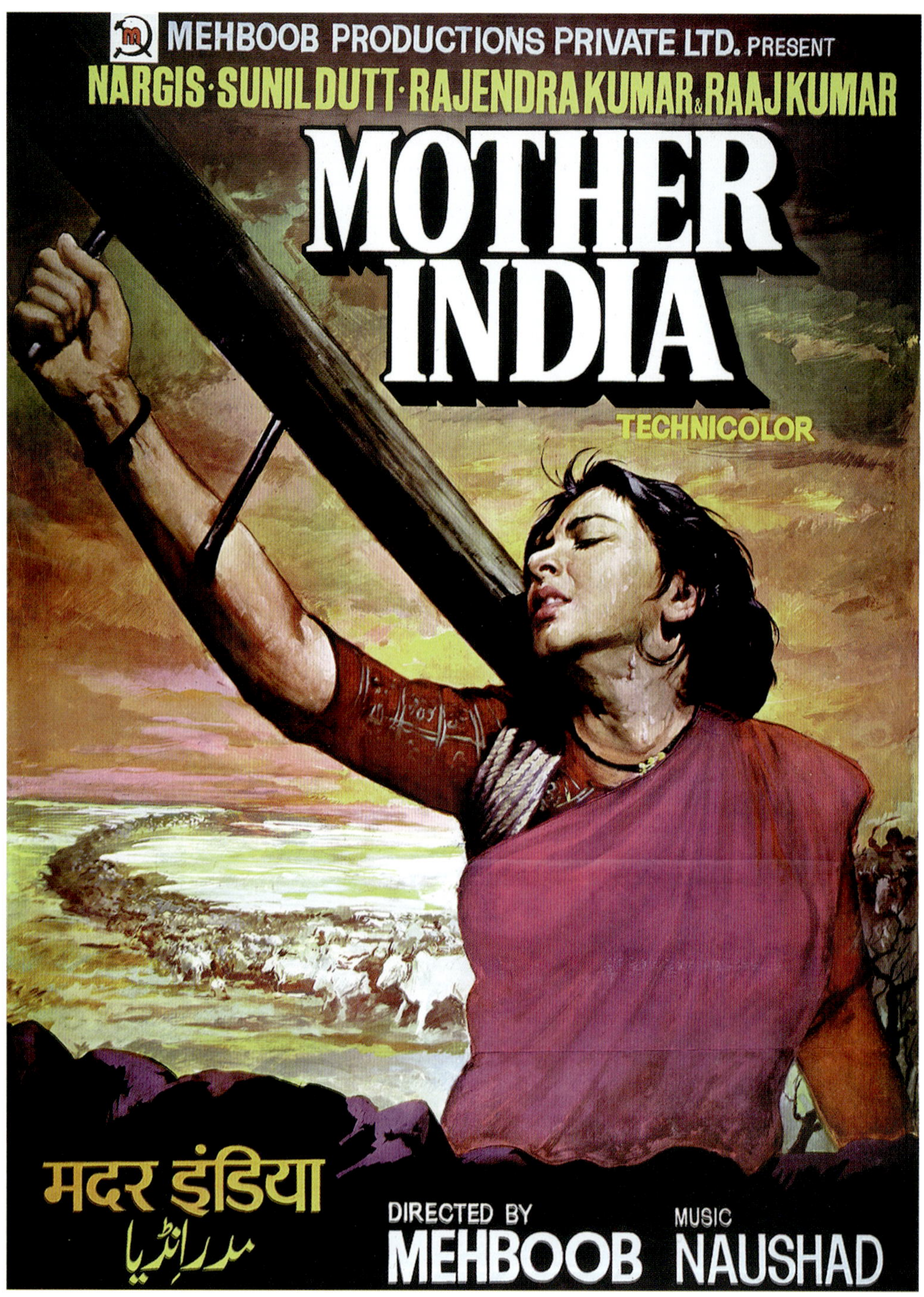

Advertisement for the film *Mother India* (1957).

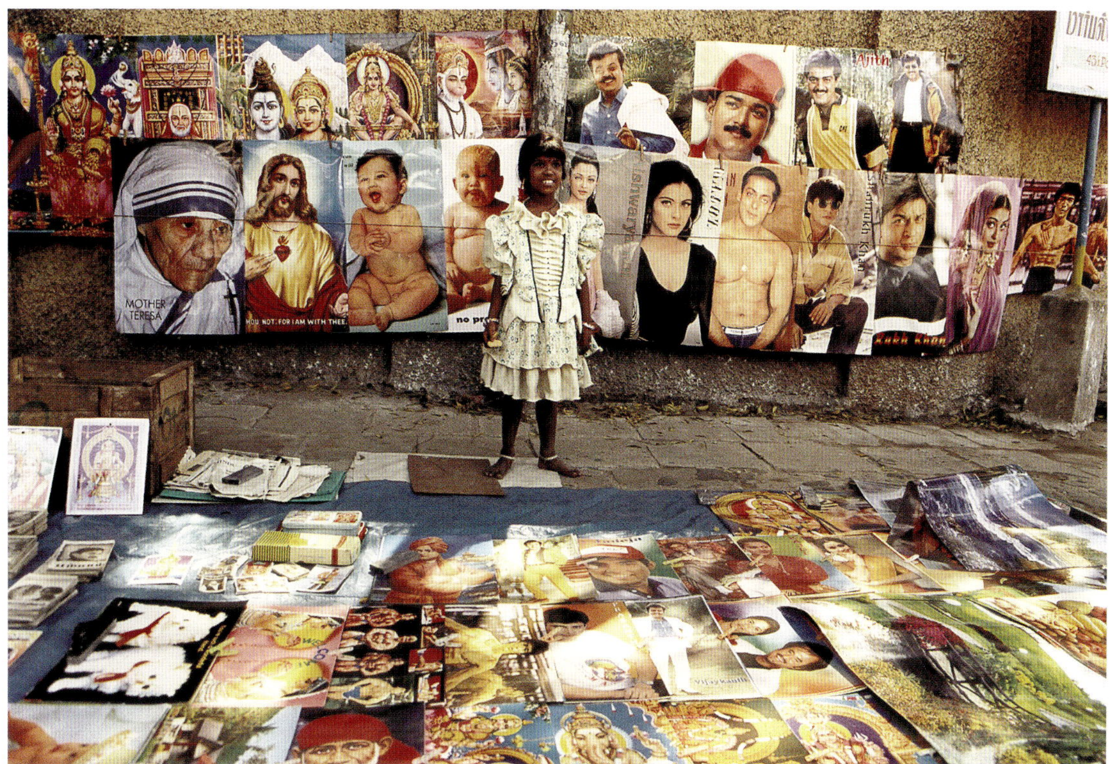

Jonathan Torgovnik, posters and memorabilia of film stars on sale in Chennai, 2000.

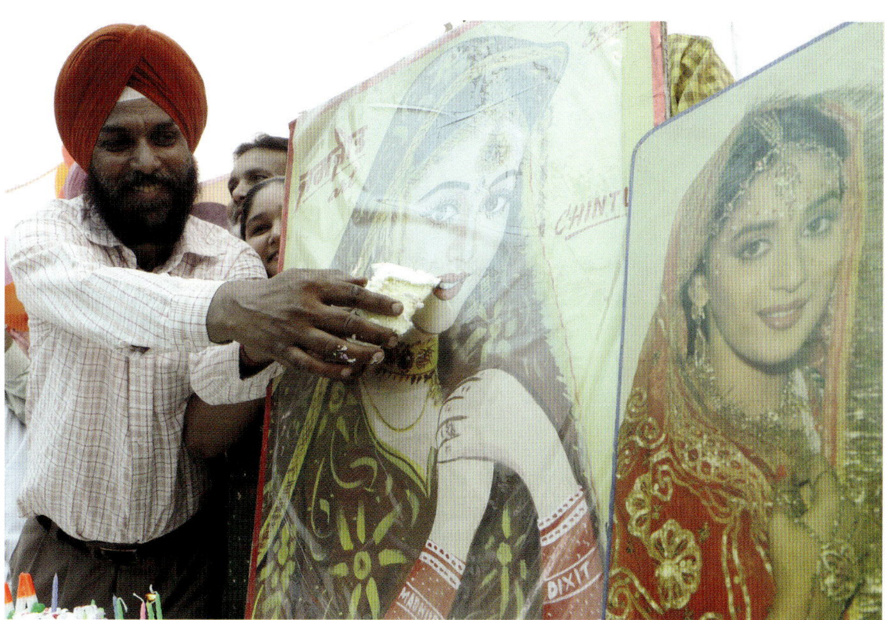

Man celebrates the 44th birthday of a Bollywood film actress by presenting a birthday cake to her poster image, 2012.

but also as the inexpensive, mass-produced prints known as bazaar or calendar art; more recently they have passed under the less derogatory term 'god posters'.[33] While pictures of fat babies and lush landscapes are abundantly represented, religious themes (largely Hindu but also comprising Muslim, Sikh and Christian content) dominate the market.[34] Muslim subjects and folklore, including images of shrines in Mecca and Medina, Quranic calligraphy and portraits of local saints and their tombs and miracles, are all in strong evidence.[35]

And yet, while god posters remain unchallenged, the Bollywood poster is in free fall. A form that dates to the middle of the twentieth century, these hand-painted posters advertised each new film's release. Based in Mumbai, the Indian film industry is lively and ambitious, but also unafraid of mixing historical features with romances, or musical comedies with serious drama. Bollywood posters breathe deeply of the genre's carnivalesque air. Until the 1980s, colour photography was rare; artists hand-painted coloured posters, often basing their designs on black-and-white stills but creating montages with liberal interpretation. Beginning in the 1940s and culminating in the 1970s and early 1980s, the style of these advertisements became more and more marked, often sizzling with only slightly repressed sexuality and dazzling with their wild expressionist brushstrokes and florid hot colours, coupling raw emotions with escapist fare. This approach was labour-intensive, with artists not only copying images but also creating their own montages and typefaces; nevertheless, they were printed in large runs and distributed nationally, being found in barber shops and the shopfronts of *paan* (betel nut chew) vendors and tea stalls as well as the publicity hoardings of Mumbai and New Delhi.

Beginning in the 1980s, painted publicity has been replaced by posters printed from photographs, usually stills taken on location during shooting. Instead of asking a Bollywood painter to work up an image a day or two before the film's release, these ads were created weeks or even months before an actual release. The new system cut into painters' livelihoods; when large-format digital printers were introduced, their numbers decreased even further. As one poster painter put it, the cinema is 'about money and hand-painted art doesn't fit in because of two aspects: it takes too much time and it is way too expensive'. As one reporter said: 'the fantastic made way for the facsimile'.[36]

There are two sides to any poster – its message and its style. While Bollywood posters' message stays on target, their visual style has changed radically. When American-style publicity and digital posters pushed aside the old handmade posters, some say they 'lost much of their Indian charm'.[37] As one Western journalist put it, the 'beautiful painted posters that decorated city streets all over India' are gone.[38] And yet, many Indian filmgoers care little about the aesthetic differences between digital and hand-painted images; as a fan offers a piece of birthday cake to two images of the screen idol Madhuri Dixit on her 44th birthday, it matters little whether one image is painted and the other a touched-up photograph. The enchantment of the cinema, its ability to fire the imagination and to shape dreams for millions of people, remains unchanged.

However, hand-painted Bollywood posters are defended with a ferocity that has yet to dim. The terms of this nostalgia are often muddled and emotional, based on the lamentations of ageing makers who mourn the passing of the great days of the painted Indian poster and collectors who snap up old works or well-known Bollywood classics when they appear on the market. Succinctly summing up these attitudes, the BBC has called the hand-painted Bollywood poster a 'victim' of India's technological and economic explosion.[39] But, like a heinous crime, the backlash is often more visceral than carefully thought out. As one Mumbai poster entre-preneur noted:

> Many of our artists see the digital posters of today as equivalents of fast food and the hand-painted posters of the past as a lovely home-cooked meal by a mother.

More succinctly, one artist insisted: 'When digital posters came in, our industry sank like the Titanic.'[40]

But these posters are often invested with a wonderment that transcends grandma's apple pie or a doomed passenger liner. With brooding heroes and sulky sirens depicted over-sized, in raw, fluorescent colours, these posters are often described in fantastic terms. Dealers now hunting down older, hand-painted posters express emotions more commonly found in a love letter. As one put it, a hand-painted poster is written with blood, sweat and tears. It conveys raw emotions and energy to the reader whereas the digital poster is like a digitally typed letter – it is lifeless.[41]

With collectors' emotions running high, what once formed a routine if riotous backdrop to south Asia's vibrant street life is now becoming a rare and precious thing, cosseted by collectors and shown in museums. The hand-painted Bollywood poster is rapidly becoming an *objet d'art*. Hand-painted posters offer a gorgeous release from the banal photo stills that dominate commercial cinema. Unlike a beautiful sunset, Bollywood paintings emerge from the human imagination, brought into being through a maker's touch. They are enchanted with a power that, as Gell would have it, comes out of our idolization of technique, casting a spell over all of us.

At a pitch only slightly slower than that of India, critics and collectors worldwide blame digital posters for usurping hand-painted posters. In recent years, West Africa developed its own booming film industries. Lagos, for instance, has given birth to 'Nollywood', itself modelled on Bollywood. In Ghana, a scrappy 'mobile cinema' industry emerged in the 1980s, relying on roving entrepreneurs who travelled the country setting up temporary cinemas using little more than a TV, VCR and gas-powered generators. Local sign painters, long relegated to creating visual advertisements on businesses and shopfronts across English- and French-speaking West Africa, were commissioned to paint posters for local and foreign films, as with a poster from 1986 advertising *The Spy Who Loved Me*. Often created on burlap bags originally used to store flour, these posters hastily announce their own ephemerality. And yet here, too, hand-painted movie posters wither in the cold glow of the computer.[42]

But do posters made on computers really announce the end of wonderment? Newer West African posters suggest otherwise, bringing the hand-painted into the realm of digital enchantment. A new entry into the vivid visual culture of West Africa, the 'street news' posters circulating in Nigeria, Ghana, Ivory Coast and Benin emerged in recent years as a component of broadening democracy and the lifting of censorship. Sometimes called 'almanachs', or 'calendriers', street news posters have a shared ancestry with Indian and Chinese poster-calendars. Both derive from nineteenth-century calendars distributed by the British colonial administrators or marketers. Yet, while all are descended from an imperial past, they are, at best, distant cousins today. Moreover, in the cultural melting pot of coastal West Africa, Hindu god posters and calendars were commonly imported by Indian traders, beginning in the late nineteenth century. The imagery of the latter has become part of the indigenous or Vodun visual culture. Thus, it has been common to find a diaspora of Hindu posters and calendars for sale in Ivory Coast markets.[43]

Whatever their origins, the posters in West Africa aim to cover stories succinctly, elbowing their way into a tale and rapidly getting to the heart of the matter. With low literacy rates (roughly 65 per cent of Nigerians, for instance, are functionally literate), many buyers 'read' such posters in place of other media. Like West Africa's painted signs, these contain multiple narrative 'cells', communicating easily comprehended stories and carrying limited text; indeed, because they are often printed in several languages, including Hausa Igbo and Yoruba, as well as pidgin English and sometimes French (if they are also meant to be sold in French-speaking countries), there is little space for long, textual distractions. They also announce a fantastic world of vicious soldiers, gloating cannibals and smirking bureaucrats who use naked farmers as footstools.

As social observers, street news posters function differently from newspapers and magazines. Not only is written language kept to a minimum, with short headlines, captions and speech balloons, but they live short, topical lives. Bought and displayed in homes or small shops and outdoor kiosks, bars and hairdressing salons, their calendars are of minimal practical use, hidden as they are in tiny print and almost always crushed into the bottom of the poster. Typographically, they can be unsophisticated and show clear limitations. Their makers, for example, are often incapable of operating the shift key. But for a poor and only semi-literate audience, the toilsome business of alternating upper- and lower-case letters, apostrophes and other grammatical niceties are pointless irritations, while proper parts of speech only slow the narrative down. Often sold alongside newspapers, some depict current events or highlight wins by local or national sports teams. But many other themes are even more flamboyant than the tabloids and street gossip.

If the punctuation and diction of these stories lack the niceties of souped-up prose, they can still be rich and satisfying, full of sad beauty, bawdy adventure, political wisdom and especially wild surmise. Sensational themes face down national politics, accidents or funerals of celebrities. Some subjects, for example tales of cannibalism, human sacrifice or organ harvesting, deal with titillating hearsay or urban legend. By using multiple cells, their makers can fill space rapidly, presenting various scenes; when showing multiple viewpoints, they allow the viewer to soar above the mundane, while simultaneously presenting themes from the underside of life. In the years immediately following military rule, when the Nigerian press sank under state repression, nimble and explicit street news posters often critiqued the old regime. 'Death Does Not Take Bribe', from 1999, for example, depicts the late General Sani Abacha bringing a box full of money to an enthroned devil; ironically referring to Nigeria's former ruler as 'our great hero', in a larger box the poster shows Abacha bringing the same box to Christ on Judgement Day. A smaller cell shows the late general burning in hell.

Not too surprisingly, street news posters do not subscribe to journalistic objectivity, and neither do they disclose personal material like political essays, diaries, letters or satirical paragraphs. Instead, they carry solemn warnings against the loss of one's values and valuables, doling out titillation and admonition at the same time. At 'chop houses' or barber shops, posters allow the illiterate or those with limited reading skills to engage with the public sphere, playing the part of the cracker-barrel philosopher but also coexisting with a world of enchantment filled with malicious spirits and were-animals, witches and Satan. At their worst, they provide watered-down gossip and a few bottomless anecdotes. Full of hasty despair and quick anguish, they often tell magical stories. Indeed, in the age of modernity, they hark back to the griot telling stories. Nevertheless, like the storytellers of yore, they work as a kind of social lubricant, encouraging conversation but also re-enforcing shared moral, political or religious values. A poster explaining Sharia law, for example, uses a typical cartoon-strip format to identify fornication, theft and other salacious or venal crimes that

'Death Does Not Take Bribe', 1999.

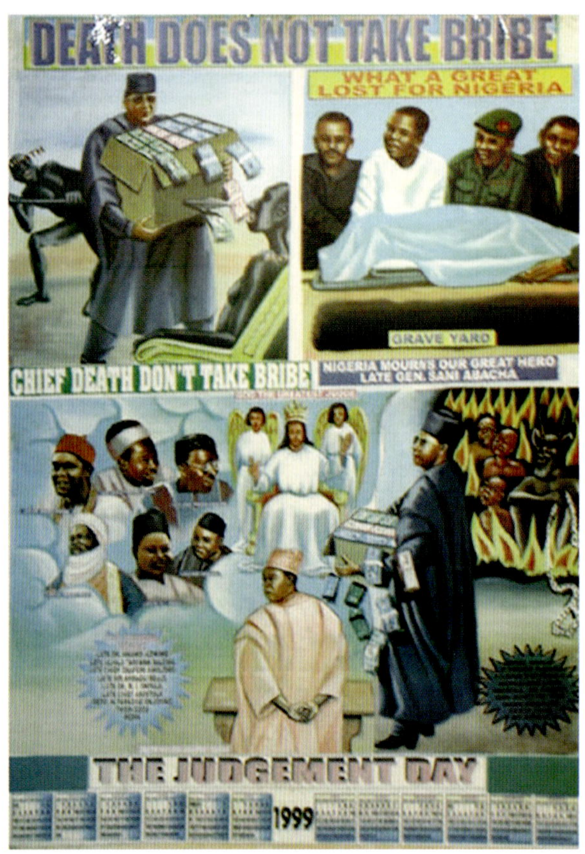

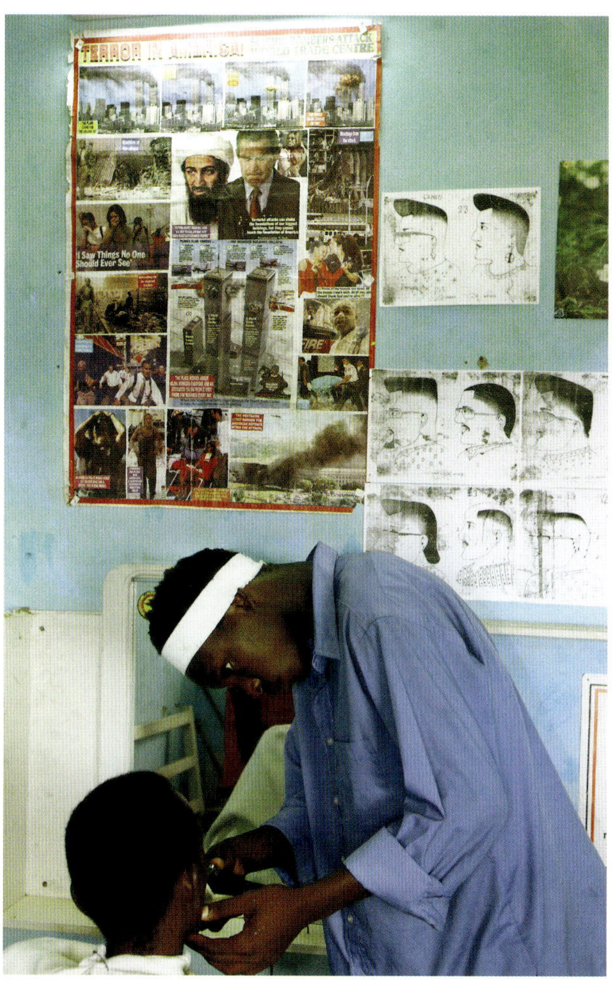

Marco Longari, barber shop in Burundi displays posters about the 9/11 attacks, 2003.

justify, in Muslim religious law, punishment for their perversions; other Islamic posters teach the proper rituals surrounding washing or praying. Conversely, Christian posters frequently decry converts who still practise animism or are on speaking terms with the devil. But these posters also ring with the power of society's standards; cannibals are brought to justice, for example, while violently forcing initiation rites on university students in secret clubs is decried. They combine the golden companionship of the tavern with the pastor's moralizing sermon against life, as seen from the underside.

At least one scholar has called these 'a new generation' of posters, which are replacing the hand-painted vignettes that dominated the earliest street news posters. Instead, these newer posters use scanners, photographic images circulating freely on the Internet, computer photo-processing programs and computer graphics. More recently, photo-based images collaged together on the computer and representing events like the capture of Saddam Hussein or the collapse of the World Trade Center in New York, pirate imagery and stories from cable news and websites.[44] Nevertheless, such imagery exists side by side with the traditional and hand-painted. The barber shop in Burundi displays a street news poster from Nigeria alongside a hair-styling chart drawn by hand and recalling the hand-painted signs once so common. While these digitally made posters are widely accepted, they still evoke the magic that shimmers just beneath the surface of the most commonplace, everyday world.

Unlike in India, however, this has been achieved more carefully. Indeed, the shape-shifting magic of hand-painted images is often

combined with descriptive, photographed images. As the scholar
Audrey Gadzekpo notes, photos may increasingly be taken from
the Web and collaged into a poster composition. The magic of photo-
processing programs allows 'news' poster-makers remarkable latitude,
but also echoes and magnifies emotional truisms. Faces of newsmakers
are digitally collaged onto other people's bodies; parties whose paths
never crossed in real life are placed side by side. As proof, Gadzekpo
points to a Ghanaian poster from 2008 showing Barack Obama and
John McCain in a race on foot, with both politicians' heads superimposed
into a sports image.[45] In the poster of 2011 about Internet fraud, the
eyes of a 'Sakawa boy' are collaged onto the head of a dog. Other
posters combine hand-painted cartoon imagery with photographs.
In these cases, a 'type of local news that could not be documented
by photos but only by painted images' is documented. Thus magical
transformations of were-beasts into humans and other wildly fantastic
events of witchcraft, cannibalism or the sale of human parts fill
out posters that otherwise rely on photographic imagery.[46] That is,
computers oozing their own incomparable kind of magic tricks, evoking
enough wonderment to pass a communal test of belief, allow these
poster-makers to be parodist, historian, poet, clown, fable writer,
satirist, reporter and griot all in one.

Bridging Useless Spaces

There are many reasons why Reza Abedini's poster 'Bridge: The Visual
Language of Reza Abedini' discreetly announces the designer's
exhibition to a Dutch audience by using Latin letterforms, but a
key to the show's content remains in the delicate tracery of Persian
script. The calligraphic effect is where Abedini's range of design
activity, including 'graphics' and 'books', is clearly featured. As in most
of Abedini's work, a kind of cultural bartering takes place; like the
poster's silhouetted figure of a man dressed in nineteenth-century
military garb, the poster ties East with West. The further we probe,
the increasingly revelatory the poster becomes; its cross-cultural
references are meant to be savoured and investigated. The man's
Western-style regalia is replaced with an elegant cascade of Farsi
lettering. Recalling Iran's Qajar dynasty, the period in the nineteenth
century when Western forms were imported in an attempt to 'modern-
ize' the country, the poster's references overlap and impinge on one

Reza Abedini, 'Bridge: The Visual Language of Reza Abedini', 2006.

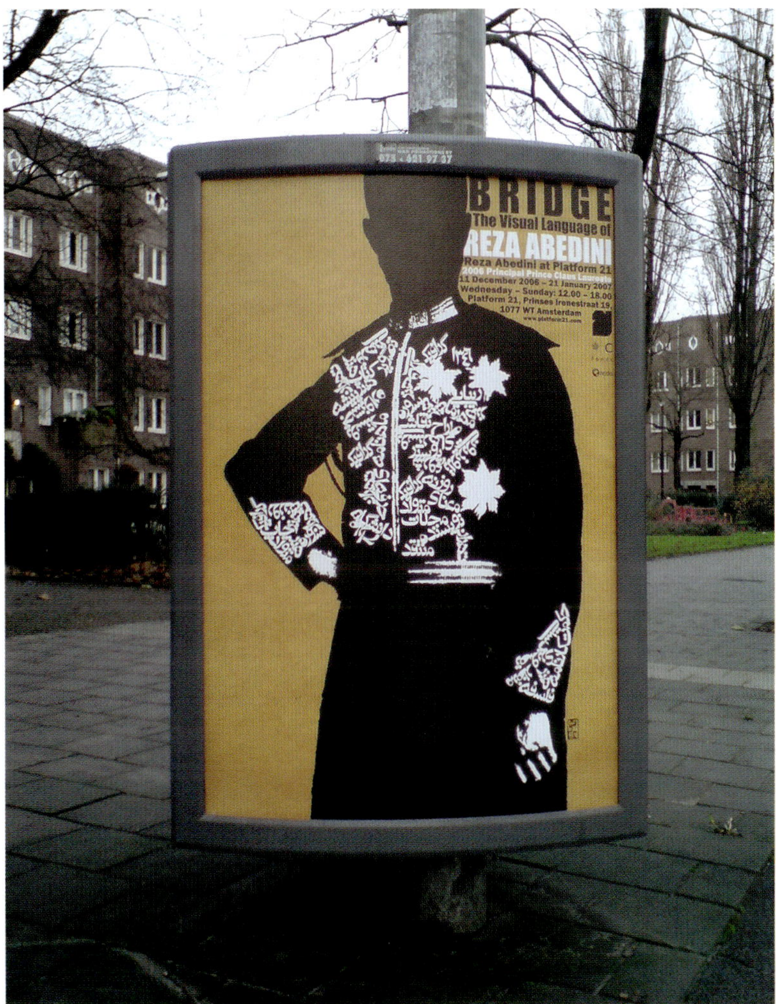

another. The man's swagger recalls the pomp of the Persian court,
as well as the moment when photography swept the shah's inner
circle as a fashionable hobby. Nevertheless, for Abedini, the period's
Westernization signalled 'a disaster for Persian script'.[47] Instead, Abedini
speaks casually of the magic of calligraphy, and his posters stand in
for a kind of 'retraditionalization' of Iranian culture, bridging past and
present, East and West, but each on singularly Persian grounds.

A striking polyglot, Abedini consciously chose the poster format,
evincing a deep sympathy with the form. For all that, his posters bristle
quietly with creative tension. Even native Farsi speakers find Abedini's
calligraphic script difficult to decode. As with the most decorative Iranian
manuscripts, understanding and appraisal are intentionally delayed,
often forcing readers to take the composition in for a moment of

aesthetic contemplation before undertaking the task of decipherment. But the biggest revelation is how Abedini remains utterly modern while navigating conservative Islamic scribal culture. He deftly infuses his work with a sense of wonderment; it is a talent worth saving, to inspire less gifted mortals.

In the culture of Islamic Iran, famous for its reticence on all issues aesthetic, calligraphy is deemed among the greatest of arts. More than the study and practice of visual mark-making, writing in script is an admission of spiritual ardour; it is the means of employing a holy craft. After all, calligraphy transcribed God's word in the form of the Quran. Here, the Quran is not 'mere' script; today as well as then, as missionary and author Constance Padwick put it, the written word is like 'the twigs of the burning bush aflame with God'.[48] The text of the Quran is strictly faithful to God's message. It does not convey a narrative about holiness; in itself it is 'a textual object of divinity'.[49]

Abedini's exhibition 'Bridge: The Visual Language of Reza Abedini' (2006–7) is testimony to the powerful physical presence of Arabic script. The show itself was filled with text, featuring three-dimensional sculpture of key phrases from Persian poetry and even a hologram of Abedini, his body covered with script. In the past, to be worthy of transcribing such wisdom, traditional calligraphers' training was both mental and physical; a scribe, it was said, acquired a 'sixth finger' when he gradually developed a superior talent. Such attainment came only after years of practising religious faith and mystical purity; calligraphy was practised while observing prayer, religious rites and chastity. It may explain, very indirectly, why a talented scribe could only gain the acceptance of experts and authorization to sign his own works after decades of study.[50] And with true respect, the Quran's texts are fiercely and loyally passed along, reiterated and exhibited widely. Centuries after Muhammad died, the unshakable words of the Quran are fully integrated into the streetscapes and architecture of traditional Islamic cities. Quranic verses have worn lines of script on the faces of mosques, over doors of homes, as ornament on government buildings or communicating with public banners. For all this, Abedini believes that the arrival of print technology in Iran and its application to Persian script was an unmitigated disaster.

In the West, printing is practised out of necessity, sometimes with struggle and not always with a clear idea of what is taking place; the Islamic approach to writing is utterly alien. Long exposed to printing,

Persians first encountered block printing when the Mongols introduced printed money to Iran in the late thirteenth century. Nevertheless, the Chinese-made currency was widely disdained and finally abandoned.[51] A Christian Armenian press was established in Jolfe in the seventeenth century, but its influence did not spread. Instead, the antecedents of modern Islamic typography may be traced to book publishing in Europe. Firmly and conveniently, Gutenberg's printing press transformed Western society; attempts to bring this change to the Islamic world were slower. That the alphabets of Muslim countries often use fluidly concise cursive scripts led many early observers in both Europe and the Middle East to doubt that the printed word could adequately – let alone elegantly – transcribe Arabic and Farsi texts. This was no esoteric point. Abedini observes passionately that, regarding printed books, 'the structure of graphic design in Iran is totally Western, but we use the Persian writing system on it . . . It doesn't connect things together'.[52] The failure to develop linkages and ligatures in printing, Abedini insists, proved more than the inability of printing presses to make bridges between letters; in the minds of many, when divested of technical differences, there remained an atmosphere of malign mystery, leagued with deep incomprehension and mistrust. Only with nineteenth-century lithography and twenty-first-century computers would this change.

With the Westernizing Qajar dynasty in the nineteenth century, Persian print culture began to develop, at first in a series of quick spurts, then as part of a larger flow. Nevertheless, posters arrived almost as an afterthought. Lithographic presses were used for books and newspapers, an honest compromise since they already catered to the wealthy and literate. At best, posters were gradually introduced in the early twentieth century and usually addressed consumers, touting products promoted by Western companies. It was not until 1941, after his ascent to the throne, that the monarch Shah Pahlavi also began to circulate political posters in the form of rather focused and regal portraits. At Tehran University, a graphic design department was founded in 1950; the education here was modelled on that found in Western art schools. This limited poster culture makes it all the more surprising how, with lightning action, the form rapidly developed during the 1977–9 Islamic Revolution.

Abedini insists that 'Graphic design in Iran can be divided into two separate periods: designers that studied before the revolution, and

Gran Fury/ACT UP, 'You've Got Blood on Your Hands, Ed Koch', 1986–7.

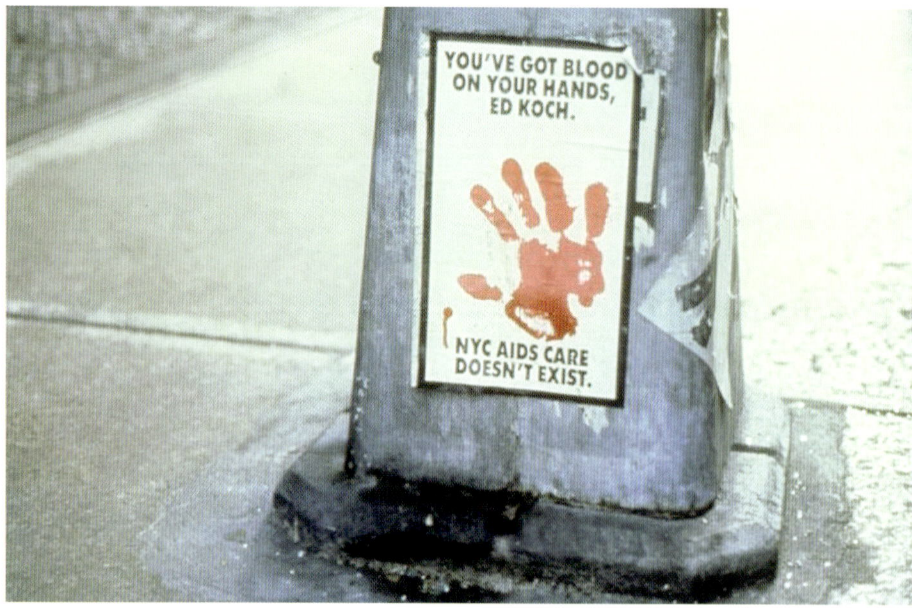

those who studied after the revolution.'[53] If Persia's history with print-ing is short, the poster was an ideal vehicle for the Islamic Revolution's programme of reinventing tradition – or 'retraditionalization'.[54] During the early years of the Islamic Revolution, posters were hung in streets and alleyways, usually on highly receptive walls. Along with tape recordings of sermons, photocopied leaflets and other non-official communications, posters emerged as a dramatically simple form of 'small media', that is, tools of resistance against a state that controlled television and radio.[55]

By the late 1970s, Iranian poster designers drank from a deep well of visual sources. Indeed, through the late 1970s and into the 1980s, activists worldwide aspired to an aesthetic slickness very different from the rough graphics of Medu and the Atelier Populaire. In the United States, for instance, groups like Gran Fury and ACT UP (AIDS Coalition to Unleash Power) imitated the dominant forms of corporate advertising in posters like 'You've Got Blood on Your Hands, Ed Koch'. Here, the groups used the contrast value of a primitive, blood-red handprint disrupting an otherwise-tidy poster of polished type and careful composition. During the Iranian Revolution, militants valued the poster, toying with a variety of messages and swerving between the epithetical and threatening and the visionary and utopian. In 1979, for instance, student radicals gave an embittered press conference before the occupied American embassy in Tehran, decorating their dais with a poster reading: 'Shah and His US Trained and Equipped Army Gear Up for Further Massacres'. Their stylistic sources were equally varied, including the International Style, Russian Revolution, Andy Warhol and even Baroque paintings, as well as a range of Iranian painting traditions.

After the rise of the Islamic Republic, this visual eclecticism vanished in the twinkling of an eye. Indeed, some Muslim critics questioned the motives of graphic designers, associating them with the permissive school of rhetoric in which right and wrong do not exist and there is no foundation for style or context. At its worst, they argued, graphic design is little more than images that have been

> simplified into a series of dots, lines, surfaces or colours . . . generally used to promote the spirit of a consumer society that is at present ruling the industrial communities of our world. In short, graphic art is the creation of compositions that convey straightforward and blunt messages.[56]

But Reza Abedini took a different approach. Claiming the designed poster as an 'opportunity', he climbed the potent wave of re-traditionalization and rode it in.

Perhaps if the Revolution had unfolded differently, Abedini might not have turned to the poster format, which so perfectly

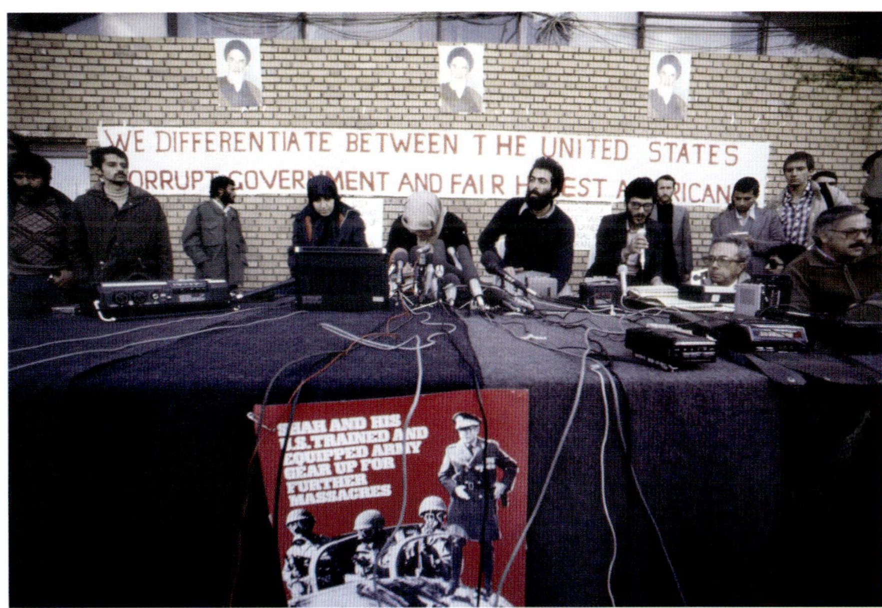

Iranian Students at the US Embassy, 1979.

allowed him to probe the 'problem' of Iranian calligraphic tradition. To be a calligrapher in Iran, even today, is to be something of a scholar and a poet – or if not a poet at least to shelter the transmigrated soul of a dead one. But graphic design, he asserts,

> is defined by Western designers . . . you share the writing system . . . you share the images, and type, somehow based on the history of graphic design but you should realize the invitation of type, moveable type, is based on value and the spirit of writing systems in the West.[57]

Both politically and aesthetically, he used these posters to make a personal rebellion against Western typography. Recalling the moment in the Qajar dynasty

> two hundred years ago when printing systems came . . . they found out that the writing system doesn't work with these machines because the words here are completely different as the Roman system. What they did . . . was to force the Arabic and Farsi systems to be as close as possible to the Roman system to be printed on this machine.[58]

The Westernizing Qajar dynasty played with Western technologies like photography and printing; unsurprisingly, the elegantly masculine silhouette on Abedini's 'Bridge' poster, itself taken from a Qajar-era photograph, hinges on its experimental fervour; keeping its calligraphic tradition intact, its digital tools allow the unencumbered use of Latin and Arabic lettering.

Reviving Persian calligraphy in the age of the computer is no simple matter; using the poster format to do this provided a growing, buoyant freedom. Although the calligraphy on Abedini's posters appears written by hand, in fact it was made on a computer. The sense of liberation, intelligently self-cultivated and unencumbered by the frozen forms typical of Latin printing presses, created a boom in Persian calligraphy. In the hands of an artist like Shirin Neshat, whose films and photographs are saturated with a steady breeze of calligraphic texts, written language becomes a backdrop for a larger political critique. For Abedini, however, calligraphy provides a different commentary. Clearly there is no replacement for a skilled

hand that bridges one stroke of the brush to another, but rather
Abedini reacts to the very form of calligraphy itself. Early typog-
raphers, Abedini observed,

> neglected the characteristics of Persian scripts and tried to
> prepare them for printing systems just as they did for Latin
> characters. Therefore, they adopted and adjusted Persian
> letters into blocks, transforming them in order to make them
> suitable to be used repetitively and in junctions. But . . . [this]
> was just the beginning of numerous problems with Iranian
> type . . .[59]

As Abedini saw it:

> Even digital type is based on this system. We do Arabic type on a
> computer, but still the mentality of designing a type is based on
> this. Just in the last few years actually we've been able to get rid of
> some of these problems like useless distance between the letters.[60]

Abedini proves that, when carefully attended, computer
technology can reinforce the free-swinging lyricism of hand-written
Arabic or Farsi. But, more to the point, letterpress printing has dominated
Western thinking about graphic forms since the 1450s. Its separation
of text and images, for example, leaves little room for conceiving an
image-like text. That said, Abedini carefully shapes individual letters
and coaxes them into broader patterns, all the while disrupting the
baseline, entwining letters and images into complex designs. If the
very act of writing in the Middle East can be deeply expressive, then
Abedini uses letterforms, including both the stocky, assertive Latin
alphabet and fluid shapes from written Arabic and Farsi, to build on
long-established traditions.

Abedini leans towards the most decorative of calligraphic
conventions, but he is also sensitive to their magical meanings.
His fluid and carefully arranged compositions use the Nastaliq and
Shikasteh styles, merging text and image. However, posters like the one
advertising the artist's exhibition 'Siah Mashq' point to deeper Persian
traditions where words were believed to form a kind of under-armour.
Warriors, for instance, would go into battle wearing undershirts covered
with written prayers. Confronted with an exhibition of his work in Qom,

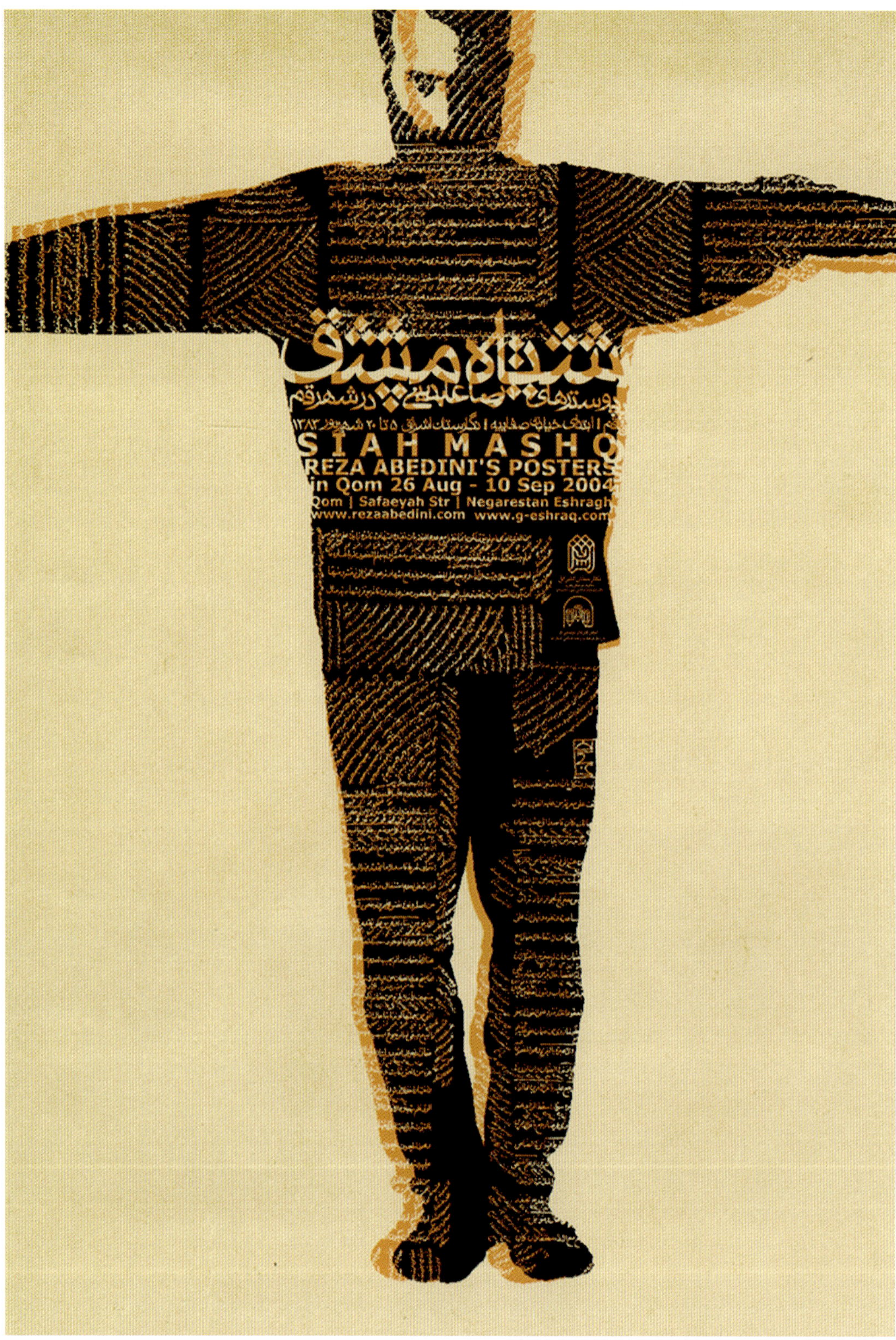

Reza Abedini, poster for the artist's exhibition 'Siah Mashq', 2004.

an ancient site of Islam in Iran, Abedini faced a tricky task. Abedini armours himself with words. Perfectly formed letters flit, skirt and skip across the computer screen and printed poster, alike. Words pack silhouetted figures densely, often leaving them surrounded by wide, empty spaces. In some posters a single word hangs in space. Abedini's fluid and carefully arranged compositions make it almost impossible to separate one element from another.

While Abedini sees globalization as 'a horror', his re-tradition-alization of Iranian posters places him in a curious relation to global audiences in the age of the Internet. The desktop revolution has allowed any casual user enormous power, providing clip art and fonts, as well as WYSWIG printing, to large numbers of untrained poster-makers. But, as some historians observe, 'The tools of design' have been 'momentarily confused with the skills of designers'.[61] Practised with passion and precision, digital typesetting and design have expanded the possibilities of what professional designers can achieve. But Abedini's re-traditionalization also points to another issue. In 'Bridges' and elsewhere, he presents an intriguing inversion of the Westernization of design. Fully sensitive to how the West has treated and mistreated Islamic scripts, he instead treats Latin forms in a curious way, using them in arabesque swirls and twists that are so incomprehensible that they might as well be the writing of elves. But the skill and wonderment that Abedini brings to his poster production has attracted international attention. Abedini's 'Bridge' poster from 2007, for example, marks the honorary exhibition held in the Netherlands when he won the Prince Claus prize. And the influence is clear for a generation of designers in the Middle East who see something different.

Shepard Fairey and the Eighth Wonder of the World

> It's late on a muggy Saturday night in Hollywood, and guerrilla artist Shepard Fairey is hanging by his fingers from the ledge of an abandoned building. Moments earlier Fairey was pasting an 8-foot-high portrait of the late World Wrestling Federation star Andre the Giant on the building's wall, but things have suddenly taken a dramatic turn.
>
> Fairey got about half of the colossal poster up before some rent-a-cops came a-callin'. In full Wu Tang-ninja 'they'll never take

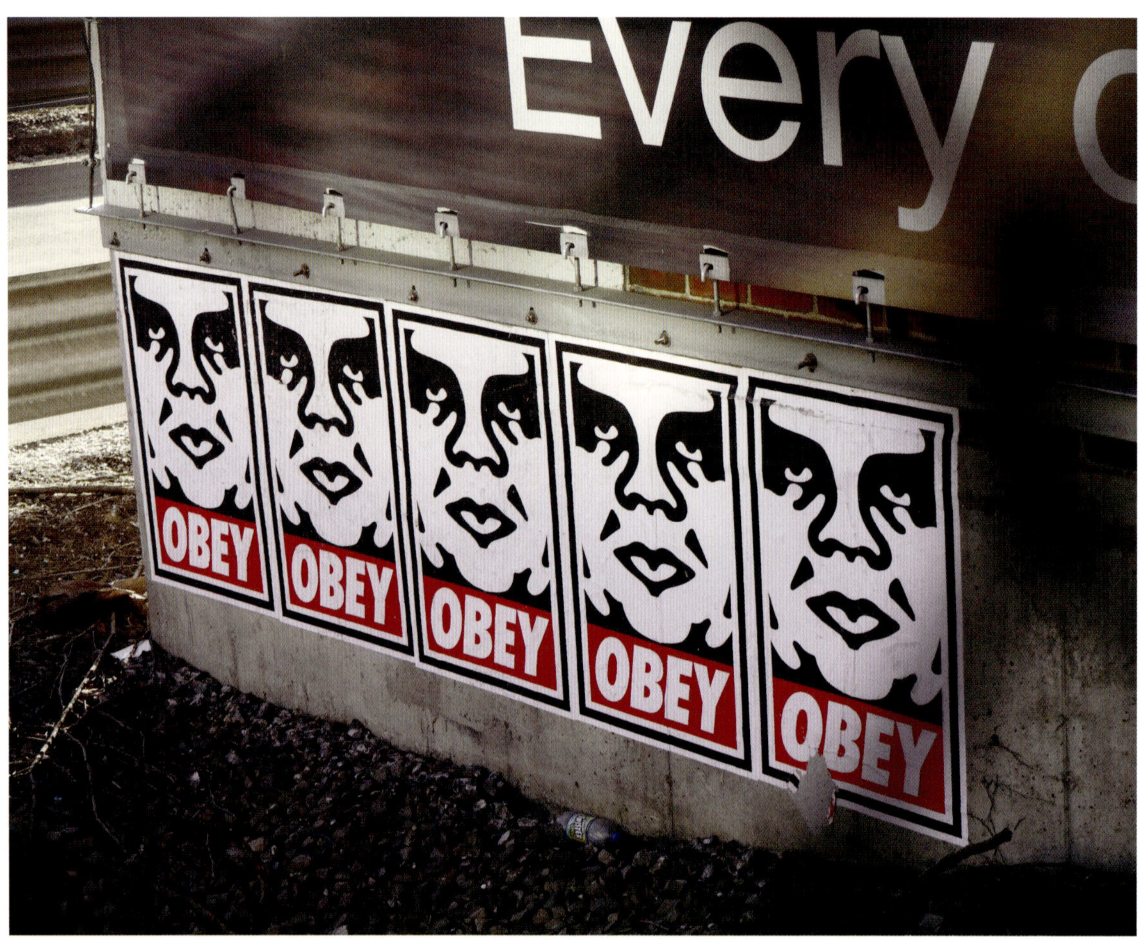

Shepard Fairey, 'Obey', c. 1999.

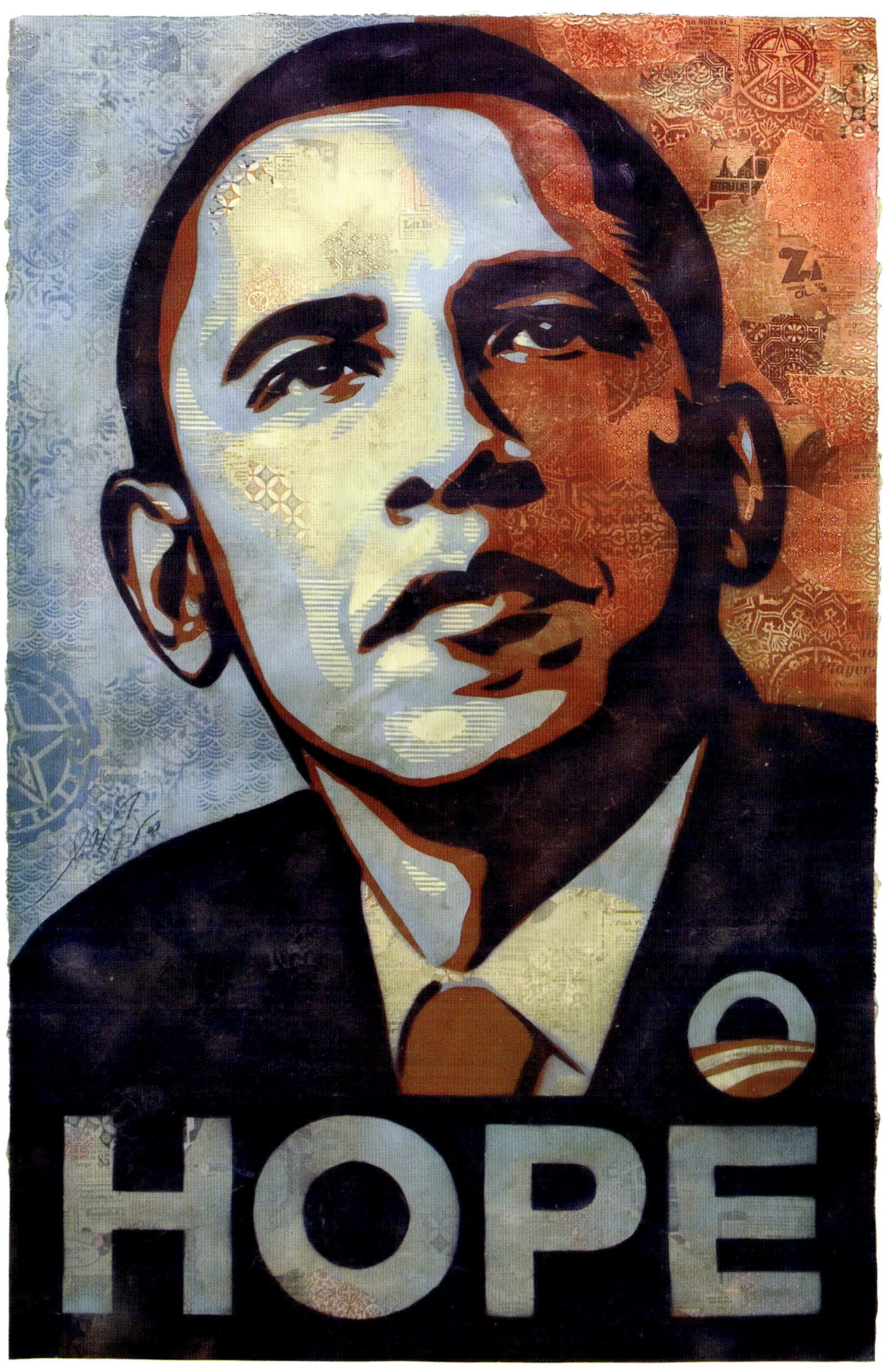

Shepard Fairey, 'Hope', 2008.

me alive' mode, he hid from view, scrambling to the edge of
the ledge while the private security guards radioed for backup.

Before the donut patrol surrounds the block, Fairey drops
12 feet to the concrete sidewalk below and hightails it across
the street where other members of 'the posse' wait.

'This kind of thing almost never happens,' explains Fairey, 30,
panting from the run. 'It's very rare that I have any problems in
LA – especially this soon out.'[62]

Shepard Fairey is an enchanter. By the time he designed his now-famous
poster for Barack Obama's election campaign of 2008, he had already
gained fame for his 'Obey' series. Staring out from bus shelters, lamp
posts and derelict urban walls, Fairey's 'Andre the Giant Has a Posse'
image was an underground cult classic of the 1990s. Mysterious,
brooding and pregnant with possible allusions, the grainy, black-and-
white image attained the designer's goal, as he put it in a Manifesto
of 1989, to 'reawaken a sense of wonder about one's environment'.[63]
Whether construed in semiotic terms, as an 'elaborate joke of putting
out this empty signifier',[64] or more poetically, as 'a mysterious muse,
an invitation to search for meaning',[65] Fairey's 'Andre the Giant' poster-
and-sticker project adds a wrinkle of mystery and enchantment to the
urban landscape.

The Polish sociologist Zygmunt Bauman argues that 'mystery' in
the modern world is reviled; modernist orthodoxy, he insists, lays claim
to rationality. Any argument to the contrary is no more than 'a barely
tolerated alien awaiting a deportation order'.[66] Postmodernism, by
contrast, introduces a form of 're-enchantment' by which 'we learn
to live with events and acts that are not only not-yet-explained, but
inexplicable'. Indeed, the imagery seems to float 'free of even the
creator's rationalizations; even knowing his name and his face doesn't
destroy the self-perpetuating mystery'.[67] Fairey's project – that is, the
posting of mysterious stickers and posters, often under cover of night
and frequently using illegal spaces – employs both worldly and
unworldly enchantment.

It would be easy to imagine that Fairey rose to prominence
rising upwards like an eagle riding a warm updraft. When Fairey
chose the French professional wrestler André René Roussimoff
as a subject, he was already treading mythic ground. Rich, feted,
famous and now dead, he was marked for note. By the mid-1980s,

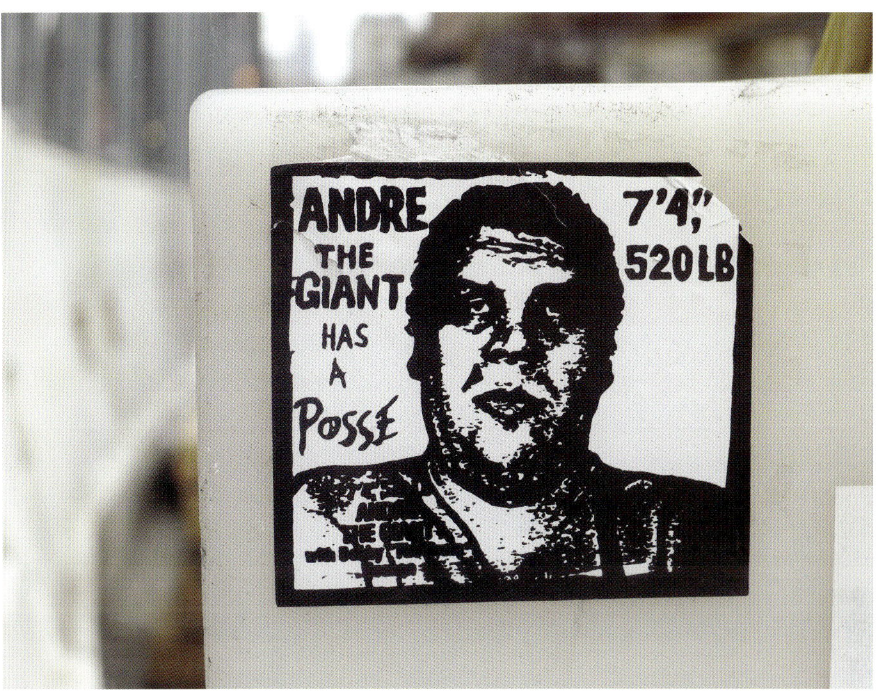

'his size, his cheerful personality, and his surprising agility in the ring'[68] had earned Roussimoff fame and fortune as one of the World Wrestling Federation's top draws; the Frenchman even played a role as a comic sidekick in Rob Reiner's *The Princess Bride* (1987). In 1989, while still enrolled at Rhode Island School of Design, Fairey demonstrated to a friend how simple imagery can be translated into stencils, making a simple monochromatic icon of an Associated Press photograph of the wrestler. Squeezing the ominous portrait inside a thick black border, he added the (probably false) statistics touted in WWF promotions – '7′4″, 520 lb' – in the upper right and the crucially enigmatic phrase 'Andre the Giant Has a Posse' along the left. Combining his interests in skateboard culture, graffiti art and Dada absurdism, Fairey began printing the image and text onto small stickers and soon found himself surprised by the image's power; from street lamps and stop signs there stared out the puckish face of André, and he was genuinely surprised to see that 'it was having an effect on more than the crowd it was intended to effect [sic]'. From the start, his 'gnomic stickers and posters'[69] introduced an element of mystery into the urban streets of the northeast; an early pivotal moment occurred when a local Providence newspaper offered a reward to anyone who could explain the 'upstart enigma' that was turning up on street signs and back

273

alleys. He clearly tapped into a need for mystery that at least one commentator has called 'freemasons for the twenty-first century'.[70]

The sticker-and-poster campaign led Fairey to claim his 'Andre the Giant' image as a kind of free-form 'Rorschach test'.[71] But it also follows on at least a decade of guerrilla-like posting by groups like Gran Fury. Fairey recalls that 'before the Andre the Giant Has a Posse work I had started doing these dogmatic self-righteous "Stop Racism, Question Authority" didactic works'. But this approach lacked the allusiveness of his 'Obey' campaign, whose vagueness is part of its mystery. Uttered sardonically or with secret pride, 'obey' is isolated; but given a special twist, it is like putting a special spin on a ball. For Fairey, enchantment, or what he calls 'a certain leeway for interpretation', is fundamental.[72] Looking back at his development, Fairey surmised:

> when I got into the Andre thing I thought that it needed a
> little bit of mystery . . . the audience needs to wrestle with
> the meaning a little bit.[73]

In an article titled 'Andre the Giant Is Watching You' (2005), journalist Cody Goodfellow noted that

> he watches from STOP signs and lamp posts, the back of
> bus benches, the ceilings of public restrooms . . . creating
> an illusion of a secret society like the Church of the Subgenius
> or the Tristero conclave in Pynchon's *Crying of Lot 49*.[74]

Wired magazine, the mouthpiece of the digital age, reacted to Fairey's 'Giant' stencils and posters with bafflement, unable to 'decide if André is a joke, a cult, or a Madison Avenue trial balloon'. Editor and author Steven Heller characterized the project as 'a trademark of alienation'.[75] By the mid-1990s, he was billed as 'a modern-day trickster'.[76] His fans have been described as a cult, filled with 'acolytes [who] spread the odd Obey gospel to the ends of the earth'.[77] Behavioural scientists and marketers might deem the project a 'meme', that is, an image or concept that spreads from person to person like a virus.[78] But Fairey snaps at his troops and barks hidden commands: obey, hope. Fairey himself deserves, if nothing else, an award for sheer pith; his brevity in English usage leaves the language unimpaired but almost points to the absurdist, anti-consumerist French Situationists as an inspiration.[79]

With the 'Obey' project, however, part of the magic rests not in the digital making, but in how Fairey used modern technology to make, as he put it, 'low fi' art. Indeed, his first image of André the Giant was little more than a cut-paper stencil of an image he had seen in the newspaper. The most sophisticated technology that he used was a photocopier that made his sticker in multiples. He would later claim that his move to posters was simply based on access to materials: he discovered how to jam machines to make free copies. But the process and format actually brought his work into direct dialogue with earlier public posting practices. His first sticker was produced in 1989, five years after the introduction of the Mac. And yet his most basic image could have been produced 30 or 40 years earlier. In some ways, it is almost a reaction against digital sleekness. At the same time, it also rejects the strategies implicit in traditional poster advertisements that push consumers to purchase goods and services; propaganda posters urge us to follow orders. The 'Obey' campaign offered no clear way for viewers to act on the posters' demands. It was a publicity campaign for a non-existent product. As McCormick put it, Fairey's underground work illustrated a form

Shepard Fairey wheat-pasting, 2009.

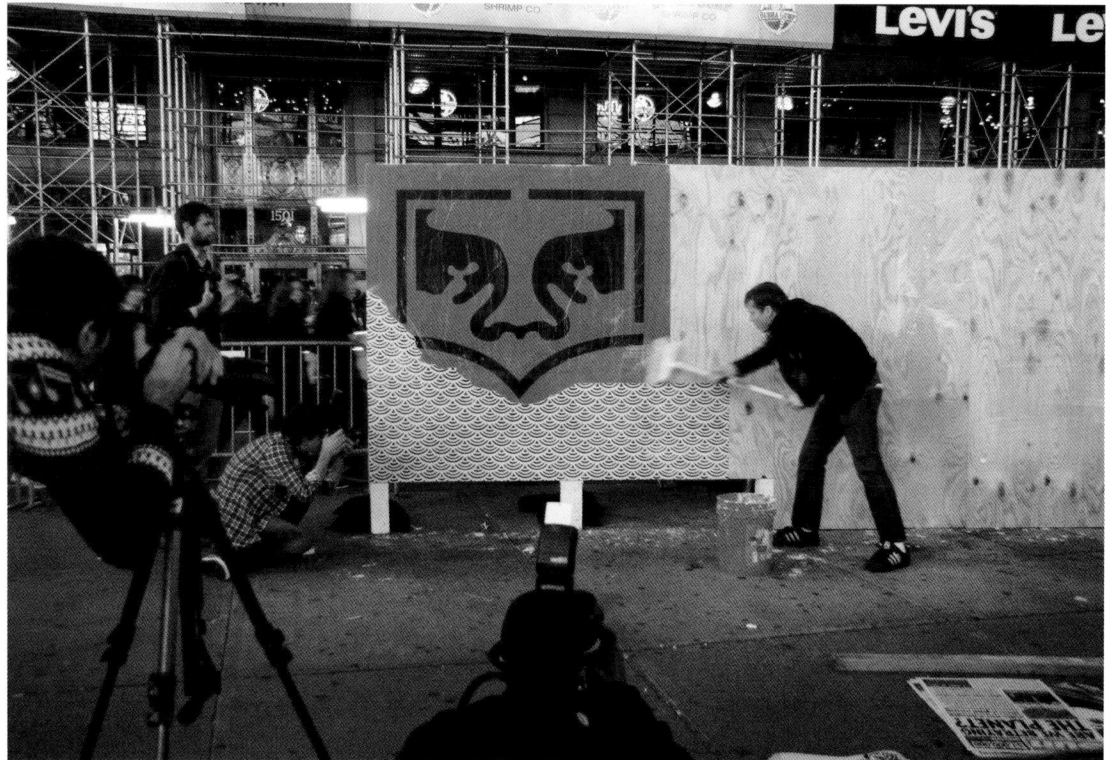

of semiotic confusion 'on a very simple level of grabbing people and making them question what that sign is'. In semiotic terms, the entire 'Giant' campaign can be read as a reflection on the condition of postmodernity itself, or, as critic Peter Schjeldahl described, 'yanking my mind into a placeless jet stream of abstract associations'.[80] This confusion or absence of meaning has been understood in multiple modes. Some observers interpret the campaign negatively, as a sinister and potentially threatening conspiracy. In many ways, this reading recalls Roland Barthes' theorization of the 'terror of the uncertain sign'.[81] But, for others, it is part of a larger revitalization of posting itself. In some ways Fairey's visual work is so concise, he has been so enigmatic, that he sometimes seems to have short-changed himself, like someone with nothing more to say yet with time to fill. Shepard Fairey got out of this predicament by a simple trick: he repeated the composition again and again.

If part of the enchantment enfolding Fairey's work lies in its low-tech look, the poster-maker also shifts meaning to encompass the artist's practice and performance. Where Jacques Villeglé pulled down street posters and put them into galleries and museums, Fairey makes the act of putting posters up central to his practice – it is a performance in itself. The older poster format helped him realize that 'This thing that I'm doing has power but I really don't have to answer to it.' Fairey's use of the public space, sometimes called 'postering', adds a provocative twist to his brand of postmodern enchantment. Indeed, the word 'poster' is becoming both a verb and noun.

In some ways, Fairey's practice parallels the earlier work of street artists like Keith Haring. Not only did Haring reclaim poster space, drawing on the black paper that covered expired posters hung in the New York Subway system, but he too moved quickly through the city, stealthily imbuing poster spaces with chalked pictures of barking dogs, zapping spacecraft and radiant baby. In a rather poetic way, he reclaimed the empty space set aside by the Metropolitan Transit Authority and used for paid advertising. But, in their self-conscious primitivism, the very drawings stand out against the carefully produced commercial posters surrounding them. Single-handedly, Fairey reclaims the spaces claimed for sophisticated, computer-generated posters. Haring would go on to design posters as well, but he recognized the wonderment of his drawing, claiming that it brings 'together man and the world. It lives through magic'.[82]

Klara Lidén, *Untitled (Poster Paintings)*, 2010.

For artists like Haring and Fairey, 'wild style graffiti', quickly 'thrown up' on walls in and outside big cities in the 1980s, was a deep inspiration. But he and many other artists of their generation see graffiti as providing, as Fairey put it, creativity

> without compromise. No govt. censorship, no gallery owner
> to reject you. It's about a pure, uncompromised manifestation
> of your art and ideas whether people like it or not.[83]

Fairey's practice clearly imitated the guerrilla-style street art that emerged from the graffiti scene and was against authority figures – an idea that caused him to quiver with revulsion. But a shadow of gloom seems to hang over each posting, as if he knows how hopeless his cause is. Paper gives graffiti a form of permanence, but the graffiti artists also provided a model for postering as a new form of performance. He would use ladders to get at inaccessible places, climb walls to evade capture and surreptitiously slap stickers on signs and walls while seeming to walk down the street casually. Whether their work be spray-painted or wheat-pasted, the street artists whom Fairey admired the most associated art-making closely with illegality. In this milieu, stealing paint and paste was sometimes considered part of one's practice, and illegality carried its own cachet. In both the poster and sticker worlds, getting arrested means recognition, as one practitioner reflected, 'comparable to the prestige an artist gets with his first gallery or museum show'.[84] Arrested in Philadelphia, Long Beach and New York, Fairey was even arrested minutes before he was scheduled to appear at a gala at the Institute of Contemporary Art in Boston in 2009. For Fairey, such 'street art is not only an act of expression, but also of defiance' – a position that echoes earlier graffiti artists.[85]

Fairey's act of postering most resembles the derring-do of graffiti art, but his remains a practice best understood within the larger bill-sticking tradition; poster hangers were once the embodiment of modernity, and the billsticker's rambles represented more than traced new physical and social geographies, albeit a status hidden from anyone who lacked a practised eye. In his critique of enchantment from 1976, the psychoanalyst Bruno Bettleheim made a strident entreaty for the continued telling of fairy tales to children and conducted a series of detailed examinations of Hansel and Gretel, Little Red Riding

Hood and several others. Titled 'The Uses of Enchantment: The Meaning and Importance of Fairy Tales', his argument suggests that the graphic and often dark stories told by the Brothers Grimm were essential to children's psychological development, helping them deal with the 'psychological problems of growing up and integrating their person-alities'.[86] But we might also say that Fairey's work, while not warning us to avoid scary witches offering gingerbread houses to eat, does reinvest the real world with a kind of poetry. Fairey's stealthy act resembles in many ways the practice of Nouveau Réaliste artist Villeglé. Swapping mysterious sunglasses for enchanted beanstalks, Fairey taps into a newer folklore whose vocabulary includes malevolent aliens and storybook giants. But, unlike the Brothers Grimm, who used symbolic figures like evil witches to help children divine secret truths that may help them cope with neglect, serious harm and death, Fairey's fables allude to a different, dark sphere. His measure of enchantment alludes to fears of lost control of our public spaces, of surveillance and Orwellian fantasies of social control. He reminds us that we exist in a very real and never entirely knowable world. The very materiality of posters has become the focus of numerous artists in recent years. Klara Lidén echoes the Nouveau Réalistes in reverse: rather than slash posters apart, Lidén brings them together. Gathering advertisements, fliers and even dissident posters like Fairey's from the streets, Lidén glues them into thick, slightly unruly blocks; adding a monochrome sheet to the top of her polyphonic pile, she erases or silences all messages, whether commercial, political or subversive. The resulting jumbles – wrinkly, ragged and with edges frequently shot through with shards of sharp, saturated colour – remain resolutely mute, suggesting an open horizon as much as a closed mouth; again, they draw our attention to the enduring physical presence of the poster itself.

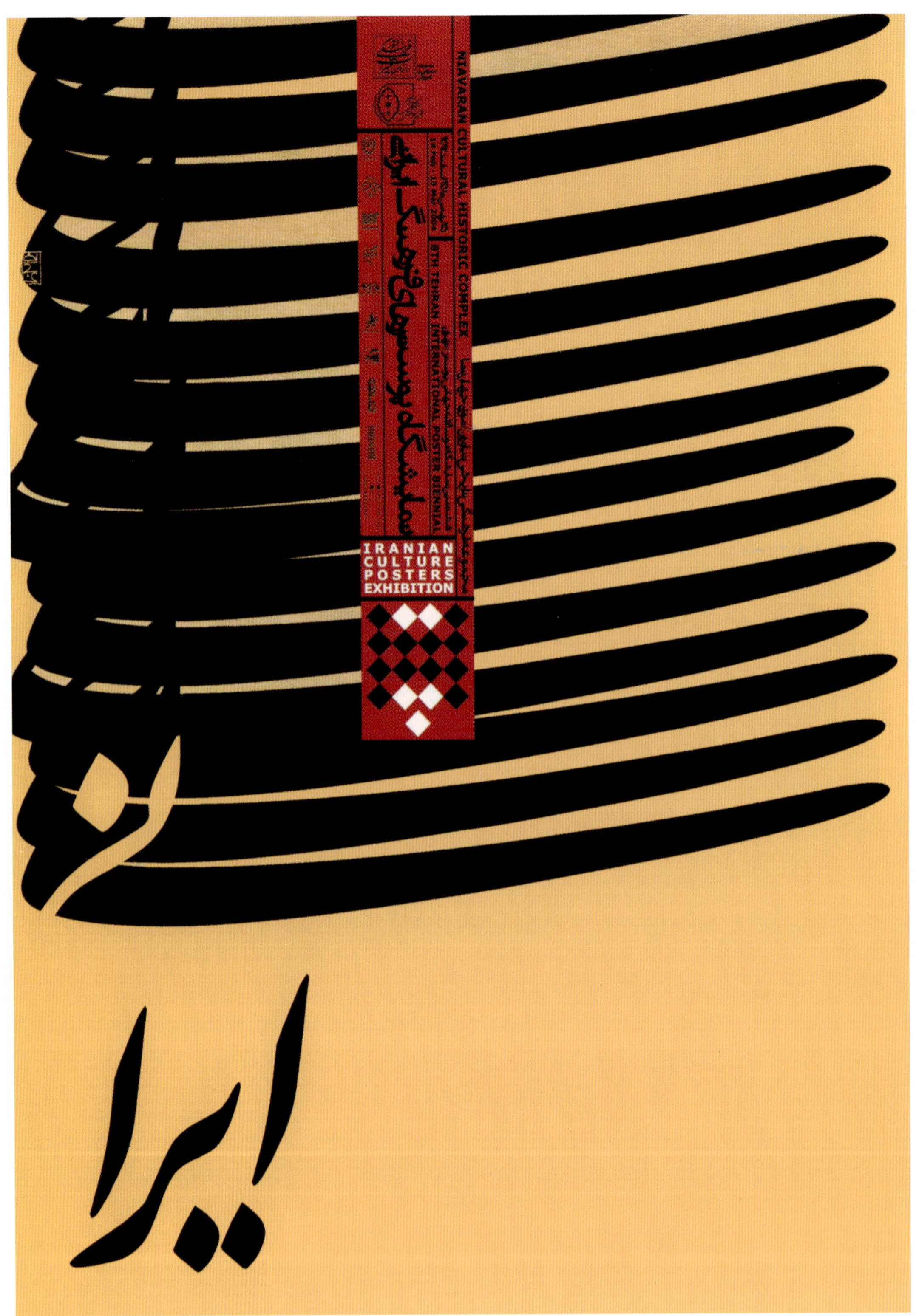

Reza Abedini, poster for the 'Iranian Culture Posters Exhibition', 2004.

EPILOGUE: POST-POSTERS?

A jauntily dressed man clambers onto the counter of a fast-food joint and places a poster over the menu. The same man pushes through a darkened bar where football fans watch a match on a wall-mounted television. He jumps on a chair and tries to place his poster next to the screen; incensed fans shout him down. Finally, he finds the perfect place for his poster – a road sign. Smiling with satisfaction, he gazes on his work as tyres squeal and a car plunges into a ditch. This 30-second public-service ad, issued by the Federal Road Safety Corps of Nigeria (FRSCN), highlights an unusual safety hazard in the weeks leading up to Nigeria's national elections in 2011: the 'poster wars'. Throughout Lagos, the country's largest city, political placards were plastered indiscriminately over bridges, motorway dividers, major roads and expressways.[1] Election-related material became so ubiquitous that it engulfed Lagos.

Loud and abrasive political cousins to the street news poster, the election placards might be dismissed as tenacious but unwelcome evidence of Nigeria's fragile new democracy. After the country's military regime ended in 1999, posters of all kinds evolved. Lagos has had a puzzling relationship with them, including periods when they have flourished and, more recently, blissful stretches of time when they have been reined in. After the elections of 2011, the cacophony again faded. Until then, posters papered the urban landscape like a kind of political wallpaper and giving a 'roiling migraine to many residents'.[2] As a local lawyer put it, the government was little more than a purpose-ful shadow and 'should wake up to its responsibilities and rid the streets of such ugly posters'.[3] Others felt that the postings 'debeautify the state'.[4] As another Lagos-based lawyer put it, the sight of so many handbills and posters on public buildings 'gives a very ugly picture and connotes poor organization of the state'.[5] In a city like Lagos, where power cuts are common, access to clean water is limited and more than 70 per cent of the city's residents live in slums, it may seem odd that posters have received so much negative attention. And yet, with firm authority, the local government declared its own war against posters and in 2006 founded an agency specifically 'to show Lagosians that it means business'.[6] Its measures were dramatic and effective. Almost immediately, one newspaper reported, 'officials of the agency usually prowled the state like hungry lions, seeking posters to remove',[7] even establishing special mobile courts that tried and fined lawbreakers arrested on the spot. In a pseudo-protective flutter, several officials wearing business suits, accompanied by journalists, 'descended on the giant hoardings, which dotted the Lagos landscape, and cut them down'.[8] To maintain the city's newly clean streets, high-tech tools were purchased and quickly flushed away illegally pasted posters. As a local official told reporters: 'In other parts of the world, outdoor advertising is serious business. People don't just put posters and billboards just anywhere.'[9]

And yet, the hurly burly of urban Lagos actually does sound like other parts of the world or, more specifically, like a revised and updated version of Dickens's world. Moreover, the torments suffered by Lagosians recall the anger of Charles Garnier and his contemporaries in Paris who insisted that brash new posters were destroying the revered city's landscape. Like Lagos, the French capital was renowned for its dense and often wild postings for political campaigns, which spared no monument, even appearing at the foot of the Arc de Triomphe. Not asking for permission to post on private property, bill posters routinely worked at night, covering entire districts and surprising property owners with their sense of impunity.

For all the complaints, it is easy to forget that paper shreds and rots. Newer plastic and vinyl posters rip, tatter and drop, clogging storm drains and canals. Ephemeral or not, there is no escaping posters' quick, sly decay – that is, their sheer materiality. No one drove into a ditch because their e-mail covered a road safety sign. Half a continent away from Nigeria, South African photographer Zwelethu Mthethwa's ongoing portrait series records the inhabitants and interiors of Cape Town's shanty towns. Seen from the outside, rusty, corrugated iron homes belie richly decorated interiors. With a kind of dizzying cheer, bright new posters – usually printers' overruns – are used for insulation as much as decor. No digital poster ever kept someone warm.

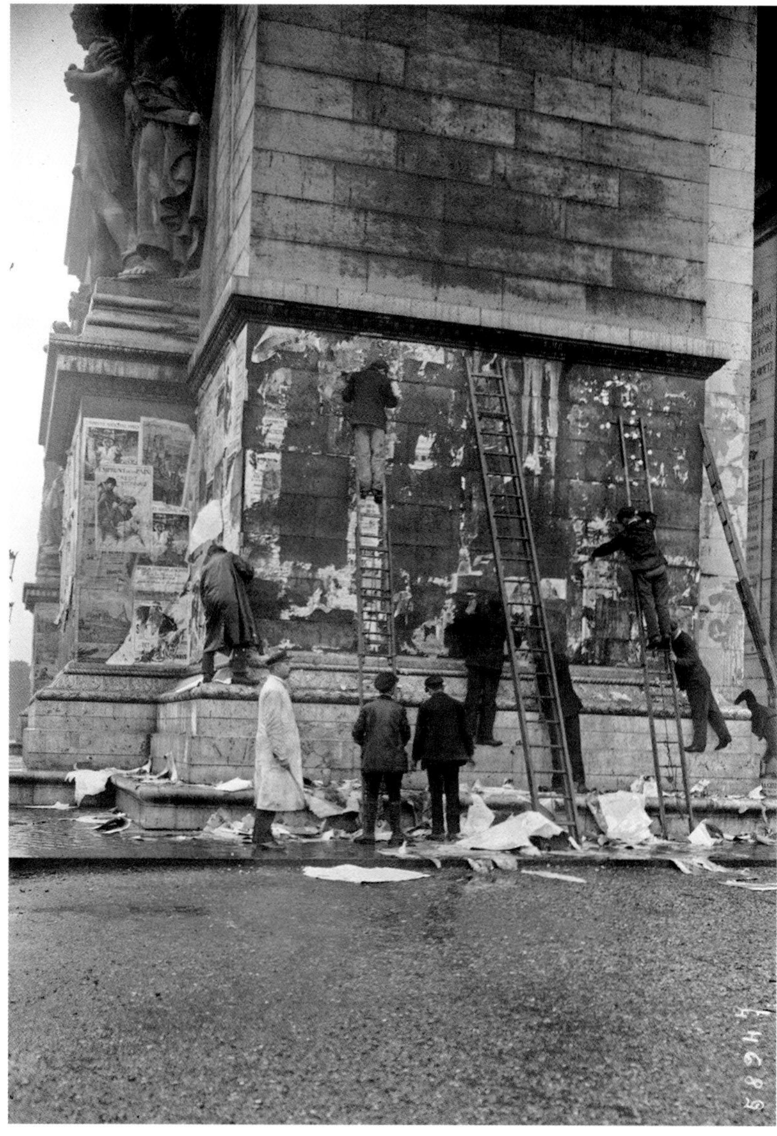

Light years from both Lagos and Cape Town, Silicon Valley's network administrators map a digital world composed of sprawling systems of information. Many networks gel, as if by themselves, following their own rules and protocols, but however different each may be, they must all communicate with each other. If different technology standards must be knitted together to form an overall pattern, still information technology and networking professionals have managed to see the larger picture. Where, most of all, do they go to find a roadmap to these systems? They are all available on a 'Network Communication Protocols Map' poster. And, while this

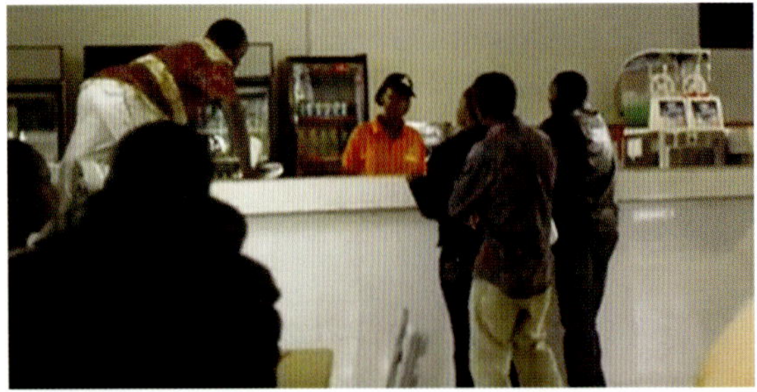
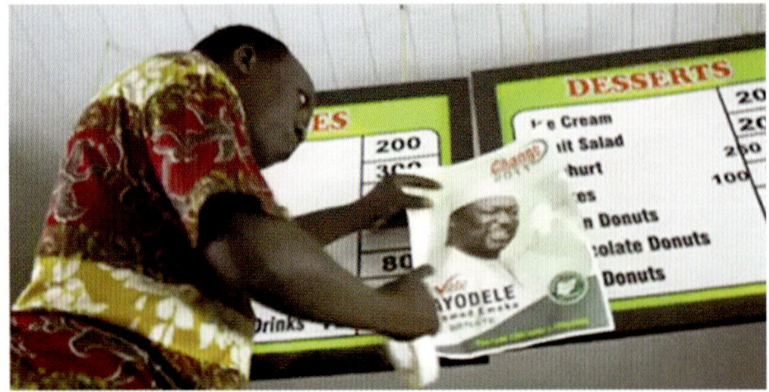

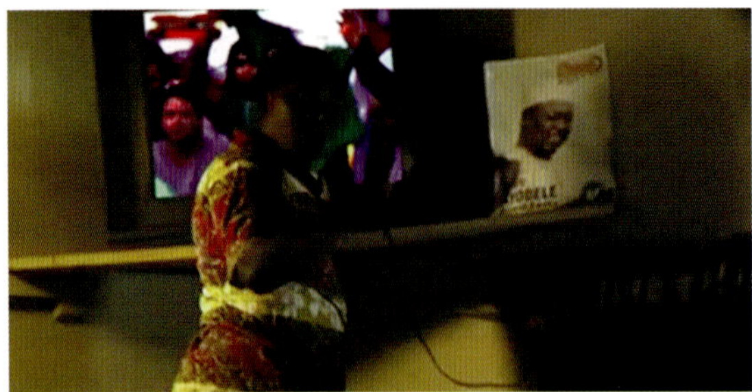
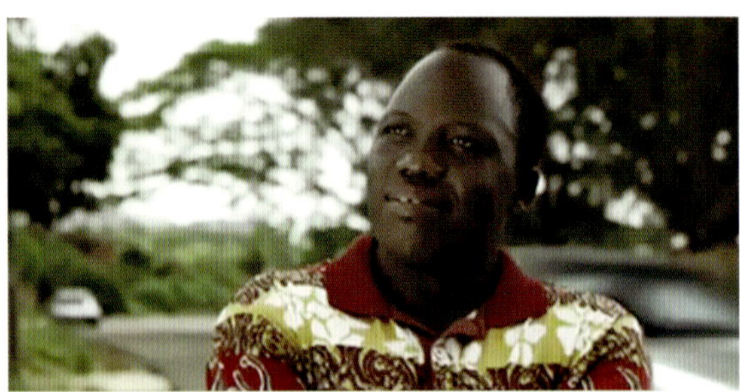
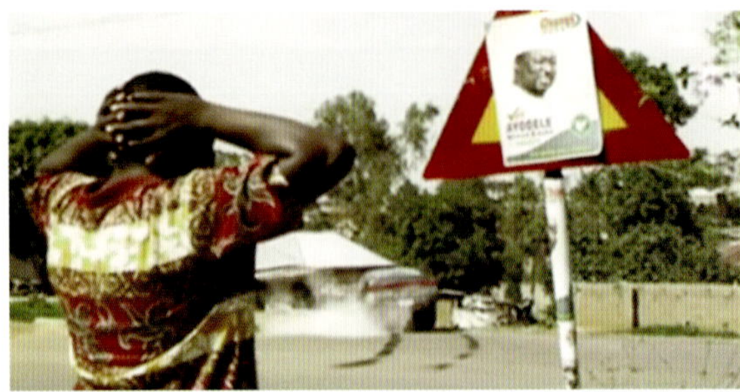
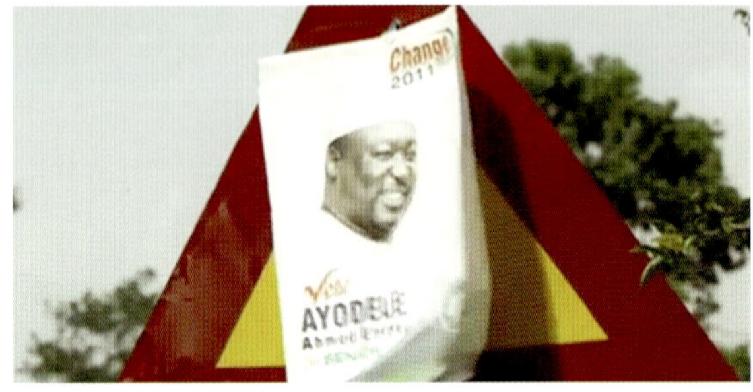

poster-map provides a handy, quick and concrete reference guide, it graces technology administrators' offices worldwide. It makes concrete something utterly invisible. One source for these posters, Javvin Technologies, has a site overflowing with user testimonials for the poster. One satisfied user reported:

> I am an IT engineer. I have the Javvin Map of Communication Protocols hanging on my office wall. It helps me get an instant answer to many network and communication questions.

Others see the poster as an advertisement that doubles as a way to connect with digital clients. Another buyer recalled:

> It was last holiday season . . . I purchased a few copies of Javvin's Map of Communication Protocols. I framed them and gave them

Zwelethu Mthethwa,
Untitled, 1999.

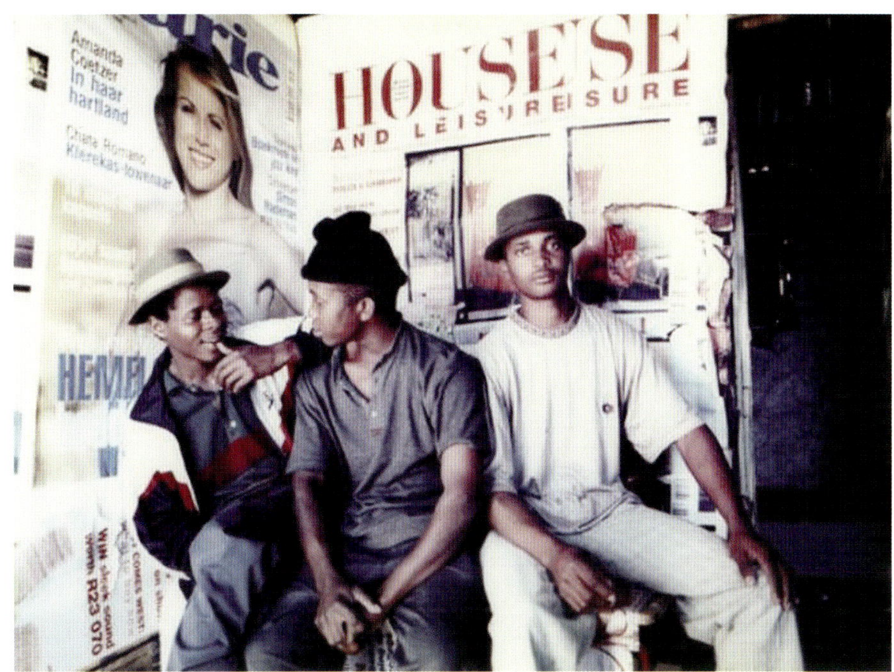

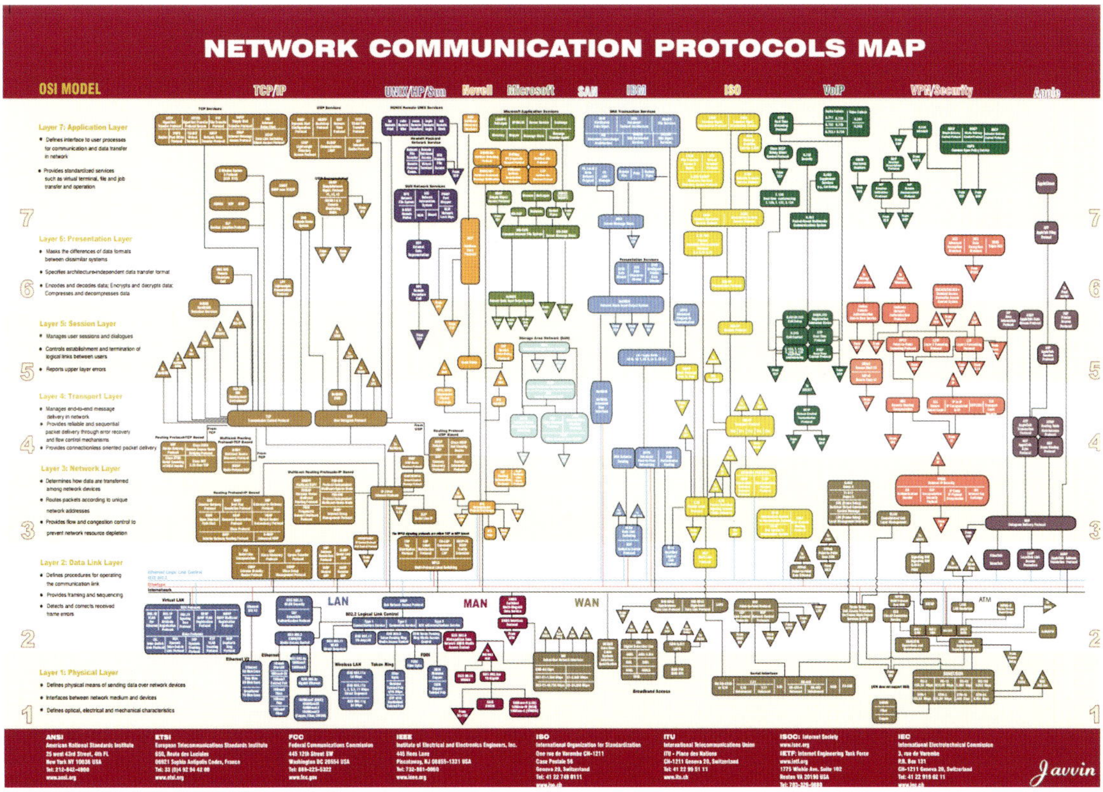

'Javvin Network Protocols Map', 5th edition, *c.* 2010.

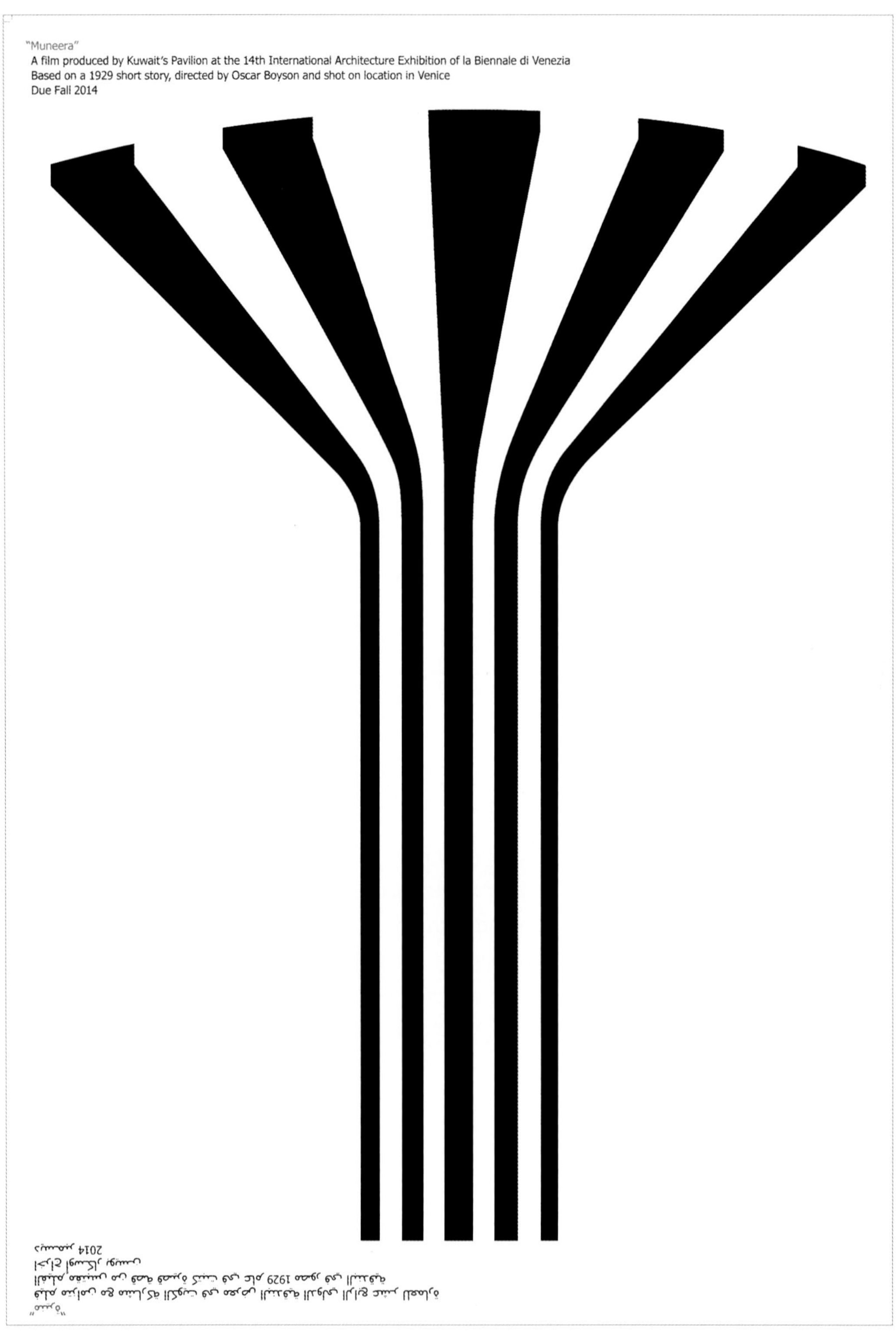

Dexter Sinister's poster for the Kuwait Pavilion at the 14th International Architecture Exhibition of the Venice Biennale 2014. The poster can be hung and read in either orientation and shows an inventive approach within the established billsticking tradition. On a global basis, designers continue to make posters for exhibition, using traditional bills placed on walls.

to my customers as holiday gifts. They were very delighted. The pictures have been hanging on their walls since then and remind them everyday of our wonderful relationship.[10]

Depending on one's vocabulary, it can be easy to speak of a new golden age for the poster. They thrive when hung indoors, like the Network Communication Protocols Maps, or outdoors, in the manner of Fairey's 'Obey' posters. Best of all, they are still a valid form of communication in Los Angeles and London. Or such is the premise of this book. But a second and equally important truth also emerges: if we look beyond media elites and see the development of posters as a global phenomenon, the picture widens. April Greiman and Shepard Fairey may continue to design posters, but other poster makers have emerged in Lagos and Hyderabad. Over the years we have taught ourselves, and been taught, to observe developments in design only within a relatively small slice of a larger world.

For some time, there has been a mistaken idea that global graphic design is nothing more than the Westernization of design forms worldwide; beneath the rhetoric of interconnectedness across national and ethnic lines, this argument goes, Western styles and values are spread. The result is a homogenization of culture. This may well be the case in some corners of the globe. But posters are a stubborn and resilient form and continue to develop in new ways entirely outside the West. This is a process that exists plainly. Nevertheless, in order to see it, we must shift our gaze away from Stefan Sagmeister in New York to poster-makers in Tehran and Accra. As we broaden our understanding of the presence as much as the poetics of posters, the digital will, no doubt, continue. But the dialogue between digital and non-digital, West and non-West, begs a broader rethinking of design. The poster is dead. Long live the poster.

REFERENCES

Introduction

1 Alain Weill, *The Poster: A Worldwide Survey and History* (Boston, MA, 1985), p. 21.

2 For example, H. R. Woestyn, 'Posters for the Churches', *The Poster*, 2 (June–July 1899), p. 250, and Earnest Elmo Calkins, *Modern Advertising* (New York, 1905), p. 97.

3 'The Lay Figure: On the Possibilities of the Poster', *Studio International* (March 1917), p. 52.

4 Will M. Clemens, 'The Collecting of Posters', *Printers' Ink: A Journal for Advertisers* (10 June 1896), p. 6.

5 W. S. Rogers, *A Book of the Poster* (London, 1901), p. 25.

6 Blaise Cendrars, *Le Spectacle est dans la rue* (Paris, 1935).

7 Hansard, 'Orders of the Day' for 25 November 1947, Finance Bill, Mr William Hall, hansard.millbanksystems.com, accessed 20 September 2012.

8 Maurice Rickarts, *The Rise and Fall of the Poster* (New York, 1971), p. 39.

9 John Barnicoat, *A Concise History of Posters, 1870–1970* (New York, 1972), pp. 246–7.

10 Angharad Lewis, 'Introduction', in Malcolm Frost, Angharad Lewis and Aidan Winterburn, *Street Talk: The Rise and Fall of the Poster* (Mulgrave, Victoria, 2006), p. 42.

11 Elias Khoury, *White Masks* [1981], trans. Maia Tabet (New York, 2010).

12 Sharjah Art Foundation, 'Projects' for 2009, 'Faces, 2009', www.sharjahart. org, accessed 1 August 2013.

13 Arjun Appadurai, ed., *The Social Life of Things: Commodities in Cultural Perspective* (Cambridge, 1986).

14 Dagmar Finkova and Sylva Petrova, *The Militant Poster, 1936–1985* (Prague, 1986), p. 8.

1 Consuming Words on the Street: 1840–1950

1 Charles Dickens, 'Bill-sticking', *Household Words* (22 March 1851), p. 601.

2 William Henry Pyne, ed., *The World in Miniature: England, Scotland, and Ireland* (London, 1827), p. 235.

3 Walter Benjamin, *Selected Writings,* vol. I: *1913–1926* (Cambridge, 1996), p. 456.

4 Susan Sontag, 'Posters: Advertisement, Art, Political Artifact, Commodity', in *Looking Closer 3: Classic Writings on Graphic Design*, ed. Michael Bierut et al. (New York, 1999), p. 196.

5 André Mellerio, *La Lithographie originale en couleurs* (Paris, 1898), reprinted in *The Color Revolution*, trans. Margaret Needham (Rutgers, NJ, 1978), p. 97.

6 Quoted in Camille Lemonnier, 'Quelques opinions sur les affiches illustrées', *La Plume*, CX/4 (5 November 1893), p. 495.

7 See Elizabeth Guffey, 'Socialist Movements and the Development of the Political Poster', in *A History of Visual Culture* (Oxford, 2010), pp. 42–54.

8 Louis J. Rhead, 'The Moral Aspect of the Artistic Poster', *The Bookman*, 1 (1895), p. 312.

9 'Horrible London; or, The Pandemonium of Posters', *Punch, or The London Charivari*, XCV (1888), p. 170.

10 *Journal officiel de la République française* (1880), pp. 6212–13.

11 Sontag, 'Posters', p. 200.

12 Vyvyan James, 'The Poster Academy', *Art Record: A Monthly Illustrated Review of the Arts and Crafts*, I (1901), p. 97.

13 Joris-Karl Huysmans, 'Le Salon de 1879', in *L'Art moderne* (Paris, 1883), p. 9.

14 Roger Marx, *Masters of the Poster, 1896–1900* (New York, 1977), p. 7.

15 Ibid.

16 William Morris, 'The Lesser Arts', in *Selections from the Prose Works of William Morris* (Cambridge, 1931), p. 170.

17 Quoted in Lemonnier, 'Quelques opinions', p. 496.

18 Miriam R. Levin, 'Democratic Vistas – Democratic Media: Defining a Role for Printed Images in Industrializing France', *French Historical Studies*, XVIII (1993), p. 83.

19 Ernest Maindron, *Les Affiches illustrées* (Paris, 1886–95), p. 2.

20 'An Interview with Francis Jourdain by Henri Perruchot', in *Aspects of Modern Art: An Anthology of Writings on Modern Art from L'Oeil* (London, 1957), p. 8.

21 Dora Vallier, 'Braque: La Peinture et nous, propos de l'artiste recueillis', *Cahiers d'Art*, XXIX (1954), p. 16.

22 Alexandre Henriot, 'Soirée chez un amateur d'affiches', *Le Monde Moderne*, VI (1897), pp. 181–92.

23 Charles Hiatt, *A Short History of the Illustrated Placard, with Many Reproductions of the Most Artistic Examples in All Countries* (London, 1896), pp. 101–2.

24 Alain Weill, *The Poster: A Worldwide Survey and History* (Boston, MA, 1985), p. 31.

25 'The Curiosities of Advertising', *The Century*, XX (1880), p. 612.

26 H. Hazel Hahn, *Scenes of Parisian Modernity: Culture and Consumption in the Nineteenth Century* (New York, 2009), p. 66.

27 Margaret Holmes Bates, 'The Way He Works', *Fame*, IX (1900), p. 356.

28 Ibid., p. 355.

29 Quoted in Catherine Gudis, *Buyways: Billboards, Automobiles, and the American Landscape* (New York, 2004), p. 12.

30 Bates, 'The Way He Works', p. 356.

31 David M. Henkin, *City Reading: Written Words and Public Spaces in Antebellum New York* (New York, 1998), p. 77.

32 Hahn, *Scenes of Parisian Modernity*, pp. 61–72.

33 Quoted in Gudis, *Buyways*, p. 22.

34 Quoted in Weill, *The Poster*, pp. 165–8.

35 Émile Zola, 'Une victime de la réclame', in *Oeuvres complètes: Le Feuilletoniste, 1866–1867* (Paris, 2002).

36 'The Lay Figure', *Studio International*, XVII (1899), p. 212.

37 Louis J. Rhead, 'The Moral Aspect of the Artistic Poster', *The Bookman*, 1 (1895), pp. 312–14.

38 Charles Garnier, 'Les Affiches agaçantes', *Gazette des Beaux-Arts* (December 1870), pp. 490–91.

39 Richardson Evans, *The Age of Disfigurement* (London, 1893).

40 Ibid., p. 183.

41 Richardson Evans, 'Architecture and Advertisements', *Journal of the Society of the Arts*, XLII (1893), p. 41.

42 Artemas Ward, 'Bad Advertising', *Fame*, VI (1897), p. 357.

43 William F. Haitz, 'Hitching the Newspaper Campaign up with the Poster', *The Poster*, XI (1922), p. 37.

44 Gudis, *Buyways*, p. 25.

45 Ibid.

46 Henri Mouron, *A. M. Cassandre* (New York, 1985), p. 120.

47 Interview with Louis Cheronnet, *L'Art Vivant*, XLVII (1926), p. 13.

48 Dawn Ades, 'Function and Abstraction in Poster Design', in Dawn Ades et al., *Poster: The 20th-century Poster: Design of the Avant-garde*, ed. Mildred S. Friedman (Minneapolis, MN, 1994), p. 36.

49 Giorgio de Chirico, 'Salve Lutetia', *Bulletin de l'effort moderne*, XXXI (1927), p. 8.

50 In Robert Desnos, *Nouvelles Hébrides et autres textes, 1922–1930* (Paris, 1978), p. 466.

51 See, for example, Victoria E. Bonnell, *Iconography of Power: Soviet Political Posters under Lenin and Stalin* (Berkeley, CA, 1999).

52 David A. Gray, 'Managing Motivation: The Seth Seiders Syndicate and the Motivational Publicity Business in the 1920s', *Winterthur Portfolio*, XLIV/1 (2010).

53 Gennifer Weisenfeld, 'Selling Shiseido: Cosmetics Advertising and Design in Early 20th-century Japan' (MIT, Visualizing Cultures, 2010), www.ocw.mit.edu, accessed 13 September 2012.

54 Christopher Pinney, *'Photos of the Gods': The Printed Image and Political Struggle in India* (London, 2004), p. 31.

55 Ibid., p. 100.

56 Ades, 'Function and Abstraction', p. 25.

2 Trashing Tradition: 1945–1965

1 'Headline People (1962)' [video], www.britishpathe.com, accessed 12 September 2012.

2 Jacques Villeglé and Catherine Francblin, 'L'Art, c'est le vol', *Beaux-Arts Magazine*, 291 (2008), pp. 64–9.

3 Jean-Marc Huitorel, 'Jacques Villeglé: "Oui" Rue Notre-Dame-des-Champs (22 octobre 1958)', *Art Press*, 348 (2008), pp. 20–22.

4 Charles Matlack Price, *Poster Design: A Critical Study of the Development of the Poster in Continental Europe, England and America* (New York, 1922), p. 364.

5 M. de Wyss, *Rome under the Terror* (London, 1945), p. 183.

6 Kristin Ross, *Fast Cars, Clean Bodies: Decolonization and the Reordering of French Culture* (Cambridge, 1996).

7 Jacques Villeglé, *A Theater without Theater* (Barcelona, 2007), p. 150.

8 Tom McDonough, *The Beautiful Language of My Century: Reinventing the Language of Contestation in Postwar France, 1945–1968* (Cambridge, 2011), p. 82.

9 Matt Ford, 'The Physics of Peeling and Tearing', www.arstechnica.com, 2 April 2008.

10 Interview with Nicolas Bourriaud, in *Jacques Villeglé*, ed. François Bon, Nicolas Bourriaud and Kaira Cabanas (Paris, 2007), p. 132.

11 See Hannah Feldman, 'Of the Public Born: Raymond Hains and La France déchirée', *October*, 108 (2004), p. 83.

12 J. I. Biegeleisen, *Poster Design* (New York, 1945), p. 5.

13 Roger Parry, *The Ascent of Media: From Gilgamesh to Google via Gutenberg* (Boston, MA, 2011), p. 117.

14 David Ogilvy, *Confessions of an Advertising Man* (New York, 1963), p. 127.

15 'British TV History: The ITV Story Part 4', *Teletronic: The Television History Site*, www.teletronic.co.uk, accessed 19 October 2012.

16 Quoted in 'Polish Posters', *Communication Arts*, XIX/1 (1977), p. 86.

17 Ibid.

18 Parry, *The Ascent of Media*, pp. 117–88.

19 John Ruari McLean, *Jan Tschichold: Typographer* (London, 1975), Appendix 3.

20 Quoted in Dawn Ades, 'Function and Abstraction in Poster Design', in Dawn Ades et al., *Poster: The 20th-century Poster: Design of the Avant-Garde*, ed. Mildred S. Friedman (Minneapolis, MN, 1994), p. 41.

21 Julian Stallabrass, *Gargantua: Manufactured Mass Culture* (New York, 1996), p. 178.

22 David M. Henkin, *City Reading: Written Words and Public Spaces in Antebellum New York* (New York, 1998), p. 79.

23 Ades, 'Function and Abstraction in Poster Design', p. 36.

24 Jacques Villeglé, 'L'Esthétique de la rue', in *Urbi & Orbi* (Mâcon, 1986), p. 10.

3 New Art, New Space: 1960–1980

1 Jane Gollin, 'Posters for all Seasons', *Art News*, LXVI/8 (December, 1967), p. 22.

2 John Garrigan, 'Introduction', in *Images of an Era: The American Poster, 1945–75* (Washington, DC, 1975), p. 10.

3 David Kunzle, *Posters of Protest: The Posters of Political Satire in the US, 1966–1970* (New York, 1971), p. 14.

4 Walter Benjamin, *The Arcades Project*, trans. Howard Eiland and Kevin McLaughlin (Cambridge, MA, 1999), p. 406.

5 Interview in *Freedom on the Fence*, film (dir. Andrea Marks, 2009).

6 Mariusz Knorowski, *Muzeum ulicy: Plakat Polski w Kolekcji* (Warsaw, 1996), p. 13.

7 See James Aulich, *Political Posters in Central and Eastern Europe, 1945–95: Signs of the Times* (Manchester, 1999), p. 21.

8 William G. Rosenberg, ed., *Bolshevik Visions: First Phase of the Cultural Revolution in Russia* (Ann Arbor, MI, 1990), p. 253.

9 Interview, *Freedom on the Fence*.

10 See David Crowley, 'Henryk Tomaszewski: Affiches tekeningen', *Journal of Design History*, IV/4 (1991), p. 260.

11 Florian Zieliński, 'Social and Political Art in the Frame of the Polish People's Republic', in *100th Anniversary of Polish Poster Art*, ed. Krzysztof Dydo (Krakow, 1993), p. 40.

12 Ibid., p. 34.

13 Crowley, 'Henryk Tomaszewski', p. 260.

14 Interview, *Freedom on the Fence*.

15 Ibid.

16   See, for instance, Jirina Siklova, 'The Gray Zone and the Future of Dissent in Czechoslovakia', *Social Research: An International Quarterly*, LVII/2 (1990), pp. 347–63.

17   Zieliński, 'Social and Political Art', p. 40.

18   Crowley, 'Henryk Tomaszewski', p. 260.

19   Quoted in Kevin Mulroy, ed., *Western Amerykanski: Polish Poster Art and the Western* (Seattle, 1999), p. 100.

20   Zieliński, 'Social and Political Art', p. 31.

21   Ibid.

22   Jan Lenica, 'The Polish Poster School of Art', *Graphis*, XVI/88 (1960), p. 136.

23   Charles Rosner, 'Posters for Art Exhibitions and Films: A Lesson from Poland', *Art and Industry*, XLVII (1948), p. 52.

24   Interview, *Freedom on the Fence*.

25   Crowley, 'Henryk Tomaszewski', p. 260.

26   Herbert Gold, 'Pop Goes the Poster', *Saturday Evening Post* (23 March 1968), p. 33.

27   Philip Meggs, *A History of Graphic Design* (New York, 1998).

28   Manuel Gasser, 'The Poster Craze', *Graphis*, 135 (1968), p. 59.

29   Maurice Rickards, *The Rise and Fall of the Poster* (New York, 1971), p. 39.

30   Ibid., p. 103.

31   Susan Sontag, 'Posters: Advertisement, Art, Political Artifact, Commodity', in *Looking Closer 3: Classic Writings on Graphic Design*, ed. Michael Bierut et al. (New York, 1999), p. 196.

32   Gollin, 'Posters for All Seasons', p. 22.

33   Owen Edwards, 'Sign of the Times: Bob Dylan', *Smithsonian.com*, www.smithsonianmag.com, June 2010.

34   Paul Nini, 'Across the Graphic Universe: An Interview with John Berg', www.aiga.org, 30 October 2007.

35   Dominic Lutyens, 'Interview with Milton Glaser', *The Independent* [London] (6 January 2001), p. 18.

36   Interview in *Milton Glaser: To Delight and Inform*, film (dir. Wendy Keys, 2008).

37   Milton Glaser, 'Polish Paper Cuts', *Push Pin Graphic*, 33 (1961).

38   'Posters', *Horizon*, IX/4 (1967), p. 104.

39   Milton Glaser, *Graphic Design* (New York, 2012), p. x.

40   Gasser, 'The Poster Craze', p. 59.

41   Gollin, 'Posters for All Seasons', p. 23.

42   'Nouveau Frisco', *Time*, LXXXIX/14 (7 April 1967), p. 69.

43   Sontag, 'Posters', p. 216.

44   John Luhr, 'The Blurred Graphic Image of Lincoln Center', *Print Magazine* (May–June 1967) p. 20.

45   Ibid.

46   Sontag, 'Posters', p. 208.

47 Ibid.

48 'The Coolest Things: Personality Posters and Psychedelic Posters', *Newsweek*, 69 (1967), p. 8.

49 Paul Grushkin and Dennis King, *Art of Modern Rock: The Poster Explosion* (San Francisco, 2004), p. 11.

50 Gollin, 'Posters for All Seasons', p. 23; Sontag, 'Posters', p. 215.

51 Jon Borgzinner, 'The Great Poster Wave', *Life*, LXIII/9 (1967), p. 42.

52 Jasia Reichardt, 'Posters! Begin Your Exciting Art Collection Now!', *Studio International*, CLXXIV/895 (December 1967) p. 249.

53 Gollin, 'Posters for All Seasons', p. 23.

54 Jean Progner and Patricia Dreyfus, 'The Poster Revolution: Artifact into Art', *Print,* XXV/4 (1971), p. 81.

55 Sontag, 'Posters', pp. 215–16.

56 Kunzle, *Posters of Protest*, p. 14.

57 Ibid., p. 15.

58 Joan Didion, 'Marrying Absurd', in *Slouching towards Bethlehem* (New York, 2008), p. 84.

59 Hilton Kramer, 'Postermania', *New York Times Magazine* (11 February 1968), p. 30.

60 Jacaeber Kastor, 'Eye Candy', in *The Art of the Filmore, 1966–1971,* ed. Gayle Lemke and Bill Graham (New York, 1999), p. 11.

61 Paul Grushkin, *The Art of Rock: Posters from Presley to Punk* (New York, 1987), p. 71.

62 Progner and Dreyfus, 'The Poster Revolution', p. 81.

63 Ibid.

64 Quoted in Grushkin, *The Art of Rock*, p. 71.

65 Ibid., p. 11.

66 Ibid.

67 Ibid.

68 Tom Wolfe, *The Electric Kool-aid Acid Test* (New York, 2008), p. 359.

69 Quoted in 'The Coolest Things', p. 97.

70 Jesse Kornbluth, *Notes from the New Underground* (New York, 1968), p. 119.

71 Scott B. Montgomery, 'Signifying the Ineffable: Rock Poster Art and Psychedelic Counterculture in San Francisco', in *West of Center*, ed. Elissa Auther and Adam Lerner (Minneapolis, MN, 2012), p. 361.

72 Gollin, 'Posters for All Seasons', p. 22.

73 See, for example, Mark Watson, 'The Countercultural Indian: Visualizing Retribalization at the Human Be-in', in *West of Center,* ed. Auther and Lerner, pp. 204–24.

74 Kevin Moist, 'Dayglo *Koans* and Spiritual Renewal: 1960s Psychedelic Rock Concert Posters and the Broadening of American Spirituality', *Religion and Popular Culture*, VII (2004), p. 2.

75 Quoted in 'Nouveau Frisco', p. 69.

76 Ibid.

77 'The Coolest Things', p. 97.

78 Gollin, 'Posters for All Seasons', p. 23.

79 Meggs, *A History of Graphic Design*, p. 404.

80 Moist, 'Dayglo *Koans* and Spiritual Renewal', p. 2.

81 'October Sixth Nineteen Hundred and Sixty Seven', *The Digger Archives*, www.diggers.org (accessed 3 September 2012).

82 Interview with the author, 6 March 2012.

83 Ibid.

84 'Sheila de Bretteville: Designer, Educator, Feminist', *Notes on Design*, www.sessions.edu/notes-on-design, accessed 2 September 2012.

85 Patricia Mainardi, 'Quilts: The Great American Art', *Feminist Art Journal*, I (1973), pp. 18–23.

86 Jori Finkel, interview with Sheila de Bretteville, 'Remembering the Landmark Woman's Building', *Los Angeles Times*, articles.latimes.com, 15 January 2012.

87 Interview with the author, 6 March 2012.

88 Ibid.

89 Interview with Jori Finkel.

90 Interview with the author, 6 March 2012.

91 Quoted in Alison Fendley, *Saatchi & Saatchi: The Inside Story* (New York, 2011), p. 22.

4 Fetishism and the Global Poster: 1960–1980

1 William Pietz, 'The Problem of the Fetish, I,' *Res*, IX (Spring 1985), pp. 5–17; William Pietz, 'The Problem of the Fetish, II: The Origin of the Fetish', *Res*, XIII (Spring 1987), pp. 23–45; William Pietz, 'The Problem of the Fetish, IIIa: Bosman's Guinea and the Enlightenment Theory of Fetishism', *Res*, XVI (Autumn 1988), pp. 105–23.

2 Robert Trumbull, *This Is Communist China* (New York, 1968), p. 61.

3 Zhan Yan and Zeng Huang, 'Mao Portrait Story: Image Is Everything', *China Daily*, www.chinadaily.com.cn, 8 January 2008.

4 Ibid.

5 See Melissa Chiu, 'The Art of Mao's Revolution', in *Art and China's Revolution*, ed. Melissa Chiu and Shengtian Zheng (New York, 2008), p. 6.

6 Julia F. Andrews, *Painters and Politics in the People's Republic of China, 1949–1979* (Berkeley, CA, 1994), p. 360.

7 Robert Benewick, 'Icons of Power: Mao Zedong and the Cultural Revolution', in *Picturing Power and the Peoples Republic of China: Posters of the Cultural Revolution*, ed. Harriet Evans and Stephanie Donald (Oxford, 1999), p. 132.

8 Liu Chunhua, 'Painting Pictures of Chairman Mao Is Our Greatest Happiness', chineseposters.net, originally published in *China Reconstructs* (October 1968), p. 6, accessed 30 September 2013.

9 Pang Laikwan, 'The Dialectics of Mao's Images: Monumentalism, Circulation, and Power Effects', in *Visualising China, 1845–1965*, ed. Christian Henriot and Wen-hsin Yeh (Leiden, 2012), p. 413.

10 'A Splendid Revolutionary Oil Painting: Chairman Mao Goes to Anyuan', chineseposters.net, originally published in *China Pictorial*, 9 (1968), p. 12, accessed 30 September 2013.

11 'Great and Noble Image', chineseposters.net, originally published in *Chinese Literature*, 9 (1968), p. 41, accessed 30 September 2013.

12 Svetlana Boym, *Common Places: Mythologies of Everyday Life in Russia* (Cambridge, 1994), p. 105.

13 Lorraine Justice, *China's Design Revolution: Design Thinking, Design Theory* (Cambridge, 2012), p. 48.

14 John Saar, 'A Country Being Worked Very Hard', *Life*, LXX/16 (1971), p. 34.

15 Jung Chang, *Wild Swans: Three Daughters of China* (New York, 2003), p. 278.

16 'Sikkim–Chinese Border, Prelude to a Skirmish', *Life*, LXIII/13 (1967), p. 4.

17 Xiaomei Chen, 'Growing Up with Posters in the Maoist Era', in *Picturing Power and the Peoples Republic of China*, p. 107.

18 Lincoln Cushing, 'Revolutionary Chinese Posters and their Impact Abroad', in Lincoln Cushing and Ann Tompkins, *Chinese Posters: Art from the Great Proletarian Cultural Revolution* (San Francisco, 2007), p. 11.

19 'The Angry Din of China's Joyless New Year', *Life*, LXII/7 (1967), p. 38.

20 Saar, 'A Country Being Worked Very Hard', p. 32.

21 Theodore H. White, 'Journey back to Another China', *Life*, LXXII/10 (1972), p. 50.

22 Justice, *China's Design Revolution*, p. 50.

23 Chen, 'Growing Up with Posters in the Maoist Era', p. 105.

24 Arthur Danto, *Andy Warhol* (London, 2009), p. 114.

25 Luis Hernández Serrano, 'Fifty Octobers of a Poster', www.upec.cu/noticias/octubre12/24/05.htm, accessed 24 October 2012.

26 Alejandro de la Fuente, *A Nation for All: Race, Inequality and Politics in Twentieth-century Cuba* (Chapel Hill, NC, 2001).

27 Quoted in David Craven, *Art and Revolution in Latin America, 1910–1990* (London, 2006), p. 94.

28 Susan Sontag, 'Posters: Advertisement, Art, Political Artifact, Commodity', in *Looking Closer 3: Classic Writings on Graphic Design*, ed. Michael Bierut et al. (New York, 1999), p. 209.

29 Quoted in Shifra Goldman, 'Painters into Poster Makers: Two Views Concerning the History, Aesthetics and Ideology of the Cuban Poster Movement', *Studies in Latin American Popular Culture*, III (1984), p. 169.
30 See Sadira Elfrieda Rodrigues, 'Neither Red nor Black! Cuba, Africa and the Politics of Posters', MA dissertation (University of British Columbia, Vancouver, 2003).
31 Luis Camnitzer, *New Art of Cuba* (Austin, TX, 2003), p. 110.
32 Craven, *Art and Revolution in Latin America*, p. 75.
33 Carleton Beals, *Great Guerrilla Warriors* (New York, 1970), p. 2.
34 Quoted in Trisha Ziff, *Che Guevara: Revolutionary and Icon* (New York, 2006), p. 24.
35 Gene M. Tempest, 'Anti-Nazism and the *Ateliers Populaires*: The Memory of Nazi Collaboration in the Posters of *Mai '68*', BA thesis (University of California, Berkeley, 2006).
36 Pierre Bernard, interview by Gene Tempest, 4 July 2006. Regional Oral History Office, Bancroft Library, UC Berkeley, Social Movements Archive.
37 Josh MacPhee, 'Street Art and Social Movements', www.justseeds.org, 17 February 2009.
38 Atelier Populaire, *Texts and Posters from the Revolution* (Indianapolis, IN, 1969), preface.
39 Jean-Paul Ameline and Benedicte Ajac, *Figuration Narrative: Paris, 1960–1970* (Paris, 2008).
40 Pierre Buraglio, interview by Gene Tempest, 5 July 2006. Regional Oral History Office, Bancroft Library, UC Berkeley, Social Movements Archive.
41 Gérard Fromanger, interview by Gene Tempest, 8 July 2006. Regional Oral History Office, Bancroft Library, UC Berkeley, Social Movements Archive.
42 François Miehe, interview by Gene Tempest, 22 June 2006. Regional Oral History Office, Bancroft Library, UC Berkeley, Social Movements Archive.
43 Eric Seydoux, interview by Gene Tempest, 13 June 2006. Regional Oral History Office, Bancroft Library, UC Berkeley, Social Movements Archive.
44 Bernard, interview by Gene Tempest.
45 Atelier Populaire, *Texts and Posters*, preface.
46 Fromanger, interview by Gene Tempest.
47 Atelier Populaire, *Texts and Posters*, p. iv.
48 Fromanger, interview by Gene Tempest.
49 Atelier Populaire, *Texts and Posters*, preface.
50 Judy Seidman, *Red on Black: The Story of the South African Poster Movement* (Johannesburg, 2007), p. 75.

5 A New Golden Age – Digital Enchantment: 1980–2014

1 Alfred Gell, 'The Technology of Enchantment and the Enchantment of Technology', in *Anthropology, Art and Aesthetics*, ed. J. Coote and A. Shelton (Oxford, 1992), p. 43.

2 'The Language of Michael Graves', www.longhauser.com, 'Work'/'Posters', accessed 3 December 2012.

3 Paul Rand, *From Lascaux to Brooklyn* (New Haven, CT, 1996), p. 99.

4 Quoted in John Mendenhall, *High Tech Trademarks* (New York, 1985), p. 5.

5 Mick Winter, *Scan Me: Everybody's Guide to the Magical World of QR Codes* (Napa, CA, 2010), p. 20.

6 April Greiman, interview with Archie Boston, video (Los Angeles, 1987).

7 April Greiman and Aris Janigian, *Something from Nothing* (London, 2001), p. 16.

8 Zuzana Licko and Rudy Vanderlans, 'The New Primitives', *I.D.*, XXXV/2 (1988), p. 60.

9 Josh Berger, Sarah Dougher and Plazm, *100 Habits of Successful Graphic Designers: Insider Secrets from Top Designers on Working Smart and Staying Creative* (Gloucester, MA, 1995), p. 145.

10 Quoted in Liz Farrelly and April Greiman, *April Greiman: Floating Ideas into Time and Space* (New York, 1998), p. 10.

11 Greiman, interview with Archie Boston.

12 Quoted in Rick Poynor, *No More Rules: Graphic Design and Postmodernism* (London, 2003), p. 96.

13 Farrelly and Greiman, *April Greiman*, p. 13.

14 'Does It Make Sense?', *Design Quarterly*, 133 (1986).

15 Lotte Buch, 'Uncanny Affect: The Ordinary, Relations and Enduring Absence in Families of Detainees in the Occupied Palestinian Territory', PhD thesis (University of Copenhagen, 2010), p. 82.

16 Interview with Steven Heller, 'Richard Hollis: A Concise History', *Print* magazine, www.printmag.com, 15 March 2012.

17 Mahmoud Darwish, *Memory for Forgetfulness: August, Beirut, 1982* (Berkeley, CA, 2013), p. 53.

18 Sarah Smiles, 'The Propagandist Making "Martyrs" of Militants', *The Age*, 1 September 2006, p. 12.

19 Susan Taylor Martin, 'Scenes from a Reporter's Notebook', *St Petersburg Times* online, www.sptimes.com, 11 April 2002.

20 Laura Deeb, *An Enchanted Modern: Gender and Public Piety in Shi'i Lebanon* (Princeton, NJ, 2006).

21 Mahmoud Abu Hashhash, 'On the Visual Representation of Martyrdom in Palestine', *Third Text*, XX (2006), p. 397.

22 Penny Johnson, 'The Eloquence of Objects: The Hundred Martyrs Exhibit', *Jerusalem Quarterly File*, XI–XII (2001), p. 90.

23 Lori A. Allen, 'The Polyvalent Politics of Martyr Commemorations', *History and Memory*, XVIII/2 (2006), p. 127.

24 Deeb, *An Enchanted Modern*, p. 57.

25 Robert Fisk, 'Street Life: Beirut – Martyr to a Unique School of Heroic Art', *The Independent*, www.independent.co.uk, 'News'/'Article Archive'/[December] 1998, 14 December 1998.

26 Ibid.

27 Ibid.

28 Allen, 'Polyvalent Politics', p. 120.

29 Hashhash, 'On the Visual Representation of Martyrdom', p. 400.

30 Allen, 'Polyvalent Politics', p. 115.

31 Mikkel Bille, Frida Hastrup and Tim Flohr Sørensen, eds, *An Anthropology of Absence* (New York, 2010), p. 84.

32 Arden Stern, 'Sign Writing in Lusaka: Zambia Design and Culture', in *Design and Culture* (forthcoming, 2015).

33 Kajri Jain, *Gods in the Bazaar: The Economies of Indian Calendar Art* (Durham, NC, 2007), p. 16.

34 Ibid., p. 50.

35 Yousuf Saeed, 'An Image Bazaar for the Devotee', *ISIM Review,* XVII (2006), p. 8.

36 Esha Mahajan, 'Bollywood Posters Script a Sequel in Art', *Times of India*, timesofindia.indiatimes.com, 30 June 2011.

37 Ben Barnier, 'Artist Keeps Bollywood-Poster Making Alive', abcnews.go.com, 11 June 2007.

38 Laura Allsop and Lianne Turner, 'Bollywood Poster Painters Face Extinction in Digital Age', edition.cnn.com, 23 June 2011.

39 Humphrey Hawksley, 'Bollywood Technology Kills Poster Art', www.bbc.co.uk, 16 July 2003.

40 Mahajan, 'Bollywood Posters Script a Sequel in Art'.

41 Allsop and Turner, 'Bollywood Poster Painters Face Extinction in Digital Age'.

42 Wendelin Schmidt, 'Mass Media and Visual Communications', *Third Text*, XIX/3 (May 2005), p. 307.

43 See, for example, Dana Rush, 'Eternal Potential: Chromolithographs in Vodunland', *African Arts*, XXXII/4 (1999), pp. 60–75.

44 Wendelin Schmidt, 'Mass Media and Visual Communication: Popular Posters in West Africa', *Third Text*, XIX/3 (May 2005), p. 310.

45 Audrey Gadzekpo, 'Street News: The Role of Posters in Democratic Participation in Ghana', in *Popular Media, Democracy and Development in Africa*, ed. Herman Wasserman (New York, 2011), p. 116.

46 Schmidt, 'Mass Media and Visual Communication, p. 312.

47 Jim Quilty, 'The Man Who Went Digital with Persian Letters', *Daily Star Lebanon*, www.dailystar.com.lb, 'Culture' section, 27 February 2007.

48 Constance E. Padwick, *Muslim Devotions: A Study of Common Use* (London, 1961), p. 199.

49 J. R. (Wayne) Osborn, 'The Type of Calligraphy: Writing, Print, and Technologies of the Arabic Alphabet' (PhD thesis, University of California, San Diego, 2008), p. 28.

50 Sonia Rezapour, *The Splendor of Iran*, vol. III (Yassavoli, 2007), pp. 32–3.

51 Karl Schaefer, 'Mediaeval Arabic Block Printing: State of the Field', in *Historical Aspects of Printing and Publishing in Languages of the Middle East: Papers from the Symposium at the University of Leipzig*, ed. Geoffrey Roper (Leiden, 2014), pp. 7–13.

52 Quoted in Rick Poynor, 'A Man Apart', *Creative Review*, XXVII/5 (2007), p. 46.

53 'Reza Abedini', *Grafist*, IX (2005), p. 10.

54 Pierre Bourdieu, *The Algerians* (Boston, MA, 1962), p. 155.

55 Annabelle Srebmy and Ali Mohammadi, *Small Media, Big Revolution: Communication, Culture and the Iranian Revolution* (Minneapolis, MN, 1994), p. 8.

56 Habibollah Ayatollahi, *The Book of Iran: The History of Iranian Art*, trans. Shermin Haghshenas (Tehran, 2003), p. 313.

57 Reza Abedini, interview, Gestalten.tv [podcast], news.gestalten.com, May 2012.

58 Ibid.

59 Ibid.

60 Quoted in Kasia Cieplak-Mayr von Baldegg, 'Western Font Design Meets Persian Calligraphy in the Work of Reza Abedini', *The Atlantic*, www.theatlantic.com, 1 October 2012.

61 Johanna Drucker, *SpecLab: Digital Aesthetics and Projects in Speculative Computing* (Chicago, IL, 2009), p. 326.

62 Stephen Lemon, 'Andre the Giant Bombs the World!', *Salon*, www.salon.com, 22 June 2000.

63 Shepard Fairey, 'Manifesto: A Social and Psychological Explanation', in *OBEY: Supply and Demand, The Art of Shepard Fairey* (Boston, MA, 2006), p. 7.

64 Lemon, 'Andre the Giant Bombs the World!'.

65 Joshuah Bearman, 'Behind Obama's Iconic HOPE Poster', *Huffington Post*, www.huffingtonpost.com, 11 November 2008.

66 Zygmunt Bauman, *Postmodern Ethics* (Cambridge, 1993), p. 33.

67 Cody Goodfellow, 'Andre the Giant Is Watching You', *Obey*, www.obeygiant.com, accessed 15 December 2013.

68 Ibid.

69 Peter Schjeldahl, 'Hope and Glory: A Shepard Fairey Moment', *New Yorker* (23 February 2009), p. 138.

70 Goodfellow, 'Andre the Giant Is Watching You'.

71 Fairey, *OBEY: Supply and Demand*, pp. 89–90.

72 Iain Aitch, 'Stick 'em up', *The Guardian* (25 November 1999), p. A12.

73 'Art, Culture, Politics: A Conversation with Shepard Fairey', The Norman Lear Center, USC, www.learcenter.org, accessed 10 September 2013.

74 Goodfellow, 'Andre the Giant Is Watching You'.

75 Colin Berry, 'The Medium has No Meaning', *Wired*, 4.08 (August 1966), at www.wired.com; Steven Heller, 'Interview with Shepard Fairey: Still Obeying after all These Years', *AIGA*, www.aiga.org, 4 June 2004.

76 See, for example, 'Manufacturing (Dis)content', Walker Art Center, Education Department, press release, 4 February 2000.

77 Noah R. Brier, 'Buzz Giant Poster Boy', *American Demographics*, XXVI/5 (2004), p. 12.

78 Rick Poynor, *Obey the Giant: Life in the Image World* (London, 2001), p. 177.

79 Steven Heller and Louise Fili, *Stylepedia: A Guide to Graphic Design Mannerisms, Quirks, and Conceits* (San Francisco, 2006), p. 228.

80 Schjeldahl, 'Hope And Glory', p. 79.

81 Roland Barthes, 'Rhetoric of the Image', in *Image, Music, Text*, ed. and trans. Stephen Heath (New York, 1977), p. 37.

82 Quoted in *Documenta 7: Kassel*, vol. II, exh. cat. (Kassel, 1982), p. 144.

83 Shepard Fairey, 'Provocative Questions', unpublished interview transcript from *I.D.* magazine, *Obey*, www.obeygiant.com, accessed 2 December 2013.

84 Jen Darr, 'Stick It', *Philadelphia City Paper* (14–21 January 1999).

85 Fairey, *OBEY: Supply and Demand*, p. 295.

86 Bruno Bettelheim, *The Uses of Enchantment: The Meaning and Importance of Fairy Tales* (New York, 2010), p. 14.

Epilogue: Post-posters?

1 Gbenro Adeoye, 'The Poster Wars of Lagos', *Gbooza!*, www.gbooza.com, 10 March 2011.

2 Stella Odueme, 'Nigeria: Lagos Beauty Now Challenged by Mutilated Election Posters', *Daily Independent*, allafrica.com, 20 May 2011.

3 'Posters Deface Lagos – Stakeholders', *PM News*, www.pmnewsnigeria.com, 16 April 2012.

4 Odueme, 'Nigeria'.

5 Quoted in 'Posters Deface Lagos'.

6 Adeola Balogun, 'Cleaner City via Sanitation of Politics Posters, Hoardings', *Nigerian Best Forum – NBF/General Topics*, www.nigerianbestforum.com, 26 February 2011.

7 Seye Ojo, 'Poster War in Lagos', *Daily Sun*, archive2.sunnewsonline.com, 16 March 2011.

8   Balogun, 'Cleaner City'.

9   'LASAA, Not a Revenue Generation Body', *This Day Live*, www.thisdaylive.com, 6 February 2011.

10 'Give Him a Network Protocols Poster', *Javin News* on *PR Web*, www.prweb.com, accessed 12 October 2012.

SELECT BIBLIOGRAPHY

Ades, Dawn, et al., *Poster: The 20th-century Poster: Design of the Avant-garde* (Minneapolis, MN, 1984)

Alexandre, Arsène, et al., *Modern Poster* (New York, 1895)

Aulich, James, *War Posters: Weapons of Mass Communication* (New York, 2007)

—, and Marta Sylvestrová, *Political Posters in Central and Eastern Europe, 1945–95: Signs of the Times* (Manchester, 1999)

Barnicoat, John, *A Concise History of Posters* (New York, 1979)

Bestley, Russell, and Ian Noble, *Up Against the Wall* (Hove, 2002)

Biegeleisen, J. I., *Poster Design* (New York, 1945)

Bogart, Michele Helene, *Artists, Advertising, and the Borders of Art* (Chicago, IL, 1995)

Bonnell, Victoria E., *Iconography of Power: Soviet Political Posters under Lenin and Stalin* (Berkeley and Los Angeles, CA, 1999)

Breitenbach, Edgar, et al., *The American Poster: A Brief History* (New York, 1967)

Camnitzer, Luis, *New Art of Cuba* (Austin, TX, 2003)

Constantine, Mildred, and Alan Maxwell Fern, *Word and Image: Posters from the Collection of the Museum of Modern Art* (New York, 1968)

Crowley, David, *Posters of the Cold War* (London, 2008)

Davidson, Russ, and David Craven, *Latin American Posters: Public Aesthetics and Mass Politics* (Santa Fe, NM, 2006)

Flood, Catherine, *British Posters: Advertising, Art and Activism* (London, 2012)

Foster, John, *One Thousand Indie Posters* (Beverly, MA, 2011)

—, *New Masters of Poster Design* (Gloucester, MA, 2006)

Frost, Malcolm, et al., *Street Talk: The Rise and Fall of the Poster* (Mulgrave, Victoria, 2006)

Gallo, Max, *The Poster in History* (New York, 1974)

Glaser, Milton, *Graphic Design* (New York, 2012)

—, *Design of Dissent* (Gloucester, MA, 2005)

Grushkin, Paul, and Dennis King, *Art of Modern Rock: The Poster Explosion* (San Francisco, 2004)

Hahn, H. Hazel, *Scenes of Parisian Modernity: Culture and Consumption in the Nineteenth Century* (New York, 2009)

Henatsch, Martin, *Die Entstehung des Plakates: eine rezeptionsästhetische Untersuchung* (Hildesheim, 1994)

Henkin, David M., *City Reading: Written Words and Public Spaces in Antebellum New York* (New York, 1998)

Heyman, Therese Thau, *Posters American Style* (Washington, DC, 1998)

Hiatt, Charles, *A Short History of the Illustrated Placard, with Many Reproductions of the Most Artistic Examples in All Countries* (London, 1896)

Images of an Era: The American Poster, 1945–75, exh. cat., National Collection of Fine Arts, Washington, DC, et al. (Washington, DC, 1975)

Kauffer, Edward McKnight, *The Art of the Poster: Its Origin, Evolution, and Purpose* (New York, 1937)

Kramer, Dieter, and Wendelin Schmidt, eds, *Plakate in Afrika* (Frankfurt, 2004)

Laver, James, and Henry Davray, *Nineteenth-century French Posters* (London, 1944)

Le Coultre, Martijn F., and Alston W. Purvis, *A Century of Posters* (Aldershot, 2002)

MacPhee, Josh, ed., *Celebrate People's History: The Poster Book of Resistance and Revolution* (New York, 2010)

Maindron, Ernst, *Les Maîtres de l'affiche* (Paris, c. 1900)

Margolin, Victor, *American Poster Renaissance* (New York, 1975)

—, Ira Brichta and Vivian Brichta, *The Promise and the Product: Two Hundred Years of American Advertising Posters* (New York, 1979)

Marx, Roger, *Masters of the Poster, 1896–1900* (New York, 1977)

Matlack Price, Charles, *Poster Design: A Critical Study of the Development of the Poster in Continental Europe, England and America* (New York, 1922)

Miescher, Giorgio, and Dag Henrichsen, *African Posters: A Catalogue of the Poster Collection in the Basler Afrika Bibliographien* (Basel, 2004)

Moore, Colin, *Propaganda Prints: A History of Art in the Service of Social and Political Change* (London, 2010)

Müller-Brockmann, Josef, *Geschichte des Plakates / Histoire de l'affiche / History of the Poster, 1914–1996* (London, 2004)

Pica, Vittorio, *Manifesto: arte e comunicazione nelle origini della pubblicità* (Naples, 1994)

Quintavalle, Arturo Carlo, *Manifesti: storie da incollare* (Milan, 1996)

Reaves, Wendy Wick, *Ballyhoo! Posters as Portraiture* (Washington, DC, 2008)

Rennie, Paul, *Modern British Posters: Art, Design and Communication* (London, 2010)

Resnick, Mark, and R. Roger Remington, *The American Image: US Posters from the 19th to the 21st Century* (Rochester, NY, 2006)

Salsi, Claudio, ed., *Advertising and Art: International Graphics from the Affiche to Pop Art* (Milan, 2007)

Scott, David, *Poetics of the Poster: The Rhetoric of Image-Text* (Liverpool, 2010)

Seidman, Steven, *Posters, Propaganda, and Persuasion in Election Campaigns around the World and through History* (New York, 2008)

Stallabrass, Julian, *Gargantua: Manufactured Mass Culture* (New York, 1996)
Timmers, Margaret, ed., *Power of the Poster* (London, 1998)
Weill, Alain, *Encyclopédie de l'affiche* (Paris, 2011)
—, *The Poster: A Worldwide History and Survey* (Boston, MA, 1985)

Stallabrass, Julian, *Gargantua: Manufactured Mass Culture* (New York, 1996)
Timmers, Margaret, ed., *Power of the Poster* (London, 1998)

—, *The Poster: A Worldwide History and Survey* (Boston, MA, 1985)

ACKNOWLEDGEMENTS

My thanks are due to many people who have taken an interest in the subject of this book, including Kim Detterbeck, Carma Gorman, Michael Golec, Raiford Guins, Jim Housefield, Gen Hyacinthe, Stuart Kendall, Paul Kaplan, Jane Kromm, Michael Lobel, Victor Margolin, Jason Pine, Matt Resnick, Simon Sadler, Louise Sandhaus, Brooke Singer, Bobbye Tigerman and Sarah Warren. I also owe thanks to Purchase College funds for faculty development, the Richard B. and Noel S. Frackman fund and the Strypemonde Foundation. And, as ever, to my parents George and Mary Ellen, as well as Matt and Ellen, a large source of patience, love and support.

PHOTO ACKNOWLEDGEMENTS

The author and publishers wish to express their thanks to the following sources of illustrative material and/or permission to reproduce it:

Courtesy of the artist (Reza Abedini): pp. 268, 280; ADAGP/DACS: pp. 100–101; from *Les Affiches Illustrées*: p. 10; AFP/Getty Images: pp. 247 (top), 250, 253 (foot), 259; Agence Rol, photo courtesy Bibliothèque Nationale de France: p. 58; photo courtesy Archive.org: p. 61; © ARS, NY: pp. 25, 176; The Art Archive at Art Resource, NY: pp. 32, 124 (© Copyright Peter Max); © Artists Rights Society (ARS), New York/ADAGP, Paris: pp. 76, 180; © Artists Rights Society (ARS), New York/ADAGP, Paris/Estate of Marcel Duchamp: pp. 118, 119; Associated Press: p. 247 (foot); Banque d'Images, ADAGP/Art Resource, NY: p. 203; © Bruno Barbey/Magnum Photos: pp. 217, 220; courtesy of the artist (Uri Baruchin): p. 38; © Bettmann/CORBIS: pp. 40, 135, 169; photo courtesy Bibliothèque Nationale de France: pp. 44, 50, 52, 132, 147, 218, 223; Bildarchiv Preussischer Kulturbesitz, Berlin/Art Resource, NY: p. 120; © Jonathan Blair/Corbis: p. 215; © Bowstir Ltd 2010/mankowitz.com: p. 146; Sheila de Bretteville/Otis College of Art and Design Library: pp. 171, 172; British Library/Robana via Getty Images: p. 87; photos © The British Library Board, London: pp. 192, 210; courtesy Marc Brunner: p. 246; © Henri Bureau/Sygma/Corbis: p. 265; © Rene Burri/Magnum Photos: pp. 201, 204; CCI/The Art Archive at Art Resource, NY: p. 136; © Christie's Images/Corbis: p. 107; Contact Press Images: p. 196; Cooper-Hewitt, National Design Museum, Smithsonian Institution: pp. 140 (gift of Sara and Marc Benda), 238; Cooper-Hewitt, National Design Museum, Smithsonian Institution/Art Resource, NY: p. 31 (top); courtesy of Corita Art Center, Los Angeles: p. 128; CRG Gallery, In Situ/Fabienne Leclerc, and The Third Line: pp. 34–5; from *Current Advertising*, July 1902: p. 60; © D. R., Harry Shunk: p. 88; Davis Museum at Wellesley College, Wellesley, MA/Art Resource, NY: p. 123; photo by Evans/Three Lions/Getty Images: p. 82; Evening Standard/Getty ImagesData: p. 179; courtesy Shepard Fairey/ObeyGiant.com: p. 270; Gamma-Keystone via Getty Images: pp. 78, 105, 189; courtesy Steve Garfield, Shepard Fairey/ObeyGiant.com: pp. 271, 273, 275; photo Jaar Geerlings: p. 261; courtesy Getty Images: pp. 21 (foot), 39, 77, 85, 96, 99, 126, 148, 153, 161, 183, 187, 190, 199,

INDEX